International Business: The Canadian Way

Edited by
Herman O. J. Overgaard
Wilfrid Laurier University

Maxime A. Crener
University of Ottawa

Bernard Z. Dasah
University of Ottawa

Alfred L. Kahl
University of Ottawa

**KENDALL/HUNT
PUBLISHING COMPANY**
Dubuque, Iowa

Crookell-Wrigley: CANADIAN RESPONSE TO MULTINATIONAL ENTERPRISE
Reprinted from the Spring 1975 issue of the *Business Quarterly*, by permission of the School of Business Administration of the University of Western Ontario.

Crener-Kahl: FIRA and the Exodus of Direct Investment from Canada
Reprinted from the November/December 1979 issue of *Cost and Management*, by permission of the Society of Management Accountants of Canada.

Litvak-Maule: THE EMERGING CHALLENGE OF CANADIAN DIRECT INVESTMENT ABROAD
Reprinted from the Spring 1978 issue of the *Business Quarterly*, by permission of the School of Business Administration of the University of Western Ontario.

Ross-Banting: IMPROVING CANADA'S GLOBAL COMPETITIVENESS
Reprinted from the Autumn 1981 issue of the *Business Quarterly*, by permission of the School of Business Administration of the University of Western Ontario.

Gordon-Richardson: WHY MANUFACTURE IN CANADA?
Reprinted from the Winter 1977 issue of the *Business Quarterly*, by permission of the School of Business Administration of the University of Western Ontario.

Crookell-Graham: INTERNATIONAL MARKETING AND CANADIAN INDUSTRIAL STRATEGY
Reprinted from the Spring 1979 issue of the *Business Quarterly*, by permission of the School of Business Administration of the University of Western Ontario.

Scrivener: INTERNATIONAL MARKETS OR DIE
Reprinted from the Spring 1979 issue of the *Business Quarterly*, by permission of the School of Business Administration of the University of Western Ontario.

Distefano: MANAGING IN OTHER CULTURES: Some Do's and Some Don'ts
Reprinted from the Autumn 1972 issue of the *Business Quarterly*, by permission of the School of Business Administration of the University of Western Ontario.

Ronen-Kraut: SIMILARITIES AMONG COUNTRIES BASED ON EMPLOYEE WORK VALUES AND ATTITUDES
Reprinted from the Summer 1977 issue of the *Columbia Journal of World Business*, by permission of the Graduate School of Business of Columbia University.

Kee: CANADA'S CULTURAL BARRIER
Reprinted by permission from the Summer 1977 issue of the *Marquette Business Review*.

Moller: THE MULTINATIONAL EXECUTIVE: Patriot or Traitor
Reprinted from the Spring 1972 issue of the *International Journal of Accounting Education and Research*, by permission of the Center for International Education and Research in Accounting of the University of Illinois.

North South Institute: THE CANADIAN ROLE: Bridge Builder or Fence Sitter?
Reprinted from *The North South Encounter: The Third World and Canadian Performance*, 1977, by permission of the North South Institute.

All other articles in this text have been reprinted by permission of the authors.

This preliminary edition has been printed directly from the editors' manuscript copy.

Contents

Part IV: Canadian Export Strategy (continued)

Part V: Canadian Market Penetration Strategy   405

Preface

There was a day, not so long ago, when interest in international business was largely restricted to a limited clan of hardy foreign traders. However, the surge in modern transportation, mass communication and technology began to pull nations closer together as well as to increase the business connections among the countries of the world. The world is now often referred to as a global village of interdependence -- for no nation, at least in the short run, now has all the resources required for the optimum functioning of its economy.

There has arisen, therefore, not only a tremendous growth in international business but also the creation of new institutions. Consequently, international business has been attracting increasing interest as a field of concentration in schools of business administration at both the undergraduate and graduate levels.

Furthermore, international business has become, not without cause, an urgent subject of study for businessmen and all who are concerned about international affairs. The fact of the matter is that the profits accruing from international business and the increases in production and employment through which these profits are earned are in jeopardy mainly because of misunderstandings and confusion about the relations of business to political principles and social values. This confusion exists in the advanced countries as well as in the less developed nations where subsidiaries of multinational firms have been established.

To say the least, international business requires and deserves the attention of all in every nation -- the political scientist, the economic theorist, the government official, the journalist, the businessman, and the student.

INTERNATIONAL BUSINESS -- THE CANADIAN WAY emphasizes the need for such attention from the Canadian viewpoint. Canada is unique in many respects. It is the next door neighbour of the United States and experiences the proliferation of U.S. multinational corporations with their sometimes extraterritorial effects. It is also the host country for foreign direct investment by multinational firms of non U.S. origin. In addition, it is the base for several large Canadian firms and banks which operate outside Canada. Above all, the bicultural and bilingual nature of Canada is a uniqueness that very few nations enjoy.

It is reasonable to say that to effectively transact international trade in the present day milieu requires the mastery of more than one language for, so maintains the draft report of the Task Force of Canadian Federation of Deans of Management: "the unilingual international business executive is almost a contradiction in terms." Hence, it can be said that Canadians are in the enviable position of being among the best qualified for international business operations.

Canada is the ninth largest international trading nation in the world on a per capita basis, hence such trade is vitally important to Canada. In 1980 nearly thirty percent of the Canadian Gross National Product was derived from exports. This was double the Jananese and triple the American figures. Approximately half of all the goods produced in Canada are exported. Nearly half of all the exports and over eighty percent of the exports of Canadian manufactured products originate in Ontario.

The pattern of world trade is undergoing basic changes and Canada must prepare for more intensified competition in export markets. There is, therefore, a need for a book such as this one which presents a variety of readings preparted by both academic, business and government authors to expand the reader's horizons while at the same time presenting some controversial issues from a Canadian point of view.

I
Canadian
Nationalism
and
International
Business

Canadian Response to Multinational Enterprise
by
Harold Crookwell and Leonard Wrigley
Professor   Associate Professor
University of Western Ontario

1. INNOVATION AND CANADIAN CONTROL: THE POSITIVE APPROACH

A fundamental economic objective of Canada is the development of industry that is both innovative and Canadian controlled. Without innovation there is no economic growth. But without Canadian control, the viability of the country as a sovereign state is at risk.

Since the end of World War II, industry in Canada has been innovative. In the result, the Canadian people enjoy a high standard of living. Indeed, the authoritative English journal, The Economist, using broad measures, placed Canada first amongst all countries in 1973 for quality of life. On the narrow measure of per capita income, Canada was fourth in the world. On such data, it is clear that Canadian industry is advanced in innovative activity. However, the cost has been a loss of national control of the economy to an extent without parallel in the modern world: 58% of Canadian manufacturing industry (and no less than 80% for the technologically advanced sectors) is today under foreign domain.

New government legislation, the Foreign Investment Review Act is designed to redress the situation. Henceforth, there are restrictions on the sale of domestic firms to foreign-based firms. Clearly, the government intends that existing domestic firms will remain Canadian. But this is a negative approach. And there is a price to it. The unintended consequences of the Act will be a severe reduction in innovative activity within Canada. Given the present characteristic strategies of Canadian domestic firms, the goals of innovation and Canadian control are in conflict.

In Canada, the domestic firm competes on cost. That is, it competes in the market through having the lowest cost of production at the point of sale. By contrast, the foreign owned firm (subsidiaries of multinational enterprise) competes through product innovation. Unless the domestic firms are able and willing to change their strategic posture, the conflict cannot be resolved.

Ability to change originates in technical knowledge; willingness in financial motivation. This article begins by showing how innovation is brought into Canada, and how the process favors the foreign subsidiaries. Next it shows the results in terms of progressive loss in Canadian control. Then, it considers the Foreign Investment Review Act. Finally, it presents the outline of a strategy for change from a cost-reducing to a product innovative enterprise.

2. INNOVATION IN CANADIAN INDUSTRY

In the modern world of industry, innovation is brought about through the application of new technology to improve the products that are made, or the processes employed in making them. Most characteristically, new technology is discovered and developed in the Research and Development (R/D) unit of an industrial enterprise. Thus, any consideration of innovation in Canadian industry must deal with four different things: R/D; the application of new technology, improved products, and improved processes. From this view, the results of our studies suggest the characterization as shown in Figure I, in comparing foreign-controlled with domestic firms in their major thrust towards innovation.

Our studies indicate that relatively little research is performed within Canadian industry. This is done mainly abroad. The research that is done in Canada is aimed largely at improvement of production processes, rather than new product development. There is more activity in Canada in the commercial use of new technology, but again there is bias against new product development especially by domestic firms. Most firms, domestic and subsidiary, are active in applying new technology (developed elsewhere) to improve processes in order to reduce cost. However, in general, only subsidiaries are actively using new technology to secure product innovation. There is, thus, a great difference in thrust between subsidiaries and domestics. What accounts for it? To answer these questions, it is necessary to describe the mechanics of technology acquisition.

3

FIGURE I - INNOVATION IN CANADIAN INDUSTRY: MAJOR THRUST BY OWNERSHIP

	Product Innovation	Process Innovation
Research for New Technology	1. Foreign Parents 2. Foreign Licensors to Domestic firms	1. Some Subsidiaries 2. Some Large Domestic Firms
Commercial use of New Technology	Most Subsidiaries	1. Most Subsidiaries 2. Most Domestic Firms

Technology can be made or bought. A firm with a production plant can make its own technology, 'in-house', through its own internal R/D units, connecting production to R/D through administrative links within a firm, as in Figure II (A). Or it can buy technology through a licence agreement from the R/D unit of another firm, thus linking production to R/D across the market, as in Figure II (B).

The relative advantages of make or buy depend greatly on whether what is wanted is a single piece of new technology (in the form of a set of blueprints, technical specifications and start up assistance), or a continuous flow of new technology geared to changing markets and production processes. In stable industries, where the product does not change, or changes are rare or spasmodic, it is usually enough to buy the necessary technology. Examples of such industries are lumber, ore mining, and basic foods. If new processes are required, say to offset rising wage rates or more difficult natural conditions, large firms have tended to make their new technology, thus ensuring a close attention to their own present and future needs, but small and medium firms have survived through buying their requirements.[1]

However, in secondary industries in the mainstream of the economy, what is needed for effective competition is a continuous flow of new technology. This is particularly so in industries where product improvement is a key element in corporate strategy for survival and growth in the market. The firm that competes on

FIGURE II - TECHNOLOGY, MAKE OR BUY

Firm				Firm		Firm
Production	Admin. Links	R/D		Production	Market Links	R/D

new products has a considerable edge over firms that sell the same product year in and year out, relying on low cost for survival. But to compete on new products, a continuous flow of new technology is required. And to ensure this flow, we have found that it is highly advantageous for the firm to make its own technology, to build its own $R'D$.

Canada Imports Technology

Historically, Canada has imported the vast proportion of her requirement of technology. Although her natural resources are great, her population is relatively small. Moreoever, she is a young country, especially so in terms of technical skills and institutions for developing and supplying those skills. Indeed, until recent times, imports of technology were an absolute necessity. The demand of the people for sophisticated products required skills far in excess of those existing in Canada. They imported innovation; in doing so they acquired the habit of looking outside for their critical technology requirements.

The immediate source of imported technology, has been the United States. Even though (as indicated by patents) only some 40% of technology new to Canada, was developed in the U.S.A., some 80% of it will have been transmitted into Canada from that country. Thus, the technology transfer process from U.S.A. to Canada is of great economic importance.

Because of tariffs, new technology has not been imported into Canada embodied in products. Rather, it has come in the form of knowledge, skills, and specification. Production took place within Canada, in the plants either of domestic firms or of multi-national

5

subsidiaries. But though their production plants may be similar the domestic firms have acquired their technology in ways quite different from those of the subsidiaries. The difference is important: it is at the heart of the Canadian problem.

Technology Obtained From Parent Company

The subsidiaries obtain the vast majority of their technology, fully complete and up to date, from parent company product divisions who in turn link directly into the corporate R/D centre. These divisions usually have product development laboratories where much of the work is done to commercialize ideas arising from R/D. By maintaining continuous and frequent, "face-to-face" communication with parent product divisions, subsidiaries are able to increase the speed and reduce the risk of new product innovation in Canada. For this reason there is a strong and direct link between the Canadian personnel involved in an innovation and U.S. personnel in a similar role. All are members of the same firm, and may well over time interchange roles, as career interests dictate. They will get to know each other well, and learn how to form accurate judgements on each others estimates and ideas.

By contrast, the Canadian domestic firms maintain this "continuous flow" process only through arms-length licence agreements with U.S. based licensors. As a general rule these licence agreements call for the transmission of both current and future technology from the licensor. Payment is in the form of royalties on future sales, which in turn generate the resources needed to pay the royalties. There is little risk involved on the Canadian licensee's part except he may not get quite the technology he needs and almost certainly not when he needs it. The U.S. licensor normally protects his position by two clauses in the license agreement: one, by restrictions on the markets that can be served (usually the Canadian market), and, the other, by insistence on free flow back to the U.S.A. of any product or process improvements developed by the Canadian licensor. However, although these clauses excite the Canadian government, they have little practical significance at present. As one U.S. executive put it:

"We always try to include these clauses in our licence agreements, but I don't think they are all that important in relation to Canada. We seldom get any technology flow back from our licensees because they don't do research. And they really don't constitute a competitive threat in foreign markets because they are high cost producers, in international terms, even without the royalty costs, and most of them are inexperienced in foreign markets."

Licensing has not proved as effective a method of transferring new product technology as the internal administrative process of multinationals. In the result, domestic firms have been unable to compete in product innovation, particularly at the early, most profitable, stages of the product life cycle. At the same time licensing does enable the Canadian domestic firm to survive in the mature product stage. Operating in this way over time has created habits within the domestic firm of 'follow my leader'. In consequence, as innovation has become more rapid and more important, the domestic firms have not grown with the economy. They remain small, numerous, and with few exceptions of no great significance in their own country. Spectacular exceptions cannot hide this massive fact.

Subsidiaries of Multinationals Important to Canada

It is the subsidiaries of multinationals, particularly of the technology oriented U.S. based multinationals, that are important in Canada. They have become this way through their advantageous position in the technology transfer process and through their habits of product innovation.

FIGURE III - RELATIONSHIPS WITHIN THE MULTINATIONAL

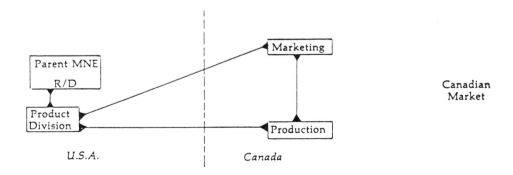

3. LOSS OF CANADIAN CONTROL

In 1970, the book value of Canadian manufacturing industry was approximately 46 billion dollars. Of this, 27 billion, some 58% was held by firms under foreign control. Table I below portrays the change over time in manufacturing industry, and compares this with other industries.

Clearly, while there has long been a significant foreign position in Canadian manufacturing industry, the great surge occurred in the 15 years between 1948 and 1963. These were the years of great growth and technical advance in U.S.A. manufacturing industry. Growth, through technical superiority, pushed these U.S. firms into Canada, characteristically, by method of acquiring an existing domestic firm and feeding it their own technology.

The result of foreign take-over has been uneven as to corporate size. Table II shows the distribution of the 46 billion dollars of assets in manufacturing industry among foreign and Canadian controlled firms by size of firm. It is clear that foreign controlled firms tend to be large, also that the multinationals have avoided almost altogether those firms under $1 million in assets. By contrast, there are thousands of small domestic firms, but not many in the $5 million to $10 million range. Furthermore, the data masks the effect of certain domestic firms, such as Massey Ferguson and Seagrams, of a size comparable to the largest abroad.

TABLE 1 - FOREIGN CONTROL AS A PERCENTAGE OF SELECTED
CANADIAN INDUSTRIES SELECTED YEARS, 1926-1970[1]

Industry	Percent Control Year							
	1926	1930	1939	1948	1954	1958	1963	1970
Manufacturing	35	36	38	43	51	57	60	58
Petroleum and Gas	—	—	—	—	69	73	74	78
Mining and Smelting	38	47	42	40	51	60	65	68
Railways	3	3	3	3	2	2	2	—
Other Utilities	20	29	26	26	8	5	4	—
	—	—	—	—	—	—	—	—
Total of Above	17	20	21	25	28	32	34	35

[1] Control for the purpose of this table is defined as more than 50% equity held abroad.

The data in the foregoing tables are taken mainly from Stat-istics Canada. Data from other sources bear out the same pattern. While there has been strong foreign (mainly U.S.) direct invest-ment in Canadian manufacturing industry since the early days of the present century, it was not until the end of World War II that the great surge got under way. Between 1948 and 1963, the industrial face of Canada was changed. The agents were mainly the U.S. based multinationals. By 1963, the majority of manu-facturing industry was in their hands. Since that time, although direct investment from abroad has continued to grow, on the whole the rate has only kept step with the general growth of the econ-omy, and of the population of domestic firms in it.

However, the growth pattern in subsidiaries and domestic firms has differed. In the decade 1963-1973, the number of sub-sidiaries has not greatly increased, but the size of each subsidiary has. Thus, the subsidiaries are larger today, than ten years ago. By contrast, the domestic firms are merely more numerous. The total population of domestic firms has increased significantly, not so the average size of enterprise. And even some of the Canadian domestic firms with sales in the $25 million + range are, in sub-stance, loose conglomerates of small, quite unrelated businesses.[2]

The result has also been uneven as to industry. Table III shows the percentage of foreign control among selected industries in 1970, as measured here by profits and sales as well as assets. On this view, foreign control is highest in the technologically advanced sectors. Firms under foreign control also tend to be somewhat more profitable, in terms of assets or sales, than their Canadian counterparts.

Comparison With Other Countries Emphasizes Canada's Position

What is of importance is the comparison with data about other lands. In the United Kingdom and other European countries, the percentage of manufacturing firms under foreign control ranges from about 10% to 15%. Canada, with 58%, is in a wholly different category. This is the heart of the issue concerning measures to restrict foreign control. Most of the government measures, and all the impending measures, follow the European pattern. They are designed to screen out foreign takeovers. But if Canada is wholly different - because of the vast difference in scale - the validity of following the same pattern is in question. Measures

TABLE II – DISTRIBUTION OF ASSETS BY SIZE OF FIRM AMONG FOREIGN AND CANADIAN CONTROLLED MANUFACTURING FIRMS, 1970

Firm Size By Assets	Foreign Controlled		Canadian Controlled		Total	
	No. of firms	Assets (billions)	No. of firms	Assets (billions)	No. of firms	Assets (billions)
25 + million	170	20.1	102	10.3	272	30.4
10 - 25 million	181	2.8	102	1.5	283	4.3
5 - 10 million	279	2.0	197	1.3	476	3.3
1 - 5 million	960	2.3	1573	3.2	2533	5.5
Under 1 million	816	0.4	5229	2.3	6045	2.7
Total	2406	27.6	7203	18.6	9609	46.2

that aim merely to hold the present position are not enough for Canada. At the same time, any measures that impede the efficiency of 58% of manufacturing industry - that part under foreign control - can hardly be considered.

4. THE FOREIGN INVESTMENT REVIEW ACT

In the last few years, the government has taken a number of steps to assist innovation and Canadian control of the economy. The Canada Development Corporation was created to acquire and assist domestic enterprises in need of finance or overall guidance. There are tax measures to assist very small domestic firms, and a new Federal Bureau Development Bank is projected to provide finance for such firms. Financial institutions, especially banks, are protected from foreign control. There is a bill to ensure a majority of Canadian directors in all federally incorporated businesses.

But the acknowledged center-piece of the government's legislative approach has been the Foreign Investment Review Act. In substance, this act ensures that foreign investment projects will be screened on the legislated critique of "significant benefit to Canada." In deciding whether a project meets this test, five factors are taken into account:

TABLE III – PERCENTAGE OF FOREIGN CONTROL OF SELECTED CANADIAN MANUFACTURING INDUSTRIES, AS MEASURED BY ASSETS, SALES AND PROFITS

Industry Ranked in approximate order of technology intensity	Assets %	Sales %	Profits %
Electrical Products	64	63	78
Chemicals	81	81	89
Machinery	72	73	78
Petroleum and Coal Products	100	100	100
Primary Metals	55	51	62
Metal Fabrication	47	45	65
Food and Beverages	31	27	29
Leather Products	22	21	25
Textiles and Clothing	39	28	55
Furniture	19	15	20
Wood	31	22	24
	—	—	—
Total — All Manufacturing	58	55	63

1. The effect of the investment on the level of employment in Canada,

2. The degree of Canadian participation in the enterprise of which the project is part,

3. The effect of the investment on technological development,

4. The effect of the investment on competition, and

5. The compatability of the investment with national and provincial economic and social policies.

The main investment projects included in the act are foreign takeovers of Canadian firms, the establishment of new businesses in Canada by foreigners, and the expansion of an existing foreign controlled firm into an area unrelated to its present activity. But the act is so framed as to permit and encourage a bargaining process. For example, the 'significant benefit' test is a policy test, not a legal test. Ultimately, it is the cabinet, not the courts, which decide that a project will be rejected or accepted.

The Act was the direct outcome of a report released in May 1972, Foreign Direct Investment in Canada, the so-called Gray report; the third, latest, and largest official examination of foreign ownership as a basis for national policy. The report has been discussed throughout Canada, taken as the basis for action by the government, and much studied in every land where the question of multinational enterprise obtrudes itself. To the extent the report is valid, the subsequent act will secure the expected result - an innovative, Canadian controlled industry.

We question, however, the validity of the Gray report. In our judgement the report rests upon an assumption which we believe to be false. In the result, we believe that the Act should be played on a low key, and should not have the central role in furthering the objective of innovation and Canadian control.

The report is based on the assumption that domestic firms can acquire new technology from license agreements (as modified to comply with new legislation) as effectively as the subsidiaries do from their parent organizations. To Herb Gray, the supervisor of the report, nothing was more objectionable than what he saw as the truncated nature of the subsidiary. But the subsidiary is truncated only from a national viewpoint. It is organically linked to a parent R/D unit. Not so the domestic firm. If, in a modern environment, a complete firm required internal R/D, then the domestic firms are not complete. They are truly truncated - help-less in an uncertain environment unless and until a foreign licen-sor sells them the necessary technology. Licensing is not an ef-ficient way to secure a continuous flow of new technology.

For something as intangible as new technology, the market system is defective. That system rests on legal obligation to comply with agreements for sale of goods. Such obligations are almost impossible to value and enforce when the goods in question are ideas, skills, and knowledge. As a result, the legislative process for dealing with patent or license infringements is slow, complex and costly. Until domestic firms are equipped with their own R/D units, we see the foreign owned subsidiaries in Canada as necessary for innovation. Licensing is not an alternative. There is no reservation in that judgment.[3]

But it is not only in its assumptions that the report, in our opinion, is faulty. The report and the subsequent Act are essentially negative in nature. Their emphasis is to blunt or hinder an initiative arising outside. Such should not constitute the centrepiece of government action. Men do not live only to fight bad things. They need positive goals to let loose the springs of action.

In the early 1960's the government attempted to stimulate more research in Canadian industry. At large, the attempt failed, and the government lost heart. We believe, however, that the attempt was in the right direction. It represents the long view. That is, it was an attempt to secure innovation and Canadian control through the positive approach of moving the domestic firm to be oriented towards product innovation and towards growth. That is a difficult and slow path to follow, slower perhaps than political tenure can endure. We believe, however, it is the right one.

5. COMPETING ON INNOVATION -
    THE CONDITIONS FOR SUCCESS

The aim should be to move Canadian industry back to the path taken for a time in the early 1960's. That is, to make progress through internal R/D. Fundamentally, it is to compete on product innovation. However, in contrast to the ideas of the 1960's, it is recognized today that an internal R/D unit, although necessary, is not itself sufficient to ensure success.

In order to compete effectively in product innovation, a firm requires a continuous flow of new technology. For a reliable flow over time, five things are necessary.

1. A team of qualified scientists capable both of creative research and development and of appreciating the facts of competition in products as well as in ideas.

2. An organizational structure to relate together the scientists with the managers of production, marketing, and finance, particularly when in conditions of high uncertainty.

3. A market large enough to enable profitable commercial exploitation of a new product, and if the costs of innovation are large, the market must be large, but not otherwise.

13

4. Finance sufficient to cover the costs (mostly, labor and equipment) in all the stages between the first concept of a new product and its subsequent introduction to the market place.

5. A strategy for growth for the firm as a whole that extends far enough ahead in time to foresee the future output from current investment in research, and what this means for the kind of enterprise the firm will become.

The changes called for within the domestic firms to obtain these five things are not easy. They are difficult. Old habits will have to be broken, and a new approach taken towards competing in the market. For such changes to occur, men will have to commit themselves and their careers and their interests to the new strategy. They will do this only if success brings rewards - for failure will surely bring penalties. Reward for success, if it means anything at all, means differential income. And there is the real choice that should be presented to Canada.

We can have both innovation and Canadian control if the domestic firms develop a strategy of product innovation. They will develop such a strategy only if there is the possibility for the managers to earn a high income. But Canada, though yet a young country, has begun to pursue the social goal of egalitarianism. We think that egalitarianism is premature - the necessary habits are not yet in place. Canada wants three things: innovation, Canadian-control, egalitarianism. In our judgment, she can have any two, but not all three, at the same time. In this, we make our position quite clear. We choose innovation and Canadian-control. We have no love for egalitarianism per se.

REFERENCES

[1] Richardson, P.R., Strategies of Process Technology Acquisition in the Canadian Mineral Industries, Ph.D. Thesis in progress, UWO, 1975.

[2] L. Wrigley and K. Dundas, Corporate Growth and Development in Canada (unpublished Memorandum, U.W.O.)

[3] A detailed examination of the licensing alternative as it applies to domestic firms will be contained in the Ph.D. thesis of Peter Killing, Manufacturing under License in Canada, in progress, UWO, 1975.

ACKNOWLEDGMENT

[1] Funds for the research on Canadian Response to the Multinational Enterprise were provided by the Department of Industry Trade and Commerce, Ottawa, and the Fund for Excellence, UWO.

[2] We are indebted to Professor J.N. Fry for his assistance in reviewing early drafts of this paper, and for his support over the past four years in the general research project.

[3] We are also indebted to Professor D.C. Shaw, Director of Research, U.W.O., and Professor M.R. Leenders, who organized the provision of funds for doctoral candidates associated with the research - K. Dundas, P. Killing, R. Falconer, and P. Richardson.

FIRA and the Exodus of Direct Investment from Canada

by
Maxime A. Crener and Alfred L. Kahl
Associate Professors
University of Ottawa

INTRODUCTION

Canada has now had a foreign direct investment policy for two years. It is time to ask the question: Is the existing policy the right one?

This paper first presents some information about the current policy and its functioning before discussing the implications of the experience to date. The paper then presents a policy alternative which may be just as effective but much less expensive.

CURRENT POLICY

The current policy is embodied in the Foreign Investment Review Act which was passed in 1973 as the culmination of developments which began back in the 'fifties.

The purpose of the Act is to review new foreign investment proposals to insure that they are beneficial to Canada, considering such factors as: net capital inflow, increased employment, increased resource processing or use of local parts and services, additional exports. Canadian participation as shareholders, directors or managers, improved productivity, enhanced technological development, improved product choice for consumers, beneficial impact on competition, and compatibility with industrial and economic policies.

The Act created an Agency which recommends to the Cabinet which makes the final decision. It created a political rather than an economic test for decision making from which there can be no appeal. Much of what the Agency does is kept secret.

A major difficulty in the Agency's mission is likely to be in assessing "significant benefit to Canada" because Canada does not yet have a clear and enforceable industrial policy. Without such a policy, the Agency must make decisions on an incremental basis.

THE FOREIGN INVESTMENT REVIEW AGENCY

For the first two fiscal years of operation, the Agency has expended more than $5.5 million and 250 man years. Are the benefits to Canada worth this cost and is there a cheaper way to obtain the same benefits?

One possibility for reducing costs would be to restructure the Agency according to service areas, such as: foreign takeovers, de novo foreign investments, and expansion of foreign-controlled firms. Such an organization might facilitate original decision making based on expected benefits and subsequent monitoring of permitted investments since the same people would then be able to follow each project from beginning to end. This would save time since these people would be more familiar with the subject matter. Hence costs should be reduced.

Instead, the Agency has been organized according to functions into three branches: Assessment, Research and Analysis, and Compliance. This type of organization poses communication problems both internally and externally.

In the first fiscal year, the Agency dealt with 150 applications, resolving 92 of them. Only 20 proposed aquisitions failed to meet the test of significant benefit to Canada, and of these only 12 were actually disallowed since the others withdrew their applications.

In its second fiscal year, the Agency dealt with 144 new applications as well as with those carried over from the preceding year, and resolved 153 of them. Only 22 were actually disallowed while 21 were withdrawn.

According to the FIRA annual reports, the majority of the acquisition proposals resulted from initiatives of Canadian businessmen who were experiencing financial difficulties.

Since this is the case and very few applications have been disallowed, it seems that the costs of operating the screening system probably exceed the benefits, if any, produced by the system. Unless these costs can be considered as "start-up" expenses which will be justified by future developments, the current situation does not offer much ground for optimism. Although one of the purposes of FIRA was to negotiate greater benefits for Canada, the Agency's policy of secrecy does not provide outsiders with adequate information; hence we assume that the benefits thus far have been rather minimal.

A major shortcoming of the Canadian system is the lack of public policy toward Canadian multinational firms since the concept of significant benefit to Canada applies equally well to both foreign and local firms. A Canadian industrial policy applicable to all firms is badly needed and should apply to all firms operating within the country regardless of their ownership.

Indeed, the Canadian preoccupation with ownership is misdirected since it is obviously the economic performance of a firm within its borders which should be of interest to the government. Up to now it has been assumed, as an article of faith, that Canadian ownership would necessarily be in the best interests of Canada, even though there is no empirical evidence to support this assumption.

OWNERSHIP AND PERFORMANCE

Concentration of attention on mere ownership of the shares of the company overlooks at least two things of fundamental importance:

1. The relation of share ownership to actual day-to-day control of the behavior of the firm.

2. The relation of either ownership or managership to the national interest.

Since at least the 1930's, the separation of ownership from actual control of the large business firms has been decried and lamented.[1] The rise of the professional manager has, in fact, severed the link between ownership and control over the behavior of the firm. It is now managership rather than ownership that counts!

18

A major study of multinational firms by Vernon[2] found that U.S. nationals in such a firm cannot be counted on to serve either the interests of the U.S. parent firm or the U.S. government nor can local nationals be counted on for unalloyed partiality to their own home territory. This recent evidence corroborates Thomas Jefferson's 1814 contention that "merchants have no country" since they care more about profits than nations.

There is, therefore, no a priori reason to believe that either Canadian owners or Canadian managers, alone or together, could or would serve the Canadian nationalist interest in the absence of some control over the behavior of the firm.

It has been asserted that Canadian ownership is likely to produce more and better quality jobs, a better standard of living and lower taxes for the population than foreign ownerhsip.[3] These are economic issues and there is virtually no empirical evidence to support these contentions; in fact, the opposite is just as likely to be true!

According to reliable sources such as the FIRA annual reports and the evidence provided by <u>Canadian Business</u>, there was an exodus of capital from Canada during 1976. These sources indicate that the majority of capital expenditures by Canadian-owned and/or controlled firms has been outside Canada, mainly in the U.S., because of high costs in Canada with lower productivity and the Canadian Anti-Inflation program.[4] It is the foreign-controlled firms which have been doing most of the investing here, according to FIRA![5]

In the past, Canada has very rightly complained about the extraterritorial application of U.S. laws. It is true that the U.S. has no right to do this but it is also true that Canada has every right to make laws to control all firms operational in Canada but has not done so. Also overlooked was the fact that Canada was obviously the second choice supplier since the prospective buyer already knew the U.S. parent firm could not supply the product from the U.S.

Foreign firms have also been criticized for not exporting enough. Obviously natural resources companies have to export since that is the reason for which they were created. Exporting is possible for the manufacturing industries only if Canada has a comparative advantage in the production of something. If exports are profitable, then and only then will they be made, even by Canadian-owned firms.

A recent study of Canadian exports discovered no evidence to support the hypothesis that foreign-owned subsidiaries operating in Canada are less export-oriented than Canadian owned firms.[6] An earlier study found that the larger the Canadian affiliate, the more likely it is to export, not only to the parent firm and sister affiliates, but also to independent firms in third countries.[7]

There is general agreement among economists that Canada provoked and encouraged foreign investment with the National Policy and its high tariff. Similar results were found by Brash[8] in the case of Australia where increases in tariffs were followed by increases in foreign investment.

The very existence of these foreign firms is ipso facto evidence that they are providing something the Canadian economy wants and is not getting from local firms.

The banking industry provides further evidence of Canadian ambivalence. Canada has only ten banks and they are protected at home from foreign competition because of the importance of the banking sector to the nation. These banks are in fact multinational firms, particularly active in the Caribbean area where they are frequently the only banks in the country. It would seem that the national interests of these countries would be better served by indigenous banks while at the same time the Canadian banks could use their resources to provide better banking services to Canadians.

There are also occasional Canadian complaints about foreign cultural influences. This is merely the result of being so close to the huge U.S. economy. Even in Quebec, which has its own language and culture, there is great consumer demand for TV cable service to bring in U.S. programs, despite the high quality of local programming in French.

Initially, the nature of early British investment in Canada led to the establishment of a still strong Canadian capitalist class which interested itself primarily in finance, commerce, transportation and utilities, since these areas best served the foreign investment. As British power waned, U.S. investment grew, particularly in the last two decades, and was concentrated in the relatively underdeveloped resource and manufacturing sectors. In the past, there was very little internal pressure on policymakers because of foreign investment since it did not represent a threat to the existing establishment until very recently.

POLICY IMPLICATIONS

If foreign investment is considered to be a public policy problem, the Canadian evidence appears to indicate that three major options exist: establishment of some type of screening process for new investments, establishment of fixed rules for domestic shareholders, directors, and/or managers, or establishment of legislation specifying the sectors of the economy from which foreign investors will be excluded.

The Canadian government opted for a screening process and set up an agency for this purpose. The Agency may not have been organized in the optimal manner but since Canada does not yet have a comprehensive industrial policy it is extremely difficult to put a really effective screening process into practical effect.

A simpler solution is to adopt legislation specifying the sectors, such as defence, where foreign investment is to be excluded. This policy is likely to be more in accord with tradition, since it leaves the greatest scope for individual initiative. This is the approach favored by the new government of the province of Quebec as well as by some of the other provinces; thus if the federal government were to adopt it as well, many of the current federal-provincial frictions would be reduced.

The other approach, specifying fixed rules for domestic shareholders, directors, and/or managers, has no empirical support for its efficacity in achieving national objectives and in any case, requires as a condition precedent, the existence of sufficient domestic funds to enable shareholders to purchase the shares, and the existence of sufficient qualified people to serve as directors and/or managers.

The U.S. is in the enviable position of having all of these necessary prerequisites. Most other countries, and particularly those still developing their economies, do not, so they should obviously avoid these kind of policies.

CONCLUSION

The Canadian experience indicates that the present foreign investment policy of Canada is probably not the optimal one, since it requires an effective industrial policy, which does not yet exist.

The alternative policy of specifying fixed rules on the participation of domestic shareholders, directors, and/or managers is also not likely to be the optimal one since it excludes people and capital which may be very important to economic development.

Therefore, the other alternative of specifying key sectors from which foreign participation will be excluded is the most likely to achieve results in conformity with national as well as provincial objectives.

[1] A. Berle and G. Means, The Modern Corporation and Private Property (NY: MacMillan), 1932.

[2] R. Vernon, Sovereignty at Bay (NY: Basic Books), 1971.

[3] J. Fayerweather, Foreign Investment in Canada (Toronto: Oxford University Press), 1974.

[4] J. Van der Feyst, "Exodus! The Flight of Canadian Capital," Canadian Business, December 1976, 13ff.

[5] FIRA, Annual Report 1975/76, FIRA, Ottawa, October 1976, p. 25.

[6] T. Abdel-Malek, "Foreign Ownership and Export Performance," Journal of International Business Studies, Fall 1974, pp. 1-14.

[7] A. Safarian, Foreign Ownership of Canadian Industry (Toronto: McGraw-Hill), 1966.

[8] D. Brash, American Investment in Australian Industry (Cambridge, Mass.: Harvard University Press), 1965.

The Emerging Challenge of Canadian Direct Investment Abroad

by
I.A. Litvak and C.J. Maule
Professor   Professor
York University Carleton University

INTRODUCTION

Direct investment abroad by Canadian companies is fast
emerging as a major topic for debate in Canada. The concern
expressed is twofold: first, such investment by Canadian businessmen is viewed as a vote of non-confidence in the state and
future of Canada's economy. Press announcements of Canadian
firms acquiring, or establishing new, commercial operations
abroad, particularly in the United States, have become a common
feature in the daily newspaper. The firms identified include both
giant corporations such as Inco, acquiring ESB a major battery
manufacturer in the United States, as well as small firms like
Hobarth and Association Studio in Monteal which intends to open a
$300,000 photo products plant in the state of New York.

Secondly, attention is drawn to the potential negative impact
of such investment on Canada's economy. For example, expanding
abroad can be an alternative to expanding at home. By producing
abroad to service local markets, unions and politicians have argued
that domestic employment is being exported. Moreoever, it is
contended, that such investment will result in a significant drop in
Canadian exports and thereby result in further deterioration of
Canada's balance of payments. Both consequences are being
highlighted in the context of Inco's recent announcement to cut
back nickel production and employment in Canada, while bringing
on stream its new nickel deposits in Indonesia and Guatemala.

The negative view of the impact of such investment on the
capital exporting country is not unique to Canada. A similar
debate occurred in the United States with much greater intensity
in the early 1970's. In response to such charges, especially triggered off by Unions, the U.S. government launched a major study

to examine the impact and effects of direct investment abroad. The findings refuted most of the charges, claiming that such investment was indeed beneficial to the U.S. economy.[1]

The purpose of this article is to present some important data on Canadian direct investment abroad; to highlight the key characteristics of Canada's major corporations with investments abroad; and to draw some observations and generalizations concerning the overseas operations of these companies.

NATURE AND EXTENT OF CANADIAN DIRECT INVESTMENT ABROAD

Canadian direct investment abroad (CDIA) almost quadrupled from $2.5 billion in 1960 to $9.3 billion in 1974.[2] By the end of 1974, the United States accounted for approximately 53% of total CDIA, United Kingdom 9%, the European Economic Community (excluding the U.K.) 6%, Australasia 5%, and Japan 1% (see Table 1). As a group, these countries accounted for approximately 85% of CDIA. Thus, most of CDIA is in developed economies. The industrial distribution of CDIA in 1974 was approximately 50% in manufacturing with more than half of it centered in the United States; 21% in mining and petroleum; 15% in utilities; 4% in merchandising and 10% in other industrial categories.

Four key observations can be made with respect to CDIA: first, most of it is located in the developed world; second, the United States with more than one-half of the total is the major geographical area of concentration; third, the manufacturing sector is the prime area for such investment, much of it centered in the United States; and fourth, most of the investment is held in subsidiaries which are 100% owned by the Canadian parent company.

Two further observations should be noted. In 1969, approximately 40% of CDIA was made by enterprises in Canada which were controlled abroad, e.g., Ford Motor Company of Canada.[3] In the intervening years, this figure may have declined somewhat for two reasons: investment abroad is being undertaken by more Canadian based and controlled firms, both large and small; and, some of the previously non-Canadian controlled firms have acquired the status of "Canadian" controlled firms because of a change in their ownership composition and/or by virtue of a reclassification of their

TABLE 1

CANADIAN DIRECT INVESTMENT ABROAD BY LOCATION OF
INVESTMENT IN 1974

CANADIAN DIRECT INVESTMENT ABROAD

I. A. LITVAK AND C. J. MAULE

INTRODUCTION

Direct investment abroad by Canadian companies is fast emerging as a major topic for debate in Canada. The concern expressed is twofold: first, such investment by Canadian businessmen is viewed as a vote of non-confidence in the state and future of Canada's economy. Press announcements of Canadian firms acquiring, or establishing new, commercial operations abroad, particularly in the United States, have become a common feature in the daily newspaper. The firms identified include both giant corporations such as Inco, acquiring ESB a major battery manufacturer in the United States, as well as small firms like Hobarth and Association Studio in Montreal which intends to open a $300,000 photo products plant in the State of New York.

Secondly, attention is drawn to the potential negative impact of such investment on Canada's economy. For example, expanding abroad can be an alternative to expanding at home. By producing abroad to service local markets, unions and politicians have argued that domestic employment is being exported. More-

vestment abroad. The findings refuted most of the charges, claiming that such investment was indeed beneficial to the U.S. economy.[1]

The purpose of this article is to present some important data on Canadian direct investment abroad; to highlight the key characteristics of Canada's major corporations with investments abroad; and to draw some observations and generalizations concerning the overseas operations of these companies.

NATURE AND EXTENT OF CANADIAN DIRECT INVESTMENT ABROAD

status by Canada's Foreign Investment Review Agency. The implications for Canada of the foreign-controlled component of CDIA may differ from that of CDIA which is Canadian controlled and which is the subject of this article.

Finally, CDIA is highly concentrated in a few large enterprises. Statistics Canada revealed in 1968 that 12 large Canadian enterprises accounted for about 69% of total CDIA.[4] Based on data collected by the authors, this figure may in fact understate the current high level of concentration of CDIA in a handful of "Canadian" based and controlled enterprises.

The data obtained by the authors differ significantly from the totals compiled by Statistics Canada. The previously noted $9.3 billion of CDIA has been compiled on the basis of flows and claims between all Canadian parent companies and their foreign subsidiaries. The data surveyed and compiled by the authors include all corporate assets located abroad, including those foreign-held assets acquired through local (foreign) financing. The difference between the balance of payments calculation of direct investment and that of overseas corporate assets is best demonstrated in a benchmark study of foreign direct investment in the United States.[5] At year end 1973, the U.S. government estimated that Canada's direct investment position in the United States was $5.2 billion compared to $3.9 billion estimated by Statistics Canada, while the balance sheet assets of Canada's U.S. affiliates according to the U.S. study totalled in the neighborhood of $24 billion. These are the data which must be collected in order to examine the full public policy implications of CDIA. For example, related to the U.S. "assets" figure for Canada, 175,973 people were employed by the U.S. affiliates of Canadian based companies.

THE CORPORATE LANDSCAPE

Canada is atypical because so much of its industry is owned and controlled by foreign investors. This phenomenon can be quickly gleaned by examining The Financial Post Top 200 industrial Canadian companies ranked by sales for 1976/77: Of the 200 companies, "68 are wholly owned by foreign parent companies, 47 are 50% or more owned, and there are another 20 where there is substantial, sometimes controlling, foreign interests".[6] About 75% of these 135 foreign owned/controlled firms have their headquarters in the United States.

A commonly accepted definition of a multinational enterprise is one that has "controlled manufacturing subsidiaries in six or more countries".[7] The parent companies of most of these large foreign controlled Canadian firms meet this condition, and the majority of them are either listed in the Fortune 500 Largest U.S. or non-U.S. Industrial Corporations.

Canada placed 39 firms on the Fortune 1976 list of the "500 Largest Non-U.S. Industrial Corporations"; however, only 22 of these firms are Canadian controlled, and they form the basis of our study of CDIA. Table 2 identifies the "Canadian contingent by sales, assets and employees. The leading "Canadian-owned" firm is Massey-Ferguson which ranked 80th on this Fortune list, and was a distant fifth to General Motors of Canada which ranked 32nd. General Motors of Canada had sales of approximately $5.3 billion in 1976 almost twice the total of Massey-Ferguson, and it is the first company in Canada to exceed the $5 billion sales figure. The other non-Canadian controlled companies whose sales exceed Massey-Ferguson were as follows (in rank order): Ford Motor of Canada, Imperial Oil and Chrysler Canada.

Table 2

CANADIAN CONTROLLED FIRMS ON THE FORTUNE LIST OF LARGEST NON-U.S. INDUSTRIAL CORPORATIONS

Company	Sales[8]	Assets[9]	Employee
	(- - - $000 - - -)		
Massey-Ferguson	2,771,696	2,305,145	68,200
Alcan Aluminum	2,656,072	3,090,239	60,000
Canadian Pacific Investments	2,152,259	4,046,339	36,948
Seagram	2,048,910	2,161,193	17,000
Inco	2,040,282	3,628,311	55,767
Canada Packers	1,609,089	314,975	15,000
MacMillan Bloedel	1,542,022	1,268,155	23,601
Steel Co. of Canada	1,379,267	1,823,723	22,691
Noranda Mines	1,250,079	2,073,207	32,649
Northern Telecom	1,127,966	698,482	25,277
Moore	1,053,241	764,262	25,964
Dominion Foundries & Steel	916,845	1,023,543	11,500
Genstar	901,097	1,221,378	10,695
Domtar	899,494	760,763	17,520
Abitibi Paper	892,984	891,000	22,000
Consolidated Bathurst	755,887	735,760	17,557
Burns Foods	732,178	162,425	6,971
John Labatt	683,336	446,626	12,150
Molson	663,015	428,063	10,695
Dominion Bridge	543,994	357,270	10,313
Hiram Walker-Gooderham & Worts	543,955	912,388	7,500
Dominion Textile	472,915	360,702	13,130

SOURCE: *Fortune*, August 1977, pp. 226-235.

27

To what extent are Canadian controlled firms multinational? Based on the Harvard criteria of "manufacturing subsidiaries in six or more countries", many of the "Group of 22" could not be considered "Harvard Multinational". On the other hand, if the criteria were altered to include firms which operate subsidiaries in at least two foreign countries, then most of these firms could be viewed as multinational.

Rather than formulate a convenient criterion to fit the "Group of 22", the authors conducted a short survey in 1977 to ascertain the companies' geographic breakdown of sales, assets and employees for 1975/76 (see Table 3). In the case of Canadian Pacific Investments, a holding company, data was obtained for two of its more improtant subsidiaries - Cominco and Algoma. A number of interesting observations can be made concerning the overseas operations of these firms.

Sales - In the case of nine companies, non-Canadian sales exceeded sales in Canada as a percentage of total corporate sales. Some of the comparisons are quite extreme, viz., Massey-Ferguson 92% vs. 8%; Alcan 83% vs. 17%; Seagram 94% vs. 6%; Inco 89% vs. 11%; Moore 90% vs. 10%; and Hiram Walker 88% vs. 12%. In every case, U.S. corporate sales equalled or exceeded company sales in Canada. Five of the nine companies had non-Canadian sales in excess of $1 billion: Massey-Ferguson, Alcan, Seagram, Inco and MacMillan Bloedel.

Assets - Unlike the sales situation, fewer companies hold more of their assets outside of Canada: Massey-Ferguson, Alcan, Seagram, Moore and Hiram Walker. Other companies with significant assets abroad are Inco (47%), MacMillan Bloedel (39%), Noranda (25%), Northern Telecom (20%), Abitibi (22%), Dominion Bridge (40%), and Dominion Textile (31%). Cominco, a subsidiary of Canadian Pacific Investments, has 37% of its corporate assets abroad. In the case of Massey-Ferguson, Seagram, and Moore, U.S. corporate assets exceed the Canadian totals.

The corporate process of internationalization has moved more rapidly in the functional area of marketing (sales) than in (assets). This may be attributed to a combination of the following reasons: first, extended and extensive exporting of goods from Canada is often a precursor to undertaking substantial investments abroad; second, Canadian controlled firms in manufacturing are

Table 3

CANADIAN CONTROLLED COMPANIES ON THE FORTUNE LIST OF LARGEST NON-U.S. INDUSTRIAL CORPORATIONS
1976
GEOGRAPHIC DISTRIBUTION OF SALES, ASSETS, & EMPLOYEES

Company	Sales Total ($000)	Can.	U.S.	U.K.	Other	Assets Total ($000)	Can.	U.S.	U.K.	Other	Employees Total	Can.	U.S.	U.K.	Other
		- - - % - - -					- - - % - - -					- - - % - - -			
Massey-Ferguson	2,771,696	8	23	8	61	2,305,145	11	26	15	48	68,200	12	9	17	62
Alcan Aluminum	2,656,072	17	21	15	47	3,090,239	48	9	16	27	60,000	31	6	14	49
Canadian Pacific Investments*	2,152,259	- - - N.A. - - -				4,046,339	- - - N.A. - - -				36,948	- - - N.A. - - -			
Seagram	2,048,970	6	68	- -26- -		2,161,193	10	- 90** -			17,000	10	- 90** -		
Inco	2,040,282	11	50	12	27	3,628,311	53	23	9	15	55,767	46	27	15	12
Canada Packers	1,609,089	85	4	4	7	314,975	82	3	5	10	15,000	79	1	6	14
MacMillan Bloedel	1,542,022	24	45	9	22	1,268,155	61	23	13	3	23,601	77	15	7	1
Steel Co. of Canada	1,379,267	88	8	- -4- -		1,823,723	96	4	—	—	22,691	99	1	—	—
Noranda Mines	1,250,079	25	25	7.5	42.5	2,073,207	75	12.5	—	12.5	32,649	85	7.5	—	7.5
Northern Telecom	1,127,966	86	9	- -5- -		698,482	80	15	- -5- -		25,277	80	12	- -8- -	
Moore	1,053,241	10	63	7	20	764,262	9	61	11	19	25,964	9	51	15	25
Dominion Foundries	916,845	90	5	1	4	1,023,543	98	2	—	—	11,500	100	—	—	—
Genstar	901,097	80	18	—	2	1,221,378	85	12	—	3	10,695	89	10	—	1
Domtar	899,494	78	15	7	—	760,763	94	3	3	—	17,520	93	2	5	—
Abitibi	892,984	40	48	- -12- -		891,000	78	22	—	—	22,000	91	9	—	—
Consolidated Bathurst	755,887	55	20	5	20	735,760	90	---	—	10	17,557	85.	—	—	15
Burns Foods	732,178	95	2	—	3	162,425	100	—	—	—	6,971	100	—	—	—
John Labatt	683,336	93	6	- -1- -		446,626	90	5	- -5- -		12,150	95	5	—	—
Molson	663,015	96	3	1	—	428,063	95	4	1	—	10,695	97	2	1	—
Dominion Bridge	543,994	67	33	—	—	357,270	60	40	—	—	10,313	55	45	—	—
Hiram-Walker	543,955	12	58	3	27	912,388	16	33	25	26	7,500	25	23	24	28
Dominion Textile	472,915	60	25	3	12	360,702	69	21	1	9	13,130	79	18	—	3
Cominco*	725,005	25	39	16	20	973,205	63	18	1.5	17.5	10,696	80	9	.5	10.5
Algoma Steel*	584,835	78	21	- -1- -		928,248	89	11	—	—	12,200	91	9	—	—

*Cominco and Algoma Steel are controlled by Canadian Pacific Investments Limited (CPI) which in turn is a subsidiary of Canadian Pacific Limited.

**Largely in the U.S.

relatively late entrants as multinationals, compared to their European and U.S. counterparts; and, third, many of these firms are in resource based industries, they are highly capital intensive in Canada, and until recently were largely export-oriented.

This scenario is changing as more Canadian companies are vertically integrating forwards and diversifying their operations through foreign acquisitions and the formation of new establishments abroad. At present, four Canadian companies have corporate assets in excess of one billion dollars located outside of Canada; specifically, Massey-Ferguson, Alcan, Seagram, and Inco. Moreoever, they are among the more aggressive Canadian companies currently expanding abroad.

Employees - As one might expect, the distribution of employees parallels the geographic breakdown of corporate assets. In addition to Massey-Ferguson, Alcan, Seagram, Moore and Hiram Walker, Inco had more employees working for the corporation abroad than in Canada (54% vs. 46%). Generally speaking, these six companies are the most internationally diverse of the "Group of 22". A key characteristic of Canadian multinationals is that the domestic market declines rapidly in importance as they internationalize their operations, and the contribution of Canadian sales to total corporate (global) sales drops significantly behind the U.S. figures.

As previously noted, four Canadian companies have overseas assets valued in excess of $1 billion each. These may be viewed as members of the Canadian billion dollar club when dealing with CDIA. Before proceeding to highlight the historical evolution of these companies, it should be noted that Brascan, a Toronto-based firm, could also satisfy the billion dollar criterion. Since it is primarily a regulated utility distributing company, it was excluded from the Fortune list. At this time, Brascan could be described as a binational firm, Canada and Brazil - with most of its operations based in Brazil, e.g., 90%+ of sales and employees, and 80%+ of assets. Another potential club member is Bata Shoes, a privately-held corporation, with headquarters in Toronto. Most of this company's activities and investments are also based abroad, but unlike Brascan they are geographically diverse.

THE BILLION DOLLAR CLUB[10]

Alcan and Aluminum

In the Western world, six large multinational companies with vertically integrated operations control approximately 80% of the aluminum smelting capacity. These six producers are Alcan (Canada), Alcoa, Reynolds and Kaiser (U.S.), Pechiney (France), and Alusuisse (Switzerland).

Two of the characteristics of the North American industry are its dependence on imported sources of bauxite and/or alumina, which the major firms have traditionally owned or controlled, and the large number of independent fabricators that manufacture aluminum products often in competition with the major producers. In Canada, these characteristics are accentuated even further. The Canadian aluminum industy is entirely dependent on imported bauxite; smelting capacity is owned 85% by Alcan and 15% by Canadian Reynolds; Canadian consumption of aluminum products is supplied about 68% by Alcan, 20% by Canadian Reynolds and 12% by imports and secondary aluminum. A very high proportion of aluminum produced is exported from Canada. Consequently, the Canadian aluminum industry can be closely identified with Alcan, and the livelihood of this industry can be seen to be very dependent on external factors.

Measured in terms of capital employed and sales of aluminum, 42% of Alcan's fixed capital was outside of Canada, and 83% of sales were realized in foreign markets. In addition, 69% of the approximately 60,000 Alcan employees work outside of Canada.

Alcan's subsidiary and related companies have bauxite holdings in seven countries, produce alumina in six, smelt primary aluminum in ten, fabricate aluminum in thrity-four, have sales outlets in over one hundred, and maintain warehouse inventories in the larger markets.[10]

Is Alcan a Canadian company? Many Canadians and foreigners alike perceive Alcan to be an American firm, not a Canadian company. However, judging by the criteria of registered ownership, location of headquarters organization, and nationality of senior management and the board of directors, Alcan is a Canadian multinational corporation. In mid-1976, the registered ownership of the more than 40 million shares of Alcan Aluminum Limited (the parent holding company) then outstanding was 49.0% in Canada, 37.3% in the United States and 13.7% in other countries. Moreover, the majority of the directors and officers of Alcan are citizens of Canada. In 1976, the Canadian government, through the Foreign Investment Review Agency, classified Alcan as a "Canadian" company, not bound by its regulations governing acquisitions and new investments into related and unrelated areas of Canadian business activity by "foreign-owned" firms.

The perception of Alcan as an American company has risen from the knowledge that its corporate roots were in the United States, and that there was majority U.S. ownership in the company until the later 1960s. At the turn of the century (July 3, 1902), the Aluminum Company of America (Alcoa) established a Canadian affiliate under the name of the Northern Aluminum Company, Limited. Some 23 years later on July 8, 1925, the corporate name was altered to the Aluminum Company of Canada, Limited, hereafter referred to as Alcan Canada, which on May 31, 1928 became the principal operating subsidiary of Aluminum Lim ited, the holding company known as Alcan. This Canadian incorporated company was assigned all of Alcoa's foreign holdings except for its bauxite operations in Surinam.

The first "corporate separation" between Alcoa and Alcan appears to have been prompted more by managerial ambition, rather than possible U.S. antitrust action. Arthur Vining Davis was Chairman of the Board of Alcoa in 1928, when two of his subordinates were competing for the Presidency of the firm: Roy A. Hunt, son of Captain Alfred Hunt, a founding member of Alcoa, and E.K. Davis, Arthur's younger brother. The split between Alcoa and Alcan allowed A.V. Davis to appoint his brother, E.K. Davis, to the Presidency of Alcan, while Alfred E. Hunt was named president of Alcoa.

On assuming the presidency of Alcan, E.K. Davis brought with him to Canada a small group of Alcoa-trained personnel who collectively were responsible for the emergence of this company as a giant industrial enterprise in Canada. Some of the Alcoa-Alcan pioneers were visible and dominant in a number of the key managerial positions and boardrooms of Alcan and its key operating subsidiary Alcan Canada up until the later 1960s.

Running parallel with the managerial changes, significant antitrust developments dramatically altered the U.S. ownership composition of Alcan, and its links to Alcoa. In April of 1937, the U.S. Department of Justice filed a complaint under the U.S. antitrust laws naming as defendants Aluminum Company of America (Alcoa), 25 of its subsidiaries and affiliated companies including Alcan and 37 of its directors, officers and shareholders. The complaint alleged that Alcoa monopolized the manufacture of virgin aluminum ingot, and the sale of aluminum sheets, alloys, bars, etc. in the United States. The case was formally ended twenty years later in 1957.

Although no wrongdoing was proven by the antitrust authorities, the Court ordered in June of 1950 that "the shareholders of Alcoa be required to dispose of their stock interests either in Limited (Alcan) or Alcoa", to ensure the future competitiveness of the U.S. aluminum industry. All the principal shareholders, except E.K. Davis, elected to sell their Alcan shares, and by December 1957 the disposition order, with a small balance of shares outstanding, was completed.

Alcan has grown rapidly from a relatively small firm to one of giant proportion, even in global terms, second only to Alcoa. The company's corporate thrust has changed from being chiefly a producer and exporter of primary aluminum to a large vertically integrated producer which increasingly consumes its own primary aluminum output in its world wide fabricating plants, producing a myriad of industrial and consumer goods manufactured out of aluminum. A major ingredient for the success of this strategy rested on Alcan's investment and penetration of the U.S. market.

Alcan's U.S. subsidiary, Alcan Aluminum Corporation (Alcancorp), which was nothing more than a sales subsidiary in 1944, emerged as the fourth largest aluminum fabricator in the United States, and its sales in 1976 would have easily placed it on the Fortune list of the 500 largest industrial corporations in the United States.

The importance of Alcan's U.S. subsidiary cannot be underestimated: in 1976, sales to third parties in the United States accounted for about 21% of Alcan's total worldwide sales, and for approximately 9% of Alcan's total capital employed. Similarly, the importance of Alcancorp's contribution to Alcan Canada, and hence its impact on Canada cannot be overemphasized: "approximately 75% of U.S. ingot imports comes from Alcan and 80% from Canada as a whole". As a result of Alcan's investment into fabrication in the United States, there is a very high degree of corporate interdependence and integration between Alcan Canada and Alcancorp. This explains why Alcan actively encourages the creation of a North American free trade arrangement, at least in primary aluminum.

In recent years, the shape of a new corporate strategy appears to be emerging; a strategy that will not necessarily be linked to the requirements of Alcan Canada, i.e., consumption of largely Canadian produced primary aluminum. In 1971, David M. Culver, currently Chief Executive Officer of Alcan Canada, projected a scenario in which Canadian smelter production would be geared essentially to North American requirements, especially those of the United States, and would play a marginal role as a supplier to other foreign markets.

Traditionally, competitive pressures have led Alcan to erect abroad local smelting operations in order to protect its dominant local position. Currently, in order to enter certain new markets or retain its position in existing markets, Alcan is being pressured into establishing fully integrated aluminum industries (self-contained ingot and fabricating systems) even in those countries where the importation of Canadian primary aluminim might make the venture more efficient. These investments are being made because of their strategic and economic importance to the general competitiveness of Alcan as a multinational enterprise, of which Alcan Canada is a part, albeit a critical one.

INCO AND NICKEL

Inco is the world's larges producer of nickel, a substantial producer of copper, which is associated with nickel in the nickel-bearing sulphide ore mines in Canada, and a major producer (from its Canadian ores) of six platinum group metals - platinum, palladium, rhodium, ruthenium, iridium and osmium. The company also produces iron ore pellets and limited quantities of gold, silver, sulphur, selenium and tellurium. In addition, through its rolling mills division with plants in the United States and Great Britain, it produces wrought nickel, high nickel alloys and welding products; and since 1974, Inco has become a major producer of automotive battery products.

In 1975, Inco supplied 38.5% of the "Free World's" nickel consumption. Its major customer is the United States which accounted for 41% of the company's metal sales in dollars, followed by Europe with 39%, and Canada with 11%. Inco supplies approximately two-thirds of U.S. nickel requirements. Although Inco has operating facilities in more than 20 countries, the bulk of its nickel is mined in Canada, and it appears that Canadian nickel deposits will continue to be an important element in the company's operations. The company is making substantial investments in developing nickel deposits in Indonesia and Guatemala, and is engaged in seabed exploration for nickel.

There appears to be an historical parallel between the emergence of Inco and Alcan as major Canadian based multinational companies. Both are of U.S. origin, the year 1902 is a critical one in their respective development, and the U.S. steel industry played a significant role in their establishment. The International Nickel Company was formed in 1902 through the merger of a number of firms in Canada and the United States, under the sponsorship of J.P. Morgan and Co. and the U.S. Steel Corporation. The head office was centered in New York, and seven of the ten members of the first corporate board of directors came from major U.S. steel firms, as did the first President of the company.

In 1916 the International Nickel Company incorporated its Canadian subsidiary, the International Nickel Company of Canada, Ltd., and partly in response to Canadian government and public pressures to refine mine output locally, it built a refinery at Port Colborne, Ontario, which came on stream in 1918.

The year 1928 is a major landmark in the emergence of Inco as a Canadian based company. Through an exchange of shares, Inco (Canada) became the parent company, and Inco (U.S.) the subsidiary. It is interesting to note that on May 31, 1928, Aluminum Limited (Alcan) was incorporated in Canada to engage in the international aluminum business. In both instances, however, while Inco and Alcan were legally incorporated in Canada, Inco's head office was based in New York, and Alcan's most senior personnel were resident in the United States as well in 1928.

Through a combination of acquisition, expansion and modernization, Inco, at the time of World War II, was the Western world's largest wholly integrated nickel producing complex, from mining to refining and primary fabrication, with subsidiary operations located on two continents, and company personnel scattered in twelve countries. An interesting similarity between Alcan and Inco arises from the fact that these two companies looked to Canada for their raw material source - in the case of Alcan, it is cheap hydro-electric power, and for Inco it is the nickel ore body. To this day, approximately one-half of the corporate assets for both firms are located in Canada, and the bulk of their Canadian output is exported to sister subsidiaries and affiliated companies, largely in the United States and Europe.

Inco, unlike Alcan, however, has been more active in diversifying its activities away from the company's traditional metal base of operation. The first major step in Inco's diversification program was the acquisition in mid-1974 of ESB Incorporated, one of the world's leading battery companies. This U.S. company is a subsidiary of Inco-Canada's U.S. subsidiary, International Nickel Company, Inc. Sales of ESB Incorporated were $598 million in 1976, accounting for about 30% of world wide corporate sales in 1976. ESB, in its own right, is a major U.S.-based multinational firm with 98 plants in 17 countries.

As a result of the ESB acquisition, the strategic importance of the U.S. market in terms of sales, assets and employees is now greater for Inco than Alcan: i.e., sales - 50% vs. 21%; assets - 23% vs. 9%; and employees - 27% vs. 6%. In terms of ownership, the two companies exhibit similar characteristics; at year end (1976), "Canadian residents of record held 49% of the shares outstanding, United States residents of record 36%, and residents of record in other countries 15%".

Unlike Alcan, however, Inco only recently moved its head office organization from the United States (New York) to Canada (Toronto), i.e., 1972. It was in the late 1950s that the most senior executives of Alcan moved from the United States to their head office in Canada (Montreal). Inco, like Alcan, was recently judged by FIRA to be a "Canadian controlled firm"; but in the case of both firms, the chief executive officers have been and are to this day citizens of the United States, although the boards of the two companies continue to be "Canadianized".

MASSEY-FERGUSON AND FARM MACHINERY

Massey-Ferguson Limited (M-F), headquartered in Toronto, is one of Canada's oldest and largest multinational operations. As an international organization, it can trace its corporate thrust into international business as far back as the 1880s. The predecessor of M-F was the Massey Harris Co. Limited which marged with Harry Ferguson Limited in 1953 to form Massey-Harris-Ferguson whose name was changed to Massey-Ferguson Ltd. in 1958. M-F is a holding company with over 100 subsidiaries incorporated in different national jurisdictions. The company operates world-wide through subsidiaries and through associates in which it holds minority interests; it manufactures in 18 countries, and sells farm machinery, industrial and constructions machinery, and diesel engines through subsidiaries, associated and franchised distributors and dealers in more than 130 countries.

With a sales volume of $2.8 billion in 1976, corporate management contends that it is the largest manufacturer, in the western world, of agricultural tractors and sugar cane harvesters; that its aggregate sales in agricultural equipment is exceeded only by the sales of two U.S. multinational competitors; and that it manufactures more high-speed diesel engine units, worldwide, than any other competing producer. M-F is not only one of the biggest firms in Canada, it also ranks as one of the world's largest manufacturers of agricultural equipment. This distinction is an important one to bear in mind when one compares the size of Canadian MNCs with those of the United States. The largest manufacturers in the United States tend to rank high among the largest worldwide, but the largest in Canada only rank high in the context of industry/-product specific categories.

The growth of M-F since the mid-1960s has been triggered off by an active program of acquisition, expansion and integration. Most of the acquisitions took place in the industrialized west, e.g., United States, U.K., Italy and Germany. In 1976 M-F had a manufacturing base of some 50 plants containing 25 million sq. ft., situated in 12 countries. This is the core of the company's manufacturing system; in addition, through corporate arrangements with associate companies or licensees, M-F manufactures in 18 other countries.

M-F has pursued a program of corporate integration in all key areas of commercial activity; however, it is in production and sourcing that the company has gained considerable success and business acclaim. The corporate policy is designed to promote maximum interchangeability of component parts, especially for tractors and combines, in order to increase production efficiencies on a world-wide basis. In the company's 1975 Annual Report, management stated:

> Highly productive results have been secured from each major capital investment through the use of our worldwide production scheduling system and our logistics network of multinational sources. In addition, product costs continue to be kept under control by product integration - switching from buy to make ... through product design and manufacturing planning, emphasis continues to be placed upon interchangeability and commonality to obtain cost benefits and sourcing flexibility.

M-F's strategy aims at sourcing complete machines for specific markets from those M-F plants which can supply them at the lowest cost. Flexibility, via interchangeability of component parts of the machine, is not simply realized by plant location, but also by phase of manufacturing which takes place in the individual plant. Corporate integration is especially evident in the North American operations of M-F, because there are no tariffs on shipments of agricultural equipment between Canada and the United States. For this reason, a group of M-F operating subsidiaries conduct the company's business in this combined market with some products manufactured in the United States and others in Canada.

In 1976, the relative corporate importance of Canada and the United States, measured in terms of sales, assets, and employees, was as follows: 8% vs. 23% (sales); 11% vs. 26% (assets); and 12% vs. 9% (employees). Employing the same yardstick for the two country comparisons (Canada vs. United States), the 1966 figures were as follows: 10% vs. 31% (sales); 18% vs. 16% (assets); and 17% vs. 11% (employees). In that 10 year interval, North America's share of the company's total sales dropped from 41% to 31% while Latin America, Asia, Africa, and Australia increased their relative sales importance. But in terms of assets, both globally and in the context of the company's North American operations, the picture is different: the United States now accounts for slightly more than one-quarter. The sales to assets ratio is approximately 1:1 and it appears that even though free trade exists between the United States and Canada, the company has opted to service the U.S. market largely from U.S. plants. While transportation costs may be a ready made explanation for establishing and acquiring U.S. plants, rising Canadian labor costs and the lower productivity of its Canadian plants led M-F's Canadian management to invest more heavily in recent years in the United States.

M-F's entry into the U.S. market parallels the approach favored by many of today's companies which invest in the United States; namely, the acquisition route. In 1910, M-F acquired an implement manufacturer located in Batavia, New York. On the other hand, M-F's rationale for first investing in the United States is somewhat atypical. E.P. Neufeld in his study of M-F notes:

> When it did obtain its first manufacturing facilities in the United States it was, paradoxically, because of the fear of free trade and not because of any attempt to circumvent the tariff. This is how it happened. Potential competition from the United States threatened to change with the 1910 campaign for reciprocity, that is, for free trade between Canada and the United States. Massey-Harris (M-F) seemed to fear that if the campaign were successful, its Canadian market would be threatened by a flood of imports from the United States. Such fears were not entirely ill-founded. To protect itself from such competition, Massey-Harris hurriedly established itself in the United States by buying into the Johnston Harvester Company...

Among North American multinationals, M-F is a pioneer; by 1908, it realized approximately one-half of its corporate sales outside of Canada. This achievement took place without the benefit of significant sales to the U.S. market. This is no longer the case; sales in the United States are significant, accounting for about one-quarter of total corporate sales; and M-F's U.S. subsidiary, Massey-Ferguson Inc., placed 18th in sales on the list of the 100 largest foreign owned companies in the United States.

SEAGRAM AND LIQUOR

The Seagram Company Ltd., like M-F, is a holding company. It is headquartered in Montreal, and multinational in scope, with operating subsidiaries and affiliates in 23 countries. The company produces a complete line of whiskies, gins, rums, brandies, vodkas, other spirits and wines and markets its brands in over 130 countries. In addition, through its subsidiaries, the company is engaged in exploration for and development, production and sale of crude oil, natural gas and related products. A further similarity between Seagram and M-F is that in addition to being one of Canada's largest firms with a 1976 sales volume of approximately $2 billion, Seagram is also the world's largest producer and marketer of distilled spirits and wines.

The history of the present day company dates back to 1928 when Samuel Bronfman and his brothers acquired the shares of Joseph E. Seagram and Sons Ltd. of Waterloo, Ontario. This Waterloo-based firm began its operation in 1857 and by 1928 was a highly respected firm. The 1928 purchase was combined with the Bronfman's owned and managed company, Distillers Corporation Ltd., to establish a new public company, Distillers Corporation Seagrams Ltd.

Bronfman's entry in the U.S. market took place some five years later (November 1933) when a distilling plant in Lawrenceburg, Indiana was purchased. Thus, the acquisition route was again employed by yet another Canadian multinational. Joseph E. Seagram and Sons Inc. was formed to operate the distillery and has since become the parent company in the United States. Expansion in the U.S. market has continued rapidly ever since. In 1976, the U.S. market accounted for 68% of total company sales and Joseph E. Seagram and Sons Inc., incorporated in Indiana in 1933 and headquartered in New York, is now an operating and holding company in its own right. It controls through stock ownership all of the affiliated distillery operations and sales companies in the United States.

In 1975, the U.S. subsidiary of Seagram Company Ltd. of Canada had a sales volume of approximately $1.6 billion, ranking third on the list of the 100 largest foreign owned companies in the United States. The relative commercial importance between the head-office in Canada and its U.S. subsidiary head-office can be whimsically contrasted from the following quote excerpted from the company's 1975 Form 10-K report, under Item 3, entitled

Properties:

The company's executive offices are located in a four story office building which the company owns at 1430 Peel Street, Montreal Quebec, and Joseph E. Seagram's executive offices are located in a 38 story office building which it owns at 375 Park Avenue, New York, New York.

That this is the case is not surprising since 68% of Seagram's sales is realized in the United States while only 6% is earned in Canada. Nonetheless, Seagram's market share in each country is comparable - 20% in Canada and over 19% in the United States.

Since World War II, Seagram's has been actively expanding its overseas operations (non-North America), while in more recent years it has been engaged in a significant diversification program away from its traditional business of distilled spirits and wines. With reference to its policy of growth through internationalization, the M-F strategy of interchangeability and flexibility appears to characterize the Seagram corporate strategy. Sam Bronfman, who until his death was synonymous with "Seagram", offered the following explanation for the emergence of his company as one of the world's leading multinationals"

I have always considered it most important that our business between the countries in which we have interests should be on the basis of a "two-way street". Let me explain. We ship our Canadian, American and Scotch whiskies to France and Italy, for example, and we ship our French and Italian products to Canada, the United States and Great Britain. This "two-way street" premise extends to all the countries where we have facilities. It is this policy which is the spine of our business. It brings and holds together our world-wide operations.

Inasmuch as 94% of company sales are realized outside of Canada, and only 10% of the company's assets are located in Canada, with the United States accounting for well over one-half of total corporate sales and assets, it is not surprising that a U.S. subsidiary of Joseph E. Seagram & Sons, Inc. handles international sales. Seagram Export Sales Co. Inc., established in New York, was formed and given responsibility for sales in over 100 countries.

41

In 1953 a major change in the company's activities was initiated. In that year the Frankfort Oil Co. of Oklahoma was purchased. In the words of Sam Bronfman:

Forseeing the requirements for energy in the 1950's and the 1960's, and the almost unbelievable demand of the 1970's, I was motivated in 1953 to cause Joseph E. Seagram & Sons, Inc. to begin investing in the petroleum industry - the energy business.

Growth through diversification received its biggest boost in 1963 when Seagram acquired Texas Pacific Coal and Oil Co., now known as Texas Pacific Oil Company, Inc. (incorporated in Delaware). This company generated total revenues of $140 million in fiscal 1975, ranking it among the top five independent producers in the United States. This Dallas-headquartered firm does no refining or consumer marketing itself; instead, it concentrates exclusively on finding, developing and producing hydrocarbons. Its major pre-occupation today is with expansion.

In 1975 exploration and development property was held in 20 states of the United States and in Alberta (by Seafort Petroleum). North American holdings, largely U.S., totalled 25 million net underdeveloped acres, while overseas acreage amounted to 8.1 million net acres. Spain, Dubai, the North Sea, Kenya and the Philippines are some of the areas in which the Seagram's subsidiary, alone or in partnership, is pursuing its exploration activities.

The management of Seagrams is committed to developing the company's oil and gas business. Business and political events since 1953 strengthened management's conviction that the need for and value of new reserves would continue to grow. This conviction involves further exploration in the United States, but Seagram also accepts the larger risks, both political and economic, that is involved in international exploration. Management believes that it is overseas where the discoveries of world-ranking new reserves will probably be made, and that this will influence Seagram's investment in the future. Current investment and Seagram's corporate strategy for the future appears to be U.S. and non-Canadian oriented, albeit, multinational in scope.

SUMMARY OBSERVATIONS

CDIA is occurring with increasing frequency through the establishment of new facilities, take-over of foreign firms and involvement in joint ventures. Much of this investment is financed through borrowings in foreign financial markets, and by investing the retained earnings of existing foreign affiliates abroad. Domestic markets saturation, drive for growth, relative scarcity of production factors (labor, capital, land, and intermediate products), access to foreign markets, need for certain raw materials, and tax and other financial advantages are some of the reasons offered by Canadian businessmen for investing abroad.[11]

In the 1960's, corporate motivation for investing abroad was largely viewed in positive terms, i.e., to grow big enough to compete successfully internationally meant the firm had to break through the small Canadian market syndrome. The bulk of this investment was undertaken by resource based firms in Canada as a means of diversifying their operations both in geographic and product terms. Motivation for investing abroad in the late 1970's has been greatly accelerated by negative considerations as well, such as Canada's high inflation rates; government controls on prices, profits, and executive salaries; strikes, union militancy, and poor labor-management relations; federal-provincial jurisdictional disputes in mining and expropriation; and the general political and economic uncertainties surrounding Quebec.

The corporate vignettes of Canada's four major multinationals indicate that regardless of their historical roots, Canadian or U.S., their investment and involvement in the United States is substantial, increasing and critical to the success of their corporate strategies. Moreover, the performance of the Canadian part of the operation is affected by what happens in the United States. While the corporate relationship between the Canadian and U.S. entities within the Canadian multinational corporation are to varying degrees interdependent, they are also asymmetrical; as is the case between Canada and the United States in terms of trade and capital. Thus, although the headquarters of each of the four corporations is based in Canada, the sensitivity of the corporate executive in Canada to what happens in the United States is very great.

In the context of the present politco-economic environment in Canada, including poor government-business relations, it is worth noting that Alcan and Inco were originally of U.S. origin. For this reason, it is not difficult to imagine that these two firms might wish to transfer their headquarters again; this time back to the United States. The move would not be a difficult one to make. Similarly, Seagram and Massey-Ferguson might see the merit of moving their headquarters. Some would argue that such a move would be more "de jure" than "de facto"; and the most likely site would also be the United States.

The probability of the foregoing scenario materializing at this time is not great, but it cannot be ruled out. If the present poor investment climate in Canada continues to deteriorate because of political as well as eocnomic circumstances, the current transfer of headquarters' organizations between provinces, e.g., Quebec and Ontario, may in due time be overshadowed by moves involving some of Canada's largest industrial enterprises with substantial operations in the United States, to the United States.

The authors are currently examining the policy implications of Canadian direct investment abroad for corporations and governments in Canada.

FOOTNOTES

[1] United States Tariff Commission, Implications of Multinational Firms for World Trade and Investment and for U.S. Trade and Labor (Washington: U.S. Government Printing Office, 1973).

[2] Statistics Canada Daily, Catalogue 11-001E, September 14, 1976, p. 2.

[3] I.A. Litvak and C.J. Maule, "Canadian Investment Abroad: In Search of a Policy", International Journal, Vol. XXXI, No. 1, Winter 1975-76, p. 161.

[4] Ibid, p. 16.

[5] The difference between the Canadian and U.S. calculations re: Canadian direct investment in the United States is due to the difference in the definition of what constitutes direct investment; a lower percentage of foreign equity ownership is employed in the case of U.S. data to indicate direct investment. The Canadian figure is taken from Statistics Canada Daily, Cat. 11-001E, Sept-

ember 14, 1976, p. 4. For the U.S. data, see Report to the Congress, <u>Foreign Direct Investment in the United States</u>, Volume 2, (Washington: U.S. Department of Commerce, April 1976).

[6]<u>The Financial Post 300</u>, Summer 1977, p. 19.

[7]Raymond Vernon, <u>Sovereignty at Bay</u> (New York: Basic Books, 1971), p. 11.

[8]All companies on the list must have derived more than 50% of their sales from manufacturing and/or mining. Figures exclude intracompany transactions and include subsidiaries more than 50% owned, either on a fully consolidated or prorata basis.

[9]As shown at the company's year-end.

[10]The following books provide a historical overview of the four Canadian multinational corporations: I.A. Litvak and C.J. Maule, <u>Alcan Aluminum Limited: A Corporate History</u>, prepared for the Royal Commission on Corporate Concentration, Government of Canada, 1977; Samuel Bronfman, <u>Little Acorns</u>, a personal history of Seagram Co., included in the company's Annual Report of 1970; E.P. Neufeld, <u>A Global Corporation</u>, University of Toronto Press, 1969; O.W. Main, <u>The Canadian Nickel Industry</u>, University of Toronto Press, 1955.

[11]See I.A. Litvak and C.J. Maule, "Canadian Multinationals in the Western Hemisphere", <u>The Business Quarterly</u>, Vol. 10, No. 3 (Autumn 1975), pp. 30-42.

Improving Canada's Global Competitiveness
by
Randolph E. Ross and Peter M. Banting
Professors
McMaster University

What must Canada do as a nation if she wishes to change her current world position? Present concerns about the structure of Canadian inter-relationships with the world economic community suggest that deeply rooted patterns must be changed if Canada is to improve her economic status. This article reports the results of a study undertaken to determine what types of research would be of greatest benefit to Canada's economic development.

A group of distinguished business executives, government officials and academics participated in a year-long Delphi study, which was used to both generate and evaluate a large number of research projects of benefit to Canada's future economic and trading relations. The results reported here are presented not as individual research projects, but rather as a synthesis of the concepts underlying the proposed research projects that were generated by our study.

BROAD SCALE CONSIDERATIONS

Any consideration of Canada's future international trade position must first take into account the broad issues of her current position and limitations. This research study identified a number of macro areas requiring study if future options are to be fully explored. These have been grouped under the categories: resources, resource-related industry, capability, market diversification, product competitiveness, liberalized trade, and rationalization of inter-governmental policies.

Resources:

Rapid changes have taken place in world-wide supply and demand for Canada's traditional natural resource products. These

changes have been initiated by increased exploration, foreign government development policies, offshore limits at sea, population
changes, increased industrialization, exhaustion of foreign dom-
estic-based supplies and political disturbances, to name but a few.
As Canada makes investment plans for her resource industries,
both industrialists and politicians must be aware of where the
future global shortages and surpluses are likely to occur. Two of
the specific areas suggested by the panel are Canada's future
forestry management and the impact of grain export policies on the
domestic livestock industry. In short, it requires careful planning
not only to marshal resources to meet export demands, but also to
provide long-term stability in both foreign sales and domestic
needs.

RESOURCE RELATED INDUSTRY DEVELOPMENT

The development of Canada's natural resource industries was
such that the equipment, machinery and certain infrastructure
elements required in the early days had to be purchased from
other countries. This pattern has not changed significantly, even
though Canada has grown and acquired the domestic technical
know-how to facilitate her resource industries. Capital equipment
is still purchased from abroad, to a great extent, rather than
being designed and manufactured by Canadian companies. The
unfortunate result of this is that, in areas where our natural
resource abundance should lead to the development of Hirschman
linkages[1] and their resultant contributions to Canada's trade in
such equipment and services abroad, little development has taken
place.

Canada could develop capital goods industries related to such
areas as forestry, mining, exploration, fish and animal processing, grain milling, storage facilities, transportation and distribution systems, and so on. These, in turn, could gain relatively
easy access to foreign markets by piggybacking their marketing
efforts on the sales of the natural resource materials, and thereby
improving the value added component of our exports.

Capability:

While the areas identified under "Resources" may suggest
opportunities for development, their rapid exploitation is likely to
be hindered by a number of factors, most of which stem from

47

domestic conditions. One project identified the following impeding conditions:

- Discrepancies between federal and provincial governments (mostly caused by politics);

- An inadequate transportation and shipping system (rail, ports, merchant fleet);

- A labor force plagued by frequent strikes, and comparatively overpriced in world labor markets;

- A relatively small population and a relatively small proportion of highly-skilled labor;

- Export and import tariffs, quotas, and barriers imposed by Canadian or foreign sources;

- Lack of Canadian capital and/or guidelines regarding the integration of foreign capital and business management;

- Ecological constraints of the fragile environment of the Canadian North.

For example, a different project pointed out that there are indications that the Canadian reputation in meeting delivery quotas and dates is declining. Reliability has always been an important factor in expanding and maintaining markets. In this regard, yet another project indicated that, except for whole shiploads, Canadian exporters are still subject to space limitations, delays, trans-shipment surcharges and other problems associated with inadequate shipping, especially to non-European destinations.

A possible approach to measuring the impact of these constraints might utilize such simulation models as Statistics Canada's CANDIDE or MIT - Forrester's DYNAMO. However, to overcome these constraints on our capabilities requires new and aggressive national policies to be developed and implemented.

DIVERSIFICATION OF MARKETS

For several years, an explicit policy objective of the federal government has been to achieve greater diversification of Canada's export markets, mainly by urging the business community to devote more effort than before to exploring and exploiting opportunities outside North America. While some firms have been quite successful in penetrating "new" markets, Canada's export statistics have yet to show any significant increase in market diversification, with the exception of B.C. exports to Japan. Although this is a long-term goal, time alone is unlikely to produce the desired results. There are several possible reasons for delays in diversification. These include management's biased assessments of various market prospects, shortage of company resources to explore other export opportunities adequately, lack of effective government support measures, etc. It is not until these reasons are identified more clearly and their significance is assessed that progress towards achieving greater diversification can be expected.

To understand the difficulties in diversification, the panel repeatedly recommended research studies of various areas of the world. These studies, however, were not focused on government policy. Rather they illustrated the need for concrete, pragmatic studies of the day-to-day commercial requirements facing international marketers.

The federal government cannot will less dependence on the U.S. market. Pragmatic measures must be taken at the enterprise level. For example, to expand into markets in less developed countries requires a total change in management attitudes and cultural assumptions.

> "Trac II may offer a superior shave,
> but it makes a lousy pencil sharpener."
>
> Rodney Mills,
> Assistant General Manager
> Gillette International

Other factors such as absence of foreign exchange coverage, lack of foreign language capability, inadequate capital to overcome non-tariff barriers, and other unrecognized obstacles must be identified, before remedial programs and policies can be developed to foster diversification of Canada's foreign market.

PRODUCT COMPETITIVENESS

A frequently identified problem in Canada's export structure is our reliance on the sale abroad of raw materials. Major industrial nations of the world use these in processing and manufacturing, thereby, capitalizing upon them in terms of value added. This raises two questions: Should Canada continue to export a high percentage of unprocessed items? Or is it feasible to increase the proportion of downstream processing and manufacturing of our natural resources?

There exist compelling - but not insurmountable - reasons for our lag in the export of secondary manufactured goods and consumer products generally. Relatively high production costs; extended transport distances within Canada as well as to distant foreign countires; unfavorable productivity levels in comparison to those of the U.S. and other industrialized countries; high import tariffs imposed on our merchandise; lack of trading aggressiveness on the part of Canadian manufacturers; all combine to restrict our economy and enshrine our cliched reputation as "hewers of wood and drawers of water."

One technique for effecting a shift, which was highly valued by business and government respondents, is a combination of export controls and a two-price system.

At present, Canadian raw materials are sold in the domestic market at world market prices, giving no margin of advantage to Canadian manufacturers. Other industrialized countries, purchasers of our raw materials, are often more competitive in third markets than Canadian manufacturers. A two-price system would offer Canadian manufacturers a cost improvement on Canadian raw materials vis-a-vis some of our world competitors, thereby permitting a more advantageous selling price for Canadian finished goods in the world market.

Beyond the basic question of this sector shift is the more fundamental issue of the competitiveness of Canadian products. To quote one panel member:

> "To most foreigners, Canada is still very much a producer and exporter of raw materials, despite the significant changes in the structure of the Canadian

economy and the gradual, though limited, increase in our manufactured exports in recent years. Diversifying the product base of our export is essentially a slow process mainly because most newly established industries must first overcome the difficulties of achieving price competitiveness in world markets. In addition to these difficulties, however, there is also the resistance which "new" Canadian products are likely to encounter from foreign customers - industrial and consumer. This is especially significant for highly differentiated products where achieving price competitiveness alone will not automatically change foreigners' images of Canadian manufacturers. Indeed, to the extent that foreign customers maintain an unfavorable image of a Canadian product, achieving price competitiveness becomes even more difficult."

One of the means by which Canadian manufacturers can improve the image of our products and differentiate them from the global competition is through industrial design. Because of an abundance of natural resources, together with heavy foreign investment, Canadian industry has neglected to develop a strong orientation toward industrial design. Meanwhile, nations with sparse natural resources, such as Japan and the Scandinavian countries, have created global opportunities through the development of unique industrial design niches.

Even with the advantage of better industrial design, continuation of low- and medium-technology manufacturing is seen by many respondents as the wrong approach. The argument is that the high growth and high profit industries in Canada belong to a small group of young, highly technological firms, which have been able to overcome material cost disadvantages, trade barriers and unfavorable foreign exchange rates by offering extremely innovative and unique products and services in global markets. They argue that Canada's growth and future economic competitiveness will depend upon her ability to encourage the incorporation of more of these young, rapid growth, high technology firms.

RATIONALIZED INTER-GOVERNMENTAL POLICIES

A unique aspect of Canada, as a major industrial trading

nation, is the apparent disagreement between provincial and federal policies, objectives and goals. This hampers our ability to present a consistent policy position relative to trading, investment and industrial development. Thus foreign businessmen and governments, when negotiating with political bodies in Canada, at times find the stated positions to be in conflict. Rather than becoming embroiled in domestic political issues, these foreign companies and government officials simply withdraw and do not engage in further negotiations. As our major trading partners increasingly approach the issue of international economic relations in terms of matters belonging to the central government rather than individual companies, Canada's ability to bargain is significantly weakened by a lack of public sector consensus.

LIBERALIZED TRADE

Canada has long been an advocate of freer trade and an ardent supporter of GATT. Canada has traditionally relied more on tariffs as protection for her industries than on the many, and more subtle, forms of non-tariff barriers favored by her principal trading partners. As tariffs are reduced, Canada is left increasingly vulnerable to crippling market disruptions from imports. These are accentuated in periods of surplus capacity, and during times when Canada experiences balance of payment problems with her trading partners.

The small size of the Canadian market makes it particularly vulnerable. Such loss of the domestic market base has been, and will continue to be, an important deterrent to expansion in many Canadian industries. This, in turn, weakens her export capabilities, as well.

There may be a need for Canada to develop safeguards against such market disruption. These safeguards should be:

- compatible with GATT rules
- effective
- capable of prompt activiation
- established prior to granting further tariff reductions

Is is noteworthy that U.S. trade legislation currently before Congress, while granting authority for substantial tariff reductions, also deals extensively with the strengthening of already comprehensive safeguard measures.

There was general agreement among panel respondents that Canada should fully understand the costs of unqualified support of "free trade" as it is practised in today's world, and become more activist in her direct intervention with the free flow of goods in a way that is similar to the responses that other governments have made regarding such liberalization of trade.

INVESTMENT AND TRADE

The impact of capital on the trading position of Canada must be viewed in the context of both direct foreign investment in Canada, and Canadian direct investment abroad.

On the capital importation side, the panel identified a number of issues which may limit Canada's exporting horizons. A common generalization is that foreign ownership of many large Canadian industries has impeded technological innovation in Canada in a number of ways, including:

- Most research and development is performed at the "home office" with minor product adaptation the only R & D function resident in Canada.

- Business planning, product design, plant layouts, etc., are performed partly or entirely outside Canadian borders.

- These result in assembly-line type, relatively low-skilled jobs together with restrictions on the development of upper level managerial skills.

- Canadian plants are frequently restricted from exploiting export markets as this would conflict with the overall interests of the multinational company.

- The process of technological transfer is both fostered (by the importation of know-how, products, and processes) and impeded (because a minimum of industrial R & D is performed here with the result that few products or processes originate in Canada).

In terms of capital exports, the experience of a number of advance countries during the post-war years has shown that foreign direct investment is one of the most potent weapons that a country can use to protect its market position and to exploit more fully the opportunities available in foreign countries. Canada, herself a major recipient of foreign direct investment for several decades, has made some direct investment in foreign ventures through both crown corporations and the private sector. But to the vast majority of Canadian firms, including many which conceivably can benefit from it, foreign direct investment appears to occupy a very low priority as a means of doing business outside Canada.

Many countries, particularly in the developing "Third World," are becoming increasingly protective of domestic production and services at the same time as they are also circumscribing foreign investment in their countries. These factors make it increasingly difficult to break into and maintain, let alone enlarge, a position in many foreign markets at a time when Canada is trying to reduce dependence on traditional markets.

IMPROVING SMALL ENTERPRISE TRADE

The majority of Canadian-owned companies (as opposed to subsidiaries of foreign parents) are relatively small and engaged almost exclusively in the domestic market. An old and continuing issue in Canada is how to encourage these firms to increase their participation in foreign markets. Many panelists suggested comparative studies of firms which have successfully exported in contrast to those which have not made such a commitment. Others have suggested that contrasting information be sought regarding firms which sell overseas versus those which restrict their exports to the U.S.A. These studies would reveal enterprise profiles along such attributes as: resource commitment to export departments, willingness to customize products for export markets, geographic location, attitudes toward Canadian banks' and other financial institutions' support, sensitivity to foreign culture characteristics, ability and willingness to explore overseas markets, definition of market scope, management perception of risks in seeling abroad etc.

If these profiles show any clear delineation between exporters and others, such information could be of enormous value in directing areas of emphasis and, perhaps, reshaping the programs of the various governments' agencies which seek to improve Canadian export performance.

In addition to profile analysis, several other issues were suggested by the panel. It was felt that investigation of how well our products are promoted in trade shows, and by trade commissioners, would be a positive future direction. The ability of smaller firms to cope with such entry strategies as joint ventures, licensing agreements, etc. or to accept non-tradition forms of payment, such as bartering, were felt to be potentially beneficial areas of investigation.

It is clear that if we wish Canadian-owned industry to increase its global presence, the constraints facing small enterprises must be addressed.

GROUPING FOR EXPORT

The respondents identified three fundamental modes of association for improving export performance. These are export consortia, trading companies, and producer cartels. Whatever form it may take, grouping for export was assigned leading importance of all the research issues suggested to improve Canada's future trading position.

As has already been mentioned, many Canadian companies, of all sizes, tend to be diffident about aggressively selling overseas - whether due to distances, difficulty of communication, language barriers, extra political and business risks, reluctance to cope with extra documentation and paper work, the slow initial returns on breaking into strange markets, costs of travel, or the shortage of experienced export managers. The limited initial prospects for sales also may discourage foreign agents from taking on new Canadian lines. Thus, Canadian firms tend to concentrate their sales efforts on the easier Canadian and U.S. markets. There may be a role for more Canadian foreign trading companies which could share these costs and risks, apply professional selling techniques, and present a common front for Canadian manufactured goods and engineering services in foreign markets. Canada seems to lag behind other industrial countries (e.g., Japan) in this field, although a few Canadian groups such as Alcan Trading, Seaboard Lumber Sales, and Canatom are already active in this area.

When trading companies and export consortia are proposed for Canada, the assumption that they apply mainly to manufactured goods is too readily made. Nonetheless, Canada cannot afford to be without alternative strategies for the marketing of its raw materials in a world where prices are decreasingly set by open market negotiations. In very few commodities can Canadian producers or government take action without reference to other producers. In a situation where there is an apparent tendency towards increasing governmental intervention in price-setting and trade directions, the Canadian government would benefit from having feasibility studies on the advantages and disadvantages of combining with other raw material exporting countries.

In short, where small companies with small domestic markets and limited resources, wish to compete in the global arena against large economic concerns, such as the Eastern European State Trading Organizations, multinational enterprises and Japanese sogoshosha, they must find a way to meet their opposition on a more equal ground through some form of association.

CONCLUSION

The beginning of this article asked the question: What must Canada do as a nation if she wishes to change her current world position? While we have attempted to synthesize the threads of our respondents' many and varied suggested research proposals, it is still apparent that the amalgam of concepts is somewhat fragmented. We believe that underlying all of the proposed approaches there is a fundamental need for Canada to introduce basic structural changes consistent with a newly established identity and mission for herself in the world economic community.

While these structural changes are as varied as rationalizing governments' policies, restructuring tax and competition legislation, the education of future managers in trade affairs, and the designation of favored industries despite political repercussions, they must be arrived at through some form of national consensus - that is, an agreed upon national strategy. For example, if Canada were to undertake the development of energy-intensive industry, it would require the support of energy-producing provinces to supply lower priced domestic energy (vis-a-vis world prices) and to encourage further development of energy production.

Japan has shown the world that successful international competition is as much a result of a common sense of national destiny as economics. Canada appears to be facing the future with a fractionated approach. What Canada must do is "get her national act together."

REFERENCE

[1] See: A.O. Hirschman, The Strategy of Development (New Haven, Conn.: Yale University Press, 1958).

II
Legal
Aspects
of
International
Business

Tariff and Non-Tariff Factors in Foreign Trade
by
William M. Karn
International Marketing Manager
Erco Industries Ltd.

After more than six years of much detailed and costly preparatory work by governments and industry, and negotiation in Geneva by the member nations of GATT, the "Tokyo Round" of multinational trade negotiations was substantially concluded on April 12th, 1979. On that date the agreements reached on the Non-Tariff Barriers to Trade were released in Geneva, followed on July 11th, 1979 by the release of detailed changes in tariff rates.

Although there are 104 member countries of GATT only 14 nations signed the above agreement:

Australia	The EEC	Norway
Austria	Finland	Sweden
Bulgaria	Hungary	Switzerland
Canada	Japan	U.S.A.
Czechoslovakia	New Zealand	

The developing nations chose not to sign these documents, but there are at least 19 including Brazil, India, Korea, Argentina, and Mexico who are expected to reduce tariffs by varying degrees.

The signatory nations then awaited approval of the US Congress of the agreements reached, prior to final formal approval. It is expected that the special side deals on steel, textiles, etc. have appeased the opponents enabling the USA to approve the agreement intact.

Hence the target date of January 1st, 1980 for implementation of the first 8 annual uniform tariff cuts was realistic.

Never before during previous trade negotiations had Canadian industry been so concerned about the possible adverse effects which might result from the trade concessions granted by our Federal Government. The report of the Economic Council of Canada which was issued on July 10th, 1975 recommending total free trade, followed by a general domestic decline, rising unemployment and drastic devaluation of our Canadian dollar were just four items which triggered a massive educational effort by industry of a Government that had lost touch with reality and which appeared to be following the recommendations of economic theorists.

The submissions and studies seem to have had the desirable effect and our negotiators are to be congratulated on the amount of "spine" they have shown in the face of most difficult negotiations. Contributing to this outcome has been the "consultative process" adopted by our Government and implemented by Ambassador J.H. Warren whereby discussions in confidence with key representatives of industry sectors and Provincial Governments were possible as negotiations proceeded. It is to be hoped that the government will build on this consultative experience in dealing with continuing trade and related industry matters.

CANADA'S TRADING PERFORMANCE - 12 MONTHS, 1980
(Millions of $)

TOTAL	EXPORTS	IMPORTS	TOTAL TRADE	PCT. OF TOTAL
U.S.A.	46,825.4	48,414.1	95,239.5	66.5%
JAPAN	4,370.5	2,792.2	7,162.7	5.0
U.K.	3,192.6	1,970.5	5,163.1	3.6
OTHER WESTERN EUROPE	7,871.1	5,018.2	12,889.3	9.0
LATIN AMERICA	3,778.2	4,006.6	7,784.8	5.4
MIDDLE EAST	1,117.2	3,016.5	4,133.7	2.9
OTHER	7,073.7	3,761.3	10,835.0	7.6
TOTAL	74,228.7	68,979.4	143,208.1	100.0

SOURCE: STATISTICS CANADA

TRADE SURPLUSES -- Millions of $

1973	1,874.0
1976	644.0
1978	2,957.7
1980	3,249.3

The above turnaround in our trade surplus has resulted in a large part from our devalued dollar.

It is also interesting to note that in spite of the attempts of our Federal Government to develop a "Third Option", we are still dependent upon our nearest neighbour the USA, for 2/3rds of our trade in 1980 compared with 68.2% in 1976.

ECONOMIC COUNCIL SUGGESTIONS FOR CANADA

In order of preference the Council reported in July 1975:

a) Total free trade,
b) Free trade with U.S.A., EEC and Japan,
c) Free trade with U.S.A. and the EEC
d) Free trade with U.S.A. and Japan
e) Free trade with U.S.A.

Agriculture and energy were excluded from the Council's recommendation for free trade.

Since 85% of our exports and 84.4% of our imports derive from the EEC, U.S.A. and Japan, our future trade will depend largely on the decisions of these three bodies.

Because we have very little economic weight to bring to bear on these countries, Canada's best hope for achieving its objectives is through the mechanism of the GATT negotiations.

"Free trade, according to the Council's appraisal of the Canadian situation, is the policy most likely to contribute to a vital dynamic and growing economy in a country that remains politically autonomous and internally united" the Council concluded.

But let us look at ourselves as others see us. The Hudson Institute has analysed Canada's rapid movement toward becoming a socialist state and observes that in terms of living standards, while we used to be second to the United States, are now placed eighth amount 15 countries, and will fall to eleventh place by 1985.

Free trade is an excellent idea, when your costs of manufacture plus transportation to market are lower than those of your trading partners. However, Canada's secondary industry which provides direct employment for 2,000,000 Canadians and the 4,000,000 others whose jobs depend indirectly on them -- is struggling with higher costs than competitors in U.S.A. -- the closest alternate suppliers. Under free trade, much of present secondary industry in Ontario and Quebec could phase out, leaving opportunities for new employment for Canadian graduates in the Northern Frontier resource extraction industries, and the secondary industry of the U.S.A.

ECONOMICS OF TRADE - Drucker's View

Peter Drucker, whose name is undoubtedly familiar to all of you, has recently published a book entitled, "The Age of Discontinuity."

In the section on economics, he disagrees with the way economists still study and teach the theory of international trade. According to their theory, trade among nations is a matter of the complementary provisions of goods and services. Drucker maintains that trade grows most vigorously between nations that are converging in their economic and industrial systems. He says that it is very difficult for U.S.A. to trade with the "complementary" economy of India and very easy to trade with the "parallel" economy of Canada.

It is always dangerous to generalize and I believe that the economists and Drucker may both be correct to a certain degree. Trade begins among nations on a complementary basis and it is our good fortune in Canada that our economy has matured to the point where our secondary industry is contributing more and more to our export volume to the U.S.A. I doubt that Drucker had analysed sufficiently the detail of our product mix which made up our total exports to U.S.A. or the history of our trade negotiations with our southern neighbour leading up to our position in 1970 when his book was published.

COMMON MARKETS OR TRADE GROUPS AROUND THE WORLD

Economic groupings or trading blocs have been organized for the mutual benefit of their members since as far back as the Rhine

Confederation in 1906. From 1946 to 1967 these had proliferated to a total of 26 such associations when the Bank of America published a full listing, which is available to those interested. Others have formed in later years, among them CARIFTA - the Caribbean Common Market - which came into being on May 1st, 1973.

The Yaounde Agreement with the EEC, by which 19 African associates of the EEC gained preferential access to the Common Market, expired on January 1st, 1975. Replacing this was the Lome Convention signed in Lome, Togo on February 28th, 1975, effective 5 years, dealing with trade and economic ties with the EEC by 46 developing countries in Africa, the Caribbean, and Pacific areas.

THE GENERAL AGREEMENT ON TARIFFS AND TRADE

The most important of all alliances is the General Agreement on Tariffs and Trade, which is a contractual arrangement dealing with the commercial relationships of 100 nations, 90 full members plus 10 associate members, as of 1973 engaged in international commerce. The only major nations that are not signatory to the GATT Convention are USSR and China.

Its objectives are:

1) To help raise the standards of living,
2) To help achieve full employment,
3) To help develop the world's resources,
4) To help expand the production and exchange of goods,
5) To promote economic development.

It systematically promotes the reduction and stabilization of tariffs, the removal of trade restrictions among the contracting nations and provides for regular consultation among them on trade policies and problems. GATT is the out-growth of the unsucessful efforts by the United Nations to establish an International Trade Organization. At the Havana Conference of 1947, which drafted the I.T.O. Charter, the participating nations conducted tariff negotiations between themselves and formulated the basis for the general agreement which became effective on January 1st, 1948.

The operation of the GATT is co-ordinated by a small secretariat headed by an Executive Secretary, located in Geneva. Its annual budget of somewhat over half a million dollars is obtained by contributions from member countries on the basis of their external trade.

The major features of the Agreement are:

1) Mutual guarantee of most favoured nation tariff treatment.

2) Reduction of tariff barriers through multilateral tariff conference.

3) Elimination of quantitative restrictions with some exceptions.

4) Freedom of transit.

5) Non-discrimination in the application of allowable restrictions, with certain exceptions.

6) Simplification of customs formalities.

7) Prevention of dumping and subsidies.

8) A general escape clause.

GATT has greatly exceeded its initial prospects and has become an effective mechanism in promoting trade expansion. Member nations, having reached agreement on certain tariff matters during the "Kennedy Round" promptly began attacking other impediments such as restrictive trade policies and practices.

Since inception, GATT members have held formal tariff negotiating sessions as follows:

<pre>
Geneva - 1947
Annecy - 1949
Torquay - 1950 - 1951.
Geneva - 1956
        - 1960 - 1961
        - 1964 - 1967 (Kennedy Round)
        - 1973 - 1979 (Tokyo Round)
</pre>

The U.S. Trade Bill introduced in April 1973, and passed by Congress after many delays, at the end of December, 1974, enabled the "Tokyo Round" to take place.

SIGNIFICANT TARIFF CONCESSIONS BY CANADA'S MAIN TRADING PARTNERS

1. U.S.A.

More than $4 billion of our exports to the USA will benefit from the 40% reduction on a trade-weighted basis. After full implementation of the MTN results, 80% of current Canadian exports to USA will enter duty free, and over 90% will face duties of 5% or less, including trade under the Auto Pact.

The average US Tariff on manufactured goods will be approximately 5%.

Certain of the agreements on non-tariff measures, when implemented, in particular, the Agreement on Subsidies and Countervail, and Customs Valuation should benefit Canadian exporters.

2. THE E.E.C.

More than $1 billion of our exports to the EEC will benefit from tariff reductions averaging about 30%. The average EEC tariff on industrial products will fall from 8.7% to 6%.

3. JAPAN

In 1973, Japan became the third most important customer for Canadian exports. Our 1978 sales to Japan of $3.1 billion included $2.1 billion of agricultural and fisheries products, and basic industrial materials requiring further manufacture, and Japan is now Canada's second largest customer.

Progress has been made on the thorny problems of Japanese tariffs on manufactured goods. A reduction of almost 31% was achieved. After full implementation, the average duty on imports from Canada will be 4.8% and from all MFN sources 5.6%.

The problem now remaining is commercial -- trying to persuade the Japanese to import that which they themselves can manufacture.

PACIFIC RIM MARKET

Because half the world's population borders on the Pacific Ocean, the "New West" or Pacific Rim market is becoming of prime importance to Canada. For purpose of definition "Pacific Rim" includes all countries in East and Southeast Asia and Oceania, but excludes U.S.A., USSR, and that part of Latin America which borders on the Pacific Ocean.

Since 1960, Canada's sales to Pacific Rim countries have ranged in value from 7% to 10% of our total exports, while our purchases from those same countries have made up from 3.7 to 7.0% of our total imports. In 1974 we sold them $3.32 billion and purchased goods worth $2.2 billion.

It is interesting to note that in 1971, China emerged as Canada's 6th largest buyer of exports, with 12 month purchases of $240 million. Occupying position 1 to 5 in value of our exports in that same period were United States, Britain, Japan, West Germany and the Netherlands. China's purchases from Canada in 1976 fell to $196 million ($504 million in 1978).

Some economists have observed that hard nosed economics rather than political considerations seem to determine the direction of trade by China. It was the view of several Canadians who participated in the Canadian Solo Fair in Peking in 1972 that China will seek as much technical information as possible from industrialized nations at little cost and endeavour to expand her own industry to supply her needs rather than import.

THE DEVELOPING NATIONS

During 1971, 34 developing nations met in Geneva to tackle 3,600 separate proposals for improving trade relations with each other and with the rest of the world.

Just before the conference began the United Nations Conference on Trade and Development (UNCTAD) approved offers by 18 industrialized countries, including Canada, U.S.A., EEC, and Japan, to extend duty preferences to the underdeveloped countries on a nonreciprocal, nondiscriminatory basis.

The Canada offer was as follows:

(1) duty-free entry for imports from developing countries of a wide range of manufactured and semi-manufactured goods which at present are duty-free only if imported from countries entitled to the British Preferential Tariff;

(2) tariff reductions amounting to at least one-third of the Most-Favoured-Nation Tariff rates on most other manufactured and semi-manufactured goods originating in developing countries;

(3) tariff reductions of varying magnitude, in many cases complete removal of the tariff, on a selected list of agricultural products of special interest to developing countries;

(4) no quantitative limitations on imports of goods eligible for preferences;

(5) goods which have not been wholly produced in a developing country would still qualify for preferences if a substantial percentage of the value of the goods was attributable to the industry of a developing country. Provided other preference-giving countries are prepared to adopt similar rules of origin, Canada would treat as "local content" the value of processing performed in any developing country instead of just that performed in the country of export.

Although these nations did not sign the Tokyo Round Agreement, it is expected that the general improvement in the international trading environment should benefit all countries.

ADJUSTMENT ASSISTANCE

The Canadian Government is planning adjustment assistance programmes to:

(a) assist our companies in exploiting new export opportunities,
(b) assist firms and employees to adjust to the expected rising import competition.

NON-TARIFF FACTORS

1. Agreements on Subsidies/Countervailing Measures and Anti-Dumping

The Subsidies/Countervail Agreement is composed of three main parts which relate to:

1. the imposition of countervailing duties against injurious imports;

2. multilateral procedures to deal with foreign subsidies which affect Canadian production and trade and to reinforce the existing prohibition against export subsidies,

3. settlement procedures.

The major immediate benefit to Canada will be the U.S. agreement to apply a test of material injury before imposing countervailing duties against dutiable imports.

During the negotiations the major participants, including Canada, agreed that the establishment of parallel injury criteria and administrative procedures for both anti-dumping and countervailing actions would be highly desirable and accordingly appropriate revisions of the Anti-dumping Code have been negotiated.

2. Agreement on Technical Barriers to Trade

All countries utilize product standards for legitimate purposes such as the protection of consumer interests. Barriers to trade, however, can be created by disparities among countries in product standards and related certification systems. Difficulties may also arise with respect to methods for determining conformity with such standards.

The Agreement on Technical Barriers to Trade is intended to facilitate trade by obliging signatories to take account of the restrictive effect which product standards and certification systems may have on international commerce. It will provide guidelines for activities in this area and encourage the development and use of internationally agreed standards wherever possible.

3. Agreement on Government Procurement

Most governments discriminate in varying degrees in favour of local suppliers and these practices can be important barriers to trade. The Agreement creates a set of rules designed to ensure that suppliers from each signatory have an opportunity to bid on certain foreign government contracts.

4. Agreement on Import Licensing

All countries make some use of licensing requirements whereby a license or permit must be obtained prior to import. Barriers to trade can arise from the administration of these requirements.

The Agreement on import licensing elaborates existing GATT provisions by embodying a set of principles and guidelines intended to reduce and eliminate where possible the unnecessary trade restrictive effects which can arise from the administration of import licensing requirements. The Agreement applies to all import licensing requirements except those maintained for reasons of national security.

5. Agreement on Customs Valuation

The new international agreement on customs valuation will establish uniform standards to be applied by governments in determining the value of imported goods for purposes of levying ad valorem rates of duty. The agreement requires signatories to use as the value for duty the price at which goods move in international trade (the "transaction price") or its equivalent.

Canada is asking for a 4 year delay in implementing this new method of valuation, since the negative impact on our industry could far exceed all other benefits of the Tokyo Round combined.

6. Agreement on Trade in Civil Aircraft

The Agreement on Trade in Civil Aircraft provides for the elimination of tariffs and quotas on January 1, 1980, on all civil aircraft, engines, parts, airborne avionics, ground flight simulators, repairs and overhaul. It also sets out obligations respecting a range of non-tariff measures including technical regulations, aircraft purchases and government financial assistance. Canada, the USA, Japan, the European Community, Sweden and Switzerland are expected to participate.

7. While the above agreements on major issues should prove beneficial there remain many other barriers to trade which include:

    Packaging
    Labelling
    Documentation
    Concessional Financing
    Quotas
    Domestic Preferences

CARNETS

Canada has now adopted some of the five international customs conventions which constitute the "Carnet System". These are described as follows:

(1) E.C.S. Carnet - the original convention covering Commercial samples.

(2) A.T.A. Carnet - being broader it will ultimately succeed the E.C.S. Carnet.

(3) Professional Equipment Carnet.

(4) Containers Carnet - at present applicable to units in transit by road only.

(5) T.I.R. Carnet - International transport of goods in above containers.

With the rapid growth of containerized movement of merchandise the Customs Co-operation Council in Brussels, working with the Economic Commission for Europe, expanded their Carnet system to facilitate international trade. U.S.A. has acceded to these conventions.

CANADA'S TRADING OUTLOOK

In spite of immediate problems, we must be objective and recognize that our future economic well-being is more dependent upon our trade with the U.S.A. than with all others combined.

Since protectionism of one nation breeds protectionism by others, it is imperative that barriers be lowered as soon as possible.

We in Canada should study very closely the strengths and techniques of our trading partners--American, European, Japanese--eliminate the credibility gap between Government and Industry, and co-operate intelligently in all public and private sectors to retain our progress to date and to achieve our objective of more favourable trade in the future.

The International Trade Rules as they Relate to Tariff and Non-Tariff Barriers to Trade

by
John F. Donaghy
Office of the Canadian Coordinater
For the Multilateral Trade Negotiations
Government of Canada

The General Agreement on Tariffs and Trade which constitutes the major multilateral instrument setting out international trade ground rules was developed after the Second World War as part of a package of international economic instruments aimed at stabilizing the post-war economic situation and facilitating international exchanges on a multilateral basis. Conceived in conjunction with the International Monetary Fund and the International Bank for Reconstruction and Development (or "World Bank"), it marks a determination among its drafters to establish a hedge against any recurrence of the wide-spread protectionism and "beggar-thy-neighbour" policies of the Great Depression and immediate pre-war era.

The Agreement has two major objectives: (1) to provide an agreed contractual framework among trading countries on the rules which should govern international trade (it is the principal trade agreement of which Canada is a signatory and governs our trade relations with all our major trading partners in the Western World, including the U.S.A., the European Communities and Japan); and (2) to work toward liberalization of world trade in order to improve the framework for the maximization of international exchanges. Indeed, as soon as the Agreement was itself negotiated and signed in 1947, GATT signatories began the first round of multilateral trade negotiations. The Tokyo Round, completed in mid-1979, was the seventh general round of such negotiations carried out under the auspices of the GATT. Some have been large, others small, but all have represented successive steps towards the reduction and, in some cases, dismantling of barriers affecting international trade.

All major western countries are members of the GATT, together with over 50 third world or developing countries. Several of the state-trading countries of Eastern Europe are also members. At last count, total membership stood at 85, with another 30 or so countries which apply the Agreement provisionally or on a de facto basis. Among the main trading countries which are not included in these numbers are the Soviet Union, the People's Republic of China, Mexico and Venezuela. In Canada's case – as in the case of most other western industrial countries – trade relations with this latter group of countries tend to be governed by bilateral trade agreements, the major provisions of which invoke GATT principles of most-favoured nation (MFN) and non-discriminatory treatment. One can give a good deal of credit for the fact that world trade has increased more than ten-fold since 1950 to the negotiated trade liberalization carried out under the GATT and, perhaps equally importantly, to its contractual rules which serve as the framework within which that trade is carried out. This framework provides an effective and recently well-used vehicle for settling trade disputes between and among its members in an atmosphere where the role of both power politics and relative economic clout is minimized.

I. General Background to the "Tokyo Round" of Multilateral Trade Negotiations

Earlier GATT negotiations focussed primarily on industrial tariffs. In the Kennedy Round, concluded in 1967, tariff cuts covered about $40 billion worth of world trade and resulted in overall tariff reductions averaging about one-third from pre-existing levels. There was, however, only very limited success and no systematic effort to deal with non-tariff barriers (or NTB's) to trade. The successive rounds of negotiations since World War II have had the effect of reducing the relative impact of tariffs and in the lead-up to the Tokyo Round, the effects of NTB's on trade flows have become more visible and more significant.

The "Tokyo Round" involved the largest number of participants ever to engage in multilateral trade negotiations – 98 countries, including some some as Venezuela, Mexico, Bulgaria, Thailand and Iran which are not GATT members. The commencement of the negotiations was itself prefaced by:

- the initiation of a post-Kennedy Round GATT preparatory work in November 1967, to

i) identify and accumulate an inventory of non-tariff measures;

ii) compare relative tariff and trade structures of major industrialized countries, both by overall level of protection and by sectors; and

iii) identify barriers to trade in agricultural products and discuss possible ways and means to reduce or eliminate these.

- a September 1973 Ministerial meeting in Tokyo which adopted the Declaration officially launching what came to be known as the "Tokyo Round", most of the actual negotiating activity subsequently took place in Geneva where GATT headquarters are located.

- the January 1975 enactment of the U.S.A. "Trade Act of 1974" defining the U.S.A.'s negotiating mandate, after which delegations began taking up residence in Geneva - the start of substantive negotiations dates from this period.

The Tokyo Declaration of 1973, set out, in very broad terms, the scope of these very complex and comprehensive negotiations;

- they sought the expansion and liberalization of world trade through progressive dismantling of obstacles to trade;

- they took particular account of the trade problems of the developing countries (i.e., developing countries were not expected fully to reciprocate concessions they obtained from industrialized countries);

- six specific aims were identified:

i) a _tariff negotiation_ employing appropriate formulae of as general application as possible;

ii) the reduction or elimination of NTB's and their trade restricting/trade distorting effects and bringing these under more effective international disciplines;

iii) the consideration of possibilities for coordinated reduction or elimination of all barriers to trade in selected sectors, as a complementary technique;

iv) the examination of the adequacy of the multilateral <u>safeguards</u> system;

v) on <u>agriculture</u>, an approach which, in line with the general objectives, took account of the rather special characteristics and problems in this sector;

vi) the treatment of <u>tropical products</u> as a special and priority sector for negotiations.

A fall-out from the energy crisis which arose after the inauguration of the negotiations was a greater awareness of and interest in increased security of supply for essential renewable and non-renewable resources.

The U.S.A. "Trade Act of 1974", constituted the mandate with which the United States entered into substantive negotiations in early 1975. Countries such as Canada with parliamentary systems of Government had no need to seek prior enabling legislation but were not prepared to begin negotiating until the USA Congress had delegated a meaningful negotiating mandate to the Administration. The main elements of that U.S.A. mandate were that:

- USA tariffs could be cut by 60% if over 5% and eliminated if 5% or less; and

- USA NTB's could be removed, reduced or harmonized through international agreements, subject to submission to Congress for acceptance or rejection within a specified period of time.

II. The Tokyo Round in Context

It is instructive, given the current difficult world economic environment, to recall some elements of the backdrop against which the Tokyo Round itself, emerged almost a decade ago. The period before the 1973 Tokyo meeting was characterized by a number of quite adverse international developments, the significance of which has, with the passage of time, tended to be forgotten.

Serious protectionist pressures in the United States in the early 1970's were reflected in the turn-around in the attitude of the major U.S.A. labour unions, away from their traditional outward-looking views on both foreign policy and freer trade. They had become apprehensive that American imports of manufactured products, encouraged in some cases by multinational corporations, meant the export of jobs to foreign countries. Congress had before it, at roughly the same time as it began considering the initial draft of what became the "Trade Act of 1974", the highly protectionist Burke-Hartke Bill.

In that same period, major disequilibrium in the U.S.A. balance of payments, accompanied by significant international monetary instability, led to the American economic measures of August 1971, including the across-the-board 10% import surcharge and a discriminatory "job development tax credit", both of which seem now to have faded into contemporary history. At the time, these measures represented major challenges to international cooperation and to the international trade and payments system itself.

The decade leading up to Tokyo was also marked by the growth of regional economic groupings, notably the emergence and subsequent enlargement of the European Communities (EC). There was also a proliferation of free trade or preferential arrangements between the EC and other European countries on the one hand and those in Africa, the Mediterranean and the Caribbean on the other. These developments posed additional challenges to the multilateral trading system represented by the GATT. For Canada, as one of the few industrialized countries without a domestic market of at least 100 million consumers or free access to one, they tended to increase concerns about relative isolation and our ability to remain internationally competitive.

It was against this setting and an emerging attitude of commercial confrontation between the United States, the EC and Japan, that these three major trading powers led the efforts to launch and actively support the convening of new Multilateral Trade Negotiations. They say these as a way to resolve some of the problems confronting their trade relations, to contain protectionist pressures and to avoid a backsliding from the accomplishments of international economic cooperation which had characterized the post-War period and proven to be of such mutual benefit.

Even after Tokyo, the pace of change in international economic relations accelerated and intensified. Some began to question the relevance and the importance of multilateral trade negotiations that an objective of further liberalizing international trade in a world economic environment which was very different (given, for instance, the rise of OPEC) than it used to be.

But negotiations like the Tokyo Round are not instruments for crisis management, nor are they designed to deal with cyclical problems. Rather, they have more fundamental, long-term aims to improve the international allocation of resources through more efficient division of labour and greater specialization. In many cases, trade liberalization contribute to structural changes that may already be made necessary by changes in technology and comparative advantage. In other cases, it can provoke these changes and, coincidentally improve, productivity. For many industrial sectors in Canada and throughout the world, greater access to markets and increased international competition are major factors for any expansion of production and improvement in productivity. The theory of comparative advantage has certainly been modified in recent economic practice, but it remains essentially valid. Trade barriers abroad have, both during the Tokyo Round and since, been cited as an important constraint to Canada being able to increase its resource-based exports of processed and manufactured products.

It proved to be an encouraging sign for the trade negotiations that, during both the first and second OPEC-inspired "oil crises" of the 1970's, governments were determined to contain and avoid the risks inherent in measures such as artificial monetary devaluation, import restrictions or export stimulation and devices to reestablish the equilibrium in their balance of payments, in the aftermath of the energy crisis. This reflected a consciousness that, not only would such measures escalate through countermeasures by other governments (thereby neutralizing desired effects) but they would also lead to an atmosphere of increased international confrontation.

III. Events during the 1973-79 Negotiations

The following is a thumb-nail sketch of the negotiating activities which took place under the main headings of the negotiations.

Tariffs

- initial efforts concentrated on elaborating a general tariff plan for industrial tariffs, which would include a tariff-reduction formula of as broad a scope as possible.

77

- to be workable, agreement on a tariff plan had to reflect the overall interests of all main participants.

- it was evident from the outset that, in addition to any mathematical formula for reductions, the tariff plan would have to encompass rules for phasing in the reductions and for the full or partial exception of certain specific tariff items from the application of the formula (there was, however, a limitation on the total number of exceptions which any participant was permitted to make); there proved also to be provisions for longer periods over which staged reductions could be implemented, as well as other elements of flexibility to take account of particularly sensitive competitive situations.

- as it emerged, the tariff formula targetted on a trade weighted average reduction in industrial tariffs of about 40%; by the time the dust settled in mid-1979, that average proved to be about 1/3 for the ten largest participants taken together but it was closer to the original 40% mark trade both ways between Canada and its three largest trading partners, the USA, Japan and EC. A presentation of average tariff cuts achieved, phased in normally 8 annual steps ending January 1, 1987, is contained in Table I.

Table I
AVERAGE REDUCTIONS ON INDUSTRIAL PRODUCTS

		TRADE WEIGHTED AVERAGE*	
	Base Rate	Concession Rate	Percentage Reduction
(A) By Canada			
GATT Bound Rates	15.9%	10.0%	37.1%
Applied Rates	11.9%	8.3%	30.2%
(B) By the U.S.A.	8.2%	5.7%	31%
(C) By the EC	9.8%	7.2%	27%
(D) By Japan			
GATT Bound Rate	10.8%	5.4%	50%
Applied Rates	6.9%	4.9%	28%

* All MFN Imports on Dutiable Tariff Lines Only.

- the result also involves a considerable harmonization effect – that is, higher tariffs are cut by greater amounts than lower ones, thereby compressing peaks and valleys within individual tariff schedules as well as reducing the differences in average tariff levels between one country's tariff schedule and another's.

Non-Tariff Measures (NTM's)

- in GATT parlance, NTM's are government or government-related practices and requirements, other than tariffs, which have a restrictive or distorting effect on trade.

- examples are: export subsidies; countervailing duties; import quotas or embargoes; import licencing requirements; customs documentation and procedures; product and safety standards; packaging and labelling requirements; government procurement policies and practices; anti-dumping; discriminatory tax practices; and customs valuation systems.

- in some cases, the overall Tokyo Round objective was eventual agreement to an international code of conduct elaborating or interpreting existing GATT rules (e.g. in matters such as standards or government procurement).

- in others, the objective was the negotiated removal of specific barriers (e.g., certain licencing requirements, quantitative restrictions, or customs documentation formalities).

- in either event, the result was foreseen to reduce or, in some cases, eliminate the trade restricting or trade distorting effects of such barriers and to bring them under improved international scrutiny and discipline.

- the outcome of the negotiators' efforts was new or revised international instruments on subsidies and countervailing duties, government procurement, customs valuation, import licensing, technical barriers to trade and anti-dumping duties.

Sectors

- initial work focussed on areas where a sectoral approach (as opposed to a barrier-by-barrier approach) might be employed as a complementary technique to achieve maximum possible trade liberalization.

- Canada advocated such negotiations in resource-based sectors as non-ferrous metals and forest products where it could serve as a vehicle for advancing our particular interests in attacking barriers which constrain the attainment of further processing in Canada prior to export.

- this technique did not receive general support and the outcome of the negotiations in these product areas went less far than Canada initially hoped - although important and very useful concessions were negotiated on some forest products and non-ferrous items of interest to us, especially into the U.S.A. market.

- although not initially advanced as a candidate for attention, a sectoral agreement did evolve on civil aircraft and parts and is already proving to be of particular benefit to Canada; among other things, this accord extends duty-free treatment to civil aircraft and specifically-dedicated parts and is to have the question of its parts and components coverage reviewed with a possibility of expanded coverage within the first 3 years of its operation (i.e., - before January 1, 1983).

Safeguards

- the overall objective was to examine existing emergency mechanisms allowing for temporary imposition of increased protection in emergency circumstances to determine whether changes might be contemplated; the guiding principle was a determination that trade liberalization achieved in the Tokyo Round and earlier should not be frustrated or undermined by arbitrary or inapprorpriate recourse to quotas, increased tariffs or other measures of protection while, at the same time, leaving open the possibility of recourse to such measures where demonstrably justified.

- in general, except in the area of textile trade where a separate international arrangement is in place, pre-existing GATT rules allow for imposition of temporary restrictions in situations arising from injurious imports, but only under conditions where notification and consultation takes place, where the measures are applied on an MFN basis and where there is scope for retaliatory action by or compensation in favour of adversely affected trading partners.

- in the event, agreement proved elusive during the Tokyo Round and this piece of unfinished business is being discussed further; meantime, the existing GATT rules continue to apply.

Tropical Products

- in this area, after an exchange of requests and offers, most developed countries implemented a selection of specific tariff concessions of direct interest to developing countries in 1977; Canada's concessions, in the form of both reductions in MFN rates and improvements in certain General Preferential Tariff rates, were implemented via a Budget measure in April, 1977; since the, additional modifications to Canada's GPT have been made, consistent with the implementation of changes in the MFN rates as agreed in the Tokyo Round; further potential changes to the GPT are the subject of current Tariff Board references.

"Framework Group"

- work here focussed on ways in which existing international rules might be amended to deal, inter alia, with trade among developing countries, examining in particular where it would be appropriate to agree to "special and differential measures" for developing countries and for consideration of amendments to a range of other GATT provisions (e.g., covering balance-of-payments import restrictions; export control measures).

- no formal agreements emerged from the work of the "Framework" groups, although a series of texts constituting more or less agreed common understandings were developed and will serve as a basis for ongoing work in the GATT, especially in respect of procedures for the settlement of disputes between and among member countries.

IV. Canadian Interests in General

Canada is highly dependent on international trade, with about 25% of our GNP exported. The limited size of the Canadian market reinforces the need for improved access to foreign markets, if our industries are to achieve optimum economies of scale amd become or remain internationally competitive.

The results of the Tokyo Round provide a major opportunity to facilitate the achievement of Canadian objectives in the areas of the further processing of resources prior to export and the encouragement of internationally competitive Canadian production. Tariffs, non-tariff barriers, and, particularly, the escalation of trade barriers with the degree of processing had been pinpointed as major constriants to achieving these objectives. Trade barriers of various types had also been flagged as impeding market access for Canadian manufactured goods and agricultural products.

Canadian participation in these negotiations (as in any others) carried with it the presumption of reciprocal reductions in our own tariffs and liberalization of the NTB's we maintain. In common with other particpating countries, however, Canada had to be satisfied at the conclusion of the negotiations, that concessions offered were fully matched by advantages gained (i.e. that, in the words of the Tokyo Declaration, "mutual advantage, mutual commitment and overall reciprocity" were achieved).

In working to achieve Canada's general objectives, the negotiators sought a mix of gains in foreign markets and concessions on the Canadian side which would represent a reasonable outcome from the perspective of the various regions of Canada. They also looked for a result to which, on the basis of the Government's consultations with them, it was considered Canadian industries and producers could adapt and profit over the years which followed. Also very much in mind were the benefits which would accrue directly and indirectly to users and consumers of imported and competing domestically-produced goods and the benefit to all groups likely to flow from the improved economic performance which could be anticipated in the more competitive post-Tokyo Round environment.

All in all, on the basis of stated reactions since the event, the results of the negotiations seem to be regarded as reasonable by Canadians both as to their substance, where various economic interests are concerned, and relative to the sorts of general and particular objectives we had originally in mind.

The process of consultation with the Provinces and the private sector in the course of the MTN was an essential ingredient to the measure of success achieved and a significant "plus" in terms of relations between the Federal Government and the many constituencies of Canadian interests which make up our country. That the process was equally appreciated by the groups which participated was made very clear in the consultations themselves and in correspondence received since the results were announc-ed. For their part, Canadian Ministers took note in the press release of July 11, 1979 of the valuable contributions made by businessmen and others through these consultations and went on to say that "they wished to assure the provinces and the private sector interests concerned of the Government's determination to maintain and further develop the consultative process with respect of Canadian policies on industrial development and trade".

In a country like Canada, it proves especially helpful to have provincial perspectives on trade policy issues brought to bear not only in areas where their own regulations and responsibilities are in play, for example, liquor board marketing practices or product standards, but also more generally where the international framework importantly affects trade and economic development opportunities for their parts of the country. The views of businessmen, organizations and individuals involved directly in Canadian production and trade proved valuable in the elaboration of sound policy decisions and negotiating positions. This was true not only in the evolution of the priorities and directions which our Tokyo Round negotiating team were asked to pursue, but in the "fine tuning" for the final results where quick, up-to-date and informed responses were essential. This being said it remains true that final decisions inevitably rested with the national Government, given the numerous and often conflicting regional and sectoral interests constantly at work in the Canadian economy.

This process of information gathering, input and consultation during the Tokyo Round, both on the record and in confidence, allowed the Government to arrive at positions which represented a reasonable and broadly-accepted consensus as to what had to be done in the circumstances facing us. The outcome, while inevitably open to criticism by some who would like us to have achieved more, by some who would say we went too far in their particular product area and by some who would say we did not go far enough in terms of their interests was the product of the most extensive consultative arrangements yet put in place - arrangements which were important in themselves because, otherwise, there could easily have been a heightening, if not an exaggeration, of regional or sectoral concerns - simply because not all dimensions of a problem were known or because of fear that behind the veil of secrecy one Canadian interest might be being sacrificed to another. Table II outlines in more graphic terms the decision-making process in Canada during the key final two years of the negotiations and gives a sense of the extent to which inputs gleaned from the consultative process were fed into policy formulation in Ottawa.

To a very large extent, the valuable contacts and mutual sense of confidence and trust established during this critical period of the trade negotiations continue to serve us well in the post-Tokyo Round period as other trade issues come to the fore and require attention.

V. The Tokyo Round Results as They Relate to Canada

The following are some of the general indicators of what the Tokyo Round results mean for Canada.

For any specific Canadian interest, the perspective no doubt varies but what follows gives a sense of the overall outcome with particular reference to industrial tariffs:

1) the ten main trading countries agreed to cut their industrial tariffs by about one-third, overall;

2) Canada agreed to reciprocal reductions of somewhat less than 40 percent on industrial products exchanged with our three main trading partners taken together;

3) The extent of duty-free entry in Canada/U.S.A. trade has grown further to about 80 percent of everything Canada exports to the U.S.A. will be duty-free once the concessions are fully implemented; this is up from 70 percent today) and almost 95% of our exports will enter the U.S.A. at rates of 5% or less by 1987; the figures for U.S.A. imports into Canada are lower but nonetheless significant;

TABLE II

THE TOKYO ROUND OF MULTILATERAL TRADE NEGOTIATIONS:
DECISION-MAKING PROCESS IN CANADA DURING THE SUBSTANTIVE NEGOTIATING PHASE (1977-1979)

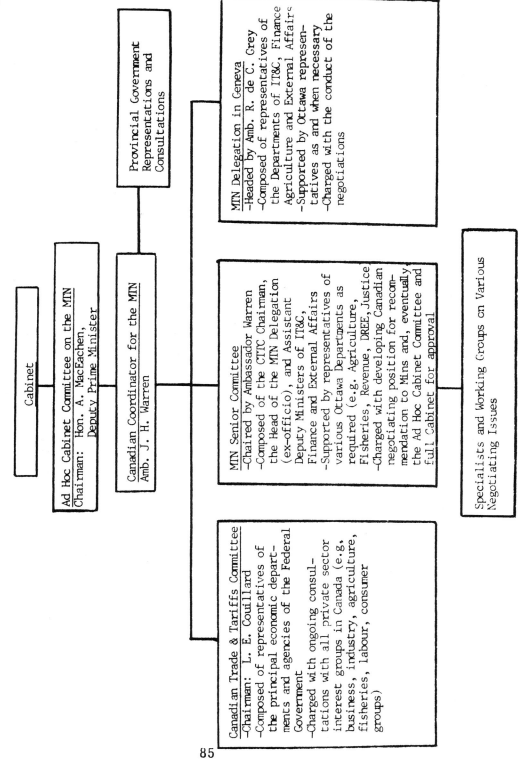

Cabinet

Ad Hoc Cabinet Committee on the MTN
Chairman: Hon. A. MacEachen,
Deputy Prime Minister

Canadian Coordinator for the MTN
Amb. J. H. Warren

Provincial Government
Representations and
Consultations

MTN Delegation in Geneva
-Headed by Amb. R. de C. Grey
-Composed of representatives of
the Departments of IT&C, Finance
Agriculture and External Affairs
-Supported by Ottawa represen-
tatives as and when necessary
-Charged with the conduct of the
negotiations

MTN Senior Committee
-Chaired by Ambassador Warren
-Composed of the CTTC Chairman,
the Head of the MTN Delegation
(ex-officio), and Assistant
Deputy Ministers of IT&C,
Finance and External Affairs
-Supported by representatives of
various Ottawa Departments as
required (e.g. Agriculture,
Fisheries, Revenue, DREE, Justice
-Charged with developing Canadian
negotiating position for recommendation to Mins and, eventually,
the Ad Hoc Cabinet Committee and
full Cabinet for approval

Specialists and Working Groups on Various
Negotiating Issues

Canadian Trade & Tariffs Committee
-Chairman: L. E. Couillard
-Composed of representatives of
the principal economic departments and agencies of the Federal
Government
-Charged with ongoing consultations with all private sector
interest groups in Canada (e.g,
business, industry, agriculture,
fisheries, labour, consumer
groups)

85

4) Post-MTN U.S.A. tariffs on manufactured goods will average about 4 percent; those of Japan and the EC will be about 6 percent and those of Canada, about 9 or 10 percent;

5) Canada - like many other participants - made reductions or comparatively small reductions in tariffs on such sensitive items as textiles, clothing, footwear, ships and rail cars; and

6) There will be time (8 annual steps beginning the first of January 1980 as a general rule) to adjust to Canadian tariff reductions and to take advantage of new export opportunities as access to the U.S.A. and other markets is progressively improved.

On the export side, Canadian manufacturers have already found interesting potential in a great number of areas including machinery, papers, aircraft, agricultural equipment and parts, other high technology sectors and Canadian whisky.

On agricultural products, tariff concessions agreed by our major trading partners cover over $1 billion worth of Canadian exports. Included among these are a wide range of fairly deep tariff cuts obtained from the U.S.A. which has, in a number of important cases, agreed to phase-out or reduce disparities as between Canadian and U.S.A. rates (for example, on corn, high quality beef, soybeans and potatoes). Some rather interesting results were also obtained on meat products, certain berries and processed vegetables into both the EC and Japan and on aged cheddar cheese to the EC. Agricultural and fisheries trade also benefits from the agreements on non-tariff measures. For a number of fisheries products, foreign tariff concessions are proving helpful to both East Coast and West Coast producers, although the degree to which other countries proved willing to open their markets for fish and fish products during the Tokyo Round was admittedly less than we had hoped.

On the non-tariff side, as earlier indicated, agreements negotiated on subsidies and countervailing duties, technical barriers to trade, government procurement, import licensing procedures and customs valuation. Revisions were also agreed in the Anti-dumping Code. When fully implemented, these agreements bring under better control many of the most difficult non-tariff barriers which have confronted our exporters. Particularly desirable gains have been achieved in "transparency" with respect to the practices of governments which can otherwise impair access to other markets. Moreover, improved international surveillance and dispute settlement procedures will help ensure that anticipated benefits are, in fact, realized. This is an area where close scrutiny by governments will be important to successful implementation at the international level. In a sense, the Tokyo Round codes are only as good as governments choose to make them by ensuring that the surveillance and dispute settlement provisions work to maximum advantage. We in government looking to interested parties in Canada to keep us fully informed of any problems which may need to be addressed with respect to the application of these codes by other countries.

So far as Canadian implementation of the MTN results is concerned, staged tariff reduction began January 1, 1980 and legislation is being addressed by Parliament in respect of non-tariff measures, notably provisions relating to Canada's capacity to deal with unfair or injurious import practices, e.g., countervailing duties, anti-dumping, safeguards and valuation. In all of these cases, procedures are being followed to allow for maximum comment and consultation with the private sector prior to the introduction of legislation. The same is true for changes proposed in the Made/Not Made-in-Canada tariff provisions and for possible modifications to our General Preferential Tariff regime. The process of developing prospective legislative or regulatory changes to permit Canada to implement the Geneva agreements on non-tariff barriers is already underway. Extensive legislative changes were not and will not be required to permit Canada to implement these codes (other than the one on customs valuation), but the occasion is being taken to streamline and modernize our existing legislation with respect to imports to ensure that we in Canada have the capability to take advantage of those measures permitted under the existing and recently-revised international trade rules. On customs valuation, Canada made clear to its negotiating partners that, since the agreed code requires significantly greater changes by Canada than by any others, we needed a 4-year grace period before implementing the changeover. We made it a further condition of our acceptance of this code that, should we find individual cases where the transition to the new valuation system results in significant losses of protection which would otherwise be available, we reserve the right to make appropriate adjustments in nominal tariff rates to recoup - but do no more than recoup - any such losses. A specific Tariff Board reference is looking into this matter and public views are being solicited.

VI. A Look Toward the Future

There are those who would say that, for at least the first three or four years after the Tokyo Round, the international trading community should not expect anything more than a pause to allow for full and effective implementation of what has so recently been agreed. To an extent, they are right; it is important to ensure that Tokyo Round commitments are lived up to and that the codes, in particular, are given a good test of operation. Others could equally argue that to stand still on efforts to liberalize trade is automatically to increase the risks of governments caving to protectionist pressures, whether general in nature of sector-by-sector. For the latter group, it is important for the overall health of the multilateral trading system (a system which has served and continues to serve Canada well) to have in train a positive program of work or a trade policy initiative to aim toward even further achievements in international trade cooperation. In either event, the elements of a trade policy agenda for the 1980's are already emerging and, whether or not addressed in a comprehensive or coordinated way, will require the attention of the main trading countries over the next few years. Possible inclusions on that agenda include such Tokyo Round leftovers as

-   new or expanded international rules on emergency safeguard actions going beyond or interpreting the existing GATT Article XIX;

-   possible revisions to the limited existing internation rules on export taxes and export controls; and

-   examining the prospects for expanded coverage under the Civil Aircraft and Government Procurement Agreements (it will be recalled that, on the latter, EC inability to put on the Tokyo Round talbe those of its Member State entities buying communications, electricity generating and transport equipment meant that the current coverage is more limited than might otherwise have been the case).

Other challenges pushing their way onto the agenda will almost certainly include

- finding ways to encourage meaningful integration of the more advanced of the developing countries (i.e., the newly industrialized countries or NIC's) into the system;

- devising some improved basis of reciprocity for relations with state-trading countries;

- achieving something real on agricultural and fisheries trade liberalization;

- examining where and if international rules or disciplines might be applied to current barriers to trade in services (e.g., insurance, banking, construction, engineering, shipping); and

- dealing with the trade distorting practices of multinational enterprises and, associated with those, the tendency of governments to provide attractive investment incentives and/or to extract trade-related performance requirements as conditions for approving foreign investments.

III
Canadian Production and Marketing Strategy

Why Manufacture in Canada?

by

J.R.M. Gordon and Peter R. Richardson
Dean   Associate Professor
Queen's University

Recent public pronouncements by Canadian industrialists indicate that within ten years Canada will no longer have a viable secondary manufacturing sector.[1] The implication is that we will return to our original role as hewers of wood and drawers of water coupled with a new major activity as government employees. This reversion to a resource economy coupled with a major service sector is the result of a loss of competitiveness in our secondary manufacturing industry. The recent decline in the value of the Canadian dollar and adverse economic statistics such as inflation, unemployment, and the adverse balance of trade, have served to further emphasize the trend.

Manufacturers themselves, when discussing the plight of Canadian secondary manufacturing industry, refer to many problems such as the attitude of labor, the drop in productivity, the increase in wage rates and government interference as being prime factors leading to the deterioration of profitability. Many manufacturers indicate that if they now have the choice, as they had ten or twenty years ago, of whether or not to locate in Canada they would no longer do so. In fact their pronouncements raise a very serious question as to why anyone would want to manufacture in Canada.

Canada needs its manufacturing firms. Along with resource companies these firms are the source of exports which finance the country's imports. Their taxes and the taxes paid by their employees finance the growing public sectors of the economy. Furthermore, manufacturing output must grow in the future if the economy is to remain healthy. D. Peters has estimated that the Canadian labor force probably will grow by 2.5 million people in the next ten years. About 2 million new jobs might be created in the

the service and construction sectors, the other 500,000 must be created in productive industries.[2]

In spite of the general doom and gloom in the manufacturing sector there are indications that some Canadian manufacturers can compete successfully and profitably. Recent testimony in front of the Senate Committee on Foreign Affairs has drawn attention to the problems of the secondary manufacturer but at the same time emphasized that such companies as ATCO, and Northern Telecom have been successful and are recognized internationally for their accomplishments.[3] These companies appear to have developed specific manufacturing and corporate strategies which can succeed in spite of the Canadian base from which they operate.

Faced with this paradox of both corporate failure and instances of success, we have attempted during the summer of 1977 to gain a greater appreciation of the general problems and issues facing Canadian secondary manufacturers as well as specific manufacturing strategies which appear to have been successful. Rather than draw our inferences from either aggregated economic statistics or published accounts we have visited and interviewed approximately 25 manufacturing firms in Southeastern Ontario and discussed with their chief executive officers the nature of their operations and difficulties associated with being resident in Canada. On the basis of these interviews we feel we have gained an appreciation of some of the perceived problems facing secondary manufacturers in Canada as well as a pattern of successful strategies. These initial observations and hypotheses will form the basis for more extensive research and analysis, however, we feel at this time it is useful to report our findings as they may elicit useful comments and suggestions.

THE NATURE OF THE PROBLEMS

The decision to locate a manufacturing operation in Canada is a strategic commitment which usually will not be changed for a number of years. Once in a Canadian location, firms do not relocate frequently, even though the business environment may change considerably. Consequently, management must be certain that the different elements of the strategic decision fit together. A major mistake at the time of plant construction is difficult to alter later.

Amongst the executives interviewed, we found considerable agreement that the environment had indeed changed and that elements once considered favorable to manufacturing in Canada were no longer so. These problems and issues have also been reported in the business and economic media as being commonly cited by Canadian manufacturers as deterrents to profitable operations.

LABOR

Probably the most commonly mentioned issue facing Canadian manufacturers and affecting their ability to be competitive internationally is that of wage rates in Canada. By and large, wage rates in secondary manufacturing are reputed to be at least equal if not in excess of those in the United States. In many instances the differential reported more than exceeds the difference in the value of the dollar at this point in time. The second related issue is that of productivity. Although a variable which defies precise definition, most of the manufacturers to whom we talked were comfortable to relate it in straight physical effort terms with an equivalent work force in the U.S. In general, they report that productivity in the United States is higher, and some of them specifically talk in terms of 25% to 30%. The net effect of these two variables is that labor costs in Canada are higher.

Manufacturers requiring a labor force with special skills and training appear to be more inclined to import these skills by using foreign workers who want to emigrate to Canada rather than developing their own training programs or being able to obtain these skills locally. This problem apparently extends into the managerial and technical ranks as well given that several executives reported that practical production managers were more readily available in the U.S. The inference was that Canadian graduates were well trained analytically and made better staff employees rather than line managers.

There appears to be deep concern amongst the managers interviewed about the attitude of labor at all levels and society in general. Their concern extends from the breakdown of the work ethic through to the negative image that society has of the private sector and the role of profits.

PROCESS TECHNOLOGY AND SCALE

A number of firms complained that they could not match the production costs of their competitors in the United States because of the lack in Canada of a market large enough to provide equal economies of scale. One firm in the electric motor industry considered that compared to its sister plants in the United States its process was obsolete. The manager of the plant told us that whereas in the Canadian plant 80 styles of motors are produced in batches along three assembly lines, in the U.S. the same motors would each be produced on a single line, with the attendant economies of scale. However, another firm in the same industry reported no such problems. The strategy of this firm was only to bring into Canada those motors which could justify production on a line basis. As a result the layout of its plant looked very much like one in the United States. In general, firms which could not produce on the same scale as comparable plants in the United States considered process technology to be a serious problem and an important contributor to higher costs.

The problem of higher wages and lower productivity than in the U.S. is compounded because in Canadian plants, where volume is typically less and therefore capital employed cannot be as specialized, the plants are more labor intensive. Companies that have attempted to substitute capital for labor in order to overcome this disadvantage reported that the cost of capital equipment capable of handling the diversity of product necessary to serve the Canadian market is high in this country.

FINANCING

Concern about finance for the support of Canadian manufacturers was expressed by many executives. All too often, they were unable to obtain either initial financing for a new venture or continued operating finance once in business. The concern expressed strongly ten years ago that Canada did not indeed have a strong venture capital market appears to be evidence once more. Those firms including government agencies, which are reputedly operating in the venture capital market are in general supporting only successful and established businesses.

The role of the banks and their attitude towards smaller manufacturers came in for considerable disparagement. In particular Canadian manufacturers, or at least those we talked to, seem to feel that the Canadian chartered banks were quite willing to lend money when it wasn't needed but when it was they become extremely difficult to deal with, and in fact were prone to call loans. One executive interviewed told of his frustrations of dealing with a Canadian chartered bank which subsequently led him to deal with the U.S. owned Mercantile Bank. Finally, when his firm sold out to a large U.S. company because of the owner's wish to retire, he found the Canadian chartered bank suddenly returning to the scene to ask the new U.S. owner if there was anything that the Canadian bank could do to help. In particular, concern was expressed over the unwillingness of Canadian banks to deal with companies who became heavily dependent upon international markets.

GOVERNMENT

The level of taxation faced by Canadian manufacturers coupled with the bureaucratic paperwork escalation, focused criticism on government rather than praise for incentive programs. Few firms acknowledged major gains due to special aid programs but most were aware of the red tape involved in obtaining aid.

Most specific criticism of government related to customs activities. Many firms found it necessary to import materials or components and had thus had first hand experience. The hassle involved in obtaining rapid clearance or duty drawbacks had led most of them to experiment with a variety of ports of entry or even establish facilities across the border.

GEOGRAPHY

The role of geographic location and climate drew mixed reaction. The dispersion of the Canadian market does create significant distribution cost, but for some manufacturers with low value to weight ratios their Canadian location is an advantage. Firms located along highway 401 serving the Toronto-Montreal market felt they had a distinct advantage. Most firms acknowledged some problems created by climate, especially heating, but these did not seem severe.

Geographic location for a number of firms in the Southeastern Ontario area represented a distinct personal advantage. Rural locations coupled with recreational opportunities had become an attractive feature for personnel. Many claimed that they would have difficulty retaining their key people if the firm moved to a major urban site.

The problems described above represent an impressive and sometimes overwhelming array of disincentives faced by Canadian secondary manufacturers. Most of these have been individually well aired in the press and should come as no major surprise to anybody concerned with manufacturing in Canada. However, taken together, they raise the question: "Why manufacture in Canada at all?" Parenthetically, as indicated earlier, we have found a number of firms who have succeeded in spite of these problems.

SUCCESSFUL MANUFACTURING STRATEGIES

Some Canadian owned manufacturing firms and U.S. subsidiaries operating in Canada are successful. We hypothesize that this is so because they have developed a logical and consistent strategy based on analysis of market needs, an understanding of critical environment factors, a sense of personal interest in doing a particular task, and finally, harnessing particular strengths and recognizing constraints imposed by weaknesses within their own organization.

We have identified four classes of company which seem to be successful. In general, executives in these firms could not see any real problems to manufacturing in Canada. They appeared able to operate in this country without feeling they could not compete with foreign firms, and importantly, they were all profitable. Each of these four general categories are: (1) product superiority, either in terms of technical product leadership or high quality; (2) process superiority, which in firms we examined meant either technical process superiority or a unique combination of two or more processes within the same firm; (3) management philosophy and style, leading to the ability to compete economically in cost sensitive markets, in spite of the Canadian disadvantages cited above; (4) customizing the product package, which generally involved a unique combination of product, process and engineering skills without necessarily technological superiority.

Two other groups of firms were identified which appear to be able to survive and grow in Canada. However, these succeeded largely because of advantages not brought about by management

96

skills. The first of these groups contained firms which had distinct locational advantages which either led to a particular image of a Canadian firm in a market sensitive to national identity, or economies associated with distribution of products having a low value of weight ratio, such as concrete products or paper products. The second group included firms enjoying direct government support or protection, which may in some cases mean that the company had its losses fully underwritten by the government. This latter category is more and more becoming a fact of life in Canada, and possibly in most developed economies. Hopefully, this strategy maintains an organization which provides employment in the short term, and may in the long run provide particular expertise which can be exploited profitably.

FOUR CASES OF SUCCESS

Case 1: The Product Innovator

Located in a small Ontario town, the product innovator sells coals to Newcastle. More precisely, 60% of the electronic devices it markets are sold to Japan. Eighty percent of its total output is exported. The device costs around $30,000 to buy, but its initial cost is relatively insignificant in proportion to the operating savings that a user can make. The founder of the firm is its chief executive and was responsible for the innovation which became the basis for the firm's commercial success. The innovation did not come about accidentally but was developed specifically to bring the firm into business.

Since its founding, the company has grown in size, but though the volume of product has increased, the basis for competition has remained the company's technological lead. The president of the firm readily admits that competition on the basis of cost would cause the firm to close within a matter of months. The production process is neither designed for maximum efficiency, nor is it evaluated on that basis. Like many other firms, the cost of raw materials are probably higher for the firm than they would be for competitors in Europe or Japan. However, the company president says that such matters do not concern him greatly.

The major task for the company is to continue to produce a product that will out-perform its competition in the specific applications for which it is intended. Three major tasks are perceived by the firm's management in this respect. The first is to develop an engineering and design group which can continue to beat the competition to the market with product innovations. The second task is to develop a marketing network and track record that ensures the company is known as the "Rolls-Royce" of its market segment. The third task is to produce a device which is absolutely reliable in operation. All of these tasks can be performed as well in Canada as in any other country in the world.

Case II: The Firm with the Process Niche

Once upon a time there was a small Canadian manufacturing firm that had a small machine shop and a plating business. Located in a busy industrial city, the firm had lots of business, but like its local competitors the problem of rising costs always had to be dealt with. Profitability suffered particularly in periods of slow business when the competition between local machine shops was very high and prices would be reduced to "ridiculously low levels" just to keep the plant operating.

However, the firm occasionally obtained jobs which required both the machining and plating skills of the firm. Over a period of time management observed that profitability on such work was far higher than on jobs which involved only one part of the business. Before too long the firm realized that they had an unusual combination of process technologies which were required by certain manufacturers for their components. Customers brought parts to show them which had been machined by one factory and plated by another. The quality was terrible. The machine shop would blame the plater, and vice-versa. Consequently, to find a firm that incorporated both technologies was important.

The small Canadian firm realized that there were only a few potential customers in Canada for such a combination of skills, so its management commissioned a reputable market research consultant to locate customers throughout the world who had need of the specific skills they had to offer. One thing led to another, and in a relatively short time the company was acknowledged as a world leader in certain machined and plated products. Customers came from as far afield as Sweden to utilize their skills.

Now although the firm had this initial advantage the president realized that other firms could do the same thing. Consequently, in addition to the combination of technologies, the firm distinguished itself by its meticulous quality control procedures and also by specializing in the production of certain items so that the plant could be set up on a basis that closely resembled a production line. So far, everyone is living happily ever after.

Case III: The "One-Off" Firm

This firm is located in Ottawa, and its management readily admit that they could not compete with foreign firms on the basis of costs: "one important reason for which is the fact that we have to compete with the government for qualified scientists and engineers and so have to pay inflated salaries ..." However, the firm's chief executive has developed a corporate strategy which does not involve competition on this basis. The firm produces custom power generation units for special requirements. High manufacturing costs and low volume mean that the firm could not compete in non-custom markets for such products. However, a core group of engineers has been developed which possesses specialized knowledge and skills. Over many years the company has developed an international reputation of being able to design power generation units for complex applications. Consequently, firms requiring such products approach this firm for quotations. When the firm is competing against international rivals not on the bais of cost, but product performance under specific and often unique conditions, its engineers produce a custom package which other design teams find hard to match. Purchasers are not so much interested in the initial cost of the purchase, which may be as much as several hundred thousand dollars, but more in the operating performance and reliability of the product after installation.

Case IV: No Frills Management

Our fourth illustration of success in Canada is different from the previous ones in that the product is one that is purchased on the basis of price. Anyone can manufacture the product. Consequently, to be competitive a Canadian firm has to maximize the volume of output so that overhead costs are spread over a greater number of units, and also to minimize the cost of this output. According to most Canadian manufacturers these tasks are almost impossible to accomplish in this country. However, the president of this fourth firm is apparently able to do what others are not.

Volume maximization is accomplished by being able to sell to private brand distributors, as well as to sell the company's own brand which accounts for roughly 50% of sales. This policy enables the company to invest in equipment and a degree of vertical integration that its competitors cannot justify. For instance, the company has introduced an electrostatic paint dipping line similar to that used by major automobile manufacturers. Not only does this process ensure high quality product surfaces, but it is also the least labor intensive and most economical in its consumption of paint.

High volume output alone is not sufficient to result in low cost production. Another major factor is the company's location in a small Ontario town between Montreal and Toronto. According to the company president the costs of land and operating the plant are lower than would be the case in a major city. Furthermore, the people in the factory are aware that continued employment in the area is to a great extent dependent on the success of the firm.

Management's concern for cost minimization is communicated to the work force in a variety of ways. Line supervision does not allow workers to remain idle. During machine downtime or a production changeover workers are utilized to carry out indirect tasks for which other firms often employ specific people. The president and his manufacturing management provide leadership in a variety of ways so that workers are brought to realize that their productivity has a direct bearing on the future viability of the firm. As a result incentive payment schemes have not been necessary to motivate hourly paid employees.

The company's approach to production does not mean that management are unwilling to invest. The president is convinced that one of the best ways to reduce costs is to spend money on high performance equipment. Nevertheless, within the firm there is a general aversion to labor or equipment that is not productive. A further example of the company's determination to remain "lean" is the low number of overhead staff employed. Only 20 out of 180 employees are not directly involved with production.

A further strategic move to cut costs is the firm's degree of vertical integration. Management had decided to integrate as much fabrication activity into the operations of the plant as possible. To accomplish this task the high volume of output described previously was a necessary condition. As a result the plant is now one of the largest in the world in the manufacture of its product line.

In short, the total corporate strategy in this firm is concerned with cost minimization. However, in contrast to traditional approaches, both management and the work force have approached the cost minimization task in a creative spirit, largely as a result of the leadership given by the company president. In consequence, not only can the firm survive in the Canadian market, but it is exporting as well.

THE CONCEPT OF MANUFACTURING POLICY

Our intention is not to propose an "industrial strategy" for Canada. We do not subscribe to the schools of thought that Canada should remain 'a hewer of wood and a drawer of water' or that 'technology is the key' to our problems,[4] or that for Canadian manufacturing 'small is beautiful'.[5] The research has indicated that firms of different types and sizes can be successful. However, from the firms we have interviewed one particular theme emerges, not necessarily unique to the Canadian situation, but possibly requiring greater emphasis given the environmental factors affecting manufacturing in this country. This theme is the need for an explicit manufacturing policy related to corporate strategy and combines with the basic idea of limiting corporate activities to those things that can be done well. What results is a focussed manufacturing effort.[6]

The idea of developing a manufacturing posture based on explicit recognition of corporate strategy is not new.[7] However, it does require the conscious consideration of defining what business the firm is in and what it must do well to succeed. Specifically, this approach involves the identification of the key variables which affect both service and price. In our view, too few manufacturing organizations are fully cognizant of how the consumer views the output of the production system.

We view the production system as being composed of two major dimensions, one to be thought of as 'hardware' and one 'software'. The hardware specifically relates to the equipment and process technology (EPT). Decisions relating to the EPT involve, by definition, a long term commitment: the acquisition, installation and implementation of plant and equipment cannot be easily reversed or changed. In fact, as we have seen, one of the competitive advantages that some Canadian firms have related specifically to the process they have developed and employ. For instance, the development of mini-mill steel making capability within this country and the successful use of numerically controlled machine tools are two examples of EPT decisions which have resulted in profitable operations for small Canadian companies.

The software component of production systems relates to managerial and control systems. Again, we have seen one Canadian company which through management leadership both in terms of personal example and motivational systems has made itself economically competitive with much larger U.S. firms. This dimension should not be restricted to involve just sophisticated management schemes. Much of the success which we have seen in this particular area relates to line leadership which we think has been ignored in less successful organizations.

Once a company has identified its own corporate strategy, and within the framework defined what is necessary in terms of the performance of the production system, it still faces problems of corporate resource availability. The art in formulating a manufacturing policy, epecially in the Canadian environment, appears to revolve around the exploitation of particular strengths without having all of the advantages available to firms in larger and more developed countries. Specifically, we have seen companies which have decided that their distinctive competence will be technical expertise, whilst recruiting key personnel to relatively small centres of population on the basis of quality of life factors as opposed to straight economic considerations. The recognition and exploitation of the fact that technical experts may not necessarily be attracted by the bright lights but rather by the smell of the woods seems to have played a rather interesting role in a number of successful companies we have visited.

Finally, the key to successful manufacturing policy is its implementation. It is one thing to develop a model for a successful production system; it is another to actually get it working. Typically, in the companies that we have viewed, this task has been the responsibility of one individual. These individuals appear to demonstrate strong leadership skills, basic analytic tough mindedness, an awareness of human sensitivity and ultimately, decisiveness. Such individuals have been critical to smaller organizations, which in spite of the problems, have been successful in the Canadian environment.

CAN CANADIAN MANUFACTURING SURVIVE?

Our research provided evidence that firms of all kinds have problems in Canada, but that firms of all kinds can be successful. In the list of firms that we classed as not being successful, a substantial number were those that were in industries where cost competition is prevalent. However, there were also a number of industries where innovation is important. In fact, probably the greatest disaster we encountered was a government owned electronics company. Our list of successes included firms which competed on the basis of cost and others on innovation.

Innovative firms in our sample which continued to be successful were those that remained in markets which did not 'mature' and become cost competitive. These firms manufactured products which were of high value added, low volume, and where production line economies were of little importance. Firms that tried to use their technical skills as the basis for high volume production encountered problems. Perhaps the single most significant example of this situation is the case of Electrohome, which finally had to move its television production from Canada to Taiwan, after being held up as somewhat of ideal for Canadian industry.

Firms in Canada can be competitive on a cost basis with foreign firms. The number of firms which are able to be so is probably small because of the nature of the task. The case cited in this article demonstrates the thought and creativeness that is essential for success in this manner. Management in this company was single-minded in the pursuit of cost reduction. All strategic decisions were made with the single purpose of increasing volume and efficiency. However, at the same time, the work force was not alienated. It was made ware of the company's task if it was to survive and so became an integral part of the strategy. The evidence from other firms competing on a cost basis is that not sufficient managers are able, or willing to be cost-efficient in Canada.

Two key lessons emerge. Firstly, focus on doing a few things well rather than trying to be all things to all people. The recognition of one's distinctive competence and then the development of purpose around that competence appears to be important in the success of most of the companies studies. Put another way, Canada is not a country which has the resources to use a club to solve problems, but rather a rapier.

Secondly, it appears paramount that companies formulate and implement a manufacturing policy. Within the general framework of manufacturing policy there are at least three key variables that have been fundamental in the success of many companies. One is the importance of new technology, and although this has been stressed on many past occasions, it still remains a key factor for Canadian industrial strategy. Another factor is the role of training and education in the development of practical managerial and technological personnel. We do not feel that our educational orientation is sufficiently practical and related to the development of line leadership and responsibility. Finally, although it is easy for managers to blame government and society in general for the deterioration of the work ethic, this blaming is not going to solve the problem. Human dignity associated with doing a job well still exists. Manufacturing organizations must recognize their own responsibility in creating an environment whereby individuals take pride in their work and satisfaction from being associated with a successful organization.

FOOTNOTES

[1] Peters, D., Speaking to the Canadian Manufacturers' Association, Montreal, June 10.

[2] Peters, D., Speaking to the Canadian Manufacturers' Association, Montreal, June 10, 1977.

[3] Testimony by chief executives of both firms to the Senate Committee on Foreign Affairs, Ottawa, Spring, 1977.

[4] Kates, J., quoted in the Globe and Mail, Toronto, June 30, 1977.

[5] Bullock, J., Jr., quoted in an article in Quest, February, 1977, p. 40.

[6] Skinner, W., "The Focussed Factory", Harvard Business Review, May-June, 1974.

[7] Skinner, W., "Manufacturing - Missing Link in Corporate Strategy", Harvard Business Review, May-June, 1969.

International Marketing and Canadian Industrial Strategy

by
Harold Crookwell and Ian Graham
Professor   Strategist
Univ. of W. Ontario   Graham Fiber Glass Ltd.

It is not surprising that a country endowed as Canada is should have large and persistent trade surpluses in agricultural and raw materials-based products. Nor is it surprising that large and persistent trade deficits in secondary industry should provide the compensating balance in the trade account. This is no more than a reflection of the theory of comparative advantage. Of late, however, there has been a shift in the nation's willingness to export her raw materials - especially the non-renewable ones, but no corresponding reluctance to continue to expand finished-goods imports. In the result, the trade balance had declined over $4 billion in the five year period from 1970 to 1975. The resulting massive current account deficits and corresponding massive debt borrowings abroad have contributed to a weakening of the Canadian dollar.

There seems, at present, no prospect that the problem can be rectified by increasing exports of raw and fabricated materials. Most forecasts are for weakening metals prices and greater oil imports. Nor does there seem, at present, the will to reduce consumption of imported finished goods, and the country cannot go on for long borrowing long term to finance current consumption and retain respectability in the international economy. As a result, the focus has come down increasingly on how to get Canada's secondary and service industries to improve their international competitiveness and hence their share of foreign markets.

This article deals with some facets of the latter problem. Who are Canada's exporters in secondary and service industries? Where do they export or invest? What channels of distribution do they use? What is the nature of their competitive advantage? How many are foreign-owned firms? The data that follow are based on interviews with 148 firms in Canada that are active in foreign markets. The representatives of the sample is as yet uncertain, but 119 of the firms were responsible for foreign sales of about $6.4 billion. These were not all export sales. Included were sales abroad from foreign production by subsidiaries of the responding firms. A breif statistical profile of the sample firms follows.

The sample firms on average derived 25% of their revenues from abroad in 1976. They were evenly distributed as to size. Most were Canadian-owned firms in secondary or service industries active primarily as exporters. There were however 42 foreign subsidiaries (mostly of U.S. parents), and 25 subsidiaries of Canadian parents.

AGGRESSIVENESS IN SEEKING FOREIGN MARKETS

An overwhelming majority of respondents claimed to be actively searching for new opportunities abroad. This is a welcome and refreshing response even from a sample of firms chosen for their involvement in foreign markets. It is presumably a reflection both of the financial attractiveness of foreign arkets to the firms, and of the depressed state of domestic markets during 1976. As the following data show, an active search posture was claimed by both indigenous and foreign-owned firms.

Aggressiveness of Sample Firms in Seeking New Opportunities Abroad

	Seeking Actively	Seeking Passively
Indigenous firms	83	17
Foreign subsidiaries	29	12

Firms already heavily involved in foreign markets seemed somewhat more active in seeking new opportunities abroad than did firms not so heavily involved. The difference was not dramatic, but did seem to confirm that the experienced firms had developed better mechanisms for spotting new opportunities, and were the more likely to expand international operations. In general, this finding held for foreign subsidiaries as well as indigenous firms.

STATISTICAL PROFILE OF THE SAMPLE FIRMS

Percent of Sales in Foreign Markets	Small Firms Sales Less than $10 mln.	Medium Firms Sales Between $10-50 mln.	Large Firms Sales Over $50 mln.	Total
Less than 25%	25	5	15	45
Between 25-50%	14	10	16	40
More than 50%	32	8	11	51
TOTAL	71	23	42	136

Primary International Activity	Canadian Owned	Foreign Owned
Export of Goods	71	38
Export of Services	13	2
Wholly-owned subs.	9	1
Joint ventures	8	—
Licensing	1	—
	102	41

Percent of Firms in Industry Sectors According to their Predominant Output		Average ($ Mln.) Foreign Sales
End Products	59	$ 20.1
Fabricated mat.	30	149.3
Crude materials	9	59.4
Services	21	10.0
	119	

The Effect of Experience on the Search
for New Opportunities Abroad

Experience level of sample firms	Seeking Actively	Seeking Passively
foreign revenue less than 50% of total	71	25
foreign revenue more than 50% of total	41	4

FOREIGN MARKETS OF GREATEST INTEREST TO CANADIAN FIRMS

Firms were asked to identify geographic regions where they anticipated market potential. The United States was ranked first by more than half the respondents as the market with the greatest potential for their products. Western Europe, South America and Asia were next in preference. If one ignores the rankings and treats each response equally, the dominance of the North American market was not so evident. North America's lead fell to 21% of all responses, suggesting that if it was not first choice, it was often not selected at all. Other market areas remained in the same order of preference, but the frequency of mention was impressive, reflecting broad international scope on the part of many firms.

Target export markets did vary according to the industry sectors in which responding firms competed. Whereas 80% of firms in the fabricated materials sector said primary potential lay in the United States, the service sector was much more diverse in its interests. Only 28% expressed primary interest in the U.S. Evidently consulting and other service industries find more opportunities in the developing world than in the industrialized nations. These results do not indicate any major shifts of interest away from market regions where sample firms are currently active.

The role of the U.S. as our major trading partner is clearly demonstrated in these data. Its position as a consumer of our natural resources is also markedly evident.

Market Regions of Interest
to Sample Firms

Region	As Ranked First		Total Responses
	Canadian-owned Firms	Foreign-owned Firms	All Firms
North America (ex. Canada)	50	15	102
West Europe	14	4	78
South and Central America	6	2	78
Other Asia	4	3	63
Middle East	2	2	53
Other Africa	4	–	48
East Europe	1	1	29
Oceania	1	–	34
Total Cases	82	27	485

High Potential Future Market Regions
By Industry Sector as Ranked First

INDUSTRY SECTOR (Percents)	North America	West Europe	MARKET REGION S & C America	Asia	Other	Total
End Products	34	5	6	1	7	53
Fabricated Materials	24	2	0	3	1	30
Services	5	3	3	3	4	18
Food, Feed, etc.	4	4	1	2	0	11
Crude Materials	2	2	2	0	1	7
Total	69	16	12	9	13	119

Organization Structure by Size of Firm (Sales Millions)

Percent	Least Complex —————— Domestic Division	Export Department	International Division	International Division	World-Wide Basis	—————— Most Complex World-wide Basis
Small (<$10 mln. sales)	17	7	12	6	29	6
Medium ($10-50 mln.)	12	7	9	10	10	19
Large (>$50 mln.)	10	4		5		24

Organization Structure by Control

Percent	Domestic Division	Export Department	International Division	World-Wide Basis	No. Cases
Canadian Control	26	12	12	29	89
Foreign Control	13	6	9	10	38
					127

PERSONNEL AND ORGANIZATIONAL STRUCTURE

The average number of employees in the sample firms was 2,200. The number engaged in international activities, however, was much smaller. About half of the firms had fewer than six employees spending at least a quarter of their time on international business activities.

Respondents were asked to rank the skills they felt were "most required to implement and achieve corporate objectives in foreign markets". Excluding skills specific to the technology of the firm, foreign market development and negotiation skills stood foremost. Negotiation skills were seen to be needed in a wide variety of tasks such as sales, investing, dealing with host government and foreign suppliers, license and distribution agreements, etc. Again, when total responses were examined, skill factors such as cultural adaptability, strategic planning, and international finance were frequently mentioned.

Skill Requirements For International Personnel

Skill	First Rankings	Total Responses
Foreign Market Development	42	90
Product or Service Knowledge	26	49
Technical Knowledge	19	58
Negotiation	14	85
Strategic Planning	10	53
International Finance	5	44
Cultural Adaptability	4	53
Other	3	9
Total	123	441

When asked which skills were most urgently in need of development, executives in the responding firms referred most often to cultural adaptability and strategic planning. International finance skills were felt to be reasonably available at nominal cost through banking intermediaries.

The type of corporate organization used to cope with foreign markets varied directly with the size of the firm. The following table shows that the larger the firm the more frequently it used the more complex world-wide product division structure.

Firms tend to move to progressively more complex organization structures in response to the pressures of growth in international markets. The above results are not therefore, surprising. What is perhaps more surprising is the number of medium and large firms with relatively simple organization structures. To some degree, these can be explained either as large firms with very little international activity or as foreign subsidiaries whose structures are determined by their relationship to their parents. For example, the foreign subsidiaries in the sample were larger firms on average than the Canadian-owned firms. However, the Canadian-owned firms were much more frequent users of the complex organization structure, as the following data show.

Undoubtedly, these results reflect a number of subsidiaries that are active in foreign markets through their parents and do not therefore require in their own organizations either the complexity of the structure or the richness of skills that indigenous firms would require.

SOURCE OF COMPETITIVE ADVANTAGE

From the view that Canada is an unlikely place from which to underprice foreign markets, one might expect that Canadian firms with a record of success abroad must have developed some distinctive competence which gave them a competitive edge in foreign markets.

An attempt was made to discover how firms perceived themselves in this regard: i.e., what, in their view, was their competitive edge, and how did they come to possess it? It was expected that some firms would see their competitive edge in marketing skills - as with Coca-Cola or Standard Brands, while others would see it in product innovation - such as Xerox, Polaroid or Northern Telecom, and yet others in process engineering - such as Massey-Ferguson, Crown Cork and Seal. Furthermore, given Canada's much publicized tradition of borrowing ideas from abroad and the tendency of foreign subsidiaries to lean on their parents for technology, it was expected that relatively few firms would have developed their key competitive edge in-house.

In this, the response of our sample firms came as a surprise. Almost 80% of respondents indicated that their competitive edge

112

was developed in-house. And product performance (innovative technology) was the most frequently mentioned competitive edge (ranked first by one-third of the sample firms).

It is clear from these data that marketing skills are as important as technology for breaking into foreign markets in the view of responding firms. It also appears that in-house development of the critical "competitive edge" generates the confidence needed to enter international markets aggressively. Hence, by sampling only those firms active in foreign markets we are by selection sampling largely those whose competitive skills are developed in-house.

Competitive Edge Most Responsible for Success in Foreign Markets

	First Ranked	Total Responses
Product performance	45	97
Market skills	35	97
Production capability	30	88
Price	13	57
Parent/Affiliate Network	13	15
Total	136	354

There also seemed to be a difference in the competitive approach to foreign markets according to the size of the firm and according to the locus of ownership. Smaller firms tended to compete more on the basis of product performance than did larger firms, which tended to emphasize production skills. There was a marked absence of price competition by smaller firms.

Competitive Advantages Ranked First By Size of Firm

Percent	Product Perform	Marketing Skills	Price	Production
Small (<$10 mln. sales)	20	13	1	10
Medium ($10-50 mln.)	14	9	6	8
Large (>$50 mln.)	8	9	6	11

The foreign subsidiaries seemed to rely much more on the parent network to help them compete abroad than did the subsidiaries of Canadian parents. It is likely that Canadian subsidiaries are more autonomous than foreign subsidiaries, but the reason, it seems, is that the foreign parent has more to offer its subsidiaries than has the Canadian parent. In cases where the Canadian parent had no international experience or presided over a loose conglomerate, there would be little it could offer its subsidiaries to help them compete in foreign markets.

	How Competitive Edge Obtained by Sample Firms	
	First Ranked	Total Responses
Developed in-house	106	125
Acquired through new businesses or personnel	4	31
Licensed from outsiders	7	33
Licensed from parent or affiliate	19	30
Total	136	219

DISTRIBUTION CHANNELS USED BY GOODS EXPORTERS

International marketing is very different from exporting. Canada's auto producers export billions of dollars per year, but the activity leaves little residue of international marketing skill in the Canadian firms. The reason is that all are subsidiaries, and responsibility for non-Canadian sales is taken by and large by their parents. Even firms without foreign parents can export without learning a great deal about international marketing. They can export through local export agents or through import agents abroad, or they can sell to single customers abroad on a stencil brand basis. The firm that sells directly to its foreign customers through its own sales force will develop a much better knowledge of its international markets, and will need a broader range of in-house international marketing skills.

It was encouraging to note that the distribution channel to foreign markets used most frequently by the sample firms was, in fact, their own in-house sales organization. As the following data indicate, overseas import agents were the second most frequently mentioned channel, although in most cases they were used as a secondary rather than a primary channel - perhaps in market areas too small to support direct selling.

The data also suggest that firms progress to channels closer to the market as they grow, with the exception of those foreign subsidiaries tied to parent channels. More smaller firms used export agents than did medium and large firms, while almost 80% of large firms used an in-house salesforce. Often there are working capital costs to in-house selling that smaller firms are hard-pressed to afford.

Distribution Channels Used By Goods Exporters

Channel	Total responses
In-house Salesforce	100
Import Agent	64
Parent	51
Export Agent	44
Total	(259)

It is interesting to note that a significant number of medium and large firms continued to use channels that tended to isolate them from their markets. This may indicate an inefficiency in their operations that could be resulting in inadequate market information and hence increased risk of being caught unaware by sudden market changes.

Sales Channel By Size of Firm
Goods Exporters

	Export Agent	Import Agent	In-House
Small	12	6	15
Medium	6	10	18
Large	5	3	16

SUMMARY AND CONCLUSIONS

From the sample of firms studied to date, it would appear that the United States is likely to remain Canada's leading trading partner. Government moves to encourage more trade with Europe and Japan, are not refelected in the strategies and forecasts of Canadian finished goods exporters.

Foreign subsidiaries in Canada are, naturally, wedded to parent channels into foreign markets and relatively few have developed international marketing skills of their own. Many indigenous firms use import or export agents to relieve them of direct international marketing responsibility. The result is a shortage in Canadian secondary industry of in-house skills in international marketing. This is not surprising. A nation with a history of exporting raw materials and primary products cannot be expected to have a rich supply of the kind of skills needed to sell differentiated finished goods abroad. Nevertheless a surprising number of the firms sampled did mention the use of an in-house sales force in at least some markets. There is clearly room here for greater management training efforts and for government policy attention.

Such policy attention as is given must discriminate between Canadian-owned and foreign-owned firms, not due to nationalistic fervor, but simply because the nature of their activities requires different stimulus to increase international sales. And the stimulus is needed whether or not Canada enters a free-trade agreement with the U.S. In fact, it would make a lot of sense to provide such stimulus as a necessary prelude to a free-trade agreement.

An unexpected number of firms had developed a critical competitive edge from which to sell into foreign markets despite Canada's high cost structure, and most had developed it in-house. It seems firms have trouble moving aggressively overseas on borrowed technology. Product innovation was the leading type of competitive edge followed by marketing skills and process engineering. Perhaps the most encouraging finding of the survey was that 80% of the firms sampled claimed to be seeking new opportunities in foreign markets. It would appear that constructive incentives for firms to develop in-house product development and international marketing skills would be put to use by Canada's international business community, as long as they did not consume in red tape the scarce managerial talent that needs to be out winning foreign markets.

International Markets or Die
by
Robert C. Scrivener
Chairman of the Board
Northern Telecom Ltd.

You may conclude that my title was exaggerated for effect. I can assure you that is isn't. It says just what I believe. The future of this country depends upons its ability to be a successful, major world trader in manufactured products, in technology and knowhow as well as in its traditional role of selling natural resources, agricultural products and energy.

It has been said that survival is the strongest human instinct. However, those who survive usually demonstrate certain characteristics. They know their environment. They condition themselves to live in it. They know their opponents and their strengths and weaknesses. They know their own strengths, weaknesses and vulnerabilities and they move to increase the first and minimize the others. They don't leave things to chance. They recognize change and adapt rapidly to it.

If you were to look around the nations of the world to identify those that have demonstrated those characteristics over the past couple of decades, you might name Japan, West Germany, South Korea or Switzerland. You would not name Canada.

These highly successful countries in world trade have recognized that international trade methods and patterns are changing significantly. They and others understand the role of governments in supporting their domestic industries with extensive financial credits for their foreign customers and other inter-governmental arrangements.

Canada must accept the fact that the United States is and will be its biggest and best customer. Expansion of Canadian sales of all kinds to the U.S. therefore is our number one priority.

Trading opportunities elsewhere in the world will be many and significant and must also be vigorously sought out by Canadian producers and manufacturers with full government support equivalent of that provided to our competitors by their governments.

Because Northern Telecom is a leader in the high technology electronics industry of telecommunications and data processing, I want to concentrate my remarks on the American and world-wide opportunities as an illustration of what can be done in the sale of advanced products and technological knowhow.

We have recognized that the electronic world of the fugure will depend upon, and fall to, countries which have developed highly successful high-technology industries and which have mastered the art of software and the science of the semiconductor.

In many, if not in most countries, they have protected their own markets with non-tariff barriers while they have penetrated the markets of others through government sponsorship of R & D, special export subsidies and the creation of world-scale companies or consortia.

Our competitors recognize that many countries do not have the financial resources to pay for the technologies, industries, systems and products that they need. They have, therefore, become leaders in providing low-cost government-to-government loans.

Many of these facts are being perceived in Canada today. Unfortunately, we still tend to cling to the philosophies and realities of the past. We still haunt ourselves with that Canadian inferiority complex that says: if its big, good and successful, it can't be Canadian. And, if it is Canadian, break it up.

Canada is one of the few world-trading nations that does not have a domestic or base market of at least 100 million people. In the world of fast-changing high technologies this is a massive handicap and, unless we compensate for it, it could be the root of our downfall.

My comments will focus on high-technology industries because that is our interest and the area of our expertise. What I say, though, applies equally to other areas of international trade which are as important to us.

High technology depends for its life, for its sustenance and for its thrust, upon research and development. R & D consumes dollars like a child eats toffees in a candy factory. Northern Telecom for example expects to spend $135 million this year, after close to $100 million last year.

Companies in the U.S., Japan, or in the European Economic Community, usually can pay for the cost of their R & D through sales in their domestic market or through government subsidies.

When they take their products into international markets, their R & D costs, their launch costs and other new-product expenses have already been paid. They are operating on an incremental cost and pricing basis.

For most Canadian high-technology companies - certainly for us - if they had the whole Canadian market to themselves they could not pay their R & D bill from their Canadian sales. They have to sell in international markets to raise the revenues to pay for the R & D that will provide the new products and systems that will permit them to protect their domestic markets and to sell in international markets. That is the vicious circle that Canadian high-technology companies face every day. For them, and for Canada, it is literally: international markets or die. Not die this week or next week, but slowly and surely die.

Why this insistence on Canadian high technology and Canadian R & D? Why not just import them?

Good questions and important questions. The answers to them will determine whether Canada will be an industrial trading force in the future or whether it will be a fringe market for those who do develop their own technologies.

Technological sovereignty and the ability to control our own industrial destiny is one reason for the development of Canadian high-technology companies and R & D centres.

Our own technology and R & D means jobs in Canada. It means the development of new products, new industries, new manufacturing methods - all of the elements that go into creating a successful, competitive, international enterprise.

High technology, particularly in the form of the electronics industry, is the key to improving the productivity of existing manufacturing and resources processing industries - a must if we expect to maintain employment in Canada and a position in international markets.

If we do not develop our own technologies, it is doubtful that we will ever really be in a position to compete internationally with any degree of constancy and surety. We will be forever buying our technology from others - after they have milked from it the competitive international advantages.

Having, I hope, sold you on the concept that we must have, and must support, Canadian high-technology companies, I must tell you that even if we had the best and largest high-technology companies in the world, we would still have a whale of a lot of trouble making much headway, under current conditions, in overseas markets.

Most of the industrial nations are spending huge amounts of money to develop their high-technology and electronics industries. For instance, Japan and the United Kingdom are spending about $1 billion each to develop their semiconductor technologies and industries. France and West Germany are taking similar action.

Naturally, with that kind of investment they, and other countries, are very protective of all aspects of their high-technology and electronics industries. They, therefore, usually through some form of non-tariff barrier, exclude foreign competition and reserve the domestic market for their own companies.

That, at least, is how it works in my industry. In Europe, other than token direct sales, local manufacture and licencing of technology, sales to the government-owned-and-operated telecommunications systems are made only by a domestic circle of "preferred suppliers". "Preferred suppliers" is a European euphemism for cartel.

The situation is different in Japan only to the extent that restrictions on our sales are even more difficult. Sales for a number of reasons, all of which add up to non-tariff barriers, are restricted to Japanese companies.

During the current GATT negotiations we urged on a number of occasions that Canadians not agree to any tariff change without receiving assurance that all non-tariff barriers also come down. To do otherwise is to open up our high-technology markets even more - and they are already among the world's most open markets -while leaving Canadian manufacturers to face the same old problem of markets closed by non-tariff barriers.

One of the major battlegrounds of international trade is in the developing countries, including China. Here, it is not only the technology that sells. It is the seller's ability to provide the best possible financial terms that often - perhaps, I should say usually - clinches the deal. We are working hard on opportunities in China and are delighted at the $2 billion trade credit advanced by EDC to China for purchases from Canada.

We are negotiating with China. If the Chinese decision was purely technological, they would probably choose us as a major telecommunications and technology supplier. The Chinese are seeking low-cost government-to-government loans for most of their purchases and the new EDC credit may be the clincher.

As I have pointed out, our prime thrust is to become a major factor in the U.S. market where we are known and accepted and where technical standards are the same as ours.

Success in the overseas markets is going to demand much more work and the expenditure of large amounts before major sales are achieved. This is expensive and can only be paid for by profitable success in Canada and the United States.

First, I suggest that we rid ourselves of negative thinking that we have inherited or imported, and look at our international trading problems in terms of the future and not of the past.

The Clyne Commission recently issued its report on Telecommunications and Canada. I commend it to each of you. It has a message about international trade that goes far beyond telecommunications. It is a message that should be heard.

This committee is one of the most representative Canadian task forces that we have seen in a long time. Its members covered business, the arts, media, communications, science, and, of course, it had an economist.

Here are a few of its recommendations. The federal government should:

-- in high-technology industries, actively foster the formation of large, Canadian-owned firms through mergers and consolidations, in order to achieve production volumes necessary to compete in domestic and export markets

-- be prepared to provide low-cost financing to foreign governments to facilitate export sales

-- revise the combines law to reflect the need to rationalize the (electronics) industry and develop large companies

-- encourage research and development through very substantially increased tax rebates on all research and development expenditures

-- recognize the fundamental importance of a secure domestic market base to the development of high-technology industries

-- support on a selective basis, qualified Canadian-owned firms through contracts for both research and development and production

-- provide tax incentives to encourage the flow of venture capital into high-risk electronics undertakings.

The Clyne Commission has provided a blueprint for success in the development of Canadian high-technology industries and for national competitiveness in international markets. In doing so, it has told us we must fight fire with fire.

It has challenged Canadians to discard views and precepts on corporate size and vertical integration that may have validity in larger countries such as the U.S., but not in Canada. They only hinder our national development.

Perhaps none of this is new to you. However, if we are to win the battle; if we are to have viable Canadian electronics and high-technology industries; if we are to be a successful major element in international trade, then all that I write about today has to be said time and time again. Canadian business and Canadian governments must come to understand the urgency of our national problem.

IV
Canadian
Export
Strategy

The Export Challenge
by
James M. McCavity
President
Canadian Export Association

Introduction

A striking measure of the significance of exports to the Canadian economy today is that, in value terms, one half of all the goods produced in this country is sold in foreign markets. Equally surprising to most Canadians is that close to one half of all the goods purchased for consumption or use in Canada is imported.

You are probably aware that in Canada's "Gross National Product" ... the sum total of the value of annual output of the goods-producing and service industries ... the former accounts for nearly 50 percent, the latter slightly more. Since one half of the output of goods-producing industries is sold in export markets, it is apparent that close to 25 per cent of this country's total annual "income" is derived from export sales ... that means 25 cents in the dollar in every Canadian pay cheque.

Thus future economic growth in Canada will be measured by our ability to maintain an internally competitive position and to sustain a rate of export growth that will be in proportion to the growth in population. If our goods-producing industries cannot continue to sell at least 50 percent of their output in foreign markets, the budget of every Canadian household will be adversely affected.

This surely is the most important challenge facing Canadians in the years ahead, what I call the "export challenge", because upon our ability to meet it will depend not only our standard of living but also the degree to which this country can cope with its rapidly growing social problems.

In this discussion, I propose to review briefly the history of Canada's trade; recent and current export performance; the outlook for exports in the years ahead; Canada's export objectives and the factors that will have an important bearing on their achievement; and finally steps that can be taken by Canadians to achieve the volume and diversity of export growth needed to ensure a "full-employment" economy.

History of Canada's Trade

From its earliest years, Canada has been a vigorous trading nation. Long before Confederation, the early settlers produced fur and fish for export in order to buy with the proceeds the things that they could not find or produce at home. Over the years, the pattern of export trade expanded to include wood, grain and minerals, and later processed products such as pulp and paper.

The successful development and export of these primary resource commodities tell the story of Canada's earlier pattern of economic development as a nation. From the beginning, as today, Canadian producers collectively have turned out goods on a scale far exceeding that required for their own use or consumption.

As is the case with developing countries at present, industrial and economic growth in Canada brought an increasing demand for imported industrial equipment and consumer goods, so that the need to earn foreign exchange from exports has mounted steadily over the years.

In this century, there have been significant changes in the structure of Canada's export trade as the manufacturing sector has grown and become more diversified. The pace of change accelerated in the 1930s with the introduction of the British Empire tariff preference scheme, which resulted in the establishment in Canada of many U.S.-controlled factories.

But the most remarkable expansion of industrial capacity took place during World War II and in the post-war years, when an expanded and modernized Canadian industry was smoothly converted to peace-time patterns of production and was thus in a position to supply the exceptionally strong demand, at home and abroad, for industrial and consumer goods.

Recent and Current Export Performance

While the export of crude industrial and agricultural commodities is still a very important factor in our economy, their share of total exports has declined substantially over the past decade. So too has the share of fabricated materials such as pulp, newsprint and metal ingots, as the export of manufactured products has jumped from 11% in 1963 to about 40% of total merchandise exports today.

The rapid growth in exports of manufacturers since 1963 can be attributed to many factors:

(i)   the sudden enhancement of international competitiveness of Canadian industry resulting from the devaluation of the C$ exchange rate in 1962, to 92 1/2 cents U.S.

(ii) special intergovernmental arrangements: e.g., the Canada-U.S. Automotive Products Agreement and the Canada-U.S. Defence Production Sharing Arrangement. The "Auto Pact" alone has increased exports of automotive products from $80 million to over $3 billion annually (1965 - 1972).

(iii) "market forces", notably the rapid increase in the international trade of manufactured products which has risen, in the past decade, at a much higher rate than trade in raw materials.

(iv) Production rationalization programs implemented by foreign-controlled multinational corporations which have resulted in the manufacture for export of many end products and components by the rapidly growing number of subsidiaries located in Canada. Today, U.S. subsidiaries account for about two-thirds of total exports of manufactures, 32% if automotive products are excluded.

(v)   Export financing facilities provided by the Export Development Corporation, and Canadian International Development Agency programs.

(vi) Tariff preferences for some Canadian products exported to Britain, Australia and other Commonwealth nations, an advantage which we no longer enjoy as a result of U.K. entry into the European Community.

Since 1963, the total value of merchandise exports has risen from $6.8 billion to nearly $20 billion in 1972, an average annual increase of about 13% which is greater than the annual average growth of GNP. However, it should be noted that it is only slightly higher than the average increase recorded by the OECD* nations collectively. In the first five months of this year, total merchandise exports rose by 14.7% over the same period last year.

As the volume of exports has risen, there has been a significant change in the direction of our trade. Canada's exports to the U.S. have risen from 55 percent in 1963 to about 70 percent, while exports to Britain have fallen from 15 to less than 8 percent of the total. Exports to Japan have trebled since 1960, outpacing the growth of exports to the U.S. While we have lost considerable ground since 1964 in the EEC and the rest of the world in terms of market share, sales to Pacific Rim markets have gained about 10 percent annually.

Those who may be interested in detailed exports statistics by commodity or by market can obtain them from Information Canada. A most useful Monthly Summary (#65-002) may be obtained for $2.00 per annum.

An analysis of the export statistics of recent years reveals two facts that are important to all Canadians:

(i) Increasing dependence upon the U.S.A.: It is apparent that we have "too many eggs in one basket" in that, in light of the growing protectionist sentiment in Washington, we are much too dependent upon the whim of Congress as well as the unpredictable fluctuation of the U.S. economy.

(ii) Heavy dependence upon the automotive and aerospace industries whose exports are largely governed by bilateral agreements that are subject to change, and also are highly vulnerable to wide fluctuation of demand.

* OECD - Organization for Economic Cooperation and Development, Paris, France

Increasing Demand has Been a Key Factor in our Export Success

While it is anticipated that the demand for many important commodities will continue to grow in our major markets, there are some obstacles on the horizon, such as the following:

(i) Rising protectionism in the U.S.A., evidenced in the U.S. Trade Reform Act of 1973 now before Congress. President Nixon is seeking powers not only to reduce tariffs and eliminate other trade barriers, but also to impose quotas and other restrictions if and when imports threaten to injure U.S. industry.

(ii) Since Britain has joined the European Common Market on the basis of the EEC common external tariff, the terms of access for Canadian exports to Britain are being greatly changed: only about 36 percent of our exports will continue to enter duty-free compared with about 94 percent at present; our industrial exports will face the common tariff and the Commonwealth preference will disappear, while competitors in Europe will have free entry. Our agricultural exports will be in an even worse position as the inward-looking common agricultural policy makes use of levies, subsidies and various other protective devices.

(iii) a large proportion of the recent gain in exports to off-shore markets has been in raw materials, for most of which Canada no longer enjoys a monopoly. New sources of supply are emerging in countries with a more attractive tax climate and lower costs, which threaten to bring increasing competition in the years ahead.

(iv) the persistent increase in ocean shipping costs has become a serious deterrent to export initiative, especially for those whose cargoes are not suited to containerization.

One important export objective must be to sustain rapid growth in exports of manufactured, fabricated and processed products on as broad a scale as possible for a most compelling reason on which I would like to dwell for a moment.

Canada today has the fastest growing labour force in the western world. About 290,000 new jobs must be created each year in the next decade in order to hold an "acceptable" level of unemployment. <u>Growth of demand in our relatively small domestic market cannot be expected to generate sufficient expansion of industrial activity to provide the necessary volume and variety of employment opportunities</u>. While the exports of crude industrial and agricultural commodities are of utmost importance to the economy, their producers are becoming increasingly capital intensive. So it is to the manufacturing sector, and the service industries which cater to them, that we must look for most of the new job opportunities needed.

It has been patently clear over the past decade that Canada's export trade was becoming much too highly dependent upon the U.S. market, particularly the exports of labour-intensive manufactured products (the U.S. took 86% of Canada's exports of "end products" in 1972). It is easy to say that we must export more to overseas markets ... but not so easy to do. Tariffs and non-tariff barriers, rising ocean freight costs and local competition make it difficult.

The international competitive position of Canadian producers has been greatly enhanced as a result of currency revaluations over the past year, particularly in the case of competitors located in Japan and West Germany. Most experts seem to believe that the C$ will continue close to parity with the US$ so that it can be hoped that this advantage will continue to encourage Canadian export initiative for some time to come.

However, a recent survey conducted by the Canadian Export Association indicates that, despite this advantage in export pricing, there are many reasons why it may be difficult to obtain a significant increase in the exports of manufactured products. Over 200 manufacturing firms have been given a questionnaire relating to exports to the expanded European Community, in which one section deals with reason why they do not export (or sell more than they do) to EC countries. Out of the first 100 replies, the following are among the principal inhibitions listed:

- 29 show high ocean freight costs
- 28 show high costs in Canada (labour, materials, etc.)
- 23 indicate that affiliated plants outside Canada supply the EC market, including some that are Canadian-owned
- 23 say that there are too many competitors in the EC

- 14 produce products not appropriate (or no demand)
- 9 either have licensees in Europe or are producing under license here which prevents export to Europe.

It is interesting to note that only 7 firms said the tariff was too high, and that another 7 face prohibitive non-tariff barriers, such as government procurement policies in the case of electrical power equipment.

In the past two years, there has been much discussion (and considerable consternation) in Canada about the new tax-free entity set up in the U.S.A. known as the "Domestic International Sales Corporation" (DISC). Any U.S. exporter of goods or services, or a group of them, can set up a DISC quickly and cheaply to obtain a substantial reduction in tax on export income.

The implications of the DISC for Canada are serious. The principal benefits to be derived by a U.S.-based corporation in setting up a DISC would be:

(a) the ability to defer U.S. corporate tax on export profits indefinitely, to the extent that such earnings can be utilized for export-related purposes or invested in export-related assets up to a 95% limit. DISCs could retain tax-free the greater of 4% of the value of gross export sales or 50% of the net overall profit on export sales.

In fixing his ex-factory price to his DISC, new regulations this year enable a manufacturer to use only direct labour and material costs so that the profit retainable by the DISC is thus going to be considerably enhanced.

The big advantage obviously is the increased availability of cash for export development and marketing, and for export-related investment by the DISC's parent; a DISC may make loans to parent or related manufacturing companies for new equipment, R&D, etc. that can enhance export performance.

Thus, the DISC would be a most attractive tool for any U.S. exporter having a continuing need for reinvestment in export-oriented facilities, and heavy export development and marketing expenses.

131

(b) to the extent that the prolonged tax deferral enables an American exporter to reduce his export price (some estimates run as high as 10% in capital intensive industries), he would be in a much better competitive position in world markets.

What are the implications for Canada? DISC could have a very serious impact in these ways:

(i) Corporations based in the U.S., Canada or elsewhere will have a powerful incentive to expand production facilities in the U.S. to cope with future export growth, rather than in other countries.

(ii) U.S. subsidiaries in Canada, which collectively account for about one half of this country's exports of manufactures, may have a difficult time competing with their U.S. affiliates in foreign markets, with the likely result that current production for export would be diverted to U.S. plants where possible.

(iii) Canadian companies with plants in the U.S. (or in a position to build them) would likewise have a strong incentive to export to world markets (including Canada) from the U.S., and to build or expand plants there.

(iv) to the extent that American producers are enabled to shave export prices as a result of the DISC scheme, Canadian companies will have new tough competition both in foreign markets and at home (even if prompt and effective antidumping action is taken, our domestic producers stand to suffer in that price cuts offered by U.S. firms inevitably tend to force domestic prices down, whether or not they achieve penetration).

Given the need for rapid and sustained growth of direct investment in Canada in the years ahead, and despite the serious threat that current exports of manufactures could be badly hurt, the Canadian Export Association believes that, in the long run, the most damaging effect of the DISC may be a drastic deterioration in Canada's ability to attract new direct investment in industries with the capability of achieving rapid growth via exports and import replacement.

The 40% tax rate and fast write-off provided for manufacturers by Finance Minister Turner recently will, it is hoped, help to offset at least some of the harmful effects of the DISC. Our Association has been pressing for over two years for a withdrawal of the proposed "reform" in Canada's tax treatment of foreign source income as a further step needed to cope with the DISC. The New Income Tax Act contains measures which would curtail the use of off-shore subsidiaries (including sales companies), through which many Canadian exporting firms have been enabled to compete abroad because (up to now) dividends from such subsidiaries have been exempt from tax. Mr. Turner has postponed the implementation of these measures to 1974, for further study. Because in effect the U.S. has simply "brought home" the off-shore tax-haven company by setting up the DISC scheme, it seems fairly sure that Ottawa will have to find a way to keep Canadian firms on a competitive tax basis.

Factors Affecting Future Export Growth

In addition to those reviewed above, there are other factors which will have an important bearing on Canada's ability to achieve her essential export objectives. Let me state these briefly and not necessarily in order of importance:

(i)   Growth in exports of primary materials cannot be taken for granted for many reasons. As evidenced in recent years, agricultural exports will fluctuate considerably due to supply and demand factors, and for most of the important industrial materials and fabricated commodities such as newsprint, Canada has many new competitors around the world. Other factors are: shortage of plant capacity, inflation in Canada, imposition of export controls on some commodities to cope with domestic price/supply problems.

(ii) Perhaps the most important development in the international trade environment will be the round of multilateral negotiations opening this week with a meeting of Ministers of all GATT nations, to which many of the non-GATT developing nations have been invited. It is expected that there will be some reduction of tariffs but the most important objectives are to eliminate or reduce certain non-tariff barriers and to reform GATT Article 19 which covers safeguards (action taken in the case of economic crisis, e.g., employment or balance of payments). The demands of Third World nations for preferential treatment of their exports may be a difficult yet important item. In the next few weeks, the terms and scope of the negotiations should be made known, at which time our Government will start its consultation with Canadian industry.

(iii) Growth of exports can be achieved only to the extent that productive capacity is enlarged or modernized, i.e., it will be dependent upon growth of direct investment; the amount of investment capital required to create one new job today, in most goods-producing industries, is at least double the amount needed ten years ago ... and this is growing rapidly in some industries on account of the public demand for pollution control.

(iv) All of the above implies that this traditionally capital-hungry nation is becoming more so as each year passes. Paradoxically, against the mounting need for growth of direct investment in the private sector, the Government of Canada is today in the process of formulating various policy measures which threaten to deter such investment:

- the new tax legislation, which is clearly designed to achieve "fairness and equity" at the expense of economic growth.

- Canada's policy on foreign control of industry, soon to be announced, may discourage foreign corporate investors if it follows the line that has been indicated by certain government spokesmen in the past year.

- prolonged uncertainty surrounding the proposed labour bill and the new Competition Act, which contain many features which would make this country a less attractive place in which to do business.

(v) In many of the so-called "growth industries" (e.g. petro-chemicals), only the huge markets of the U.S.A., the EEC, Japan and the USSR are sufficiently large to support production at optimum levels of efficiency. In some industries, the economies of scale are becoming increasingly important with the development of new technologies.

(vi) The fragmentation of Canadian secondary industry which has developed over many years, and continues to grow because of regional development programs: even in the case of those products for which the Canadian market (plus export outlets) could provide the scope for say two or three efficient plants, we may find several times that number of inefficient enterprises which are unable to meet foreign competition in export markets, or at home without costly tariff protection.

Canada's Response to the Export Challenge

In summary, it is apparent that Canada has three separate export objectives for the years ahead:

(i) to sustain sufficient growth in total exports to maintain a viable balance of payments position and an acceptable standard of living in Canada.

(ii) to boost exports to offshore markets so as to reduce our dependence upon the U.S.

(iii) to achieve rapid and sustained growth in both the volume and variety of exports of manufactured, fabricated and processed products in order to keep unemployment at an acceptable level, and to ensure the increasing tax revenues needed to cope with social problems.

It is also apparent that the extent to which Canada will attain these objectives will be governed by factors that can be divided into two categories. First, the external conditions over which Canada will have little or no control, such as protectionism and demand levels in major markets, nontariff barriers, rising costs of ocean shipping, etc. This leaves us with the domestic factors and the steps which must be taken by Canadians to maintain the necessary climate and conditions ... in short, Canada's response to the export challenge. I consider this the most vital issue in this discussion, both for the students who will soon be embarking on careers and for those of you who are now in business.

Time will permit only a brief outline of the sort of climate and conditions that we (all Canadians) must strive to create and maintain. Some of the initiatives rest with the Government, others

135

with citizens who hold responsible positions in industry and organized labour:

(i) Government Initiatives

- a more dynamic export policy which would give a high priority for the preservation of Canada's international competitive position, and for export support and promotion, in the consideration of all government policies.

- re-appraisal of the proposed tax reforms that would adversely affect foreign trade and investment. The objectives of fiscal policy today should be to ensure industrial growth, and to maintain Canada's competitive position in terms of trade and investment.

- a policy on foreign control that will not discourage the development of new enterprises in Canada by foreign-based corporation, on the grounds that there is not enough Canadian capital or new technology available to create the large number of new job opportunities needed.

- new labour legislation designed to restore responsibility and common sense in the collective bargaining system; for a nation so dependent upon keeping foreign customers happy, it is absurd that we should continue to be plagued with strikes and work stoppages in both goods-producing and service industries to the extent that we have witnessed in recent years.

- while government spokesmen continue to boast that inflation has been checked in Canada, such a victory will not be conceded by the business community until the upward pressure of government expenditures has abated and wage demands are brought in line with gains in productivity.

- bold new initiatives are needed to sustain growth in the high-technology industries such as petrochemicals, aerospace and electronics, which must somehow be enabled to export in large volume in order to survive in their world of giants. While exhaustive studies have been undertaken by government-industry teams, and such incentive programs as IRDIA, PAIT and GAAP are proving beneficial, there is need for action today, in the form of decisions as to whether or not these industries have a future in Canada, and the necessary measures and resources to implement them.

- steps are needed to reduce fragmentation of industry (a) by encouragement of mergers, consortia, and joint ventures in production and marketing especially in export-oriented industries and (b) by amending rules governing regional expansion programs so as to eliminate projects for which feasibility studies indicate an inefficient or doubtful future in an already over-crowded industry.

- finally, there is need for prompt action relating to other Government policies now under consideration: the enhancement of technological research and development in Canada, broadening of the Industrial Development Bank, improvements in export financing facilities, and so on.

(ii) Industry Initiatives

- While the development of a successful export business involves a good deal of executive time and effort in addition to an allocation of capital and productive capacity, I can assure you that it has proved highly rewarding to many Canadian firms whose exports have kept their plants busy during the recessions in Canada over the past years.

- In most Canadian secondary industries today, some enterprises are enjoying the benefits of substantial exports while others (making the same products) for one reason or another have not yet got involved; not only in the national iterest but also fo the benefit of the shareholders, it behooves every manager to "think export" and constantly to seek out export opportunities.

- As you will be hearing in lectures to follow, export business can be started without any great investment in financial and human resources, if one takes advantage of the services available ... statistical, marketing, financing, packaging, documentation, shipping, etc. ... which may be easily obtained through government sources, freight forwarders, trade associations, agents, etc. (about which you will learn in the next few weeks).

- the main prerequisites to a successful export business are: an "exportable" product, aggressive management, maximum efficiency to achieve internationally competitive pricing, quality products and packaging, availability of sufficient capital or credit to undertake expansion of inventories and production, some knowledge of export techniques and trade practices, and careful attention to foreign customers especially in respect to deliveries and after-sales service. Essentially, the requirements are the same as in the case of an Ontario manufacturer selling to customers in another part of Canada, in the face of import as well as local competition.

- no matter how much the Government may do to improve the climate and conditions for export, it is up to the managers of industry to make the decision to get involved. One of the main corporate responsibilities today is to contribute as much as possible to the solution of Canada's social problems and one way of doing so is to participate in the development of export trade.

(iii) Labour Initiatives

- there is a growing need today for recognition, on the part of all employees, of the fact that (a) a business cannot continue to operate, let alone expand, without a never-ending program of re-investment in plant and equipment, (b) that such investment capital must come either out of after-tax profits or from outside sources, (c) that investors will not put money into an enterprise unless the potential return is competitive with that obtainable in other investments.

- in short, the need in labour/management discussions today is for ways and means of ending the "not-enough-profits" crisis which has been one of the main reasons for the slow-down in new direct investment in past years. Employees who think that an increase in profits would be at the expense of

138

wages are mistaken: from 1960 to 1965, profit margins in Canadian industry rose faster than incomes so that labour's <u>share</u> of national income fell, but <u>real take-home pay</u> of the average Canadian worker rose 11.5 percent in that period, as a result of increased industrial activity.

- adult employees with children soon to enter the work force should be becoming concerned over the lack of available jobs for them; in a very important way, those employed today have a responsible role to play in achieving the necessary industrial expansion.

- an improvement in productivity can be just as effective as a cut in taxes in sustaining the international competitiveness of Canadian industry.

- every time a work-stoppage takes place, the company's relationship with (and future contracts from), a customer is at risk; a large proportion of Canada's exports is in industrial commodities and equipment, newsprint, etc. which are needed in accordance with a rigid delivery schedule; seasoned exporters know how difficult it is to retrieve a lost customer in a far-off country.

Conclusion

In this article, I have barely skimmed the surface of a complex and interesting subject. I hope that I have demonstrated that it is one of vital importance to every Canadian whether or not he or she may be directly involved in export operations.

As indicated earlier, growth of demand in Canada's relatively small domestic market cannot be counted on to raise industrial activity sufficiently to provide the job opportunities and tax revenues that will be required in the years ahead. Sustained export growth can ... and must be achieved or we may one of these years find that one of the fastest growing items in our export statistics is people. It is a challenge which, I suggest, commands an all-out team effort.

Canada's Export Challenge
by
Anthony Fenn, President
Canada Wire and Cable (International) Ltd.

<u>Preamble</u>

I have been involved in international business since the early 1950's. In those days I was living and working in Nigeria and was at the sharp end of exporters' "spears". We imported and sold mainly building materials, and contractors' plants and machinery from the U.K., Europe, and U.S.A. We also exported cocoa, palm products, groundnuts, and some minor produce such as ginger, through Marketing Boards.

Being at the receiving end of the export efforts of others, one learns a great deal about the frustrations that our own customers overseas endure if one does not understand their markets, their environment, and the way in which they are obliged to conduct their businesses.

I came to Canada some 19 years ago, and my role was reversed to that of an exporter of manufactured goods. I then began to learn something about the frustrations of exporting and the difficulties of always satisfying the exact requirements of our customers overseas. More important, perhaps, I started to learn why it is <u>essential</u> for a country such as Canada to export and why a high proportion of those exports should consist of manufactured products.

My presentation is intended to help you to better understand what you, as potential exporters, may expect to experience, and to encourage you to take up the Export Challengs in your careers, which I know you will find, as I have, to be absorbing, satisfying, and rewarding.

1. INTRODUCTION

I picked up some comments by the Chairman of Standing Committee on Foreign Affairs - Hon. George C. Van Roggen, who was proposing a Trading Bloc with U.S.A.:-

- "One out of every 2 jobs in goods producing industry in Canada is dependent upon exports to U.S.A. in one way or another".

- "An unfavourable balance of trade with U.S.A. of $7 billion per annum".

- "If Canada remains behind a tariff wall, we are going to continue to suffer from:

    - Fragmented secondary manufacturing
    - Small domestic market
    - High degree of foreign ownership
    - Minimal amount of R. & D.
    - Wide variety of products with limited specialization.

Canada, if not a member of a trading bloc, will become progressively more isolated "- versus - E.E.C., Comecon countries, U.S.A. and Japan". To my mind a Trading Bloc with U.S.A. is however, only one alternative open to us. We have another:- Global Exports.

If we develop our global exports:-

- Our 'fragmented secondary manufacturing' will become more cohesive.

- Our 'small domestic market' will become greatly enlarged.

- With internal prosperity and expanding global markets, the influence of U.S.A. foreign ownership will diminish.

- R. & D. will be increased to meet the needs of other markets, and not merely that of the U.S.A.

- Larger and more diverse markets will dictate greater specialisation. I suggest a blend of the two - Bilateral freer trade with U.S.A.

- Expansion of our global markets

- is the answer we should be looking for.

Regarding freer trade with the U.S.A., in any business negotiation, the person with the clout usually dictates the terms of the
deal.

To put ourselves into a stronger bargaining position with the
U.S.A. or anybody else when the Trading Bloc issue and Tariff
decisions are under discussion therefore, we need to have an
established trading position worldwide.
Our global market will not only give us better bargaining
power at these discussions - it will also cause Canada to become a
more interesting country for overseas and domestic investment.

2. WHY EXPORT?

Unemployment has resulted from an expanding work force and
a depressed domestic economy, which in turn has resulted in
higher taxation and living costs.

"Make work" schemes of governments are seldom, if ever,
cash/profit generating - so whilst present conditions continue, we
will have unemployment, and will have to bear the cost of benefits
for the unemployed.

High unemployment, which is a direct result of a depressed
national and global economy, also adds to the fires of inflation.

We all know the effects of inflation - ever increasing living
costs; devaluation of our currency, dissatisfaction of the work
force with their diminished "take home" pay - strikes - more
government interference and controls, - "a dog chasing its tail".
There is only one practical solution to these problems. We have to
trade our way out of them, and this is unlikely to be accomplished
within our limited domestic market. It is not easy under present
world conditions, but we have to export, - and to create more jobs
we have to export more manufactured products.

Other important reasons for exporting are:-

1. To obtain revenue from the outside into our economy. In the extreme, if our sales are limited to within the Canadian family alone, all we will be doing is to reallocate our wealth among the family members. This will not contribute towards generating more real national wealth, but it can add to social problems.

2. The world is changing rapidly, distances are becoming shorter through air travel, and no country in the world can afford to be isolated. Even China has not recognized this. Exporting ensures a greater Canadian involvement and understanding of the world, its peoples, and the different customs and traditions.

3. Canadian industry and business is generally cyclical, and if activity can continue for the export markets when the Canadian scene is depressed, employment can continue and manufacturing costs will be reduced.

4. Canada is a prime market for exporters from other parts of the world. By exporting ourselves, we protect ourselves against dumping from overseas. We can apply pressure by reciprocal action.

5. Exports advertise and establish our technology to other parts of the world which can have the result of tying in a market in our favour and making life more difficult for our overseas competitors.

6. Finally, as was the case with Canada Wire, export markets have led to profitable joint manufacturing ventures overseas. No reduction in exports, but a change in content.

You might say, "well, we have always been exporters from the days of the fur trade, and we still are", but it is extremely important that our exports are balanced so that we do not, with our raw materials, equip our international competitors to become predators in our domestic or export markets to the detriment of our Canadian manufacturing industry. Our exports, in other words, have to be balanced with manufactured goods playing an important part in the product mix. (Here government policy could play a major part). To achieve this balance, we have to concentrate on four fundamental factors - minimising manufacturing costs, improved productivity and quality, easier and more competitive terms and financing, and top quality service.

If we cannot equal or better our international competitors, in at least two of these fundamentals, we cannot hope to compete with them, or to defend our position in our market right here in Canada.

3. WHAT IS NEEDED TO BE A SUCCESSFUL EXPORTER?

We must have products to sell, of a quality and at a price that world markets need.

For a start, this demands ongoing re-examination of our efficiencies, of our raw material prices, our labour, transportation, and other costs. It is too easy to continue with the traditional, but often unsuccessful methods whilst we sit behind tariff barriers. Time is running out as GATT conclusions have now been reached.

Secondly, it also demands a better knowledge of the markets to which we hope to sell. Such knowledge can only be obtained by travelling to those markets, talking with customers, learning on the spot of specifications, packaging requirements, and any other peculiarities - such as their non-tariff barriers, port congestion, local distribution methods, methods of payment, etc. etc.

Once markets have been identified, customers and agents established, they must be closely monitored and nurtured. You cannot switch exports on and off to provide an overspill for domestic manufacturing capacity when domestic demand is slack. To export you must be dedicated, and your overseas customers must be given at least equal treatment to that of the best of your customers at home in Canada.

This calls for a change in the general attitude of most Canadians, who have, over the years, lulled themselves into a euphoric frame of mind as a result of a generally strong domestic economy. Despite exhortations from governments and some real financial assistance towards market studies and the like, few Canadians are as yet prepared to believe, or accept, that times have changed, and that our economy will continue to be troubled unless we adapt to these changing times.

144

Thirdly, we have to make use of the changes that the world has forced upon us, and to find ways to profit from them. "Trading" is a living organism, which to survive must be able to adjust quickly to change. If conditions remained static, there would be few new opportunties, and certainly no challenge.

To summarize and expand a little on my previous comments therefore, the following must be recognized in becoming a successful exporter:

- Change in our general attitude is needed

- Our inferiority complex towards exporting in competition with other more practiced industrial nations. We can compete, and we must develop confidence in ourselves.

- There are complexities of currencies, languages, cultures and customs overseas, which should not be a deterrent.

- Our hesitancy in meeting changes head on, and in looking for the new opportunties that they always present.

- Our awareness of government help that is available. We must use all the aid funds we can collect. Your taxes subscribe to them. You will hear of these from later speakers.

- Training and education in international business should be emphasized.

Finally, we must overcome the delusion that the U.S.A. is our only export market.

Government Sector

I have mentioned government aid to exporting, and it would be unusual for anybody to make a presentation of this sort without a word or two about our governments. Government financial assistance is available in various forms, but, a word of warning:

We have allowed ourselves to become over governed, and as a result we too often look to government to solve our problems for us. They cannot do so. They do not have the "hands on" skills or experience of business or industry - and remember - political goals are short term - quite the opposite to industry - which has

145

to have <u>long term goals</u>. Unfortunately, our governments have become so provincially and politically oriented that they tend to overlook the real needs of Canada and Canadians.

Controls of any kind impede trade, and act as a disincentive to business and industry, but we are severely controlled.

We must learn to make our voices heard, to ensure that our parliamentary representatives carry our messages to those who manage (or 'manipulate'?) our lives and our economic futures. Certain rules of course are necessary within any civilized community, but it is our individual responsibility to see that our representatives in government are aware of, and are prepared to listen to and to heed the voice of business and industry. Beyond heeding our considered wishes and recommendations to facilitate profitable global trade, we should resist all government interference in our area of management.

Does anybody know of one nationalized industry in the world that is really efficient, competitive and profitable? Air Canada? British Steel? Polystar? Sidbec?

- Government should provide the right environment to allow the private sector to flourish.

Enough of the political scene .... I am only interested in politics to the extent that they inhibit our initiative and enterprise and by errors of omission, or commission, damage our country and its economy.

However, there are other difficulties we have to face and to elaborate still further on the impediments to exporting, we in Canada, have certain disadvantages all of which can be overcome with enthusiasm and determination:-

- Vast distances and high freight rates to ports. The St. Lawrence freeze up, resulting in rail and road freight to alternative ports on the East Coast - or West Coast. (Don't forget the West Coast Ports, and the fact that the Pacific Rim countries are becoming an increasingly important area for targeting exports). Be imaginative - we ship to Central and South America by road to Florida on returning road transport.

146

- Labour disputes and strikes. Exporters have steamers to catch, and overseas business appointments to keep. Mail strikes, for example, delay documentation, which can result in demurrage charges at the destination. Strikes also damage our reputation for reliability.

- Limited and irregular sailings from Canadian Ports - because of the present low level of offshore export trade.

- The floating Canadian $ and other currencies. This often has dramatic effects on pricing and costs, and you must protect yourself effectively in your contracts. The depreciated value of the Canadian dollar does give us an edge in world markets, and helps to offset our higher manufacturing costs and lower productivity - as compared with the States. But industry should gear itself to compete without a currency advantage.

- Canadian standards and specifications are not necessarily similar or acceptable to an overseas customer. Can you, therefore, manufacture to his standards economically?

- Reciprocal business is often expected and particularly from Comecon countries. If you can offer it you gain an advantage.

4. PRACTICAL STEPS TO TAKE
    IF YOU HAVE NEVER EXPORTED BEFORE

Having heard how difficult it is, having heard what has to be overcome, and having, as I am sure you all have, determined that, despite these difficulties, exporting must go on, how does one go about it if you have never exported before? There are certain things which have to be carried out, some of which are not different from what would have to be done to expand domestic markets in Canada, except of course, the environmental climate into which the goods will be going.

- Firstly, market studies are necessary, and these can be begun from various sources in Canada - government libraries, Banks, other exporters. Take time - not cursory - Plan.

- Having established the most likely countries and markets for the product from all Canadian sources, visit those countries

147

and continue your survey on the spot. Canadian trade posts will be most helpful; you will learn about competition; probably about pricing levels; peculiar packaging necessary; terms and selling practices and any other quirks that may exist. Then during the same visit select potential agents for your products but do not commit long term. The agent must prove himself first.

- On your return home, you will have a much better idea what you can hope to achieve, and this is the time when you should check your manufacturing capacity, examine your costs if you have to manufacture to different specifications from those that you use in Canada, and generally weigh the situation and assess what you can supply against possible future demand. You must decide whether you are prepared to quickly add to your manufacturing capacity in order to keep your overseas customer supplied in the event that the product "takes off". This can, and does happen, at a pace far greater than you would expect it to happen in Canada. You owe it to your Agent/Customer to continue your support. Follow up service.

- You will examine the currency differences, shipping rates, port problems, documentation problems, pricing practices, whether you are going to insure your exports against payment by the customer and the terms that you are able to offer him.

- You will check the bank facilities for raising letters of credit in an overseas country, or for collecting on your behalf through a bank draft. Most of the major Canadian banks can guide you in this respect, and can tell you whether the country has a good payment record.

- If you are new to the game, a lot will be gained by discussing with experienced Canadian exporters a "Piggy Back" scheme whereby a Canadian company with the know how can guide you into the market and sell your products, taking them from your plant and delivering them to your customers overseas. (CWI OFFERS THIS SERVICE).

- As a new exporter (or as a traditional exporter) you must never forget that you are inevitably encroaching on somebody else's market, or alternatively you may be creating a new market that others will attempt to invade by improving upon your performance as soon as you have made it worth their while. Keep ahead and on top. Commercial intelligence.

The export environment is a jungle, and is extremely competitive, but having committed yourself to exporting, you must stick with it. It cannot be switched on and off in favour of domestic circumstances and domestic customers. You must honor all commitments that you make, including deliveries - despite the difficulties of catching the right steamer and so on - and you must commit yourself to engaging and educating staff to maintain your export efforts. Staff are extremely important people; they are your ambassadors overseas; they need to be self starters; and they need a cool head in sometimes extremely difficult and trying circumstances.

5. GENERAL TIPS

Before concluding, I offer a few general tips, some of which may seem to be all too obvious, but nonetheless, are sometimes forgotten. Some are a deliberate repetition of what I have already said in order to emphasize them.

- <u>You have to go out to get business.</u> It won't come to you. Circular letters around the world announcing your wares and services will generally get you nowhere. Keep moving, follow up, and don't look to government to do the job for you.

- <u>You must research your markets</u> and then spend time in those markets making your contacts, your friends. Regular follow up contact by visits, telex, telephone, mail, etc.

- <u>You often must have patience</u> and be prepared to visit a market several times before you receive your first order. After this, it may take off quickly. If it takes off quickly, you have to be prepared for it. If not, keep working at it.

- <u>Exporting and establishing an export market (or markets) is costly</u> in transportation, hotels, in time, sometimes in health, and often in family disruption. This is why, I reiterate that you have to be dedicated before you take it on - and continue to be dedicated.

- The world is a very big place despite the fact that distances are now so much shorter through rapid air travel, so do not waste time flogging a dead horse. Exploit your successes, but do not dissipate your efforts and your resources in areas where success looks doubtful. Use the "rifle" rather than the "shot gun" approach when doing your marketing exercise. Visit - You'll very soon acquire a 'gut' feeling about a market or product.

- Make full use of all resources available to you - Government aid, Banks, agents overseas, EDC, and also do not overlook the fact that there are experienced exporters in Canada who will be prepared and happy to help you.

- Having made your initial sales, establish a "manufacturer to user" relationship, even though you will normally be working through an agent in the overseas country. Visit.

- If you do not already have it, I recommend that you learn a suitable language. Generally speaking, Spanish is almost essential south of the Rio Grande, and it will help you in Europe. German and French can be helpful in Europe, and English and French in the Middle East and Africa. The Far East and Australasia is conditioned to using English.

- You must learn to pace yourself. Travel is glamourous if you are going on a vacation, but on business it can be exacting. Ease up on airline 'hospitality'. Adjust to time changes. Rest.

- Do not be seduced by the hospitality, the climate, and the attitudes of an overseas country. You are there to do a job and you gain respect if you stick to the main objective of your visit there. But be prepared to spend more time negotiating and socializing than you would expect in North America. Make friends. Invite them to Canada to see your operation.

- You must be ready to negotiate and to reach trading compromises on the spot overseas. Communications back to your head office are not always easy, and you must have sufficient flexibility to close a deal without having to refer back in changing circumstances. Training and briefing of representatives before departing abroad is essential.

6. CONCLUSION

So to conclude, exporting is a challenging and usually a rewarding sector of business.

Canada needs to export, particularly manufactured products, because manufacturing usually employs more people. It will reduce inflation, taxes, cyclical risks, and import competition.

Raw materials of course will always be exported, because these are commodities which we have in Canada that are essential to others less fortunate than ourselves, but do not forget that there are other countries equally endowed who are trying to export their raw materials. Canadian raw materials exports should not be allowed to help manufacturers overseas to compete with Canadian manufacturers' products at preferential prices - or your export markets will be invaded - as will indeed your domestic market as well. (Fortunately, most resource industry products have similar global prices, from whichever country they originate).

We can, and should, export technology provided it is suitable, licensed and protected, which includes engineering, engineering services, financial services and the like. (It is not always possible in some countries to protect technology and patents).

We should not overlook the fact that we can export our cash for local overseas investment. Contrary to what many people think in this country, when you have an overseas affiliate, it generally stimulates export business from Canada as you have a friend and an ally on the spot overseas.

Canada and Canadians are still very acceptable overseas. We should use this to our advantage together with all our energies to add to our national wealth, our well-being, and to secure our future. Seeking out and successfully exploiting export opportunities will contribute considerably to the achievement of these goals.

My message therefore is - let us all work to overcome the difficulties and negative attitudes towards exporting, and let us, as a country and as a team, identify our national and business objectives and get down to the job of selling our products, our know-how, our skills - <u>into the world</u> - not merely into Canada or U.S.A.

Exports - Canada's Lifeline in the 1980's
by
Herman O.J. Overgaard
Wilfrid Laurier University

International trade has always been a significant factor in the development of Canada's economy from its early beginnings right up to the present. Canada today is the ninth largest trading nation in the world on a per capita basis.

The largest trading nation is Germany, the second largest is the United States and in third place is Japan followed by France, the United Kingdom, Italy, the USSR, and the Netherlands. Few Canadians realize how vital international trade is to the health of the Canadian economy. For example, if everyone were to receive his next pay on a pro-rata basis in the form of the various currencies earned by Canada through the sales of its goods abroad, the average Canadian would be shocked to discover how small a proportion of his pay consisted of Canadian funds.

Canadians generally think of Japan as a major exporting country -- and it is. However, most Canadians would be surprised to learn that in terms of a country's total production, Canada exported more than twice as much as Japan, and three times as much as the United States. In other words, in 1980, Canada exported over 25% of its gross national product whereas Japan exported 14% if its GNP and the U.S.A. exported only 10% of its GNP.

Furthermore, about 56% of everything produced in Canada, including agricultural, forest, mineral and manufactured items, is exported. In other words, the Canadian market purchases only 44% of what Canadians produce. On the other hand, Canada is the world's highest importer per capita.

In addition, the domestic market is rapidly shrinking as a result of the keen and growing competition from foreign suppliers in the Canadian market. This competition will become more intense as the results of the Tokyo round of the GATT negotiations are implemented.

If things go according to schedule, these agreements should be in force by 1988.

It has been estimated by the Economic Council of Canada that Canada requires approximately 300,000 new jobs every year to accommodate the annual additions to its labour force. These jobs can only be provided if Canadian firms are successful in developing export markets.

The role of international trade in a nation's economy is among other factors, related to its size, its location, the diversification of its production, the types of abundance of its natural resources, and its level of income.

Among the ten major industrialized countries, Canada is unique in the degree of concentration of its international commodity trade in one market, with almost 70% of its commodity exports going to the U.S.A., whereas only 21% of the U.S. commodity exports are purchased by Canada while Japan buys only slightly more.

Canada's international trade is also affected by the fact that, next to the U.S.S.R., Canada has the second largest land mass (twice the area of Europe, excluding the U.S.S.R.) and slightly larger than that of the People's Republic of China. The U.S.A. is fourth. In contrast, China has a population of approximately one-billion and the U.S.S.R. has some 275 million, compared with the U.S. population of 230 million whereas Canada's population is only 23 million. As a result of these two factors, among others, it is often more economical to export a product from one area of Canada and import it to another region of Canada than to supply the entire requirements for the product internally. A few outstanding examples of this are coal, iron ore, lumber and petroleum.

History of Canada's Trade

From its earliest years, Canada has been a vigorous trading nation. Long before confederation, the early settlers produced fur and fish for export in order to buy with the proceeds the things that they could not find or produce at home. Over the years, the pattern of export trade expanded to include wood, grain and minerals, and later processed products such as pulp and paper.

The successful development and export of these primary resource commodities tell the story of Canada's earlier pattern of economic development as a nation. From the beginning, as today, Canadian producers collectively have turned out goods on a scale far exceeding that required for their own use or consumption.

As in the case with developing countries at present, industrial and economic growth in Canada brought an increasing demand for imported industrial equipment and consumer goods, so that the need to earn foreign exchange from exports has mounted steadily over the years.

In this century, there have been significant changes in the structure of Canada's export trade as the manufacturing sector has grown and become more diversified. The pace of change accelerated in the 1930's with the introduction of the British Empire Tariff Preference Scheme, which resulted in the establishment in Canada of many U.S. controlled factories.

But the most remarkable expansion of industrial capacity took place during World War II and in the post-war years, when an expanded and modernized Canadian industry was smoothly converted to peace-time patterns of production and was thus in a position to supply the exceptionally strong demand, at home and abroad, for industrial and consumer goods.

In the immediate post-World War II years, strong sellers' markets in international trade developed as a war-shaken world rebuilt itself to meet the belated demands of peace. Subsequently, there was a spectacular revival in the international exchange of goods brought about by the General Agreement on Tariffs and Trade (GATT) as a result of its sustained efforts to lower artificial trade barriers and introduce the principles of multilateralism and non-discrimination.

Growth in Trade

Since the early 1960's, there has been an unprecedented growth in Canada's international trade, both in absolute terms and as a proportion of the GNP. This was in line with what took place in the industrial world as a whole, but the Canadian growth was even stronger than the average. For example, in the period 1960-77, the value of Canada's exports rose nearly eight-fold for an average annual increase of 13.2%.

In view of the fact that prices have more than doubled since 1970, it is more informative to look at the changes in the volume of trade since 1960. In volume terms, Canada's commodity exports more than tripled for an average annual increase of 7.2%. This growth in volume was strongest in the 1960's and early 1970's with an annual average increase of almost 10% largely because of the impetus of a ten-fold increase in exports of finished manufactured goods (inedible end products).

While the export of crude industrial and agricultural commodities is still a very important factor in Canada's economy, their share of total exports has declined substantially over the past decade. So too has the share of fabricated materials such as pulp, newsprint and metal ingots, as the export of manufactured products has jumped from 11% in 1963 to about 40% of total merchandise exports today.

The rapid growth in exports of manufacturers, particularly from 1963 to 1974, can be attributed to many factors:

(1) The devaluation of the C$ exchange rate in 1962, to 92 1/2¢ U.S. increased the international competitiveness of Canadian industry;

(2) Special intergovernmental arrangements: The Canada-U.S. Automotive Products Agreement and the Canada-U.S. Defence Production Sharing Agreement.

(3) "Market Forces", especially the rapid increase in the international trade of manufactured products which rose in that period at a much higher rate than trade in raw materials.

(4) Production rationalization programs implemented by foreign-controlled multinational corporations which resulted in the manufacture for export of many end products and components by the rapidly growing number of subsidiaries located in Canada.

(5) Export financing facilities provided by the export development corporation, and Canadian International Development Agency aid programs.

(6) Tariff preferences for some Canadian products exported to Britain, Australia, and other Commonwealth nations.
It is interesting to note that since 1960 Canada's increase in the volume of exports of manufactured goods grew faster than that for industrial countries as a whole.

Changes in Commodity Composition of Exports

There was a significant change in the composition of Canada's exports in the period 1960-77. In constant dollar terms, the proportion of Canada's exports in finished manufactured goods (inedible) increased steadily from 8 percent in 1960 to 46 percent in 1977. It is also interesting to note that the share of manufactured products as a whole (including fabricated materials) in exports increased from 60 percent in 1960 to 77 percent in 1977. However, in the same period the share of agricultural products declined from 23 percent to 12 percent.

Changes in Geographic Patterns of Exports

As a result of this major alteration in the commodity composition of Canada's exports, there was a significant change in the importance of Canada's export markets. For example, the share of Canadian exports going to the United States increased from 56 percent in 1960 to a peak of 70% in 1969. These results reflected the autopact which increased many-fold the trade in automotive goods and the significant increases in exports of crude petroleum to the United States. Today, almost 70% of Canada's exports still go to the United States.

Another major change was the decline in the share of Canadian exports purchased by the United Kingdom, which stood at 17 percent in 1960 but declined to slightly under 4 percent in 1978. This was a drastic change considering that the United Kingdom was Canada's largest export market in 1941. In 1973, Japan replaced the United Kingdom as Canada's second largest export customer. In general, Canada's share of exports going to other industrialized countries has remained fairly constant. Interestingly enough, Canada's exports to the OPEC countries rose from 1 percent in 1960 to 3 percent in 1977. While Canada has lost considerable ground since the mid-1960's in the European community and the rest of the world in terms of market share sales to the Pacific Rim markets have gained about 10 percent annually.

Changes in Trade Performances in Relation to Production

Canada's current pattern of trade causes some concern due to its heavy and growing dependence on exports to the U.S. It is interesting to observe that in spite of attempts by the Canadian government to develop a "third option" during most of the 1970's, Canada has become more dependent than ever on sales to the U.S.A. markets which accounted for 70.4% of Canada's exports in 1978 compared with only 68.2% in 1976. While this interest by the U.S. in Canadian-made products and services is understandable, nevertheless, it is obvious that the best interests of the Canadian economy would be served if Canada could avoid having most of its eggs in one basket. Canada could and should pursue markets in other areas of the world more aggressively.

For example, in 1979, the U.S., with a population of approximately 230 million people, imported $155 billion, the European Community, on the other hand, is the world's largest trading entity with a population of over 260 million. In 1979, it imported approximately $204 billion from sources outside of the Community. Canada's exports to the EC represented 3% of the Community's overall imports compared with Canada's 23% share of the U.S. import market (versus the EC's 8% share of the Canadian market). While the EC constitutes Canada's largest overseas market, (12% of Canada's total world exports), nevertheless, in terms of opportunities, therein, Canada has still fallen considerably short of realizing its optimum potential. Moreover, only 11% of Canada's sales to the EC are fully-manufactured goods although 45% of EC imports from all sources are in this category. On the other hand, almost two-thirds of all EC sales to Canada are fully-manufactured goods. The large volume of goods and services imported by the

European Community indicates that certain other countries are doing a much more effective job of penetrating Community markets than Canada is doing.

Canada's exports to the European Community in 1979 consisted mainly of wood pulp, iron ore, nickel, zinc ores, paperboard, copper, lumber and barley. As I just mentioned, 11% of Canada's exports to the EC were in the category of finished goods, (versus 35% with the U.S.A.) and this figure has remained consistent over a number of years. This is particularly relevant in terms of our trade scope with the community. The EC actually purchased 45% in manufactured goods from outside sources. Thus it is clear that Canada has to do a great deal more in this secondary sector not only in terms of exports to the European Community but also with reference to exports to other areas of the world. The countries that seem to hold the greatest opportunities for Canadian exporters include the United States, Australia, New Zealand, Brazil, South Africa, Spain, the Scandinavian countries, the Arab oil countries, and the People's Republic of China.

Problem Areas

One problem is the growing threat to Canada's export trade from competition from countries that could have been safely ignored a decade ago. Many Canadian manufacturers today are concerned about competing against manufacturers from other countries such as South Korea, Taiwan, and Singapore, which can often produce goods of equal quality and much lower costs.

Another threat is the increase in the number of countries selling raw and semi-processed materials for which Canada previously supplied a major portion to world markets, such as copper, nickel and newsprint.

A third problem area stems from the development of cartels such as the Organization of Petroleum Exporting Countries (OPEC), the Intergovernmental Council of Copper Exportion Nations (CIPEC), the International Bauxite Association of Natural Rubber Producing Countries, the Association of Tungstin-Producing Countires, a group of Latin American coffee producers, and the Caracas Group (an iron ore association).

There is also the possibility of third world countries forming a cartel using certain commodities as leverage for purchasing goods from the developed countries.

The development of several regional trading blocs over the past two decades also pose a threat to Canadian exporters. The total population of these blocs constitute over one billion people or about 30% of the world's total with a Gross World Product (GWP) of 40% of the world's total. If Japan and People's Republic of China are included, which severely restricts imports, and which have an economy large enough to qualify as a common market of their own, the total is well over half of the GWP. These common markets are designed to give members specific advantages in trading with each other, and conversely create disadvantages for non-members, including Canada.

For Canada, as one of the few industrialized nations without a domestic market of at least 100 million consumers or free access to one, these developments have tended to increase its concerns about relative isolation and its ability to remain internationally competitive.

Attempts by the United States for example, to involve more of its economy in export trade, such as through the Domestic International Sales Corporation legislation (DISC) and efforts by other countries, including Canada, to meet these developments, have further complicated the international trade scene.

Since 1950, world trade has increased more than ten-fold, and a good deal of the credit for this unprecedented growth can be given to the negotiated trade liberalization carried out under the GATT and, perhaps equally importantly, to its contractual rules which serve as the framework within which that trade has been carried out.

The recently completed (1979) "Tokyo Round" of GATT negotiations established the target date of January 1, 1980 for implementation of the first eight annual uniform tariff cuts. In spite of this, however, the current slowdown of world trade has caused a growing concern for protectionism throughout the world. Since protectionism of one nation breeds protectionism by others, it is imperative that trade barriers be lowered as soon as possible.

At this point, it should be recalled that in 1975 the Economic Council of Canada published a report entitled "Looking Outward: A New Trade Strategy for Canada". This report recommends that Canada should adopt some type of free trade policy. The report states that "a free trade policy is not only feasible for Canada, but is the best guarantee of its national objectives".

Another problem is that competition in export markets as a whole has become more and more intensified in recent years as technological developments in the field of transportation and communications make the markets of the world increasingly available to all. If Canadians wish to retain and develop their standard of living, they must recognize that the world has become a global village, and they must be globally oriented. Napoleon's troops did not travel across Europe any faster than did the soldier's of Julius Ceasar some 2,000 years before Napoleon. But today, the world has shrunk so much in size that it has become a global village, and man can now circumnavigate the globe in a spaceship in a matter of 90 minutes, and communicate with almost any corner of the globe by radio in a matter of seconds.

As a result of such technological developments, as well as the GATT negotiations, many Canadian manufacturers are beginning to realize the domestic market is shrinking as they feel the effects of the keen and growing competition from foreign manufacturers penetrating the Canadian market.

Canadians should also look at themselves as others see them. For example, the Organization for Economic Cooperation and Development (OECD) in Paris has observed, while Canada used to be second to the United States in terms of living standards, Canada is now in eighth place among the top fifteen countries and, if the Canadian economy continues on its present course, Canada's standard of living will fall to eleventh place by 1985. Other signs of illness in the Canadian economy in 1977 included:

a) Canada had more strikes than any other country;
b) Canadian productivity was over 15% lower than than in the U.S.A.;
c) Canada was the largest borrower in the world in international markets.

While these matters have improved a great deal since 1977,

future growth in Canada will be measured by its ability to maintain an internally competitive situation and to sustain a rate of export growth that will be in proportion to its population growth. This surely is the most important challenge facing Canadians in the years ahead -- "The Export Challenge", because on Canada's ability to meet this challenge will depend not only its standard of living but also the degree to which the country can cope with its rapidly growing social problems.

Canada's Trading Outlook

Whatever the solution of these merging problems may be, the pattern of world trade is undergoing basic changes and shifts in emphasis, and Canadians must be ready for them. As Canada enters the eighties, it stands on the threshold of a new and challenging era in international trade. While the recent GATT negotiations created some of the difficulties mentioned above they also increased Canada's access to foreign markets. Thus, the next ten years could be very prosperous for Canadian industry if firms will undertake to develop their export potential.

The average Canadian manufacturer needs more output to lower his unit production costs and thus become more competitive and earn more profit. If he can increase his output by developing markets outside Canada, he will realize not only a profit on his export sales but a higher margin of profit on his domestic sales as well. Sales abroad of course, can help to offset fluctuations in the Canadian economy. Given that 85 percent of the firms in Canada are classified as "small business", it is from this sector that most of the 300,000 new jobs Canada needs every year must come.

Manufacturers will have to export in the eighties simply to survive. The fact of the matter is that the industrial capacity of the Canadian economy far exceeds the needs of the Canadian market. Particularly, Canada needs to increase exports of manufactured goods and to diversify its markets. While Canada's export performance has been impressive over the past 20 years, the need and opportunity for additional growth are there in an expanding trade environment.

Unfortunately, only a relatively small number of Canadian manufacturers are exporting. Of the estimated 26,000 manufacturers in Canada, only some 7,000 are registered in the exporters directory of the Canadian Department of Industry, Trade and Commerce, and most of these are not exporting on a sustained basis. It is estimated that some 200 firms actually account for three-quarters of Canada's exports.

During the annual meeting of the Canadian Export Association in 1979, the Ministry of Industry, Trade and Commerce at that time told exporters that Canada's exports would have to be tripled in order to eliminate the country's current trade deficit. Such a significant expansion of Canada's exports must depend to a great extent, therefore, on encouraging a much greater number of small-to-medium size manufacturers to export.

Investigations by the Canadian Government Department of Industry, Trade and Commerce (D.I.T. & C.) revealed the following reasons for rather poor performance of Canadian firms in the export of manufactured goods: a lack of management interest; lack of finances; unfamiliarity with export marketing; and fear of the unknown. It was also found that approximately 60 percent of Canada's labour force is employed by small and medium-sized firms which are mostly owned by Canadians.

In order to overcome many of the obstacles mentioned above, and to encourage small businesses to export, the federal and provincial governments have each developed a small business division as well as a variety of export assistance and incentive programs. The federal government has also established the federal business development bank with 54 branches across the country. This bank provides loans to firms that have sound business proposals but which lack reasonable financial resources. It will also provide management expertise upon request.

Through the enterprise development program, the program for export market development, trade missions, trade fairs, and many more federal programs, small businesses can research markets abroad and increase their penetration of foreign markets. In addition, provincial governments also have a variety of complimentary programs which will assist the exporter.

Other federal government organizations such as the Department of Supply and Services, The Canadian Commercial Corporation, The Export Development Corporation, and The Canadian International Development Agency are involved in sourcing and assisting Canadian exporters.

However, it should also be noted that the extent to which the growth of exports can be achieved will be significantly affected by the ability of Canadian manufacturers to modernize and enlarge their productive capacity -- i.e., on the growth of direct investment. The amount of investment capital required to create one new job today in Canada is more than double the amount required ten years ago, and this is growing rapidly in some industries due to such factors as the public demand for pollution control.

The lack of an appropriate infra-structure is also hindering the development of Canadian consortia to bid on turnkey projects abroad. This situation is illustrated by the fact that last year Canadian firms tendered only on one percent of the world Bank contracts although membership in the world Bank entitles Canada to tender on a much higher percentage of the Bank's contracts.

Canada's Response to the Export Challenge

In summary, then, it is apparent that Canada has three separate export objectives for the years ahead:

1. To sustain sufficient growth in total exports to attain and maintain a viable balance of payments position and an acceptable standard of living in Canada;

2. To increase exports to offshore markets so as to reduce Canadian dependence upon the U.S. market;

3. To achieve rapid and sustained growth in both the volume and variety of exports of manufactured, and processed products in order to keep employment at an acceptable level, and with Canada's economic and social problems.

As Canada enters the eighties, she stands on the threshold of a new era in international trade. Not only will the recent GATT negotiations create more foreign competition in the domestic market, but they will also increase Canada's access to foreign markets. For example, by the latter part of this decade about 80 percent of everything Canada exports to the United Stated will be duty-free, up from 70 percent today. Thus, the next ten years could be very prosperous for Canadian industry if firms develop their export potential.

How to Select an Export Market
by
E.C. Hill
President
Dearborn Steel Products Inc.

Selling Abroad

The export market has for most Canadian manufacturers a tremendous potential. Unlike the domestic market, each major sale abroad is different, has its own peculiarities and usually involves new problems requiring solutions. Selling abroad can be a wonderful experience. One can look back into history and read about the early traders making almost impossible journeys from one country to another trading goods for gold and other merchandise. Export financing is not new either as for several hundred years European banking houses, for example the House of Rothschild, have financed the sales and purchases of a multitude of goods.

Canada's Need for Exports

A challenge which presents itself to Canadians today, to develop more business abroad, is probably greater than it ever has been before. We must export more manufactured goods. I am not suggesting that we not export raw materials and products of our resource industries, but I am stating most emphatically that we must increase our exports of products from the secondary manufacturing sector of our industry. If we do not do so, we will be unable to employ the new people who are each year entering our labour market, as it is the secondary manufacturing part of Canada's industry and its exporting services that has the ability to provide the number of new jobs which are required each and every year for the next 7 to 8 years. Canada needs about 288,000 new jobs each and every year and with the further mechanization of our resource industry, the creation of new jobs in that sector will be very small.

Our domestic market is only so great and we cannot absorb on the home front all the goods and services we are capable of producing, so we must, therefore, export.

Canada has made great strides in the development of export markets for products from the primary resources industry and we are developing export markets too for more of our manufactured goods. Our number one customer is the U.S.A. and the bulk of our trade is directed that way. However, the Americans produce many of the items we produce and in greater quantity, so while they are our best customers, they are in many cases with third countries our biggest competitor. To balance out our trade, it is the so called "THIRD" countries of the world to which we must direct our attention in the further development of our export market.

Many people consider exports are less important to Canada than exports are to the Japanese, the British, the French, the Germans, etc. This is incorrect, as we export a higher percentage of our gross national product than any of these countries mentioned, and we are, therefore, more dependent on the export business than are they.

Consequently, we have a big job to do and the question is how are we going to do it.

Choosing an Export Market

Let us say you are an industrialist who has not really done any export business to date or to any material degree. You decide you have got to expand your business and the only way you can do so is to develop some interest and orders from abroad. The important thing, I think, at the outset is to assess exactly what you have got to sell and to spend some time in serious thought on planning your campaign strategy to successfully penetrate the international marketplace. Success in exporting begins with a proper state of mind. It is not an easy business and it is not a casual business, but it is a business which requires energy, determination and perseverance - probably to an even greater degree than has been required to date in developing a domestic market.

I might add here that if you are successful in the domestic market, there is every likelihood you can also be successful in the export market, and so let us consider you have been successful at least to a degree at home. However, if you lack success at home, I sincerely question the degree of success you can expect to achieve abroad. A strong home market base is a big asset.

Any campaign, either commercial or military, requires careful and thorough planning. When you plan an attack on the International Marketplace, plan this as a steady, permanent program and do not try any in and out procedure to rid yourself of a temporary surplus. Certainly you might be successful, but it would only be temporary and if this is your objective, I question not only your degree of success, but I suggest that such an attitude might be harmful to Canada's international reputation generally. So, if you are going to try, do your planning well and plan to stay at it.

It is important that senior members of the management team support the activities of the sales department in this campaign. Expenses will come before sales and expenses involved in international marketing are sometimes higher on a percentage basis than on the domestic field, particularly during the development stage.

Do not try to cover the whole world at once. In your initial planning, determine where you think your product or service could be of interest, select a couple of countries and start there. It is surprising, but success with a customer in one country can influence a prospective customer in another country to give you a trial order. It is important that you recognize at the outset you have to make a start somewhere. Therefore, the planning for the first order or first few orders is important.

The First Steps

Assuming that you have now decided you are going to venture out in the foreign market and you have decided on a country or a couple of countries. Now what should you do? The first thing to do is to determine if these areas are either interested or are utilizing products similar to yours. There are several ways you can get this information, but probably one of the best would be to write to the Canadian Government Trade Commissioner, or if there is one, the Ontario representative of the Ontario Department of Industry and Tourism accredited to that country, and ask him to supply you with some basic sales information. These people are with some basic sales information. These people are delighted to receive inquiries, particularly from new exporters and usually in a short space of time; and depending of course on the complexity of your questions and general requirement for information, they will come back to you with a pretty good analysis of the situation.

If you have a product which is normally sold through a wholesaler, dealer or distributor, then you should ask the Trade Commissioner for information as to who might be a suitable representative. Many successful contacts have been developed in this manner by Canadian exporters and it is a simple, easy way of getting information without heavy expense.

Approaching the Dealer

Now that you have a contact, it is important to sit back and consider your next move because this could very well be a highly important one. You have got to describe your product to the prospective dealer in such a way that he can understand it, and that he in turn may be able to check out the interest for your product in his country. Maybe you have some sales literature or a catalogue. If so, this is a distinct advantage. If not, maybe you should consider having such selling tools, depending of course on your type of product or service. These are some of the basic considerations and one may think such thoughts are almost unnecessary to mention, but it is surprising sometimes how very inept some people are when they approach the International Marketplace. You have got to tell your story and if you have something unique, you have got to talk about it. Additionally, if you are looking at a market in a country where the language is not English, you may have to consider reprinting some of your sales information, as well as some of your service information, in another language.

The language of commerce internationally is English and the runner up is probably French. Most commercial people, certainly the senior people in importing firms in other countries, have either a working knowledge of English or are quite fluent. Therefore, direct communication is not, in most cases, a problem, but the description of a product in writing, when it involves people at the consumer level, may have to be in the language of the importing country.

167

Your first letter to a prospective dealer or customer should be businesslike and should contain sufficient information as to your product or service, delivery, the prices F.A.S. a Canadian port, or if it is at all possible, and this usually can be developed by an inquiry or two, the laid down price for your product in the country involved.

If you are selling a mechanical item, particularly one which is somewhat sophisticated, the question of service, maintenance and spare parts ability will certainly come up, and if you are selling an item where initially technical assistance is a requirement, then you must give some thought to this at the outset.

One of the big problems in the international marketplace effecting the successful and continuing sales of mechanical equipment is a question of proper <u>service</u>, <u>technical assistance</u> and the <u>availability of spare parts</u>. People abroad do not want to get stuck with something that breaks down after a few months and which will require spares from Canada so the unit can be made operational again. In such instances, the ready availability of spares must be an item for early consideration. Most of us like to sell spare parts, it is good business at a good profit.

Another matter for early consideration in your basic strategy is how much of your production can you make available to the export market. Some people have found heavy demands almost at the outset, and as a result they have had to decide whether or not to expand to meet the flow of orders.

Transportation costs will be an important item. It is one the customer will be most sensitive about as frequently the cost of freight is a major part of the total price asked in the country abroad.

One thing is of paramount importance and cannot be overly emphasized. When replies come in to your first letters and they probably will come in, answer these letters promptly and completely. Try to put yourself in the position of the prospective importer and give him as much information as you can so he in turn can come back to you with intelligent information, et cetera. You will undoubtedly find that people abroad are more careful in their correspondence than are some North Americans and they appreciate working with people who reply in a prompt, business-like manner and who provide the information requested.

Do not forget that first impressions account for a great deal. Try to make your presentation, your correspondence and all your dealings with both the Trade Commissioners and prospective dealers or customers abroad not only businesslike, but impressive and without a lot of exaggeration. Give these people the feeling you are not only interested in serving them and doing business with them, but that you do business in a forthright and businesslike manner. Indecision, vacillation, carelessness and indifference to requests or inquiries can turn off a customer very, very quickly. Even though your initial contact abroad may be through correspondence, the cost of writing a letter and taking time to research information, etc. is expensive, and you should spend your time and money wisely. You should try to impress the customer properly right from the start.

Differences in a Way of Life

You will find out quite quickly business practices, while fundamentally the same in most countries, do differ in the manner of presentation, discussion and procedure. People abroad do not think exactly as do North Americans and customs vary from country to country. You must realize this right at the start. Initially, if you choose to communicate by correspondence or any other form of written message, this particular point may not be terribly important, but it will become more important as you proceed toward either conclusion of a sale or conclusion of a selling arrangement with a foreign buyer. My attitude has always been that our job is to obtain the order, and therefore I have always felt one must maintain a degree of flexibility of approach, so if it is at all possible, you follow the general routine to which the buyer is accustomed, providing of course you achieve your objective. I realize this is a pretty general statement. Another way of covering this point would be to say that one should not expect to do business in the International Marketplace exactly the way it is done in North America.

In many parts of the world, pleasantries and bits of light conversation such as inquiries about the family, mutual friends, etc., will precede business discussions to a much greater degree than is usually seen at home. You will find too that in many parts of the world, time is not considered to the same degree as it is here in North America. In North America we sometimes endeavour to move too quickly and find there are some details which should have been considered which were overlooked. I think you will find in the International Marketplace your discussions will be more thorough, and while it is still possible for certain matters to be overlooked, the likelihood of this is much less.

If any of you have had an opportunity to talk business with the Chinese, you will understand the point I have just mentioned. The Chinese are rated to be extremely thorough and astute in their business negotiations and they take an infinite amount of time and care to cover every possible point or eventuality. Consequently, when you have concluded a deal with the Chinese, the probabilities are that you will have discussed everything and anything which could possibly occur during or after a transaction. This is an example of thoroughness which does prevail in the International Marketplace, in varying degrees, depending on the type of buyer, the type of sale and the country involved. While you might consider too much time is taken up in discussing minor issues, I think we all realize that all too frequently minor issues can become very quickly major ones, and the old saying of "a stitch in time saves nine" is an appropriate phrase. Do not be impatient about prolonged contractual negotiations. It will take in all probability a considerable period of time to conclude the first order and subsequently, you may spend considerable time on additional orders, but I suggest to you that this time is by no means wasted, and it is probably very necessary.

Patience is a virtue, the saying goes, but when you are involved in international marketing, negotiations and discussions, patience is a requirement. A show of impatience on your part, either through correspondence or direct contact, may well be considered discourteous and you should not do this unless the provocation is extremely acute.

When to Travel

My comments up to now have been devoted, to a large measure, to generalities, procedures and suggestions which require your consideration prior to attacking the international market or in the initial stages of your first contacts. You may very well consumate a sale through correspondence but you may also find, as many have, the only way you are going to conclude negotiations successfully will be to have a face to face meeting with your dealer or customer. Thus, you will at some stage have to consider the prospect of traveling abroad.

The first trip or trips abroad are an exciting and new experience for those who have not done so previously, but before embarking on a trip, I caution you to plan your program very carefully.

A common mistake many make is to figure you can accomplish what you want to do in a day or so. Maybe you can, but as I have already stated, time is not as important in many countries abroad as it is at home and therefore, what you can do in Canada and the United States in a day or two days may well take you a week in another country. So, when you plan your trip leave yourself enough time to do your work and then add at least 50% more. One thing you will find is that international travel is tiring and if you go by air as most do, a long trip can be rather exhausting. Some people travel better than others and some can begin work almost immediately on arrival but most should not. A sudden change of environment, different language, new people, different food, et cetera, all have an effect on your system and a well rested and relaxed businessman is much better able to handle the rigors of negotiations than one who is not.

If you are planning a trip, probably you should plan to visit more than one place so as to improve your chances of success. If, for example, you were planning to visit Colombia, which is in the northern part of South America, maybe you should also plan to visit Peru and Venezuela. Or, if you are going to go to New Zealand, why not consider going to Australia as well, and maybe Indonesia. This may sound very elementary but sometimes people focus only on the matter immediately at hand and you might be missing a good bet if you did not take a few more days to cover a somewhat larger territory.

Before you embark on a trip, do some planning. Advise the Canadian Government Trade Commissioner of your intentions to visit the country in which he is posted, and if you are going to need his help, say so and describe what sort of help you need. He can help you with a translator, he can provide you with some secretarial service and you may very well want him or his assistant to accompany you during your initial contacts. The Trade Commissioner can arrange your appointments and in fact, if given sufficient time, can, to a large measure, arrange your whole program. But give him sufficient time to make such arrangements and to fit what you want done into his already busy schedule. Trade Commissioners are delighted to assist you, and they are particularly pleased when you decide to visit the country to which they are accredited, but most Trade Posts abroad are busy ones, and they have a lot of visitors, all of whom require some special form of attention, etc. If given adequate notice, the Trade Commissioner can do a better job for you. If you have a prospective customer or dealer as well in the territory and you have been corresponding with them, then advise them as well, and with sufficient notice, of your intentions to visit.

Personal contact plays an important part toward success in the International Marketplace. Many things can be handled easily and quickly by face to face discussions. On the other hand, be sure that prior to setting out you carefully scrutinize all correspondence of recent date with that territory and if there are any unanswered questions, be certain you are prepared to provide answers. A very good way to arm yourself for a trip is to put yourself into your customer's or dealer's position and try to come up with the questions you would ask if the conditions were reversed.

I feel Canadians have a real advantage in the International Marketplace today over many of their competitors from other countries. We at home do not realize as well as we should the very high esteem in which Canada and Canadians are held by other nations. We are thought of as the ideal country, and our citizens are accepted abroad to a degree that citizens of other countries often envy. This is an advantage and should be jealously guarded by all Canadians and should not be abused. A fine reputation is hard to win but easy to lose, and is a valuable asset. Canada has this position in most areas of the world and it must be preserved.

Let's get back to when you should travel. I have already told you to plan your trip carefully and to give others ample warning. While it is a good idea to go out and see prospective customers, do not do so prematurely. You can sense when the time is right or you should be able to. It is fine to go on an exploratory trip without first making contacts but even if you plan to do that or plan to combine business and pleasure into one trip, if you are going to seek help from anyone, including a Canadian Government Agency, give them advance notice. Sometimes an exploratory trip is necessary in advance of correspondence, etc. You alone must decide on this, depending of course on your product or service. For such a trip you may wish to apply to the Canadian Department of Industry, Trade and Commerce for a PEMD Grant (Program for Export Market Development), for which the application has to be submitted several weeks ahead of the trip.

From time to time the Ontario Government and the Federal Government sponsors a Mission to a particular marketing area and it may be possible for you to join such a group, although one must be invited and the policy in previous years has been to keep the Mission available only to people who have a current interest or who have done business in a certain area.

Buying groups also visit Canada sometimes at the invitation of either a Federal or Provincial Department. Therefore, continuing contact with both the Federal Department of Industry, Trade and Commerce and the Ontario Department of Industry and Tourism is most desirable. You may even have a prospective customer walk into your place of business. Many inquiries come in to both these Departments direct from abroad and it is important that both these Departments be aware of your present interest and intentions toward the International Market.

Trade Fairs are held in many countries on a periodic or annual basis. Sometimes the Federal Government sponsors a Canadian exhibit or pavillion, the latter holding samples of a number of Canadian products. The Department of Industry, Trade and Commerce, in conjunction with Information Canada, look after these activities, and when a Canadian exhibit is being sponsored, some assistance in the form of an absorption of freight costs, etc. is available to the exporter, along with assistance in customs clearance and general administration at the other end. If you decide to participate in one of these Fairs, it is a good idea to consider having a representative attend for at least part of the Fair period. In many cases, goods are sold to buyers during or immediately after the Fair. PEMD grants are also available for participation in fairs.

As an example, quite a number of Canadian manufacturers

displayed products at the Canadian Trade Fair in Peking in the summer of 1972. This was an opportunity to actually show the Chinese Canadian made products and as a result, many of the exhibitors achieved some immediate success in the Chinese market. Without the assistance of the Canadian Government in setting up the Trade Fair, this valuable opportunity to the exporter would not have existed.

Prices/Quotations

You have selected the market you want to penetrate but before you go very far, you have got to provide such basic information as the price to your prospect. This sounds very simple, as presumably you know what you want for your goods or services, but do you know as much as you should about the competition which exists in that particular country. In selecting an export market, you must look at the pricing situation at an early date. If your product is locally manufactured, then you must determine at what price the competitive product is being offered and then what price your product will cost laid down in that country, with import duties, etc., included. I am not going to become involved in a long discussion on prices, quotations and credit because this forms the basis of another lecture. However, one subject interlocks with another and when you are selecting an export market, you must look for one where it is possible to compete price wise. There is no sense wasting time in an area where the competition from possibly a local source is too great to overcome. You must, therefore, make this item one for early consideration.

Trade with Socialistic Countries

Many Canadian companies have been very successful in negotiating important contracts with countries having a Socialist or Communist government. We are businessmen and we should not become unduly concerned about the politics of a country, providing there is some mechanism for conducting commercial activity, and there is such a mechanism in every country. Conducting business in a Socialist or Communist country may undoubtedly be more complex than in another area but that should not be considered necessarily a deterrent. If prospects for you lie in such areas, then you should be guided by the recommendations of the Canadian Trade Commissioner assigned to that area. If you choose to attempt to succeed in those particular markets, which are often important ones, you must be prepared to plan your campaign very carefully in consultation with Trade Specialists in Ottawa, who are familiar with that particular country, as well as our Trade Representative located there.

In some cases, your products might be restricted for export to such territories depending on their strategic nature. If an export permit is required, as it is for some products to some countries, then you should consult well in advance with the Department of Industry, Trade and Commerce, who will guide you.

Communistic countries are usually extremely careful about maintaining their credit worthiness and quite often there is less difficulty in collections or financial negotiations with these than with some other countries who have a democratic government.

The question of credit worthiness is also important in your assessment of where to look for business. Depending on your product or service, you may very well become involved in credit discussions. Credit is an important part of International business and many, many sales are made on short, medium or long term credit. Cash sales are made as well and these are usually by means of a Letter of Credit which covers full payment or a down payment. If you are asked to supply terms, you should investigate not only the credit worthiness of the buyer, but the credit worthiness of the country in which the buyer is located. If your sale involves a substantial amount and terms are desired, you probably should get in touch with the Export Development Corporation, which is a Crown Corporation established to insure receivables from abroad, and this same Corporation, under certain special circumstances, will act as a financing agency for long term projects involving capital equipment. E.D.C. will give you very probably their views on the sort of terms and the premium cost for the country in question, but you will have to work through normal commercial sources such as your bank, Dun and Bradstreet or the Trade Commissioner to get financial information on the Buyer. You could also ask the Buyer for financial information, and many times this is freely available.

Do not overlook the possibilities of credit being a requirement for export, as in many cases it is.

Conclusion

People who are starting out in the export business sometimes are hesitant about asking for suggestions or advice from others who have developed experience in the International Marketplace over the years. Do not hesitate. Most executives experienced in export are quite happy to give you some suggestions and ideas as they recognize the importance of Canada's participation abroad.

Attendance at various seminars sponsored by the Canadian Export Association, the Canadian Manufacturers' Association, and Federal and Provincial Government Departments, can often times provide both useful information and new ideas.

A knowledge of documentation required to ship your product is necessary and this can be obtained from an international forwarder and there are many of these located in Canada. Your buyer will tell you in all probability what documents he needs for his own use and customs clearance.

You will find marketing possibilities change quite a bit from year to year in certain countries. For example, Chile was an active market for certain Canadian products until their economic position placed them in an adverse credit position. This situation may well now change and while countries do not always have to undergo a revolution to alter marketing conditions, the economies of many countries abroad change quite drastically from time to time. It is, therefore, very important that the people assigned to the development of the International Marketplace keep themselves well informed on the latest economic conditions and political trends in those areas in which you have a potential interest.

From time to time the Canadian Government will send a high level Economic Mission to another country to negotiate with that country a loan to purchase Canadian equipment, goods or services. When this occurs, automatically these countries become prime prospects.

New or revised Trade Agreements from time to time provide easier access for Canadian goods and it is a good idea to keep current on what is happening in this area.

The Canadian International Development Agency (C.I.D.A.)

has available substantial amounts of money which are used to finance Projects in developing countries. There are many opportunities here for the introduction of Canadian made goods and services, where payment is no problem and where sales experience is minimal.

There are a lot of countries in the world, many of them - in fact most of them - are still developing, and the need for goods and services is strong. There is also a fair supply from the producing nations. But if you are persistent and if you have a good product at a realistic price, the world can really be your oyster. You certainly will not know until you try.

Gearing up for Export Markets

by
Jerry N. Kendall, President
Venturetek International Ltd.
and
Michael Needham, Vice President
Helix Investments Ltd.

Introduction

Canada needs to broaden its market base for exports. Much of the export emphasis is going to be thrown toward Canada's secondary manufacturing industries which are less sensitive to the vagaries of government agreements and large contract negotiations. The advantage of exporting secondary manufacturing products is that there is more value added which helps the employment picture and strengthens the economy, and broadens the economic infrastructure.

Why Bother Exporting

(a) ### Basic Needs

In certain instances the motivation may be considered to come from the importing country where the need is basic to their existence. Examples of these are foodstuffs, raw materials and energy. Normally contracts are negotiated, often over a long period of time, with negotiations generally of a financial nature, often between governments. The degree of marketing input is pretty low. For example, there is, of course, Japan who must import most of their raw materials. Coupled with the currency revaluation in the last year we have seen the Japanese making enormous purchases in the world of wool, wheat, soy beans, ground nuts and other basic materials, creating shortages sometimes in the home market. Once these shortages begin to grow the Canadian exporter must beware of government intervention. For example--the restriction on soy bean exports.

This, however, is not the type of export market under discussion here.

(b) Opportunity

We now cross over from the area of <u>need</u> for export to the "opportunity" for export.

1. ### To Increase Profit Dollars
   This is quite obvious and I suppose is a blanket overall reason for exporting. Nevertheless, straight dollar profit is not always the prime motivator in a decision to go export.

2. ### To Justify a Production Facility Whose Minimum Economic Size Has Capacity Far Beyond the Needs of the Domestic Market Involved
   Here the planned profit from world markets is needed to justify the installation. An example of this could be Atlas Steels who built a flat rolled, stainless steel plant in Quebec whose capacity was three times the Canadian Market. Other examples in Canada are the De Havilland Aircraft Company, who can exist only through exporting about 80% of their sales, and, of course, the Aluminium Company of Canada.

3. ### To Achieve Outlets for By-Production
   An example of the by-product industry is uranium from the South African gold mines. Uranium is achieved at extremely little extra cost and offered around the world in competition to prime suppliers of uranium.

4. ### To Gain Foreign Currency to Balance the Country's Books
   The Japanese Company has motivated the industrialists into new production of new products aimed <u>strictly</u> at gaining U.S. dollars.

5. ### To Create a Market for a Proposed Manufacturing Operation to be Established at a Later Date
   This, of course, is a very familiar objective to Canadians who have seen branch offices of American operations develop into full scale manufacturing entities. Examples of this of course lie in the automotive and chemical industries. Fitting into this category also is the finishing plant in an export market which will adapt the raw product produced in the exporting country to local conditions and requirements.

179

6. Opportunistic - To Exploit a Short Term Advantage to the Fullest

Here we have both the truly opportunistic export such as hoola-hoops which capitalize on a world wide fad but also we have seen where companies have taken advantage of a short term need in an export market and used this to gain a foothold to carry out the necessary research to develop a long term association. The truly opportunistic situation normally requires very little effort on behalf of the exporter since the need is so great that the market comes looking for you. This type of export activity used to be much more prevalent than it is today and most companies look for long term markets which will complement their forwarding planning. The opportunistic markets are largely handled by import/export traders or brokers. Regardless of the objective for entering export markets, it is necessary to define the commercial and competitive environment and lay a plan which will ensure the attainment of the objective. It is wise to remember that most of the rules will be different from those governing the home market which again places the emphasis on thinking things out ahead of time. The plan must have the involvement of all levels of management concerned and the philosophy and strategies which it embodies must be tested and retested before implementation.

We must remember that the distance between an exporter and his customer is ordinarily much wider than at home. By distance I do not necessarily mean only physical distance. More important is the marketing distance which is created by intermediaries standing between the exporter and his customer. This produces an information gap which must be overcome, and here market research is essential.

International market data are varied and scattered. Generally, they are not as complete or accessible as in North America. However, as a general statement, virtually any data required are available in any market with the difference that the method of obtaining information may vary. They may have to be bought, traded, or induced, but they can be found. Economic studies can be justified in depth in the North American economy, but may not be in the fragmented market of Europe or Asia. A more elastic program has to be established based on the question, "Where are the best potential markets for my products?" "In what segments should we concentrate?"

There is no such thing as a mass export market. Each country is unique with the variety of languages, customs, etc. The last ten years, however, have seen a significant amount of money spent in identifying market factors to the point now that it becomes reasonable to maintain the guess part of decision making to a meaningful proportion. Do as much homework as possible before travelling to any export area.

Such sources as in the U.N. Statistical Office, Foreign Service Department, Economist Intelligence Unit, Business International, Government Trade Office, local Embassies, etc. can support our own data collection and correlation.

Researching international markets is very much a matter of innovation. One must have patience with conflicting, suspect or even absent data and be willing to use ingenuity when orthodox lines of inquiry peter out, for example, Hollow Drill Products, because of the paucity of data in foreign countries. In order to estimate the potential market in various countries, we correlated the amount of ore drilled by one unit of hollow drill and then obtained from each country its ore production figures, and in that way arrived at its potential market for our hollow drills.

Similarly we must be certain before starting out on an export program that we have the resources to support the program.

Personnel

Normally in a small company each member of management is wearing a number of hats and the thought of adding one more hat is enough to drop the idea entirely. Therefore, if it is going to be done properly, it must be a full time activity. The export program must also have the full support of senior management who must recognize that developing exports is time consuming and requires considerable investment.

The export manager must have a number of special skills which will be discussed later, but they certainly include such obvious things as languages, knowledge of currencies, transportation, and varied financial transactions.

Financial

The establishment of an export program is the same as any investment program in a company. There are considerable start-up costs, particularly related to the research phase and the initial selling programs.

Credit terms tend to be significantly extended, particularly on new products. The cost of servicing can be enormous.

The costs of investment in inventory and parts supply can be large and can be aggravated by the time to ship and delays in transportation. In addition there are costs of translations, special paper work, payment of duty, and fluctuations in currency.

All of this adds up to a sizeable investment to launch an export program. There are a number of government programs in this country and in others that are available to help the export marketer:

PEMD*- Program for Export Market Development
GAAP*- General Adjustment Assistance Programs
IDAP*- Industrial Design Assistance Program
PAIT*- Program for the Advancement of Industrial Technology
EDC - Development Corporation
Defense Sharing Agreements
Foreign Aid Programs

The Need for the Plan

Developing an export market should not be undertaken indiscriminately such as one executive writing to Canadian Trade Offices; another writing to his English friend in London; another following up a chance contact made on a 747 from Toronto to San Francisco.

A Plan, With a Specific Schedule, is Important

The plan has to first determine which export markets to analyze and then proceeds to analyze each market selected.

* These Federal Government programs are now (1979) incorporated in the Enterprise Development Programs (EDP).

182

The Plan encompasses <u>a thorough size-up of each Market's</u> <u>environment;</u> e.g. size, growth, competition, political and economic stability.

The size-up includes:

<u>The Consumer</u> - the buying habits of the consumer in this market - may well differ greatly from Canada.

<u>The Company's Resources</u> - Dollars available, man-hours available; personnel abilities; production facilities.

This kind of market research analysis applied to various markets will indicate what countries are export priorities and the type of marketing strategy required for success.

<u>Marketing Research</u>

I   <u>The First Step</u> - Arm Chair Market Research
Approach - Identify as clearly as possible, all data available in Canada. Compare with Canadian market to determine rough "guidelines" as to nature of the export market.

1. <u>Population Statistics</u> - Distribution by age, sex, literacy, areas, growth areas. - Indicator of size and growth of market.

2. <u>Economic Indicators</u> - G.N.P., industrial production, utility development and in particular, specific industry indexes -balance of trade are all used in conjunction with the above.

3. <u>Imports - Duties, Tariffs and Dumping Laws</u> - If it's low, importing becomes easier into the country, e.g. Denmark - no local producers. If it's high, then local production may be a more effective route.

4. <u>Long Term Financial Stability</u> - e.g. U.K. possible devaluation of Pound - Financial problems resulted in the 10% surcharge in the U.S.
    - S. America - Risk of inflation in Argentina and Brazil. At the same time we try to measure the political

climate, etc.; e.g. Mexicanization of foreign owned firms in Mexico, where foreign films must be at least 51% locally owned. To get around it, perhaps legal firms holding shares, etc.

5. <u>Tax Potential of Country</u> - Concessions, allowances, corporate taxes, capital taxes.

6. <u>If you are to manufacture</u> - look at <u>local labour rates</u>, e.g. problems today with people in our organizations who are paid at different rates.

7. <u>Language</u> - Belgium (2)
   - Switzerland (4 or 5)

8. <u>Transportation Costs</u>

9. <u>Legal Restrictions</u> - National/Regional/Local.

10. <u>Credit</u> - May have to give 120 days or more.

11. <u>Industrial Organizations</u> - They may have established informal or formal specifications to which you have to adhere, e.g. electrical trades and construction.

12. <u>Different Practices</u> - e.g. construction - SCAN Microsystems Limited. Estimator system in Canada and U.S.A., but quantity survey system in Europe.

II   The Second Step - Visiting the Export Market

The president and the manager to be made responsible for the export drive must prepare a preliminary assessment of the costs (in terms of $, skills and man-hours) and benefits (in terms of potential sales available) involved in developing the export market.

The task of this trip is to gather detailed, on the spot, information on the items in the following check list.

The Check List

1. <u>Local Laws/By-Laws</u> (especially important in some industries, e.g., construction).

2. Market Information
   Where the major market concentrations for the product are:
   by state, city; <u>customer name</u>. (Get telephone numbers,
   addresses; make contacts).

3. <u>Characteristics of the Market</u>
   (a) What are the sizes in $ of these concentrations?

   (b) How amenable are they to a foreign source of supply?

   (c) What are the key sales factors influencing the sale:
       <u>Price</u>; quality; service; lcoation; delivery time.

   (d) Federal and state laws as they apply to the product;
       duties; tariffs.

   (e) Freight and transportation companies and costs.

   (f) Indication of salesmen costs (salary and expenses); time
       before producing; performance level on average, e.g.,
       Budgets made on 4 units per month.

       Actually, could only do one unit per month. This made a
       great difference to cash flow and budgeted profits.

   (g) Amount of inventory to be tied up in export market:
       consignment - ouch!

   (h) Accounts Receivable - what kind of delay should be ex-
       pected:
       e.g. (a) Hospital market - 120 days plus.
           (b) Canadian banks do not give credit on U.S. receiv-
               ables.

   (i) Are service centres required?

   In short, is there a market for my product and in what quantities and over what time period?

4. <u>Analysis of best distribution channels</u>
   - direct sales; dealers; distributors.
   - purchasing behaviour; inventory methods.

- best method of <u>distribution</u> has to be selected. Meet frequently and discuss with dealers: - distributors
 - agents.
- talk to salesmen: do not kid yourself - <u>can these guys sell your product?</u>
- <u>at what price?</u>
- do you have to change the package?
- basic distribution decision is:

<u>DIRECT SALESMAN</u> vs.	<u>DEALER/DISTRIBUTION/AGENT</u>
Up front costs	No up front costs
Training delay	Less training delay
Limited exposure	Broad exposure
<u>BUT</u>	<u>BUT</u>
Direct interface to market	Frequent slow payers than direct customers
Direct control	No direct control or interface with customer
Salesmen concentrating on your product only	Salesmen selling a number of products

Decision can be effected by many factors:

(a) How good a "fit" can you find in a dealer or distributor for your product?

(b) Is your product a sophisticated sell (computer hardware) or a live sell (shirts)?

From the Assessment of the export market, environment, consumer analysis and company resources we can develop a written <u>Export Plan</u>.

This final study and approach should be unanimously approved by the Directors (frequently active in a small business) and top management.

The export manager should insist on at least a 12 month dollar commitment re the budget.

5. <u>Competition</u>
Who? Size, etc.

Has to be analyzed closely: pricing
package
distribution
delivery
quality
people (may find a source of people)

Note: Take full advantage of 50% incentive grants concerning time and travel costs made by the D.I.T.C. Market Development Section (PEMD grants).

III   <u>After returning to Home Base, the managers should then analyze the three major factors in the export decision:</u>
(a) - Finance
(b) - Management
(c) - Market

(a) <u>Financial</u>
A preliminary budget and cash flow should be prepared <u>at this stage</u>, indicating potential sales given the most <u>likely</u> distribution system; building in delays until the system operates efficiently (remember what took 15 years to effect in Canada will take more than six months to effect in the U.S.A. even though you <u>are</u> wiser).

(b) <u>Management</u>
<u>Skills and Man Power Available</u>
Along with the sales projection; budget and cash flow--an assessment of <u>who</u> will do the job ... the people, has to be made.

Are the qualified people on staff; if so, do they have the time and inclination: if not, where can we get people? How much do they cost? Should the sales team be U.S.A. or supplied from Canada?

If the preliminary study gives you the green light to proceed cautiously but aggressively (a unique stance perfected by all successful exporters) then a more <u>thor-ough</u> research of the market is <u>essential.</u>

(c) <u>Market</u>
Using the data gained through arm chair research and from

187

the trip to the market, the following points are analyzed:

(a) The geographic areas to be highlighted have to be identified specifically.

Analyze the consumer - SIC codes
- Competitor locations
- Associations
- Banks
- Trade Journals
- Government publications

It may be easier to sell to Michigan and New York and I can get back during the week and feel comfy - but - the market may be in Louisiana, Alabama and New Mexico!

(b) Are you going to sell regionally or nationally? State-wide only maybe.

(c) The customers have to be identified, preferably by account and by potential per account.

IV   Putting the Plan into Effect
He should expect this to take a minimum of 6 months.

Direct Sales:
Selection of good salesmen and servicemen - a time consuming and critical job.
Should be nationals as far as possible.
How to remunerate: Salary and Bonus
                    Commissions

Dealer Distributor:
Very critical.
Credits Checks: Dun & Bradstreet
                 Banks
                 Credit Bureaus local
                 Supplies
                 Financial statements

Contracts:
Distributor will probably require a contract covering exlusiveness of territory and a time period.
My advice before a history of good relations is developed is to:

1. Avoid exclusive agreements for large territories; and tie them into $ sales performance.

2. Limit agreement to 12 months with options if performance levels are met.

3. Put cancellation clause in.

4. Make contract and sign in Canada or at least interpretable under Canadian law.

Service Arrangments:
It will be 12 months before the successful entry into a new export market will be running smoothly, even if the export plan was excellent. However, the results of a successful export program can be dramatic not only in terms of sales and profits, but also in developing stimulating and challenging jobs for enterprising employees.

Conclusion - Increasing exports is not going to be easy.

The Science Council in a recent report was pessimistic on the future of Canadian manufacturing and consequently its chances of improving exports over the next five years. In its report of October this year, under the title, "INNOVATION IN A COLD CLIMATE - THE DILEMMA OF CANADIAN MANUFACTURING", the Science Council of Canada points out that manufacturing employment has declined from its traditional 21% of the labour force to only 19%. This has created a short-fall of some 120,000 jobs in medium and high technology industries where the greatest growth had been expected.

There is evidence that the profits in several industries are now approaching the subsistence level; below this level, a shutdown is inevitable. We cannot be sure that key sectors will survive, for example, the computer and textile industry.

If the trend continues, Canada's economy will be increasingly dependent on the resource and service industries. We will, once again, become suppliers of raw material to the North American continent. Some of the impediments to innovation of new products and processes are:

a) Canada's technological base is largely characterized by importation of components and technology through direct foreign investment. This leads ultimately to the assembly plant type of operation; for example, C.C.L., Microsystems, automobile companies.

b) The Canadian market is divided among too many suppliers--many of them subsidiaries of foreign companies. These subsidiaries are often not allowed to enter the export market, for example, McGraw Hill; Dupont.

c) The situation is aggravated by uncoordinated policies of indiscriminate support such as regional expansion programs. These sometimes help to establish non-viable industries in poor provinces, which simply move unemployment from province to province. For example, Ontario Development Council, Quebec Development Council, versus the Federal Programs, numerous examples of companies we've looked at - Hytek; MedCom.

d) Financial institutions generally avoid the risk of backing a new company with technologically based products. Nor is the Government aggressive with such support. For example, very few active Venture Capital companies in Canada.

e) Canadian management is inadequate - the educational systems produces one dimensional graduate with little appreciation of management skills.

But the fundamental impediment that the Council finds is the unwillingness of Government and business to cooperate in devising a coherent industrial strategy. (The Japanese are very successful at this and Helix has been trying for some time - it's very difficult). The Council recommended a Government business strategy stressing the establishment and development of medium and high technology manufacturing companies in fields related to our production of resources.

Above all, industry must overcome its subsidiary mentality - the main characteristics of which has been an extremely short time horizon.

We have tried to show how important exports are to Canada. The export opportunities are definitely there for Canadian firms if they will pursue export markets more aggressively.

Export Services Available from the Government of Canada

by
Milan Stolarik
Chief, Bureau of Latin America and Caribbean Affairs
Department of Industry, Trade and Commerce

D.I.T.& C. TERMS OF REFERENCE

The Department of Industry, Trade and Commerce was established in 1969 by merging the former Departments of Industry and of Trade and Commerce. Its mandate gives it responsibility for stimulating the establishment, growth and efficiency of the manufacturing, processing and tourist industries in Canada, and the development of export trade and external trade policies.

In its operation the activities of the Department can be classified under four broad headings:

(a) Product innovation
(b) Production efficiency
(c) International and domestic environment
(d) Market development

To achieve its objectives the Department offers assistance to Canadian industry through a wide variety of services and programs directed to almost every phase of business including research, development, design manufacturing, marketing and management.

DEPARTMENTAL ORGANIZATION

The Department is headed by a Deputy Minister, assisted by a Senior Assistant Deputy Minister, who has responsibility for the general administration of the Department as well as special responsibilities for trade and industry policy matters.

The five operational sectors of the Department are headed by Assistant Deputy Ministers and they have the following responsibilities. Mr. A.M. Guerin, Assistant Deputy Minister, Industry and Commerce Development, has

responsibility for specific industry sectors such as transportation industries, electrical and electronics, machinery, chemicals etc., and a number of other branches which deal with industrial policy matters. These operations are responsible for industrial development, product innovation and commodity activities of the Department.

Mr. R.E. Latimer, Assistant Deputy Minister, International Trade Relations has reporting to him the four Trade Relations offices responsible for trade policy and trade relations. These are the Office of General Trade Relations, the Office of Relations with OECD Countries, the Office of Special Trade Relations and the Office of U.S. Relations.

Mr. B. Steers, Assistant Deputy Minister, Trade Commissioner Service and International Marketing, provides a central focal point for the Department's trade development and marketing programs. He has reporting to him seven branches, namely, the Trade Commissioner Service and Canadian Regional Offices, the International Marketing Policy Group, the Defence Programs Branch, the Bureau of Latin America and Caribbean Affairs, the Bureau of European Affairs, the Bureau of Pacific, Asian, African and Middle Eastern Affairs and the U.S.A. Market Development Bureau.

Mr. P.E. Quinn, Assistant Deputy Minister, Enterprise Development, has responsibility for the Department's efforts relating to internal financial matters and external financing developments, and centralizes and strengthens the monitoring and control of departmental financial assistance programs. Mr. Quinn also has responsibility for the administration of the Program for Export Market Development.

The Assistant Deputy Minister, Policy Planning has responsibility for the macro and micro economic analyses in the Department as well as policy planning and development.

Mr. T.R.G. Fletcher, Assistant Deputy Minister, Tourism is responsible for the Canadian Government Office of Tourism and all matters pertaining to tourism in Canada.

In summary, the Department is striving to assist industry to overcome its problems and to maintain a suitable environment to develop and become competitive both in Canada and abroad. We realize that in the rapidly changing international scene we cannot afford to remain static and must be continuously innovative and progressive.

THE ENTERPRISE DEVELOPMENT PROGRAM (EDP)

Effective April 1, 1977 the Enterprise Development Program (EDP) replaced the following Industry, Trade and Commerce innovative and adjustment assistance programs:-

PAIT - Program for Advancement of Industrial Technology
IDAP - Industrial Design Assistance Program
PEP   - Program to Enhance Productivity
GAAP - General Adjustment Assistance Program
AAA   - Automotive Adjustment Assistance Program
FTIAP - Footwear and Tanning Industry Adjustment Program
PIDA - Pharmaceutical Industry Development Assistance
         Program

EDP combines the basic features of these programs and is designed to facilitate co-ordination amongst various forms of assistance making Industry, Trade and Commerce programs more accessible to Canadian industry, particularly smaller and medium-sized businesses.

The EDP Program is administered by the Enterprise Development Board and the regional Enterprise Development Boards all of which report to Cabinet through the Minister of Industry, Trade and Commerce.

EDP Objective

The overall objective of the EDP Program is to enhance the growth in the manufacturing and processing sectors of the Canadian economy by providing assistance to selected firms to make them more viable and internationally competitive.

The thrust of the EDP Program is to increase the effectiveness of the Department's industrial support programs to foster innovation and adjustment. The focus for assistance is on promising smaller and medium-sized firms, prepared to undertake relatively high risk projects in relation to their resources, which are viable and promise attractive rates on the total investment.

How EDP Works

There is a typical product life cycle through which all products pass. Generally, this cycle entails the following distinct phases:
a) concept
b) development
c) pre-production
d) production
e) marketing

Previously, incentive and development programs have been oriented to certain phases of the product life cycle. For example, PAIT was oriented to the concept, development and pre-production phases, while GAAP was oriented to the pre-production, production and marketing phases.

But, there are differing problems and risks facing a firm at all phases of the product life cycle. The corporate approach endeavours to examine all of the problems and risks facing a firm at each of the distinct phases of a product life cycle.

Standard operating policy for the EDP Program is to adopt the corporate approach to analysis, that is, to undertake a rigorous analysis of applicant firms and their proposed projects to identify viable businesses with attractive future prospects. The orientation is towards the business plan of the firm to identify present and future requirements for assistance and to tailor one or more forms of assistance under the program together with other government assistance and private sector financing into a "do-able" financing package to suit the applicant company.

This flexible approach is described as "merchant banking" flexibility. A merchant bank is defined as a financial institution which endeavours to serve its clients by identifying, structuring and providing (or arranging for) all of the types of financing, and financial and management services which are required by a firm to realize its full potential.

This approach may be described as investing in firms, not just supporting projects.

The corporate/merchant banking approach is similar to that of an investor. That is, the approach is to examine the resources of the firm (human, financial, physical and technological); to examine the market opportunities and constraints; and to examine the plans of the firm to marshall its present and attainable resources to exploit its present and future market opportunities.

The Decision-Making Structure

The decision-making structure for the program is addressed in two ways:

(a) The decision-making structure for the program is mixed private sector/public sector boards. This is designed to provide pragmatic, market-oriented decisions by using the experience of prominent businessmen in the decision-making process. Further, this provides the responsible officers with guidance and advice in the analysis of firms, and in structuring "do-able" packages of assistance.

Strict confidentiality and conflict of interest guidelines protect the competitive interests of applicant firms.

(b) Secondly, the decision making is decentralized to a greater extent with the creation of regional boards with delegated approval limits. This is designed to provide faster decision-making and an awareness of regional business conditions in the decision-making process.

Forms of Assistance

The following components of the EDP Program indicate the various forms of assistance available:

a) grants to develop proposals for projects eligible for assistance
b) grants to study market feasibility
c) grants to study productivity improvement projects
d) grants for industrial design projects
e) grants for innovation projects

f) loans and loan insurance for restructuring (plant expansion, equipment modernization, working capital, etc.)

g) special purpose forms of assistance-surety bond guarantees, footwear of tanning industries assistance, DHC-7 sales financing assistance.

Within the context of the overall objective of the EDP Program, each of the various forms of assistance has sub-objectives as described below:

(a) Grants to Develop Proposals for Projects Eligible for Assistance

In order to ensure that the more complex proposals for innovation and adjustment assistance are developed on a viable, adequately researched and workable basis, grants to partially offset the cost of qualified consultants can be provided to this end.

(b) Grants to Study Market Feasibility

Projects for innovation and restructuring often falter or fail due to problems related to markets and marketing. To reduce the risk of projects in this regard, grants to partially offset the cost of the services of expert consultants in this field can be provided before innovation or adjustment assistance is considered.

(c) Grants to Study Productivity Improvement Projects

To encourage feasibility studies of productivity improvement measures which do not require technology which is new to the firm but do involve some risk, grants to partially offset the cost of consultants qualified to conduct such feasibility studies can be provided.

(d) Grants for Industrial Design

The objective of grants for industrial design is to assist and to generally promote greater use of qualified industrial design services for products to be mass produced.

(e) Grants for Innovation Projects

The purpose of innovation assistance is to increase technological innovation in Canada where it will lead to industrial growth
and economic benefit to both the firm and to the Canadian economy. Grants can be provided to selected projects concerned with
the development of new or improved products and processes or
service capability incorporating an advance in technology and
offering good prospects for profitable commercial exploitation.

Due to the risk and uncertainty which accompany innovation
projects, this type of assistance should frequently be provided in
conjunction with other forms of assistance, for example, grants to
study market feasibility.

(f) Loans for Loan Insurance for Adjustment Projects

The basic purpose of the adjustment assistance aspects of the
EDP Program is to facilitate restructuring or rationalization of
manufacturing and processing firms in Canada by providing last
resort financial assistance. Canada's secondary manufacturing
industries frequently have considerable difficulty in meeting international competition both at home and in export markets. While
the problems are numerous and complex, one frequent problem
is that Canadian manufacturers have in many cases been geared to
serve domestic markets under protective tariffs. In order to
enhance the viability of secondary manufacturing and processing
and to permit Canadian firms to become more internationally competitive, massive private investment in restructuring operations
and modernizing equipment and facilities is required. In some
cases, usual sources of financing for this purpose are inadequate
for some smaller and medium-sized firms and in these cases, loan
insurance (guarantees) can be provided through the adjustment
assistance components of the Enterprise Development Program.

Direct loans can also be provided to viable Canadian firms
engaged in manufacturing or processing but this assistance is
restricted to cases where firms have been injured by import
competition.

Due to the risks frequently associated with the last resort
financial assistance, this type of assistance may frequently be
provided in conjunction with other forms of assistance, for exam-

ple grants to develop re-structuring proposals or grants to study productivity improvement projects.

(g) Special Purpose Forms of Assistance

The adjustment assistance aspects of the Program are occasionally utilized to structure special purpose forms of assistance to meet more specific objectives.

Three forms of special purpose assistance which are in place are:

i) Loans and grants to encourage restructuring of firms engaged in footwear or tanning industries;

ii) insurance on surety bonds for off-shore turnkey projects; and

iii) insurance on loans, leases and conditional sales agreements to air carriers in Canada and the United States to acquire de Havilland DHC-7 aircraft.

These three special purpose forms of assistance are administered by the Central Board and are not included in the delegated approval authority of the regional boards.

Who is Generally Eligible for Assistance?

As a general statement, the orientation of the Enterprise Development Program is to provide assistance to smaller and medium-sized firms engaged in manufacturing or processing activities. Firms in the service sector are, under limited circumstances, also eligible provided the provision of services provides direct, tangible and significant benefit to firms engaged in manufacturing or processing, or the project (such as an innovation project) is to be exploited by a firm engaged in manufacturing or processing activities.

As a matter of policy, the Board will restrict the availability of such assistance to cases where the benefiting manufacturing firm is eligible for assistance.

Applicants for innovation and industrial design assistance must be incorporated. Firms applying for adjustment assistance need not be incorporated to be eligible. However, it is highly desirable that all firms are incorporated before receiving assistance, not only for the Crown's benefit but also for their own benefit. The Crown prefers to deal with limited companies as non-personal legal entities. From the firm's point of view, incorporation provides protection to its principals by limiting their liability under business obligations.

Each of the various forms of assistance has certain criteria, but generally, the eligibility criteria are as follows:

a) the firm and the project must be viable;
b) for loans and loan insurance, the firm must be unable to obtain financing on reasonable terms; and
c) for grants, the project must represent a significant burden to the firm in respect of its resources.

For more information on the Enterprise Development Program, firms may contact the Program Office, IT&C Ottawa, or the nearest Industry, Trade and Commerce Regional Office.

INTERNATIONAL DOMESTIC ENVIRONMENT

Under this activity, the Department concerns itself with those Government programs that will have impacts on industrial and trade development including policies relating to competition, taxation, and imports in the domestic environment. Internationally, the Department involves itself with a wide range of trade policy activities relating to trade barriers, whether tariff or non-tariff, which control to a major degree the access of our goods and services to other countries. It also embraces GATT negotiations conducted on a multi-lateral basis and bilateral agreements on trade.

MARKET DEVELOPMENT

Canada is greatly dependent upon exports, perhaps more so than any other industrialized nation. For example, in 1980 our exports amounted to over 25% of our total Gross National Product of some $290 billion. Although a goodly portion of this was accounted for by exports of grain, raw materials and semi-manufactured goods we shouldn't lose sight that approximately 50% of our manufactured goods are exported. By comparison Japan exports some 11% of its GNP and the USA about 5%.

The USA remains our best customer taking 60-70% of our exports. While we are appreciative of this large friendly customer, the market development program is intended not only to increase our exports but to diversify our market base, and to increase the export of manufactured goods. It also involves the encouragement of a greater number of Canadian manufacturing companies to become exporters on a sustained basis.

The Department provides both services and financial assistance to achieve these objectives including:

a) Analysis of markets, opportunities and trends through the services of our International Bureaux.

b) Assistance in both the domestic and overseas fields through the regional offices in Canada and Trade Commissioner Service posts abroad.

c) Conduct of fairs, missions, in-store shows, catalogue shows, and publicity programs including the production of marketing brochures.

d) High level missions led by senior members of the government and D.I.T.C.

e) Program for Export Market Development which encourages Canadian companies to seek foreign business by sharing the costs involved in obtaining incremental sales under conditions of high risk. The government share of the costs are repayable if sales are achieved.

PEMD PROGRAM (Program for Export Market Development

The PEMD Program was initiated ten years ago and now consists of six sections. It is a flexible program and modifications to old sections and considerations of new sections to overcome identifiable impediments to the successful pursuit of exports are under continual consideration. It is intended to bring about a sustained increase in exports of goods and services.

Section A - Incentives for Participation in Capital Projects Abroad.

Section B - Market Identification and Marketing Adjustment.

Section C - Participation in trade fairs other than federally sponsored ones.

Section D - Incoming Foreign Buyers.

Section E - Assistance to Export Marketing Consortia.

Section F - Continuous Marketing.

The program has a very successful record. Up to the end of March 1980, more than 14,000 applications have been received, of which 7,000 had been approved at a cost of $37 million. Sales directly attributable to the program have amounted to $4.21 billion or a return of 113 to 1 based upon the Government share of costs.

EXPORT MARKET STUDIES

While these results are gratifying and Canada's performance in exporting has been impressive, nevertheless, opportunities for additional growth are available in a rapidly expanding world trade environment, particularly to increase exports of our manufactured goods and to diversify our markets. A relatively small number of manufacturers are participating in exports on a sustained basis. Of the estimated 30,000 odd manufacturers in Canada some 7,000 are registered in the Department's Exporters Directory and most of these are not exporting on a sustained basis.

The expansion of exports must therefore necessarily, in part, depend upon attracting a greater number of qualified Canadian companies to participate in the export market.

The investigations of the Department into the reasons for the rather poor performance of Canadian firms in the export of manu-factured goods, and a comparison with other major trading nations, particularly the Western Europeans and Japanese, had identified significant reasons for their success and revealed two areas which require our attention. First, much of our success in expanding the export of manufactured goods will depend upon attracting more of the small to medium sized manufacturers into the field. At the present time many of these, for a variety of reasons including lack of finance, lack of management time and experience, restricted product lines, unfamiliarity with export marketing, etc., feel unable or unwilling to participate. Secondly, we need to develop our ability to obtain a reasonable share of the estimated $20 billion annual market for capital projects, many of which are of the turnkey variety.

EXPORT MARKETING GAPS

Three areas in which our competitors seem to have achieved competitive advantages in their export trade were identified:

1) Trading Companies
2) Product Oriented Export Consortia
3) Capital Project Assistance

These facilities have been particularly useful in helping our competitors to gain access to export markets on a sustained basis. It appeared even more pressing that Canada effectively develop such facilities since we do not have the large and diversified industrial entities which are commonplace in Japan and the USA for instance, and which have sufficient resources to handle most export opportunities "in-house", and the fragmented nature of much of our industry.

TRADING HOUSES

A first step was taken to correct these structured trade deficiencies in 1972 when Section B of the Program for Export Market Development was amended to make trading organizations as well as manufacturing companies eligible for assistance. This action involved a calculated decision to assist competent trading companies in the private sector rather than develop a trading company under Government supervision such as adopted by some countries and provinces of Canada. There are approximately 750 trading intermediaries listed in the Department's Exporters Directory and they account for 20% of the exports attributable to all the companies listed.

EXPORT MARKETING CONSORTIA

In parallel it was realized that some manufacturers were reluctant to assign their marketing responsibilities to middlemen. The use of export marketing consortia are prevalent in several European countries (France, Belgium, Switzerland, Holland, Austria, Norway and Denmark). In France for instance, there are over 100 major export consortia in industrial sectors ranging from agricultural equipment to lace and chocolates. In Switzerland, biscuit and sugar confectionary manufacturers have formed a consortium exporting their products under a common brand name. It is also evident in some countries such as Netherlands and Denmark that national government do support these export consortia through annual grants.

The advantages of export consortia derive primarily from economies of scale and the flexibility of operation particularly for small to medium sized manufacturers. While these may pertain primarily to marketing, other benefits which can accrue include:

1) Reduction in transportation costs through volume sales;

2) Reduction in handling costs using common facilities;

3) Reduction in selling costs through large sales volume;

4) Continuity of supply costs through access to a number of suppliers;

5) Quality control and assurance by centralized inspection;

6) Greater resources and reduced costs for market research and development;

7) Rationalized production through forward market planning;

8) Reduced servicing costs using common after-sales service facilities and warehousing;

9) The ability to use and train specialists in particular phases of the marketing operation.

SECTION E

In view of the potential benefits which could derive to product oriented consortia, particularly of small and medium sized companies, approximately six years ago the Minister announced the addition of Section E to the PEMD. This new section is a two-phased one, sharing the cost of studying the feasibility of export consortia operation and where the evidence is affirmative, sharing the initial start-up expenses over a period not exceeding three years.

CAPITAL PROJECTS

As was indicated previously it is estimated that the global market for capital projects of a turnkey variety with a value from $50 to $500 million approximates $20 billion annually. Canadian firms have had limited success in obtaining contracts of this type.

Turnkey projects usually cover the entire span from design, engineering, construction, equipment procurement and installation to hiring and training local staff and financing. They are bid on a firm price basis by a single contractor, sometimes a consortium. Although they are frequently found in lesser developed countries, they are also attractive to many developed countries since they provide feasibility and pre-engineering proposals free of charge, quotations rather than estimates for decision making, financing arranged by the contractor and single responsibility for performance. Although Canada has not been very successful in obtaining complete projects, we have obtained a reasonable share of the elements going into large works such as engineering and design services and project management, and we have been able to obtain orders for capital equipment such as boilers, rails, locomotives, transmission lines, turbines and generators, etc.

In 1972 representatives of Canadian industry approached the Department indicating a willingness to undertake turnkey work abroad if the Department could provide financial assistance. As a result a study was undertaken which indicated that Canada had the technical and management capability in certain selected industrial sectors to undertake turnkey work, but that, in addition to assistance in marshalling consortia or joint ventures of companies supplying all the requisite skills, a program was required to share the very high cost of preparing bid proposals (up to 2% of the bid price) and providing assurance against the threat of crippling losses as a result of cost overruns.

The most difficult aspect of the program is providing the insurance. In consultation with the insurance industry, policies providing risk insurance, written by Canadian companies, and unavailable anywhere else in the world have been developed. We are now in the process of applying our ideas and assistance, in partnership with industry, on a trial basis in eleven projects totalling over $2.3 billion, which promise significant benefits to Canada. The experience we derive will be applied to refining our plans and developing an official program.

With involvement in larger turnkey projects, additional problems facing Canadian companies have been identified. One such area is the provision by Canadian companies of various financial guarantees. For large projects such guarantees can be very large and Canadian banks and financial institutions are not always able to issue the related guarantees based on the assets and resources of the prime contractor and/or its supplier companies. It was concluded by D.I.T.C. that Government assistance in this area would be required and it is the policy of the Department to consider these on a case-by-case basis for the assistance or guarantees required. As an example, a Canadian company was bidding on a project in the Middle East valued at about $300 million. A condition of the contract would have been the issuance of a surety of $30 million to the principal against advance payments on the contract. A Canadian bank was not prepared to issued the required surety without some participation of the Government to guarantee a portion of this sum in the event of company failure to fulfill the contract.

The Government approved one third participation, or $10 million, in this surety guarantee and this enabled the company to enter a bid of $317 million for the project. Although they were not the successful bidder, their bid was very competitive (the USSR was awarded the contract for about $300 million) and illustrates the willingness and ability of the private sector to bid on its own.

Surety coverage is now available from the Export Development Corporation on a regular basis.

Another impediment to obtain capital projects was recently overcome when the Department introduced its credit mix program to match concessional financing rates provided by our competitors. The program is also being administered by the Export Development Corporation.

SMALL BUSINESS ASSISTANCE

The Department has also taken additional steps to help smaller and medium sized enterprises, particularly relating to their equity problems. It is noted that some five million people or 60% of our labour force work for these companies which are mostly owned by Canadians. The Federal Business Development Bank has been set up, with 54 offices across Canada. The Bank provides loans to companies with sound business proposals but without reasonable financing resources. The Agency has become the focal point for government programs and services available to small business including:

a) Advice on and provision of financing
b) Management counselling service provided by NRC
c) Development and operation of federal management training programs operated by Manpower and Training
d) Management counselling services to small business operated by D.I.T.C.

This latter program has in a very short time proven to be most popular to Canadian business and includes:

a) Counselling Assistance to Small Enterprise (CASE)
b) Development of Management Courses

CASE provides an opportunity for owners and managers of small businesses to obtain at nominal costs the services of retired business executives to help them solve their technical, management or marketing problems.

First provided in Montreal and Winnipeg, CASE as been so successful that it is now being opened in six other centres including Regina, Vancouver and Toronto. Its services are available to companies with fewer than 50 employees and no more than $5 million in sales. The Federal Government provides up to 50% of the costs of engaging these consultants.

In addition to the above assistance to small businesses, an incentive program designed to help non-profit professional, industry, business or management associations to develop management retraining or upgrading courses has been established. A government grant of up to $50,000 for these courses is now available to cover up to 100% of the costs involved.

FOREIGN INVESTMENT REVIEW AGENCY

The Foreign Investment Review Agency, which reports directly to the Minister, is responsible for considering applications from foreign investors to take over Canadian companies, analysing these to determine whether significant benefits would accrue to Canada from these investments and advising Cabinet which of these should be permitted under the Foreign Investment Review Act.

Finally, in line with the decentralization of federal services, the D.I.T.C. has taken steps to augment its regional offices both as to strength and responsibility to better service industry in the various provinces as well as given greater autonomy in administering a number of departmental programs such as grants for industrial innovation, trade development, productivity enhancement and improved industrial design.

Export Services Available from the Government of Ontario
by
Jan Rush
International Trade and Investment Branch
Ontario Ministry of Industry and Trade

1. Export Objectives of the Ministry

In a recent speech, Ontario's Minister of Industry and Tourism, the Honourable Larry Grossman, stressed that "the manufacturing sector will be the international focus of attention throughout the 1980's, as developed and developing nations vie for a market share against a backdrop of a more turbulent global economic environment".

Indeed, dramatic shifts in the global economy have forced western nations to reassess both policies and programs in an effort to adjust to the changes in the international marketplace. Ever increasing production costs and widely fluctuating currency values are factors of this change. During the past decade Canada's overall share of world exports has declined by one-third.

To meet this challenge, federal and provincial agencies have embarked upon a cooperative endeavour to regain and expand Canada's place in international trade. The Government of Ontario, in an effort to encourage and support its share of the Canadian export industry, has outlined its "Export '80" objectives as follows:

a) To promote the exporting activities of Ontario-based companies.

b) To capitalize on the current competitiveness of the Canadian export industry due to a devalued dollar.

c) To strengthen our strategic sectors through the broadening of export markets.

d) To secure future growth markets by encouraging the development of export industries.

2. Consulting

The Ontario Ministry of Industry and Tourism has a team of qualified international marketing consultants who have detailed knowledge about ex-porting in major areas abroad. Their up-to-date information on foreign markets and the techniques for pene-trating them are intended to spare the client both time and ex-pense.

The Ministry's international offices help Ontario's exporters with advice on markets, agents and distributors. Other available services include the arrangement of appointments with key inter-national contacts. Also servicing the Ontario manufacturer/ exporter are 91 federal Canadian consular posts, which have in-formation on markets around the world.

3. Programs

Upon examination of a company's export interests, capabilities and products, a senior ministry consultant will assist with the development of a marketing strategy for a geographical area of export.

Consultation includes the direction of the client into the many federal as well as the provincial programs available.

A. Trade Missions - The Trade Mission program, a constant in the Ministry's activities, has been one of the most successful of all initiatives made available to Ontario manufacturers. Confirmed sales results are most impressive, and this program continues as one of the most rewarding provincial efforts in international marketing. Missions serve the purpose of intro-ducing new exporters into their first market, normally the United States. Trade Missions also help the expansion of efforts of experienced exporters into broader markets or deeper penetration into existing markets.

B. Trade Fairs/Exhibitions - Participation in Trade Fairs and Exhibitions is a long-standing program with the Ministry of Industry and Tourism. These events held at strategic loca-tions around the globe, have aided the exposure of Ontario businessmen in new or remote markets under the leadership and supervision of the Ontario government. Examples of

Trade Shows participation during the 1981 fiscal year include Saudibuild, Singapore Mining, Fabrik '81, and the London Furniture Exhibits.

C. Incoming Buyers - The Incoming Buyer program, through the payment of visitor's travel expenses, facilitates the meeting of Ontario manufacturers with foreign agents and distributors, and promotes Ontario as a world supplier.

D. Intern Program - The International Marketing Intern program provides Ontario exporters with the opportunity for developing and expanding their international marketing efforts. By paying one half of the salary of an Ontario business graduate for a maximum of two years, the Ontario government is sharing with the private sector an investment in training expertise. By focussing on the value to the exporting community of the vitality and resourcefulness of youth, the program opens doors to worthwhile careers for young Ontario graduates.

E. Trading House Community - The support and encouragement of the Trading House community as an integral part of the continued growth of the Canadian export industry has been an important objective of the Ministry. This crucial link in the export chain, identifies markets for Ontario manufacturers and extends the reach of their exporting initiatives.

F. Trade Aids - Trade Aids constitute a form of assistance available within Ontario, primarily to smaller manufacturers. This financial support is intended to help with the initial costs of entering foreign markets by the development of special promotional literature, packaging, product testing, and other trade aids.

4. General Comments

If you wish to find new areas for business expansion by exporting your products or offering your technology and processes for manufacturers abroad, you are invited to use the services of the Ontario Ministry of Industry and Tourism. These services are confidential, and are provided without cost or obligation. We invite you to make full use of one of the on-the-spot business development services. To do so, please call the Ministry's regional office nearest you, or:

Ministry of Industry and Tourism
Province of Ontario,
Hearst Block, 900 Bay Street,
Toronto, Canada,
M7A 2E6

Telephone (416) 965-5701

Brockville
143 Parkdale Avenue
Brockville, Ontario
K6V 682
Telephone: (613) 342-5522

Hamilton
Suite 601, 20 Hughson St. S.
Hamilton, Ontario
L8N 2A1

Kingston
1055 Princess Street
Suite 308
Kingston, Ontario
K7L 5T3
Telephone: (613) 546-1191

Kitchener
305 King Street West, Suite 507
Kitchener, Ontario
N2G 1B9
Telephone: (519) 744-6391

London
Suite 607, 195 Dufferin St.
London, Ontario
N6A 1K7
Telephone: (519) 433-8105

Mississauga
Suite 608, 201 City Centre Dr.
Mississauga, Ontario
L5B 2T4
Telephone: (416) 279-6515

North Bay
Northgate Plaza
1500 Fisher Street
North Bay, Ontario
P1B 2H3
Telephone: (705) 472-9660

Peterborough
139 George Street North
Peterborough, Ontario
K9J 3G6
Telephone: (705) 784-9161

St. Catharines
Box 3024 - Prov. Gas Bldg.
4th Floor, 15 Church St.
St. Catharines, Ontario
L2R 3B5
Telephone: (416) 684-2345

Sault Ste.Marie
120 Huron Street,
Sault St. Marie, Ontario
P6A 1P8
Telephone: (705) 253-1103

Sudbury
199 Larch Street
Sudbury, Ontario
P3E 5P9
Telephone: (705) 675-4300

Orillia
P.O. Box 488, 2nd Floor
73 Mississauga Street East
Orillia, Ontario
L3V 6K2
Telephone: (705) 325-1363

Ottawa
Suite 404, 56 Sparks Street
Ottawa, Ontario
K1P 5A9
Telephone: (613) 566-3703

Owen Sound
Nor-Towne Plaza, Suite 104
1131 Second Avenue East
Owen Sound, Ontario
N4K 5P7
Telephone: (519) 376-3875

Thunder Bay
435 James Street South,
P.O. Box 5000,
Thunder Bay, Ontario,
P7C 5G6
Telephone: (807) 623-3394

Timmins
273 Third Avenue,
Timmins, Ontario,
P4N 1E2
Telephone: (705) 264-5393

Toronto (Metro)
Suite 480, 5 Fairview Mall Drive,
Willowdale, Ontario,
M2J 2Z1
Telephone: (416) 491-7680

Windsor
250 Windsor Avenue, Room 227
Windsor, Ontario,
N9A 6V9
Telephone: (519) 252-3475

Ontario Ministry of Industry and Tourism

Statistics

	Ontario	Canada	%
Area (000 sq. km.)	1,070	9,977	11
Population (000s) (1980)	8,601	24,089	36
Exports '80			
(Total U.S. $ billions)	25.2	65.0	39
Fully Manufactured	14.4	19.8	73
Labour '80			
Labour Force ('000)	4,366	11,522	37.9
Employment ('000)	4,066	10,655	38.2

Ontario Exports - Top Ten	% of Total Exports
(1) Road Motor Vehicles & Parts	39.8
(2) Steel & Steel Products	3.8
(3) Chemicals, Organic and Inorganic	3.7
(4) Nickel Ores & Metals	2.5
((5) Newsprint Paper	2.5
(6) Office Machines and Equipment	2.3
(7) Communications & Related Equipment	2.1
(8) Food Products	2.1
(9) Precious Metals including Alloys	2.0
10) Aircraft & Parts	1.9

Ontario Export Markets (Manufactured Products)	% of Total Exports
(1) United States	76.8
(2) United Kingdom	3.8
(3) Venezuela	1.8
(4) West Germany	1.4
(5) Belgium-Luxembourg	1.0
6) Netherlands	1.0
(7) France	0.9
(8) Australia	0.8
(9) Mexico	0.8
(10a) Japan	0.7
(10b) Saudi Arabia	0.7

Export Services Available from the Canadian Export Association

by
James D. Moore
Secretary
Canadian Export Association

The Canadian Export Association was founded in 1943 with the objective of fostering export trade. Broadly speaking, it seeks to improve the climate, conditions, facilities and services for all Canadian exporters. The CEA is the only national organization devoting its efforts exclusively to the interests of all exporters and to the service industries who make these exports possible. We are a non-profit organization supported by fee paying members drawn from a broad cross-section of Canadian business firms of all sizes.

In addition to resource based and secondary manufacturing industries, the Association is unique in having as equal participants in its membership the full range of key export service firms including banks, factoring houses and others specializing in finance; export merchants and agents; export packing specialists, freight forwarders; trucking, rail, steamship and airline representatives; together with firms from marine insurance, communications, advertising and various types of consultants including that most important exporter of Canadian know how - our consulting engineers. This broad membership base is fundamental to the Association's belief that export trade is a highly specialized field. A field which today is a matter for professionals and that those involved in it can derive benefit from working together in a specialized national body to seek improvements more effectively with a united voice and to keep up to date on export practices and problems.

The Association has three main functions: distribution of information on developments relating to exports, assistance in problem solving for individual members and groups of members, and activities designed to ensure that governments and others whose policies and programs have an impact on Canadian exports are aware of exporters' preoccupations and concerns. The Association is administered by a Board of Directors. Reporting to the Board are the Association's working committees. The diversity of exporting interests within the Association enables these committees to draw on an extremely broad base of expertise when dealing with technical subjects and issues related to foreign trade. Indeed, it is sometimes possible for exporters to resolve problems with service industry interests within our committee structures.

As it is through the work of these committees that the Association is able to provide a constructive and influential force in formulating multi-industry points of view for the development of sound international trade policies, I think it would be useful to outline briefly the structure of our committees.

Their focal point is our Policy Development Committee. This is, as the name implies, the organ which formulates Association policy and initiates appropriate action on developments which may affect the expansion of Canada's export trade. The effectiveness of the Association's Policy Committee is greatly enhanced by standing advisory committees on technical subjects such as export financing, development aid, export traffic, capital projects and trade policy. The main policy committee and the technical committees meet periodically with officials in Government departments and agencies seeking to improve conditions, facilities and services for exporters. Their collective efforts typically result in briefs. Increasingly we are finding personal contact rather than written submissions more effective in bringing the collective views and concerns of exporters to the attention of government and Parliament. This had the added benefit of encouraging a dialogue which permits more ready identification of future government activity which, if inimical to the interest of exporters, can be discouraged before it solidifies firmly; or conversely, encouraged, if perceived to be in the general interest of exporters, in the directions which will be most beneficial.

The need for effective collaboration between the Association and Government officials is of great consequence to exporters. It is only by a "team effort" that, in today's uncertain and changing conditions, we can draw up an effective "game plan" to maintain export growth at a rate which will significantly contribute to the goals of full employment and improving the quality of life.

In addition to specialized committees dealing with the technical aspects of international trade, the Association has established a number of regional committees across the country. These committees not only input into the Association's national policies and activities but provide a focal point for dealing with issues of special regional importance and also provide direct liaison with provincial governments, all of whom have an active interest in trade promotion. Two other committees deal with the special concerns of small exporters and export trading houses.

I would now like to turn to staff activities. The Association provides the secretariat to committee membership activities, and is a central source for information on all aspects of export trade. Typically the kind of questions answered on the regular basis range from legislation and tax practices in other countries through agency contracts, duty drawbacks, tariffs, export financing problems, export documentation to advice to newcomers on export market prospects. The Association's ability to provide this service is greatly enhanced by a library containing several thousand texts, incidental papers, country reports. To indicate the scope of this library, which is available for public use, I am attaching a copy of the classification system applied to its contents. Supplementing the library is a comprehensive documentation reference filing system, and giving the information service a personal and perhaps more practical touch, frequent reference is made to the experience of other Association members who may have faced and overcome similar difficulties to the problem posed by an enquirer.

Three types of bulletins keep members up-to-date on what is happening in the world of exports:

-- A member's information bulletin keeps members abreast of Association news and a great variety of international trade matters.

-- A Review and Digest Bulletin summarizes items from a great many publications, reports and addresses of interest to Canadian exporters.

-- U.S. News, of interest to Canadian exporters, is a bulletin which deals with marketing changes in regulations - particularly U.S. Customs regulations - and other information of value to those exporting to the United States.

--   Other publications include a Documentation Guide and incidental papers of various aspects of export trade.

Through the years, the Association has established itself as an authoritative voice for an important section of Canadian business and industry. We now export more than half the goods we produce in this country, but we are particularly vulnerable to the whims of the great trading powers, Japan, the U.S.A. and E.E.C. At this time we are also faced with the tremendous challenges and opportunities for opening up new export markets arising from the gradual phasing in of the results from the Tokyo Round of GATT multilateral trade negotiations. It is therefore, I believe, essential that the export services available to you are utilized to the maxiumum if we are to continue to thrive as an exporting nation.

A. TRADE STATISTICS

1. Canadian

1.0 - General
1.1 - Export, Canadian
1.2 - Import, Canadian
1.3 - Summary of Foreign Trade

2. World

2.0 - General, World

B. COUNTRY GUIDES: (Economic reports, profiles, trade indexes, tariffs, and customs regulations, papers, etc.

* (Listed alphabetically) countries beginning with letters:

A. - B.1	F. - B.6	K. - B.12	P. - B.17	U. - B.23
B. - B.2	G. - B.7	L. - B.13	Q. - B.18	V. - B.24
C. - B.3	H. - B.8	M. - B.14	R. - B.19	W. - B.25
D. - B.4	I. - B.9	N. - B.15	S. - B.21	X. - B.26
E. - B.5	J. - B.11	O. - B.16	T. - B.22	Y. - B.27
				Z. - B.28

e.g. Australia - 1.23; Argentina - 1.19; U.S. - 23.21

B. 23.21 - United States

.21.1 - U.S. Trade Policy (Export Regulations, Etc.)
.21.2 - Doing Business in the U.S.A.

B. 29. Multinational Business Series Reports

*B.1 to B.28 - Use this guide for Sections L.3 and M.1

Library Classification System Continued

C. *REGIONAL GEOGRAPHIC AND ECONOMIC GROUPS

C.00   - General
C.1   - Africa (East African Community), (East, West, South, Central, excl. Arabic Bloc)
C.2   - Arabic countries, incl. Arabian Peninsula and adjacent territories; Persian Gulf & Middle East, and North Africa.
C.3   - Asia
  3.1   - East Asia, incl. Australasia, (NAFTA, etc.)

C.4   - Caribbean (Carifta, etc.)
C.5   - Central America (C.A.C.M., etc.)
C.6   - Eastern Europe/Russia (C O M C O N, etc.)
C.7   - Latin America (LAFTA, Andean Group, etc.)
C.8   - Western Europe - General
  8.1   - EEC
  8.12   - European Community Publications
  8.13   - Common Market Farm Reports

  8.2   - EFTA
  8.22   - EFTA Reporter
  8.23   - EFTA Annual Reports
  8.3   - Scandinavia (NORDIC, etc.)

D. INTERNATIONAL ORGANIZATION

D.00   - General
D.1   - GATT
 .1.1   - GATT Constitution, History, Law and Work Program
 .1.2   - Kennedy Round
D.2   - OECD Constitution, History, Law and Work Program
D.3   - ICC Constitution, History, Law and Work Program

E. CANADA

E.00   - General
E.1   - Economic Reports
E.2   - Economic Policy

---

*C.1 to C.8.3 - Use this guide for Sections L.4 and M.2

Library Classification System Continued

E.3   - Economic Council Annual Reports and Miscellaneous
E.4   - Finance
E.5   - Establishing a Business in Canada
E.6   - Government Assistance Programs for Business
E.7   - Business & Industry Policy - General
E.8   - Combines and Anti-Trust
E.9   - Science and Technology (R & D)
E.10 - Labour/Manpower/Productivity
E.11 - Prices, Inflation and Competition (Price and Wage Controls)
E.12 - Marketing
E.13 - Management
E.14 - Regional Publications and Policy (Provinces)
E.15 - Miscellaneous Government Reports
               - Industry, Trade and Commerce
               - Industry
               - Wheat Board
               - Canadian Commercial Corporation
               - Auditor General
               - Bank of Canada
               - Industrial Development Bank

F. TRADE POLICY

F.00 - General
F.1   - Canadian Trade Policy
F.2   - Canada/U.S. Trade Policy
F.3   - Agricultural Products Policy
F.4   - Non-Tariff Trade Barriers (Buy-American Laws, etc.)
F.5   - Canadian Treaties
F.6   - Standards

G. EXPORT TEXTS

G.00 - General (how to export, etc.)
G.1   - Policies to Promote Exports

H. INTERNATIONAL BUSINESS TEXTS

H.00 - General (management of international and multinational business)

Library Classification System Continued

I. FOREIGN INVESTMENT

I.00	- General
I.1	- Licensing
I.2	- Foreign Investment in Canada
I.3	- Multinational Enterprise

J. TRANSPORTATION AND COMMUNICATION

J.00	- General
J.1	- Trade Facilitation and Document Simplification
J.2	- Marine Transport
J.3	- Ports/Canals
J.4	- Export Packing
J.5	- Canadian Shippers' Council
J.6	- Air Freight
J.7	- Cargo Insurance
J.8	
J.9	- Containerization

K. INTERNATIONAL COMPARATIVE LAW AND TECHNIQUES

K.00	- General
K.1	- Contracts and Agreements (Organization and Sales, etc.)
K.2	- Arbitration (International Trade Disputes, etc.)
K.3	- Property Protection (Patents, Trademarks, Copyrights, etc.)
K.4	- Export Permit Controls
K.5	- Accounting

L. TAXATION

L.00	- General
L.1	- International Taxation - General
.1.1	- Double Taxation
.1.2	- Value Added Taxes (VAT, TVA)
.1.3	- Taxes and Exporters
.1.4	- Domestic International Sales Corporation (DISC)
L.2	- Canadian Taxation - General
.2.1	- Canadian Tax Law
.2.2	- Canadian Tax Reform, 1963

Library Classification System Continued

L.3   - Country Guides (see Section B, add country numbers to 3)
  .3.1   - Letter A through
  .3.28   - Letter Z

L.4   - Regional Guide (see Section C, add regional numbers to 4)
  .4.1   - Africa through
  .4.83   - Scandinavia

M.   CUSTOMS, TARIFFS AND ENTRY PROCEDURES

M.00   - General (Valuation, Anti-Dumping, Free Trade Zones,
            Effective Protection theory, CCC, etc.)
M.1   - Country Guide (see Section B, add country numbers to 1)
  .1.1   - Letter A through
  .1.28   - Letter Z

M.2   - Regional Guide (see Section C, add regional numbers to 2)
  .2.1   - Africa through
  .2.83   - Scandinavia

N.   EDUCATION

N.00   - General
N.1   - Organization of International Business Courses
N.2   - International Trade Courses and Seminar Programs
N.3   - Lectures and Miscellaneous Case Studies

O.   EXPORT FINANCING

O.00   - General
O.1   - International Finance
O.2   - International Monetary System
O.3   - Export Financing Mechanics
O.4   - Trade Terms (INCO and American Foreign Trade Definitions,
            etc.)
O.5   - Foreign Government Facilities (EXIM, FCIA, ECGD, etc.)
O.6   - Commercial Facilities
O.7   - Canadian Government Facilities (EDC, etc.)
O.8   - Canadian Dollar Exchange
O.9   - Exchange Fluctuations & Restrictions

Library Classification System Continued

P. DEVELOPMENT AID

P.00   - General
P.1   - World Bank (IBRD, IDA, IFC, etc.)
P.2   - Asian Development Bank
P.3   - Canadian Development Aid
P.4   - Inter/American Development Bank
P.5   - U.S. Aid Program
P.6   - UNCTAD
P.7   - U.N. Development Program
P.8   - Caribbean Development Bank

Q.

R. REFERENCE (DIRECTORIES, BIBLIOGRAPHIES, ETC.)

S. PERIODICALS

The Functions of the Export Department of the Canadian Manufacturers' Association

by
Hilda Duplitza
Export Advisor
The Canadian Manufacturers' Association

I have been asked to direct my remarks to the topic of Export Services available through The Canadian Manufacturers' Association. In order to give you a true picture of how the Association assists manufacturers not only to export successfully but also to get them motivated and interested in exporting, I would like to give you an overview of the activities of the Association as a whole. But first some background.

The Association was founded in 1871. The objective of the founders of the Association was to convert an agrarian backwater into an industrial national and their purpose in forming an association was to create a mechanism for the promotion of their views and policies. Modern industrial Canada is the proof that they succeeded. Canada's status as the sixth largest trading nation in the world with a population of some 23 million people who enjoy one of the world's highest standards of living, is vastly different from what it would have been had Canada remained a nation of "hewers of wood and drawers of water".

The Association which played so large a part in creating the favourable political and economic climate necessary for that metamorphosis is now Canada's oldest and largest trade association, with some 9,000 members spread across the nation; they account for close to 80 per cent of the goods produced in Canada.

The CMA has from the beginning influenced many aspects of the Canadian scene. It is in the business of communicating with governments. Its message to them is: "If you want more jobs in a stronger economy, give industry a chance". The fact that Government policies have been moving to strengthen our wealth-creating industries proves that CMA is an influential voice. The following are some recent examples of CMA recommendations to the Government that have been adopted:

- a major effort to reduce the burden of government-imposed paperwork and of business regulation in general;

- a tax break to spark new product research and development;

- gradual reduction of the tdax load on manufacturing;

- incentives that encourage people to risk capital on new ventures;

- a general attempt by government to reduce their spendings and give business a chance to grow.

All of which translates into creating a more favourable climate for exporters. Member participation is the reason why CMA recommendations carry weight in Ottawa and the provincial capitals. The fact that over 1,000 senior executives serve voluntarily on CMA's national, provincial and local committees attests to their commitment and commands the respect of governments.

By joining CMA, and taking part in the work of its committees, manufacturers have an opportunity to play a meaningful role in the development of government policies and legislation to strengthen Canada's economy. They have an opportunity to exchange views with other manufacturers who may also be potential suppliers or customers.

Representations to government are only one facet of CMA activity on behalf of the manufacturing community. CMA also helps its members by supplying them with reliable information and service, and with conference and seminars on a wide range of subjects, including an in-depth Course on the Principles and Practices of Export Documentation.

All CMA efforts are directed towards helping member companies become more competitive and successful in today's domestic and foreign markets. Let me summarize them as follows:

- CMA committees act effectively to ensure that industry has a strong collective voice in the development of government policies, legislation and regulation and that the interests of the CMA members are presented to all levels of government.

- Members are alerted about new or anticipated developments through communiques from CMA's professional staff.

- CMA staff experts also answer enquiries and help resolve problems of Canadian manufacturers on a day-to-day basis, promptly, efficiently, by mail, telephone, telex, and in person.

I would like to describe briefly the type of serices provided by the various departments of the Association. Some of these services affect the exporter more directly than others.

The Export Department assists members in all export procedures, market information, export financing, tariffs, documentation and any special requirements of foreign countries. It provides up-to-date information on foreign import restrictions and Canadian export controls; it provides multi-lingual translation services and authentication of customs documents for export shipments. The department also produces a monthly trade bulletin known as "World Trade News" featuring changing tariff and trade regulations, export opportunities and other items of interest to exporters. The Export Department also organizes monthly meetings on timely topics through the Export Forum. These meetings provide a forum for the interchange of knowledge and ideas on international trade matters and attract large audiences with varied degrees of expertise. They keep export executives informed of new global developments and help new exporters broaden their background knowledge. You will find on the display table copies of World Trade News and of the brochure outlining the Export Forum program for the 1980/81 season.

The Export Department, like all the other departments of the Association, is involved, through its national committee and sub-committees in a wide range of vital issues affecting Canadian trade policies. The objectives of the Export Department are:

- To develop policy recommendations in the field of international trade;

- To stimulate interest in doing business abroad;

- To create an awareness of the implications of international events; and

226

-   To provide a full range of export services to members.

The first objective falls in the category of indirect services and I will not elaborate except to say that they cover a wide range of issues and of government relations activities vital to Canada's ability to compete in foreign markets. My colleague from the Canadian Export Association will no doubt cover many of these same issues in more detail.

The Customs Department assists members on all import-related matters, including tariff classification, rates of duty, anti-dumping, refunds, drawbacks, appeals, documentation, import quotas, etc.

The Economics Department provides members with an overview of economic conditions in Canada and abroad and analyzes business trends to provide economic and statistical information vital to manufacturers.

The Energy Department alerts manufacturers to the significant cost savings attainable through energy management by means of a series of seminars and workshops held across Canada. The CMA energy program also alerts manufacturers to the business opportunities opened up by the rapidly changing energy scene.

The Environment Department provides information on developments in environmental regulations and legislation affecting air, water, hazardous substances, and industrial waste disposal.

The Industrial Relations and Social Affairs Department keeps manufacturers informed on such matters as labour relations, employment standards, health and safety, unemployment insurance, pensions and manpower training.

The International Affairs Department provides access to international organizations and contacts relating to industrial co-operation, aid to less developed countries, international labour affairs, and regional foreign relations.

The Legislation Department monitors and provides information on such matters as product liability, labelling and language requirements, restrictive trade practices, pricing policies, misleading advertising, corporate law developments, patents and trade marks.

The Metric Department supplies members with factual information on metrication developments in all industrial sectors of Canada and the United States.

The Public Affairs Department emphasizes the importance of the manufacturing sector in the Canadian economy. It is responsible for a broad range of information services to members, the public and government, including "ENTERPRISE", a semi-monthly publication summarizing CMA activities, for distribution to members, legislators and the media. You will find copies on the display table.

The Research and Development Department stresses to governments the importance of R&D incentives that help manufacturers develop the technology necessary to ensure that Canadian products are competitive in world markets and it assists members in keeping abreast of available R&D incentives.

The Taxation Department furnishes members with crucial data on federal and provincial corporate income, sales and excise tax matters, including the determination of taxable income and methods of calculating tax instalment payments.

The Telecommunications Department keeps governments and regulatory bodies abreast of manufacturers' concerns about telecommunication services, emphasizing that our services must be supplied on a competitive basis.

The Transportation Department provides members with information on transportation services and costs, assists manufacturers in selecting the mode and service most suited to their requirement, and advises on matters concerning carrier responsibility and liability.

The Canadian Trade Index Department is responsible for the publication of the Canadian Trade Index which is updated annually. It provides up-to-date information on more than 13,000 manufacturing companies (your actual or potential customers or suppliers) and their products. It features a classified directory of products, services and trade mark identification. You will find brochures on the display table.

The CMA also maintains an office in Ottawa. It advises and assists members in getting things done when dealing with the federal government. Specific services most in demand include:

- Introduction of members to the right Government officials;

- Contacts and follow-up for members with Government departments, boards, agencies, etc.;

- Information on contracts, successful bidders, amount of award, government incentive programs, etc.;

- Passports and passport renewals;

- Trade marks: name searches, registration of assignment, copies of patents;

- copyrights: searches, registration, assignments, copies.

Because provincial legislation has great influence on the day-to-day operations of manufacturers, the CMA maintains regional offices or divisions. They are geared to deal promptly and effectively with problems associated with the laws and regulations enacted by provincial governments. Many of their members are on important provincial government boards and commissions.

The Division staff monitors legislative developments continually, and CMA members serving on Division committees give the representational leadership needed to safeguard manufacturers' interests.

Politicians and civil servants at all levels of government know that, in the future as in the past, the CMA can be relied upon for sound constructive proposals and effective consultation. They are fully aware that through the Association and the circulars distributed to its members, they have a direct line of communication to some 9,000 manufacturers, and most of all, to the most vital segment of the Canadian economy.

But the role of the Association is not confined to the domestic scene. The CMA, including the Export Department and its standing committee, also plays a major role in two international organizations for which it provides the permanent secretariat. They are:

(a) The Pacific Basin Economic Council, known as PEBC, founded in 1976 by businessmen of the industrialized nations of the Pacific region; and

(b) The Canadian Business and Industry International Advisory Committee, known as CBIIAC. This committee is organized jointly by the CMA, the Canadian Export Association, the Canadian Council International Chamber of Commerce, PBEC and the Canadian Association for Latin America. This organization is involved in key business and industrial disciplines on which a business view is required at the international level. The areas of responsibility which are divided among the first four of its members include:

> Environment
> Labour
> Manpower and Social Affairs
> Trade
> Transportation
> Development Aid
> Capital Flows
> Inflation and Economic Policy
> Energy and Raw Materials
> Industrial Property
> Investment Disputes
> Multinational Enterprises
> Taxation

As you can see, the CMA is concerned with a very wide range of matters which directly or indirectly affect the climate in which business operates. However, the person in the export department of a company is probably more interested in resolving the problems or difficulties which crop up on a day-to-day basis. Well, the Association provides assistance to members at every stage, from the assessment of overseas market potential to the organization of an export department and the whole gamut of matters such as:

Trade terms, definitions and abbreviations
Letters of credit
Customs and consular requirements
Import and Export restrictions
Foreign exchange controls
Customs classification, duty rates, surcharges and taxes
   in foreign countries
Duty drawbacks
Labelling and marking requirements
Export development programs
Exhibitions, trade fairs and missions
Foreign licensing arrangements
Export credit insurance and financing
Marine insurance
Alignment of export documents
Multilingual translation
Certification and notarization of documents.

In addition to handling numerous enquiries from foreign potential buyers about Canadian manufacturers and their products, the Export Department assists business visitors from foreign countries in establishing business contacts in Canada.

This concludes my outline of the services available to manufacturers through The Canadian Manufacturers' Association.

Licensing

by
Lou Eckebrecht, Licensing
Lomar Trading Company Ltd.
Burlington, Ontario

Regardless of what business you are in, or what type of products you manufacture and sell, the world is getting smaller, and changing, and it is important to know what is going on and to participate in new knowledge regarding your business world-wide so that you will not be left behind by new developments, technology, know-how, etc.

Let's assume a business, which may have a product or two, or may be a custom business providing products to customers specifications, or a new business formed to manufacture a product, perhaps not yet known.

Larger companies have facilities to research and develop their own products. Smaller to medium size companies do not have the facilities, time or money for such purposes; most products are by accident rather than by design.

Therefore, if a company has one or two products, or is a service company without a product of their own, it undoubtedly will require additional products to compliment present products, or require products to provide company identification. To build a business, if they are custom builders, or if plans are to form a company and go into manufacturing, a product line must be found.

A company with a product has identification with its customers because of the product - i.e., a company is identified with the product. This brings repeat business, provides an opportunity for a more profitable company, and with regular production, costs can be reduced. A product line provides the basis for growth.

This can be done through research and development, which is usually out of the question for the companies we are discussing, or search systematically for products already on the market in other countries, that are successful, and attempt to obtain a <u>lic-ense</u> to manufacture for your market.

<u>Advantages of Licensing</u>: A Licensor will provide:

- Samples, brochures, literature and specifications for his product.

- Once contact has been made with the licensor, usually he will provide bills of material, labour by operations in time, complete material specifications so that one can determine the cost of the product in his own market.

- Complete information on equipment requirements, tooling, space and any special facilities required will be provided, with estimate of costs.

- Also, basic information on the license cost, front money, and royalty rate, usually will be provided at this point.

- Generally one can also obtain marketing information, the share of the total market in the home country, and what the total market is estimated to be, as well as any special discount structures, method of marketing, advertising, trade shows, profitability or the product, length of time on the market, and estimated growth picture.

With the information from the Licensor, you can:

- Relate the product to your own company, and facilities for manufacturing and marketing.

- Translate the material and labour costs to your own costs, determining the viability and competitiveness of the product in your market.

- Establish equipment, and tooling costs, and cost of any special facilities.

- Prepare a feasibility study based on marketing information from the licensor, and information from your own markets, with the costs determined, and prepare a cash flow for a period of say five years.

- Determine return on investment, or contribution towards profit and overhead from the addition of a new product.

- Based on Licensor's share of his market, and his growth over the period they have had the product on the market, you can determine a growth pattern.

- Licensor can advise you of his competition in his market, and where he stands in relation to their position, and you can determine your competition, particularly if the product had advantages over competition, which information would be obtained from the licensor.

- You can arrange to visit licensor, and/or other licensees who have been manufacturing under license.

You have eliminated 90% of the risk of taking on a new product or entering a new venture, before you sign any agreement.

Most important, compared to research and development which may take years, and then fail (about 80% never make the market place) licensing, taking 90% of the risk out of a new venture, provides a fast, efficient profitable way to put a new product on the market.

Disadvantages:

-- Agreement calls for front money on signing the agreement.

-- Royalty payments over the life of the agreement, (should be treated as part of the product costs).

-- License agreement may be for the life of patents, up to 17 years, or for a predetermined, negotiated time period.

Advantages:

-- A license agreement should provide you with any improvements in product design, manufacturing methods, marketing methods, etc., over the life of the agreement, and contact with other licensees so that you can keep abreast of what is going on in your business.

-- If you have or develop complimentary products, there is the opportunity to license same to your licensor, or other licensees, thus earning royalty income.

-- The licensor has a vital interest in your success, as his income from royalty depends on your success.

Licensing is the least expensive way to put a product on the market, with the least risk. The alternative is to assume 100% of the risks and develop your own products.

To find suitable complimentary products, each Province in Canada puts out monthly a bulletin with opportunities, the Federal Government issues an opportunity bulletin, Canadian Consulate and Provincial Government offices overseas have access to products in foreign countries, foreign consulates in Canada are willing to search out products, you can attend Technology Trade shows, e.g., Tech Ex 81 in Atlanta at which there will be companies from over 50 countries offering over 5,000 products, processes etc., for license.

One can engage a consultant in this field, who has a steady stream of products monthly from all over the world, and from his associates in foreign countries with clients offering products, and who can advertise your requirements to his associates and others with whom he is in constant contact.

Banks usually have information on products that are available, and are anxious to assist their clients.

Let's consider licensing out and the benefits - i.e., selling the license to someone in another country, giving him the right to manufacture and distribute your product there.

It is best to consider both export and licensing out, when the product is in the development stage, and to do a world-wide study for markets, obtaining information on import duties in foreign countries, restrictions, freight costs, what competitive products are in that market, where do they come from, are they made locally or imported, obtain brochures on same, and prices if possible, determine the method of marketing, and compare features of these products with your own, along with costing, so that you can determine if you should consider export to that market, or license.

By contacting the Canadian Consulates in foreign countries, you can obtain the above information, explaining your plans. When you receive this information back, you can examine the brochures on your competitors in foreign countries to determine your advantages and disadvantages, before you have frozen your design, and make appropriate changes if required.

A real benefit is that at this point, knowing the market in your own country, and the share you expect to obtain over say five years, and if you feel licensing is the way to go, you can estimate the royalty income from licensees over the period of an agreement, further you can determine where to patent and apply for trade mark or name protection, before you make commitments.

You know where you can license, you have contact with members of the consulates in these countries, and when the product is finalized in Canada, and on the market, you are in a position to start licensing.

Prior to this, having made the decision, you can contact consulates requesting they provide names etc., of prospective licensees. When you do this, prepare your paper work well, with brochures, full information on the type of company you feel would make a good licensee, and indicate what product lines you feel they might now be marketing. Consulates are not experts in your business, so make it easy as you can for them to assist you intelligently.

Mention any special equipment required to make the product, the market area you feel could be serviced economically and competitively from the area selected, what you feel the market is, also what you feel the licensee might do over a three or five year period against his competition, advise if exclusive or not exclusive manufacturing and/or marketing.

In addition, list the advantages of your product over known competitors in the area and any other advantages, e.g., manufacturing, marketing, etc. Also indicate any patent and trade name protection and state the basic terms of licensing, e.g., front money, royalty rate, length of license.

When you obtain the names of possible licensees, write to them with brochures, and sufficient information regarding your product, it's position in the market, advantages over competition, profitability, growth pattern, your estimate of their total market, and share they might expect, license terms, front money, royalty, term of agreement, trade names, patent protection, but at this point, not in detail.

Give the prospect a background on your company, length of time in business etc., so that they will have confidence in dealing with you.

Ask for details on their company, e.g., equipment, other products, ownership, how long in business, marketing staff, and procedures etc.

Hopefully you will receive several prospects from any one area, so that you will be in correspondence with more than one in any country. You might consider sending samples to the consulate, and making arrangements for prospects to go to the consulate and examine same.

You should at this time have prepared a suggested licensing agreement that reflects generally the terms you envisage acceptable to you and fair to the prospect. Remember, do not ask someone else to sign an agreement that you would not sign. License is a long term marriage, that has to be fair to both parties, or there will be a divorce.

Before you plan a visit to a foreign country or countries to visit prospective licensees, it is important to have more than one in any one country to talk to, and be prepared to spend as much time as necessary with any or all to satisfy their requirements.

You should have with you most, if not all of the following: samples, manufacturing and product drawings, tool drawings and descriptions, priced bill of materials with material specifications, labour by operations and timed in minutes, marketing methods, pricing, discounts, photographs of vital factory installations, and plant facilities. Be prepared to assist with a feasibility study if necessary, and be flexible with your timing. If necessary, revisit.

It is well advised if, for example, you are going to Europe, to have several countries to visit, which makes it easy to revisit.

Take along a suggested agreement with emphasis on "suggested". In some instances you might forward this ahead of time, so that the prospect can study same, and be prepared to discuss same during visit.

Before you visit a foreign country, learn as much as possible about their business policies and ethics. Remember you cannot shove a North American policy down the throat of the Mexican or Brazilian or European prospects, and if you try, you will not obtain licensees.

Front money and royalty should be based on your own operating costs and returns, and should not interfere with the competitive position of a licensee. You can determine this from your own position and what you could afford.

Information given to a licensee, should enable him to determine that the royalty you are asking can be earned.

If you are concerned about a prospective licensee who apparently is more than reasonably interested, you can request that he put up a guarantee bond for royalty to cover say your estimate of one year (at his cost). If he can obtain a bond, you probably do not need one from him.

Technology involved may determine the front money and royalty. A product with an extremely high profit margin might merit higher royalty, a more competitive product might demand a more realistic royalty. Royalty figures in percentages usually run from as little as 1/2% to 5%, and in some cases higher.

Licensing agreements may cover patent licensing, trade mark licensing, trade secret, know-how and technology. Quite often for licensing other tha patent licensing it is advisable to request the licensee to sign a disclosure agreement prior to disclosing technical and other pertinent information.

Licensing agreements generally provide the licensee with the right to: purchase finished products, components and assembly, manufacture of some components, purchase others and assembly, or manufacture complete, with rights to improvements, new developments, new products, etc.

A licensee along with other licensees and licensor are in a family, a long term marriage. They tend to help one another, exchanging ideas, methods, and costing. Procedures are quite open with the other parties, for the good of all.

A point to remember is that you are not responsible for the running of the licensee's business. This is his responsibility. It is also a good item not to oversell a license. Let the lincesee make up his own mind with the information provided.

Benefits to Licensor:

With licencees you have the opportunity to improve products, extending the life of agreements, and adding new products developed to existing agreements, and export those products that are competitive on such markets.

The first licensee will be the most difficult. Once signed and operating, it may be used as a reference to a second and so on.

Keep in contact with licensees, by mail, forwarding relevant information, or by telephone on occasions, and by visits when setting up others in same area of the world.

Invite licensees to visit you, introduce them to each other. When a new licensee is appointed, have all the others write and welcome them to the family, forwarding literature on your product, plus their own product literature.

You might consider two agreements, one for patent licensing, or trade secret, know-how, technology agreements, the other for trade mark licensing, splitting the royalty, so that after the patent runs out, there still would be income from the other.

There are some difficult areas to license, due to government regulations, e.g., socialist countries, South America. However, these are not impossible, and well worth the effort.

Is it worthwhile? Emphatically yes, to both licensee and licensor.

A Canadian company with about 140 employees, developed a product, patented it and licensed same in over 24 countries, and over fifteen years received $2,500,000.00 in royalties.

Another Canadian company with four employees and a trade secret, has in the last two years arranged ten licensees in U.S.A. and Canada, with options in three other areas of the world for licences, and is negotiating with an African company for licences in 16 developing countries.

Still another Canadian company has recently given a world licence to an American company for a Canadian development.

Many firms have built their company on licensed products. A good example is a company in the U.S.A. who took a license from a firm in Canada about sixteen years ago. A family business doing custom work with two sons in the business and four in university who planned to come into the business, which in no way could afford to take them in under the circumstances. After taking the license, they were required to move, so they rented a portion of a 40,000 square foot building. They now own the building, have put an extension on same, have acquired new efficient equipment thus reducing costs, and all six of the members of the family are employed there. Total employment has gone from 14 to approximately 75 and volume from a few hundred thousand to several millions. The original business of custom work is still being done, at about the same volume. We know of many companies who have benefited similarly from licensing in products.

Licensing out and in provides a firm with the following features:

- The only way to go international without a large investment.

- Keep up to date world-wide on its product and the industry.

- Makes it aware of competition world-wide.

- Outlet for further developments and improvements as well as new products.

- Income can be used for further developments, R & D and improvements in manufacturing methods to improve productivity and profitability.

- Source of new product ideas and improvements from licensees.

- Right to license in from licensees.

Here are some points to consider re licensing:

- Developing countries want to manufacture not import, licensing is the only way.

- Developed countries including Canada have the same desire.

- Licensing in creates employment fast, may reduce imports, and possibly export rights go with license.

- Licensing both ways is becoming a way of life in international trade.

There is a Licensing Executive Society, International, fees $50.00 per year, the only society devoted to licensing worldwide.

There is government assistance through various programs both Federal and Provincial to provide financial assistance to travel to foreign countries, attend trade shows etc.

Is it worthwhile, as a country? Definitely yes! The U.S.A. receives over three billion dollars annually from royalty agreements due to licensing.

Distribution in Foreign Trade
by
John Ross Holliday
President, Holross Inc.
International Marketing Consultant
Atlanta - Miami - Toronto

Businessmen have, in recent years, been exposed to almost daily reports of trade missions to foreign lands. Missions headed by senior statesmen, missions by groups of businessmen. Even Presidents and Prime Ministers tour the major nations of the world unabashedly touting the products of their countries. We read that citizens of Europe, Africa and of the Far East are eager for our wares. Our newspapers, if we take all reports at face value, might well lead us to believe that we have only to offer our products abroad and we will find eager buyers. The world is clamouring at our door to buy, buy, buy. Right? Well, that's not quite (to use the modern vernacular) "where it's at".

International marketing just like marketing at home does indeed represent opportunity. It also presents pitfalls, dangers and challenges, and just as at home, it demands thoughtful consideration as to the particular markets offering optimum potential. Also, careful exportation of potential market political climate, banking system, credit system, potential competition, and some dozen other critical factors. Fortunately in North American we have at our disposal as businessmen both federal and state or provincial government agencies, branches and departments, that can and will provide expert practical assistance with regard to most of these problems.

Assuming that you have used available government assistance, you know the countries with whom you want to do business ... assuming the markets you seek to penetrate are also either aware of or in need of your product ... obviously you have only to start shipping and the profits will roll in. Right? ... Wrong!

The difference between an eager customer, anxious to be served and an angry and disillusioned customer believing he has been deceived, can be summarized in just one word -- "distribution". The most inspired marketing program ever conceived cannot sell your product to a customer who cannot find it. Nor can it placate a customer who, having found and ordered your product, has experienced nothing but delay and inefficiency in getting his order filled.

You may well ask what the President of U.S. and Canadian Marketing organization could possibly know about foreign distribution. The answer is both "not much" and "a great deal".

"Not much" in terms of day-to-day problems and crises which arise in the course of servicing many types of foreign distribution organizations and for which we would, in any case, have far too little time in an article of this length. "A great deal" about the general principles which underlie not just one but most of the successful foreign distribution programs with which I and my organization have had contact.

My companies are not large ones. Demand for marketing services, such as ours, however, has over the past ten years in particular, become increasingly more international in scope. A number of my clients are U.S. and Canadian companies for whom I am involved in the marketing of North American goods and services in foreign countries. I also have foreign clients, including the governments of several countries for whom I provide international marketing assistance.

In the marketing field, North American involvement internationally is today largely of a pioneer nature. In this as in many other fields, however, we are rapidly becoming true citizens of the world. North American businessmen are increasingly pushing outward the boundaries of their trading arena. North American products are in demand in countries far from our own shores. North American capability is gaining recognition in many diverse fields. We are teaching India's technicians how to build, South Americans how to establish lumber industries and we are showing Kenyans how to develop prime beef herds.

North American marketing skills are also increasingly being put to work to help Canada to achieve success as an international business community citizen; though we are, in travelling this "road to success" in the international marketing place, finding unexpected obstacles in our path. Working with the marketing problems of U.S. and Canadian companies in foreign markets, I have in several instances watched in anguish and impotent fury as our best efforts were brought to nothing by an inefficient or incompetent distribution network. I have also had the pleasure and exhilaration of observing the success that comes to the client when a worthwhile product is successfully marketed, advertised and promoted, and a first-rate distribution system supplies and services and markets what has been created.

Obviously the purpose of distribution does not vary from country to country. It is the movement of goods from producer to consumer. Equally obviously, entry into the export market -- where you are dealing with not just one but 20 or 100 different countries -- does not change the basic purpose. Even the problems are not different; merely compounded by the greater numbers of everything -- people, houses, institutions, customs, markets -- which must be considered.

To further complicate matters, however, you will be dealing with these problems at least one step removed, and (to use a military analogy) with your lines of communication and supply greatly extended. It is this last which makes your distribution system so vital in the export market. In the home market you are in a position to perceived weaknesses or opportunities as they arise. If you are an Export Manager with 50 or 60 operations, you will be exceptional if you can visit any one of them more than once every one or two years. Your distributor is, therefore, not only your eyes, ears and mouth but very often your alter ego as well.

With so much at stake it will follow, therefore, that the choosing of the correct distributor for your particular needs will be one of the key decisions you'll have to make for each of your overseas operations. Still, even the most canny exporter cannot choose wisely unless he has something to choose from.

Let us look then, at some of the most effective means a new exporter can employ to establish contact with suitable overseas distribution channels.

(1) <u>Commercial Divisions of U.S. and Canadian Embassies and Consulates</u>

Some of those taxes we all complain about go to the trade services which are maintained by our embassies, consulates, and federal and state/provincial trade centres. Let me tell you that if all our tax dollars were as usefully spent we should have few grounds for complaint. Among the many areas in which these experts can be of immeasurable help to the Canadian businessman is the area of distribution. Their knowledge of local distribution channels is both sound and comprehensive.

Our Government Trade abroad are experts on the particular countries they serve and the distribution systems in them. They can give you information on the condition of the market in your field -- the way it is set up, and the distributors who service it. They can show you the method of calculating the landed price of your product and can outline the customary discounts, commissions, etc. Of course it is up to you to ask for help, as none of this advice will be worth much unless you take the trouble to contact them and outline your objectives and needs in clear and careful detail.

Now an important "BUT". <u>But</u>...under no circumstances can Government Services and Departments act as an extension of your sales force. They are <u>not</u>, and let me repeat that <u>not</u>, your overseas sales force and neither can, nor should, they be treated as such.

I have heard such officers complain that it is quite common for them to receive a letter from a prospective exporter which says, in effect, "Enclosed is our catalogue and price list. Orders will be accepted on a letter of credit basis at the above address. Thank you for your early attention to this matter." What such an exporter thinks when the orders do not arrive I do not know. What the embassy trade officials think when they get such a letter is not repeatable.

(2) <u>Advertising for Distributors</u>

There are several excellent advertising vehicles that have proven successful for North American exporters seeking distributors in other parts of the world.

(a) <u>International Trade Magazines</u>: Buyers' Guide editions of such publications are particularly useful in locating the best overseas distributors. If you select a magazine that specializes in your type of business you will find it can be used not only to solicit new distributors but to support your distributors once you obtain them.

(b) <u>International Newspapers</u>: Classified Advertisements in the international editions of such respected newspapers as the New York Times are read by the sort of internationally minded distributors you are seeking.

(c) <u>Overseas Newspapers and Trade Magazines</u>: All countries have trade associations and many of these publish magazines, bulletins or newspapers. Your Consular Trade Representative can usually advise you which ones to use and give you the information you need about rates, publication dates, etc.

(d) <u>"Free" Rides</u>: I use this somewhat facetious term to describe the multitude of export trade directories, trade shows and exhibitions, international freight forwarders, airlines and shipping companies which have vested interest in assisting exporters to develop trade. Making use of such assistance often costs little but time and effort and you will find you can often work with such partners to considerable mutual advantage.

(e) <u>Existing Canadian Exporters of Allied Products</u>: Let us suppose you are a manufacturer of spark plugs and you have decided to enter the export market. You know that Company X, who makes automotive hose clamps, is already successfully launched in the export markets you are considering. Do not hesitate to seek their assistance. There is no sounder advice you could get than the candid assessment of someone who's been through the mill. Working with <u>you</u> may also help <u>them</u> to cut <u>their</u> overseas costs.

Once distribution contacts have been made there are several options open to you when you decide on the form of distribution that will best suit your needs. In brief these are:

- your own overseas sales staff (seldom desirable for the beginning exporter)

- manufacturer's representatives (or commission agents)

- stocking distributors (exclusive or non-exclusive)

- warehousers (bonded and unbonded)

- individual importers (those who import for their own use but take no part in marketing)

- governments.

Each of these options has advantages which may or may not be recommended to you. Without knowing your particular problems it would be idle for me to recommend one over another. Though, in most instances you will choose your foreign distribution system by use of the same criteria you would use in the domestic market, nevertheless you will need to be wary in your choice. There can be important reasons for particular answers to particular problems. I would, therefore, like to point out some of the pitfalls that may tend to cloud your judgement when making your decision as to the type of foreign distribution system which you are going to decide upon.

(1) Don't dismiss the "hybrids"

For some reason most North American distribution operations seem to fall neatly into one of the categories I have mentioned. Whether through chauvinism or ignorance many North American exporters seem to view any operation which crosses traditional lines with a good deal of suspicion. Such suspicion is usually quite unfounded.

In Germany, for example, I know of a manufacturer's agent who, in his role as agent, encourages the companies he represents to put their stock into his bonded warehouse. When sales have been negotiated he orders goods released from the warehouse to the customer. He also takes care of billing and guarantees payments for the sales he has made. This has proved to be a highly profitable and convenient arrangement for all parties, yet I know of no North American distributor who provides this type of comprehensive service.

Before dismissing such hybrid operations as "jacks of all trades and masters of none", investigate the services offered with an open mind. It may save you time, trouble and money.

(2) Judge any distribution system solely on its performance

You may well feel this is so elementary as to be insulting. Yet we are all human and prone to subjective feelings we may not even recognize. Conditioned to believe that efficient business is conducted in a certain way, that well-run operations have a certain appearance, that a company that handles one type of goods is not equipped to handle others, we may reject any deviations from our own standards.

In the domestic market where you are operating in totally familiar territory, such instincts are usually sound. In the foreign market you may be led astray into unconsciously believing that "different" is "inferior" and thus pass up the distributor who will perform best for you, in favour of the one who seems more "familiar". Quite badly, as a new exporter you have neither sufficient knowledge nor "feel" for your new markets to judge on this basis. Proof of performance must be your only guide. All else is irrelevant.

Let me give you an example. In a city in the Middle East there is a well-known distributor whose "front office" is a tiny shop in the city's Bazaar. No polished receptionist greets the visitor, no stenographic pool clacks out its efficiency, no executive suite shields the owner from the passing parade. To make matters worse this company deals in such unrelated items as auto parts, automobiles, bicycles, bread and flour, and building materials, and runs a truck assembly plant on the side.

To North American eyes this "ticky-tacky" setup is more suited to the pedlar than the reliable distributor. What the North American eye does not see, and too often does not take the trouble to find out, is that the Bazaar has been operating for more than 1500 years and is the most prized business location in the city; the company in question owns three buildings in the same block and have five major warehouses from which it provides absolutely first-rate service to all of its clients, however varied their needs.

(3) Remember that farthest fields are not always greener

Many new exporters are surprised to find they can often arrange foreign distribution through contacts already in Canada. Whether from a fondness for expense account travelling or simple ignorance they go trotting about the globe establishing arrangements that are, in the end, less profitable than those that could be arranged without moving far from home base. The three most common ancillary distribution channels available from Contacts in Canada are:

(a) <u>Resident buyers in Canada for large purchasing concerns</u>: Just as most major North American department stores have resident buyers abroad, so do many foreign firms maintain resident buyers in this country. Even some governments maintain resident buyers in larger North American centres.

(b) <u>Third country purchasers</u>: Many large international organizations maintain buying agents around the world. For example, Aramco has third country buying offices in both The Hague and New York, which supply many of the needs of its Middle East operations. Such buying organizations are large, readily available, and can be highly profitable for those who can offer what they need.

(c) <u>Export management firms</u>: These companies make a specialty of exporting goods for sale in other countries. They may operate wither on commission or as outright buyers for resale. They will also undertake to seek sales on either a world-wide or one area basis. A number of companies of this type are located in major North American cities and they can be of real value, especially to the new exporter. One word of caution, however -- if you have other distribution arrangements be certain that your operations through these companies do not infringe or you will have a small internal trade war on your hands.

(4) Adjust your distribution system to your profit realities

Having advised you to keep an open mind about distribution systems that differ from your own, I am going to turn around and warn against going too far in accepting conditions in the export country without questions.

Let us suppose you plan to export to a country where the standard distribution pattern is (a) manufacturer to (b) stocking agent to (c) standard wholesaler to (d) dealer. After investigating your market you find you cannot keep your price low enough to interest a stocking agent. In such a case your solution is neither to adjust your price with the mad hope that some miracle of volume will intervene to offer you a profit, nor should you assume you cannot be competitive in the export market.

Instead, you should carefully investigate the possibility of eliminating (a) the local manufacturer and (b) the stocking agent and seek direct contact with the wholesalers and dealers. This is, in fact, how new distribution patterns arise and you would be surprised at how often these are initiated by exporters like your-self.

In short, although you will avoid running roughshod over local customs and sensibilities, you should be as sceptical of the foreign business contact who tells you he cannot meet your needs because "we've always done it this way" as you would be of the same attitude from his North American counterpart.

Finally, I want to talk briefly about an area which has been a major focus of my personal business career. That is the need for communication. You may seek out the most efficient expert and energetic distributor in your particular field of operations and still fail dismally in the export market if you do not keep your distributors frankly and fully informed of your company's operations with particular emphasis on its aims and objectives.

This was brought home to me in a very exasperating fashion by my dealings with a client who was entering the overseas market for the first time. Seemingly he had done everything right. He had advertised for and selected an excellent distributor; he had visited an appropriate Government trade advisor and learned all he could about the market; he had followed the seven golden rules for advertising and sales promotion and we had implemented a marketing program designed to suit the local situation. We got under-way with a push that seemed guaranteed of success. The campaign was well received, the demand was created, the distributor -- a ball of fire --produced orders and orders and orders. And there-in lay the rub. Our manufacturer had neglected to tell us that he was entering the export market only to unload his surplus production. As orders came pouring in, he was aghast, for he had neither the goods nor the production capacity to fill them.

In the jargon of the marketing fraternity that's called "a failure to communicate objectives". In layman's language it's called "stupid"!

Of necessity, we have been restricted today to broad general guidelines for establishing an effective distribution system for export marketing.

Finally, in all of your efforts, to effect entry to, and prosper in export trade, remember that the overseas market is not a goose waiting to be plucked. Rather it is a valuable bird, which, approached in goodwill, with common sense, specific objectives, proper caution and with a program based on knowledge and understanding, will surely reward you with many a golden egg.

Advertising and Sales Promotion in Foreign Trade
by
John Ross Holiday
President, Holross Inc.
International Marketing Consultant
Atlanta - Miami - Toronto

Owing to time constraints, this will <u>not</u> be a comprehensive and detailed discussion of advertising, and sales promotion programs suitable for foreign or any other kind of markets. Nor shall we attempt to cover the extremely specialized situations found in the the European Common Market or countries such as those of Eastern Europe where trade, marketing, and distribution are under government control.

What I <u>shall</u> attempt is to give you a brief resume of the purpose and principles underlying <u>all</u> successful advertising and sales promotion programs, whether domestic or foreign, proceed from that to a discussion of the sort of reorientation and revision which will usually be required if a successful domestic program is to be exported, and finally, by considering a few fables and horror stories along the way, we will attempt to arrive at some common sense rules-of-thumb that will enable you to approach your export markets with your feet firmly on the ground - not wedged in your mouths.

However the specifics may vary, the object of any advertising and sales promotion program, whether in the sophisticated markets of North America or the most primitive agrarian economy, is to move merchandise through the distribution chain. To achieve this objective, such a program must recognize, plan for, and integrate the requirements of marketing management, the sales force (whether distributor or dealer), wholesale and retail management, and the consumer. The specific links in this chain of product distribution may vary for individual companies or in various economies but the basic tenet of integrated merchandising effort of all product distribution levels cannot be ignored if optimum achievement is to be assured. You have heard, ad nauseum, of the

"Generation Gap", the "Security Gap", the "Credibility Gap" -- I sometimes wonder if future generations studying 20th Century society will see it as a gigantic Swiss cheese -- but at the risk of compounding an already overworked metaphor, I should like to suggest to you that when all the jargon has been set aside, an advertising and sales promotion program is really nothing more than a bridge over the "Communication Gap" that inevitably exists between the producer and the consumer.

To provide this essential bridge, a modern marketing program covers four areas:

Sales Planning -- the definition of product objectives, sales strategy, and market approach;

Sales Preparation -- generating enthusiasm and support for the product in the company or distributor's sales force;

Sales Presentation -- creating acceptance for the product through advertising at wholesale and retail buying levels; and

Sales Promotion -- transforming advertising communication into positive consumer response and action at the point-of-purchase.

To point out that in approaching foreign markets it is often necessary to make radical changes in our techniques, our tools and our methods is to belabour the obvious. Nevertheless, like the colonel's lady in Judy O'Grady, I believe we have a good deal more in common than meets the eye, and the basic approach and final objectives of a competent advertising and sales promotion program are the same in either foreign or domestic markets.

This then, is the general background from which we must formulate our approach to the problems faced in the export market.

To begin, let us assume that you are the manager of a successful North American company. Through a combination of competent technical innovation, efficient manufacturing practices, sound business management and inspired advertising and sales promotion, you have become a household word in the U.S. or in Canada and you have, therefore, decided to seek wider markets and increase profits in the export field.

You have delineated the markets where your greatest potential lies, completed your financial planning, taken advantage of the excellent advice available from foreign trade experts in both government and trade associations, assessed your particular needs and set up an appropriate distribution system, and are ready, at last, to plan and execute the advertising and promotion program which you know from experience will reinforce all your other efforts and produce the all-important sales.

At this point there are three courses open to you.

Reminding yourself somewhat smugly that "nothing succeeds like success", you can reflect that your program for the home market has been so soundly conceived that you are now number one in your field. Obviously you are already doing just about everything right. With presumably unassailable logic, you therefore, decide to export your compete advertising and sales promotion program right along with your product -- pausing only long enough to secure the services of a highly recommended translator.

If you are subject to attacks of fantastic good luck it just might work. More probably, all your careful business and financial planning will go for nothing and the necessary sales will not materialize. And small wonder. For you have failed to assess and revise your strategy and tactics to meet a whole new set of conditions and have thus committed all <u>seven of the deadly sins</u> that lie in wait for advertisers who seek sales in foreign markets.

What are they?

<u>First</u>, failure to change your market strategy in accordinace with new objectives;

<u>Second</u>, failure to adapt your product, your promotion and your advertising to ensure acceptance in the new market;

<u>Third</u>, failure to get maximum value from your advertising and sales promotion expenditure;

<u>Fourth</u>, failure to understand the social environment in which your sales will have to be made;

<u>Fifth</u>, failure to consider the appropriateness of media;

<u>Sixth</u>, failure to develop a domestic personality in the market country; and

<u>Seventh</u>, failure to appreciate the limitations of translation.

Any one of these failures can substantially reduce the effectiveness of your export advertising and sales promotion efforts. Taken together they presage almost certain disaster. Under the circumstances it might pay us well to examine a few of the pitfalls that lurk behind each of these omissions.

I. <u>Failure to change your market strategy in accordance with new objectives</u>

The underlying purpose of all business activity, whether in Kansas City or Karachi is the same -- to sell as large a volume of goods as possible at a price that will produce a satisfactory profit. That will not change. It's the "<u>how</u>" that must engage your earnest attention.

Consider, for example, the Campbell Soup Company. So commanding is their share of the soup market in the United States that virtually all of their promotion activity is directed towards simply increasing the amount of soup consumed. "Have You Had Your Soup Today?", "Soup for Breakfast", "Soup on the Rocks" -- it's a tribute to their success that most of us can remember these slogans. But in Canada, Campbell's faces a very different situation. Although substantial, Campbell's share-of-market is by no means so large that soup promotion will inevitably increase the sale of Campbell's. It is just as likely to promote Aylmer, Catelli, Lipton, Habitant or half a dozen other brands. In Canada, therefore, Campbell's strategy has always been to emphasize Campbell quality, variety and taste.

The lesson is plain. The commanding lead or high reputation you enjoy in the domestic market will not follow you into the export situation. Strategic redeployment of forces to meet your new market objectives is a necessity.

II. <u>Failure to adapt your product, your promotion and your advertising to increase acceptance in the new market</u>

If you're one of those who believes you can't get a cup of

coffee in the U.S.A. that's half as "good" as the one you get in Columbia you are probably, in your own terms, quite correct. But you would not be right to suspect that the coffee companies are engaged in some vast conspiracy to deprive you of the strong flavour you prefer. Coffee companies have only one aim -- to sell coffee -- and their excellent research and market testing programs have demonstrated that most Americans prefer a milder coffee. Therein lies your frustration. But therein also lies their success.

It is not enough to establish that a market exists for your type of product. You must delve further and see what benefits or modifications will make it most acceptable.

Failure to assess product benefits in the light of market needs can reduce the effectiveness of your advertising and sales promotion campaigns.

During the appalling famine in Biafra several years ago, you may recall an uproar in the newspapers when reporters found that a substantial shipment of Metrecal had been included in relief supplies from the United States. North-American oriented newspapermen were outraged to think that starving Biafrans were being urged to lose weight. The explanation (unfortunately in rather small print back behind the classified ads) put quite a different complexion on the matter, however, for relief officials pointed out that Metrecal was completely balanced nutritionally, could be shipped cheaply and easily in powdered bulk form, and required no refrigeration. As a dietary supplement for people whose diet was somewhat deficient in calories but almost totally deficient in nutrients it was virtually ideal.

In short, one country's luxury may be another's necessity, and vice versa. The wise exporter will make very sure he knows which end of his benefit spectrum is up.

III. Failure to get maximum value from your advertising and sales promotion expenditure

You will recall that in a burst of enthusiasm (some might call it arrogance) our manufacturer had all of his domestic advertising and sales promotion material translated, duplicated and shipped to his distributors and salesmen in the foreign market.

At worst, you might think it might not be appropriate or it might not all be used; and at best it will save the distributor a good deal of money and effort.

Unfortunately, you could be wrong on both counts.

As we all know, advertising and promotion costs are customarily built into the price of products in the domestic market. When this cost is built into the wholesale cost of products for export, it often happens that the product arriving at the customs barrier subject to duty on its C.I.F. selling price, must be offered to the foreign consumer at a price that puts it totally beyond reach. In such a case it will be much more practical to offer your distributor an advertising and sales promotion discount which will permit him to produce his material duty-free and thus keep your product competitive.

This pitfall is particularly deep for those who ship in-store display or point-of-purchase materials.

The bewilderment of the distributor who received a consignment of 30-foot supermarket banners and 5-foot long shelf displays for deployment in a country where 90 percent of all retail trade was conducted in neighbourhood stores with an average floor area of 400 square feet can only be imagined. In fact, it is probably only exceeded by the anguish of the overseas sales manager in France who was forced to explain to customs officials why he was importing 200 gross of company-imprinted book matches for distribution in a country where matches are a government monopoly and importing them is a crime.

A little ingenuity and consultation might have overcome all of these problems. More than one American manufacturer has successfully negotiated the tariff barrier by shipping his goods in cartons that could be easily dismantled and reassembled into effective point-of-purchase displays.

IV. Failure to understand the social environment in which your sales will have to be made

To suggest the possibility of failure in this area may seem almost insulting in these days of universal higher education and jet travel, when even the most provincial executive appreciates the folly of offering Seagram's Crown Royal as an incentive to salesmen in Moslem countries; or attempting to create a market for beefsteak and kidney pie in India.

As a matter of fact, in this area our problem is not so much to avoid falling into the obvious pits -- but rather to keep from stumbling into those nasty, little potholes created by what the sociologists call "manners and mores".

Did you know, for example, that a bride is not acceptable in advertising directed to Latin America? That an advertisement which depicted a woman in a sleeveless dress on the steps of St. Peter's would horrify Italians? That the women of of some countries would be dumbfounded by your attempt to sell them deodorants, because human body odor is considered an aphrodisiac?

This list is endless but the idea can quickly be grasped by considering the case of the unfortunate Canadian manufacturer who found it possible to make a substantial reduction in the price of a product he exported to Switzerland and rushed into print with a translation of his domestic advertisement which showed a bank robbery in progress while a headline trumpeted, "It's Better Than a Licence to Steal!" Poor fellow. He could probably have dashed through the streets screaming "Assassinate the President!" or "Kill All the Mothers" without being regarded as more than a harmless eccentric. But his failure to understand that in Switzerland banking is the foundation of the entire country's prosperity, and therefore not a fit subject for even the most harmless levity, was fatal to his aims.

V. Failure to consider the appropriateness of media

At first glance this would appear to be one of the easiest pitfalls for the sensible advertiser to avoid. It requires no great effort nor power of intellect to find out the circulation of newspapers, the per capita incidence of television sets and radios, the availability and readership of magazines, billboards, etc. However, as Disraeli put it, "There are three kinds of lies -- lies, damned lies, and statistics". Far more bright young advertisers have been led down the garden path by statistics, than have ever succumbed to sirens in low-cut black satin.

You see, it's not getting the facts that's difficult; it's knowing how to interpret them when you have them.

Now obviously, if your media data tell you that a country has an illiteracy rate of 80 percent and you are aiming for a mass market you will have the wit to stay out of print.

Equally obviously, when your data tell you that 95 percent of all households in a particular country subscribe to a daily newspaper you will leap into newspapers with all advertising flags flying. Well, maybe. But only maybe. Because I know of at least one country where the statistics are just as presented. But the statistics do not tell you that newspaper readership is customarily confined to the man of the house. If the primary market for your product is women, you might just as well deliver your message from the comfort of your armchair in Canada, for all the impact it will have.

Or, take another country where statistics clearly show that farmers are virtually illiterate, there is no electricity in rural areas, there is no national television network, and radios are owned by only one in every 200 people? Surely the only way to reach this kind of rural market is by word of mouth? Not at all. For what statistics fail to show, is that the one person in 200 who owns a radio is usually the village elder, and that the second most popular rural entertainment in that country is gathering in the village square every evening to listen to that same one radio.

VI. Failure to develop a domestic personality in the market country

There is probably nothing very wrong with advertising to Western Europe and using photographs whose backgrounds show New York, Miami, or Toronto. Yet with the same campaign, the same message, the same format, how much more effective you would be, if your photographs used a background that was very familiar to your potential customers.

International diplomacy is more than a matter of observing the niceties of protocol between governments. There is such a thing as international business diplomacy, and, like all sincere efforts to improve human relations, it can make life a good deal easier and pleasanter for all concerned.

Remember that your subsidiaries and distributors are corporate citizens of the countries in which they operate <u>first</u>; <u>your</u> subsidiaries and distributors second. Encourage your overseas people to contribute time and effort to the communities in which they are living. Make an allocation from your sales promotion budget so your distributor can sponsor the local soccer club. Adopt the customs of the business community around you, so your customers can relate to you, and your product, as one of themselves.

Finally, remind yourself and your representatives that you are not a missionary for the North American, or any other way of life.

It all adds up to the best public relations program you could possibly adopt.

VII. <u>Failure to appreciate the limitations of translation</u>

I come now, as all considerate speakers must, to comic relief.

For many years now "The New Yorker" magazine delighted its readers with reprints of the hilarious and often baffling attempts of exporters to communicate with their sales organizations and customers in the United States. Let us pause for a moment and relish this from a recent issue:

THE MYSTERIOUS AND AMUSEMENT-LOVING EAST
(items listed in an illustrated catalogue distributed by the "XYZ" Company Limited, Osaka, Japan).

Roop-The-Roop

Two rockets, accommodated each 4 persons, equipped at the edge of arm, circle vertically, having quick revolution, so that visitors have much thrill by the turning somersault.

Damboo

Four different animals go around, having the movement of up and down.
This equipment is a favourable amusement facility for children.

Octpus

Carriage, accommodated from 2 to 3 persons equipped at each top of 8 legs of octpus shaped devise. All of legs are revolved and make a movement of up and down, so that visitors have a fun to be tossed by octpus legs.

No question about it, it's pretty funny, or is it?

Knowing from our own experience how competent most Japanese businessmen are, are we right to assume that this manufacturer decided to cut corners, and translate his catalogue himself, with the aid of a 50-cent English dictionary? Or should we more logically assume that the manufacturer, in perfectly good faith, hired a translator with impeccable credentials, and sent his catalogue off to the export market, without the slightest inkling of the bloopers it contained?

To coin a phrase, it's our own story exactly.

Unless you are thoroughly at home in the language of your export market, you, like the unfortunate Japanese company are totally at the mercy of your translator.

But accurate translation can be the least of your worries. More often it is the nuances of language, not the actual words, that cause the corporate red faces, and sabotage even the best-laid advertising and sales promotion plans.

In the years immediately following World War II, a group of enterprising garment manufacturers in French-speaking Montreal decided, quite correctly, that the high quality, and practical styling of Canadian sportswear, would find a ready market in France, where the traditional concentration on high fashion and the dislocations of war, had combined to inhibit development of a domestic sportswear industry...

The promotion they planned was a model. Market surveys were made to decide just which lines would be most acceptable; government trade officials both in Canada and in France were consulted, and their advice heeded; the most important prospective French buyers were contacted; and planning and execution of a gala fashion showing were put in the capable hands of one of

Canada's most outstanding (and completely bilingual) fashion co-ordinators.

It is hardly suprising that the whole promotion went swim-mingly and the fashion show opened to an audience of expectant and interested buyers and a flattering burst of French publicity.

Imagine then, the surprise of the commentator, delivering her excellent sales message in flawless French, when she detected titters and giggles in the audience. As the show proceeded the titters turned to guffaws, the giggles to helpless glee, and the entire producton ground to its disastrous end, with all of the panache of a swimmer going down for the third time.

What went wrong?

That year the garment manufacturers of Montreal had decided to promote a new fashion shade of brown, which they called, most imaginatively, "caleche" brown. Now, if you consult a French-Canadian dictionary you will find that a "caleche" is the pictur-esque horsedrawn carriage so popular with sightseers in Quebec and Montreal. If you consult a French dictionary you will find the word has the same meaning or is not listed. What neither diction-ary will tell you is that in the street argot of Paris "caleche" is not a quaint Canadian horsedrawn vehicle at all, but an all-too-obvious by-product of the horse.

After this latter-day version of "The Perils of Pauline" you will readily understand why my second option for tackling the problems of advertising and sales promotion in the export market, has a good many enthusiastic practitioners. Following this plan you recognize the traps awaiting the unwary, modestly admit your ignorance of the market, and, through allowances, discounts and subsidies, turn the whole program over to your foreign distribu-tors, or overseas staff, to do what they think best. How easy and appealing it all sounds. There's a word for it too -- it's "cop-out".

This sort of exporter reminds me of the rich widower, who was proud that he had a son to inherit the family name and fortune, but, feeling himself wholly unqualified for the difficult occupation of parenthood, decided to hire the best, and most expensive ex-perts, and give them a free hand to do the job for him. In the early years he built a luxurious modern nursery, and installed the baby there in the care of a highly recommended nanny. A little later the child was enrolled in the country's most famous boarding school in winter, and a first-class camp in summer. Finally, his college days were passed at a foreign university with an international reputation, and between semesters he sailed 'round the world'. At length, his upbringing completed, he presented himself on his father's doorstep.

But to the father's consternation, this product of expensive but absentee upbringing, had adopted the intellectual standards of his dear old nanny, the sexual aberrations of the more disturbed pupils of his boarding school, the table manners of the woodsman guide at his summer camp, the language of his university, and the vocabulary of the sailors with whom he had cruised the world.

"He's got the same name as my son", said the bewildered parent, "but he's sure out of step with the rest of the family".

Permit your distributors and overseas representatives to mount their advertising and sales promotion programs in isolation from your general marketing strategy, and without direction or supervision from the home base, and I guarantee that though the product will have the same name as your product, you'll find it's "sure out of step with the rest of the family".

There is, of course a third way. You can:

(1) Keep your distributors or sales representatives fully informed about total company advertising, and sales promotion activity and objectives;

(2) Make available to them all your advertising and sales promotion material, but give careful consideration to their judgement of its relevance to their particular situation.

(3) Discuss fully the financial and tariff implications of all material before it is shipped from home office;

(4) Check, re-check and check again with your local people; all translated material, to ensure market acceptability and avoid language error;

(5) Read about, study, and visit your foreign markets;

(6) Grasp every opportunity to meet and talk with businessmen from the countries where you are operating.

(7) Consult with, and benefit from, the excellent Trade Commission services that the U.S. and Canada and most states and provinces maintain in embassies and consulates abroad. Also make use of the equally valuable advice available from the trade representatives that other countries send to North America.

It is tempting to announce at this point, "That's it! That's all you need to know to mount a successful advertising and sales promotion campaign in the export market". Unfortunately that is not "it". Nor is it all you need to know.

The dynamics of marketing, and the specifics of advertising and sales promotion are as complicated and as subject to circumstance as are those of any other business science; and therefore not possible of coverage "in toto" in a single seminar session. However, though international marketing expertise may not be instantly obtainable, it _is_ possible nevertheless to achieve international marketing success, as has been proved by many North American businessmen, by observing these Seven Advertising/-Promotion Rules for Foreign Trade Marketing.

These seven rules _are_ important. Indeed I would go further and say they are indispensable. They are the firm foundation on which any successful advertisng and sales promotion campaign for export markets must be built. However brilliant your creative conception... however energetic your efforts... however lavish your budget... if you build your campaign without this foundation you might better, as someone's wise old grandmother once said, "save your breath to cool your porridge".

An overseas market success, like a marriage, requires that the suitor respect, woo, and win his bride with her interests in mind as well as his own. How he conducts his suit... how he promotes his cause... his regard for her background, beliefs and customs, will largely determine the acceptance meted his proposal, and the productivity and profitability of a resulting partnership.

Happy international marriages to you all!

Documentation, Shipping, Packaging and Marine Insurance

by
Murray S. Philip
Export Manager
Johnston International Services

Because we have four subjects to be discussed this evening –
packaging, shipping, marine insurance and, documentation I will
try to keep my opening remarks to a minimum.

The four subjects I trust you will see as we go through the
material are very closely aligned. They are related and moreover,
they are reliant on one another. This I hope will show through as
we proceed. I will avoid plugging my own company. Rather I will
plug, if anything, the industry in which we are a part. I personally find it a very exciting industry and moreover we find it
exciting, in that, now and finally, the freight forwarder is being
recognized. The shipper, more and more, is coming to the freight
forwarder to utilize the expertise we have. I will stay away, if I
can, from things like export credit and export sales because,
people far more knowledgeable than I have spoken to you or will
speak to you in coming weeks on these subjects, this to avoid you
asking me questions later that are completely out of my realm.

I have to explain to you that the company I am engaged with is
involved in export air and export ocean shipments. By this I mean
all foreign markets, no U.S. business, no border business. The
freight forwarder can provide a very complete service if the customer requires it. Ideally the shipper can make a product, telephone his freight forwarder, inform him what he has to ship, send
him copies of orders and invoices or letter of credit. Armed with
this information the forwarder can start his job. He can book the
cargo on a vessel or air craft. He can arrange to have the goods
picked up at the plant and delivered to the pier, airport or terminal. He can prepare all of the documents that are required
whether it be to a country that requires consular legalization or
not. Also he can arrange insurance. He can prepare all bank

documents right down to the draft and presentation of the actual letters of credit and support documents. In the case of an open sale he can distribute the documents to overseas agents or receivers. There is a considerable difference in ocean and air shipments on all four subjects and I feel it best to consider them separately as we go along.

Marine Insurance

Marine insurance is far different than any other type of insurance coverage. As we go through this material I am sure you will see and I think you will remember that statement. People who do volume export should have their own marine insurance policy geared to cover their own products. Those who have very few export shipments would probably be better to place their insurance through a freight forwarder who has his own open policy. Frankly when you have a limited number of shipments it is not to your advantage to get into the cost and arrangement of marine insurance. Your marine insurance policy is separate, as I mentioned, and should not be considered in the same context as your other business insurance. To help you understand the principles I will try to give short explanations of the people and instruments involved in marine insurance.

The Policy: The policy is established with an agent who arranges coverage with the underwriters. Certificates are issued per shipment against the policy, and the certificates automatically are governed by the rules etc. included in the policy. Pads of these certificates are provided to the shipper by the insurance company. When the policy is arranged, the estimated dollar value is forecasted for what the shippers plan to export. This figure should be reviewed annually.

The Agent: A good agent will get to know all there is to know about the shipper's products, and in particular his packaging. The agent, through the underwriters, can provide information on packaging. Not all insurance agents have experience in marine insurance so choose him as you would a lawyer, notary or accountant.

The Underwriter: The underwriters maintain constant records and statistics on marine insurance. With this information they are able to establish rates. They are aware of such things as damage factors and they analyze the handling or packaging problems and loss factor. Most underwriters have world wide settling agents, and it is important when taking out marine insurance to make sure that the insurance people have these agents. You must leave the choosing of an underwriter to your agent. An experienced agent is more aware and must have your complete confidence.

The Surveyor: Insurance surveyors are independent and impartial. Many times a receiver decides to buy a product which may have certain specifications. To avoid having to come to Canada and inspect each shipment, he appoints a surveyor who will conduct this type of examination on his behalf. Some letters of credit request a surveyor's report particularly on shipments moving to government agencies abroad. The surveyor is used much like an adjuster would be in an automobile accident. If there is damage at destination he would be appointed by the insurer to determine the condition of the insured property and/or the loss or damage. His fee is paid for by the insurer.

Insurance Rates: These vary by commodity and more particularly are subject to the products susceptibility to damage, pilferage and loss. The world is divided into areas, and rates are applied which are based on local conditions. Things like dock, rail and truck facilities are taken into consideration, together with the political climate of the country. If there has been a history of on and off war or steady political unrest, these factors contribute to the rate scale. Insurance is a very competitive business, and it is well to check around before accepting insurance rates. It is also advisable to review these rates often.

Aside from the straight insurance rate there is a war risk rate. War risk rates rarely vary from insurance company to insurance company. War risk rates are established in one of two places, New York or London, and all insurance firms subscribe to one or the other. Even the two rate setters rarely vary. War risk is exactly what is says, the risk of war. The war risk rate to Vietnam is quite a bit higher than to London, England, for example, and for obvious reasons. Rates are established at so much per $100 value.

Export Packing as Related to Insurance: As I mentioned, insurance companies will provide information on how to export pack. It is obvious that if the material is not packaged in a manner that can handle what export cargo must go through, it will achieve a higher damage factor thus driving up the rates. A shipper is far better to have landed cargo in good shape instead of paid claims. It is all important for the shipper to know what the cargo must go through and pack accordingly, otherwise the damages will reflect in the shipper's claim performance and the rates will be adjusted accordingly. It is a safe bet to say that insurance companies rarely come out on the wrong end of such a dealing. The idea is, pay the price at source in the form of packaging, or pay higher rates later not to mention the damage to the goodwill between the shipper and the receiver.

Coverage of C & F or CIF Plus 10%: When fixing marine insurance the normal procedure is to insure for 10% over the C & F or CIF value. By adding the 10% you are automatically insuring the insurance premium as well as the goods and freight. It also helps to cover any additional costs you may incur when a claim results. Sometimes a letter of credit or client's order will ask that you take insurance out for CIF plus 20%, or I have seen it as high as 40%. This is the odd exception. 10% is the usual cover. Some credits or orders ask that the certificate be claused "including 90 days stay in customs". This is to cover some of the red tape experienced in certain countries.

Pier to Pier vs Warehouse to Warehouse: Most exporters take a policy that covers them warehouse to warehouse. For a few more cents the cargo is covered for the inland hauls at both ends. You can obtain just pier to pier coverage, if you had another inland policy that already covered your inland moves at this end and you were sure you had no problem at destination. This is more prevalent among people who have a plant here in Canada, for example, and only supply an overseas plant or principal.

General Average: General average is the most difficult type of insurance to explain to people. For example, if a ship is hit by another ship and part of the cargo is lost, the vessel operators could declare general average and all those having cargo aboard the vessel would have to contribute to the cost of the loss. Your first reaction as someone who had cargo on the vessel is, "Why must I pay when my cargo is intact?" When shipping by ocean and under the international terms that govern ocean shipping, you are responsible. The best example would be if a vessel was at a

268

point, due to weather, that she could sink unless the vessel was lightened. In the interest of saving the vessel and the balance of the cargo, the captain has the right to jettison any cargo in an effort to save the vessel and, as such, everbody pays; because, had he not done so everything would have been lost, the cargo, the vessel, and the crew. This general average rule dates very far back. It is said that the Chinese who ran rafts of tea up and down rivers many years ago used much the same principal. If you should ever be in a position that you have cargo on a vessel that has declared general average, your first step is to pass every-thing over to your insurance people as it is a very detailed matter and that is what you are paying premiums for them to handle.

My only purpose here was to make you aware of general aver-age in a very general way. It was things like general average that I referred to in my opening remarks where I said marine insurance is much different than most types of insurance.

Extended Coverage: The general cover on marine insurance is for 60-90 days after discharge from the vessel which is agreed to when the insurance policy is being established. In the event of strikes, wars or other delays, you sometimes have to watch the length of the insurance coverage to make sure you are covered. As soon as you learn of a delay, this coverage feature should be examined.

How to go About a Claim: There is no simple step, one, two, three in going about an insurance claim but, all insurance com-panies will spell out their requirements to you when the policy is taken out. It is extremely important to note, however, that you must never write, or admit to anything, without first consulting your insurance company. They can be excused from their res-ponsibility if it can be proven that you jeopardized the case by an admission of poor packaging or, that you were agreeable to ac-cepting a lesser amount than the value of the goods. You should remember you have paid the premium and only the insurance firms have the expertise to handle these matters. You may as well let them do it. You paid for this service. The consignee should not accept goods with visible external damage without notating the delivery receipt. The insurance certificate will indicate the set-tling agent and the receiver should report it immediately.

Responsibility of the Shipper as Detailed in the Policy: Again this depends very heavily on the product being shipped. If you are shipping dangerous cargo, for example, you must comply with the existing international regulations. The rules may insist on hermetically sealed drums, and if you use any other type of packing, you can violate your agreement as it is spelled out in the policy.

Using a Canadian Insurance Company: In many countries lately, we have seen where the governments issue a law that insurance on all goods imported into their country must be insured in their country. This is a move designed to keep the currency in the country. Brazil and the Dominican Republic have just recently done this and they are following the lead of other countries like Venezuela. There has been talk of Canada one day doing much the same. It has been mentioned that on government loans, etc., this practice may be adopted but it is not at the moment. For these reasons it may be well for you to acquire a Canadian insurance company. As you can see by now, I am the original flag waver.

Insurance and the Container: This subject is probably the hottest contested matter ever to be beat around by insurance people. The shippers felt that because of the added protection a container supplies, the rates should be reduced. The insurance companies protested and brought out the point that now every shipper is stowing the containers and as such there are no experienced stowage men being employed to protect against the rigors of sea travel. The big question which came to light was within the ocean bill of lading whereby international regulations state that the carrier is only responsible for $500 per package. They claim the container is a package. In the U.S.A., many judges would not take the case for fear of setting a precedent. Finally, a judge took a case where a container load of shoes were shipped from Italy to the U.S.A. and it was a total loss. The line contended in that their bill read "1 container said to contain so many cartons of shoes" as such, they had accepted 1 package and were responsible for the value of 1 package $500. The judge in his ruling stated that it was obvious that a container full of shoes was worth far more than $500. He did, however, state that this case was not to be used as a precedent but, since that case, there have been many (far too many to get into) where the receiver's claim has been honoured.

In the bills of lading you will have to watch in the value section of rules that they cover $500 per package as some foreign lines have shown 500 kroner or francs and at today's money values that is far less than $500. If you accept a bill with this type of thing, the insurance company will not be responsible.

Avoid Taking Part Settlements: If by chance you hit on a poor insurance company that recommended you take a quick or reduced payment of a claim - avoid it like the plague. By doing so you are setting yourself up and a precedent is established which will come back to haunt you. It is important to note that there are very few insurance companies who will do it.

Advising Insurance: Sometimes, in a letter of credit or order the receiver will ask that you advise his insurance company of the details of insurance so that coverage can be arranged under his existing policy. The format for this is very simple. You airmail or wire (if it is requested in that form) the following information and the receiver's policy number if you have it:

1. name of carrying vessel
2. port of loading
3. port of discharge
4. description of the goods
5. sailing date
6. marks and numbers
7. receiver's name and address
8. value and show if that is a C & F or FOB value and the currency in which it is sold.

General Information: An insurance certificate is like a cheque and is not negotiable unless it is endorsed. Many times this very simple thing is forgotten and causes delays.

Be very careful that the line does not stow your cargo on deck. This would be stated on the bill of lading. If so, advise your insurance company so that additional coverage can be provided. Then light into the carrier because in the case of a letter of credit they clearly ask for "on board" bills which means under deck. Some lines stow cargo on deck and cover the additional insurance without advising you. This is not good because the elements do damage and you also run the risk of it having to be jettisoned.

Air Freight Insurance

As you will gather, the documentation for airfreight is simpler in many ways than ocean. This is because there is not the time to get into the nitty gritty. Instead of weeks or days we are looking at hours. When we reach the documentation section you will see that the airway bill in fact doubles as the insurance certificate. Damage of part of the total aircraft load is rare. It's all or nothing if a plane is up or down at the speeds they are traveling. The airlines provide insurance rates that are very attractive and to the displeasure of many insurance agents, the rates are very hard to beat.

Packaging

The Seriousness of Packaging

Having just completed the insurance aspect, we must touch on it again in this subject. The shipper must find that thin line where he is protecting the cargo without having his packaging cost run out of proportion. In establishing a tolerable cost of packaging, many factors must be considered. The damage factor, the pilferage factor and the amount of handling the cargo must endure in transit. As pointed out in the insurance section, numerous claims cause insurance rates to rise and, taken on an annual basis, these costs can really add up.

We have discussed the use of experts in the field of packaging and, like many other specialized businesses, they are expensive. However, the shipper must realize that the ideas and packages developed by these people result in a savings for years, which automatically makes the cost per shipment less and less. It would be impossible to go over the numerous types of packaging available but I will try to outline to you better known examples of packaging solutions because the package is a solution.

Export Packing vs Normal Domestic Packing: When you add a package to a product, you add weight which adds freight. In export packing you have to be aware of some of the problems that can occur on export that would not occur on domestic. As Canadian exporters we have to be aware of climate or temperature changes. If you are shipping from Saint John, N.B. in February

POLICY OF INSURANCE   NO. 458126

ALBANY INSURANCE COMPANY

STOCK COMPANY   CHARTERED N. Y. 1811

W. J. ROBERTS & CO., INC., MANAGERS

59 JOHN STREET, NEW YORK, N. Y. 10038

$................................   ....19......

By THIS POLICY OF INSURANCE *in consideration of premium as agreed does make insurance and cause to be insured lost or not lost, for account of*

Marks and Numbers

SPECIMEN

at and from

to

in the sum of   Dollars

on   *Valued at sum insured.*

Shipped per   under deck

Loss, if any, payable to   or order,

upon the surrender of this Policy to W. J. Roberts & Co., Inc., or to the Company's nearest settling agent as per back hereof, and on the payment being made, liability under this insurance shall hereby be discharged.

This insurance attaches from the time the goods leaves the Warehouse and/or Store at the place named herein for the commencement of the transit and continues during the ordinary course of the transit, including customary transhipment if any, until the goods are discharged overside from the overseas vessel at the final port. Thereafter the insurance continues whilst the goods are in transit and/or awaiting transit until delivered to final warehouse at the destination named in the policy or until the expiry of 15 days (or 30 days if the destination to which the goods are insured is outside the limits of the port) whichever shall first occur. The time limits referred to above to be reckoned from midnight of the day on which the discharge overside of the goods hereby insured from the overseas vessel is completed. Held covered at a premium to be arranged in the event of transhipment, if any, other than as above and/or in the event of delay in excess of the above time limit arising from circumstances beyond the control of the Assured.

It is necessary for the Assured to give prompt notice to these Assurers when they become aware of an event for which they are "held covered" under this policy and the right to such cover is dependent on compliance with this obligation.

Where this insurance by its terms covers while on dock, wharves or elsewhere on shore, and/or during land transportation, it shall include the risks of collision, derailment, overturning or other accident to the conveyance, fire, lightning, sprinkler leakage, cyclones, hurricanes, earthquakes, floods (meaning the rising of navigable waters), and/or collapse or subsidence of docks or wharves, even though the insurance be otherwise F.P.A.

Touching the adventures and perils which said Assurers are contented to bear, and take upon themselves, in this voyage, they are of the seas, fires, jettisons, assailing thieves, barratry of the Master and Mariners, and all other like perils, losses and misfortunes that have or shall come to the hurt, detriment or damage of the said goods and merchandise, or any part thereof except as may be otherwise provided for herein or endorsed hereon.

Warranted free from claim for loss of market or for loss, damage or deterioration arising from delay, whether caused by a peril insured against or otherwise, unless expressly assumed in writing herein.

Notwithstanding anything herein contained to the contrary, this insurance is warranted free from capture, seizure, arrest, restraint, detainment, confiscation, preemption, requisition or nationalization, and the consequences thereof or any attempt thereat, whether in time of peace or war and whether lawful or otherwise; also warranted free, whether in time of peace or war, from all loss, damage or expense caused by any weapon of war employing atomic or nuclear fission and/or fusion or other reaction or radioactive force or matter or by any mine or torpedo, also warranted free from all consequences of hostilities or warlike operations (whether there be a declaration of war or not) but this warranty shall not exclude collision or contact with aircraft, rockets or similar missiles or with any fixed or floating object (other than a mine or torpedo), stranding, heavy weather, fire or explosion unless caused directly (and independently of the nature of the voyage or service which the vessel concerned or, in the case of a collision, any other vessel involved therein, is performing) by a hostile act by or against a belligerent power; and for the purpose of this warranty "power" includes any authority maintaining naval, military or air forces in association with a power.

Further warranted free from the consequences of civil war, revolution, rebellion, insurrection, or civil strife arising therefrom, or piracy.

Warranted free of loss or damage caused by or resulting from strikes, lockouts, labor disturbances, riots, civil commotions or the acts of any person or persons taking part in any such occurrence or disorder.

Labels Clause. In case of damage affecting labels, capsules or wrappers, these Assurers, if liable therefore under the terms of this policy, shall not be liable for more than an amount sufficient to pay the cost of new labels, capsules or wrappers, and the cost of reconditioning the goods, but in no event shall these Assurers be liable for more than the insured value of the damaged merchandise.

Time For Suit Clause. No suit or action on this policy or for the recovery of any claim hereunder shall be sustainable in any court of law or equity unless commenced within twelve (12) months next after the happening of the loss, provided that where such limitation of time is prohibited by the laws of the state wherein this Policy is issued, then and in that event no suit or action under this policy shall be sustainable unless commenced within the shortest limitation permitted under the laws of such state.

American Institute Clauses:

This insurance, in addition to the foregoing, is also subject to the following American Institute Cargo Clauses:

Craft, etc.	G. A. & Salv. Charges	Bill of Lading, etc.	Whag. & Fwdg. Charges	Sue & Labor Clause
Deviation	Explosion	Inchmaree	Carrier Clause	Both to Blame Clause
Amended F. C. & S. Warranty	Marine Extension Clauses	S. R. & C. C. Endorsement	Machinery Clause	Constructive Total Loss

SPECIAL CLAUSES

South American Clause   War Risk Insurance

While on Deck of ocean vessel under an on deck bill of lading (which must be noted hereon) are insured:
"Free of particular average unless caused by the stranding, sinking, burning or collision of the vessel, craft or lighter, but including jettison and washing overboard irrespective of percentage."

Except while on deck of ocean vessel under an on deck bill of lading: "Against all risks of physical loss or damage from any external cause irrespective of percentage, but excluding those risks excepted by the F.C. & S. and S.R. & C.C. Warranties, unless otherwise specifically noted hereon."

In Witness Whereof, *the undersigned on behalf of the said Company, has hereunto subscribed his name.*

This policy is not valid unless countersigned by

ALBANY INSURANCE COMPANY

Countersigned ....

273

SPECIMEN

NOTICE

In the event of loss or damage, report same immediately to, and arrange for a survey with the Company's Claim or Settling Agent, at the port of discharge or disaster. Should there be none at or near such port, consignee should apply to the nearest correspondent of the American Institute of Marine Underwriters, and if there be none, to the accredited representative of Lloyd's, London. THIS IS VERY IMPORTANT. Request such representative to hold a survey and issue a certificate stating the cause, nature and extent of the loss or damage, as well as the market value of the merchandise involved had it arrived in sound condition. When goods are discharged from a vessel or other conveyance in damaged condition, a claim must be filed in writing against the agents of the vessel owners or other carriers before removing goods from their custody. With respect to damage of a concealed nature claim should be filed against the carrier as soon as such damage is discovered. This will not prejudice the claim against your insurers, but neglect to do this may nullify your right to claims against them.

If claim presented abroad, exchange fixed by agreement at current rate on date of settlement. Option to the assured to collect claim (if any), under this Policy at the office of W. J. ROBERTS & CO., INC., in New York, or any agent named below, upon presentation of this Policy duly endorsed.

SETTLING AGENTS

ACCRA	**G. R. E. Assurance Group
ADELAIDE	**G. R. E. Assurance Group
ADDIS ABABA	The Arabian Trading Co. Ltd.
ALBERTA	Guardian Insurance Co., of Canada
ALEXANDRIA	Manley & Co.
ALKHOBAR	Aljabre Trading Co.
AMMAN	Anglo-Jordanian Ins. & Transport Agency Ltd.
AMSTERDAM	Langeveldt Schroder or Blom & van der Aa
ANTWERP	Gellatly Hankey & Co. (Belgium) Ltd.
ASMARA	The Arabian Trading Co. (Red Sea) S.A.
ATHENS	Insurance Offices Genka. Ltd.
AUCKLAND	**G. R. E. Assurance Group
BAHRAIN	Lloyd's Agents
BALTIMORE	†Toplis & Harding Inc.
BANDAR SHAHPUR	N. Nahai Bros.
BANGKOK	Guardian Assurance Co. Ltd.
BARBADOS	See Bridgetown
BARCELONA	**G. R. E. Assurance Group
BASRAH	The Busreh Slipway Company, W.L.L.
BEIRA	†Manica Trading Co. Ltd.
BELIZE	*The Belize Estate & Produce Co. Ltd.
BENGHAZI	Libyamar S.p.A.
BEYROUTH	Ets. P. Anghelopoulo S.A.L.
BILBAO	Messrs. Suc De J. Innes
BLANTYRE	†Manica Trading Co. Ltd.
BLOEMFONTEIN	Guardian Assurance Co. South Africa Ltd.
BOGOTA	Albingia Soc. Nac. de Seguros
BOSTON	†Toplis & Harding Inc.
BREMEN	Lampe & Schierenbeck
BRIDGETOWN	Gardiner Austin & Co. Ltd.
BRISBANE	**G. R. E. Assurance Group
BRITISH COLUMBIA	Oceanic Underwriters Ltd.
BRUNEI	Harrisons & Crosfield (Sabah)
BULAWAYO	**G. K. E. Assurance Group
CAPETOWN	**G. R. E. Assurance Group
CARACAS	Britanica de Seguros C.A.
CEBU	†Smith, Bell & Co. Inc.
CHICAGO	†Toplis & Harding Inc.
CHRISTCHURCH	**G. R. E. Assurance Group
CINCINNATI	†General Adjustment Bureau
COLOMBO	Delmege Forsyth & Co. Ltd.
COLUMBUS	†General Adjustment Bureau
COPENHAGEN	Firma Aug. Thune
CURACAO	Maduro & Curiels Bank N.V.
DAMMAM	Aljabre Trading Co.
DANZIG	†Polish Chamber of Foreign Trade
DAR ES SALAAM	General Agricultural Products Corporation (GAPEX)
DAVAO	†Ker & Co. Ltd.
DES MOINES	†General Adjustment Bureau
DETROIT	†Toplis & Harding Inc.
DJAKARTA	Union Insurance Society of Canton Ltd.
DUBAI	Gray Mackenzie & Co. Ltd.
DUISBURG	Peter Reschop
DUNEDIN	**G. R. E. Assurance Group
DURBAN	**G. R. E. Assurance Group
EAST LONDON	**G. R. E. Assurance Group
FREETOWN	Mining & General Services Ltd.
GDYNIA	†Polish Chamber of Foreign Trade
GENOA	Ditta Vittorio Pino
GIBRALTAR	*Smith Imossi & Co.
GLASGOW	**G. R. E. Assurance Group
GOTHENBURG	*Lindahl & Collin Ltd.
GRENADA	G.W.F. Franklin, O.B.E.
GUATEMALA CITY	G.W.F. Franklin, O.B.E.
GUAYAQUIL	Anglo-Equatoriana (Agencias) C. Ltda
HAGUE	N.V. Assurantiebedrijf
HAMBURG	Albingia Versicherungs A.G.
HAMILTON, Bermuda	Harnett & Richardson Ltd.
HAMILTON, Ontario	**G. R. E. Assurance Group
HAMILTON, N. Zealand	**G. R. E. Assurance Group

HAVANA	Seguros Leslie Pantin & Sons S.A.
HAVRE	Yves Chegaray
HELSINKI	O. Y. Lars Krogius A.B.
HOBART	**G. R. E. Assurance Group
HODEIDAH	Arabian Trading (Yemen)
HONG KONG	Union Insurance Society of Canton Ltd. or Butterfield & Swire (Hong Kong) Ltd.
HONOLULU	Hawiian Insurance & Guaranty Co. Ltd.
HOUSTON	†Toplis & Harding Inc.
ILOILO	†Smith Bell & Co. Inc.
ISTANBUL	†Tahsin Gok Ve Ortaklari
INVERCARGILL	**G. R. E. Assurance Group
JACKSONVILLE	†Toplis & Harding Inc.
JAKARTA	P. T. Maskapa; Asurans; Union Far East
JEDDAH	†The Arabian Establishment for Trade.
JOHANNESBURG	**G. R. E. Assurance Group
KABUL	Afghan Insurance Co. Ltd.
KARACHI	**G. R. E. Assurance Group
KEELUNG	Tait & Co. Ltd.
KHARTOUM	May Working People Corporation
KHORRAMSHAHR	N. Nahai Bros.
KINGSTON	R. S. Gamble & Son
KOBE	John Swire & Sons (Japan) Ltd.
KOPER	See Trieste
KOTA KINABALU	Harrisons & Crosfield (Sabah)
KUALA BELAIT	The Borneo Co. (Malaysia)
KUALA LUMPUR	**G. R. E. Assurance Group
KUCHING	The Borneo Co. (Malaysia)
KUWAIT	Abdulrahman Albisher & Zaid Alkazemi
LABUAN	Harrisons & Crosfield (Sabah)
LAE	**G. R. E. Assurance Group
LAGOS	Royal Exchange Assurance (Nigeria) Ltd.
LA GUAIRA	*Alexander Fox
LAUNCESTON	**G. R. E. Assurance Gorup
LIMA	H. M. Beausire & Co. S.A.
LIVERPOOL	**G. R. E. Assurance Group
LOBITO BAY	Hull Blyth (Angola) Ltd.
LONDON, England	**G. R. E. Assurance Group
LOS ANGELES	†Toplis & Harding
LOURENCO MARQUES	Rennies' Consolidated (L.M.) (Pty.) Ltd.
MACAO	*Firma F. Rodrigues (Suc. res) Ltda.
MADRID	Guardian Assurance Co. Ltd.
MAHE	Hunt Deltel & Co.
MALMO	Frick & Frick Ltd.
MALTA	See Valletta
MANCHESTER	**G. R. E. Assurance Group
MANNHEIM	Friedrich Hartmann Vorm J. Kerschgens
MANILA	Union Insurance Society of Canton Ltd.
MANITOBA	Guardian Insurance Co., of Canada
MARACAIBO	Frank B. Hill & Co. S.A.
MARSEILLES	Harrel-Courtes Assurances
MASSAWA	Gellatly Hankey & Co. (Ethiopia) S.C.
MAURITIUS	See Port Louis
MELBOURNE	**G. R. E. Assurance Group
MEDAN	†Harrison & Crosfield
MEXICO CITY	†Watson Phillips & Co. Sucrs. S.A.
MILAN	Allrisks, S.R.L.
MILWAUKEE	†General Adjustment Bureau
MIRI	The Borneo Co. (Malaysia)
MOLLENDO	Donnelly & Co. Ltd.
MOMBASA	G. F. Nasser
MONROVIA	Resident Representative—R. Woods
MONTEVIDEO	Soc. Anon Financiere Y Comercial
NAGOYA	John Swire & Sons (Japan) Ltd.
NAIROBI	**G. R. E. Assurance Group
NAPIER	**G. R. E. Assurance Group
NASSAU	R. H. Curry Ins. Agencies Ltd.
NEUCHATEL	Commissariat D'Avaries S.A.
NEW BRUNSWICK	Guardian Insurance Co., of Canada
NEWFOUNDLAND	Guardian Insurance Co., of Canada
NEW PLYMOUTH	**G. R. E. Assurance Group

NEW ORLEANS	†Toplis & Harding Inc.
NEW YORK	W. J. Roberts & Co. Inc.
NOUMEA	Les Establissements Ballande S.A.
NOVA SCOTIA	Guardian Insurance Co., of Canada
ONTARIO	Guardian Insurance Co., of Canada
OPORTO	Royal Exchange Assurance
OSAKA	John Swire & Sons (Japan) Ltd.
OSLO	Insair A/S
PARIS	Noel Chegaray
PEKING	People's Insurance Company of China
PENANG	Sandilands, Buttery & Co. Ltd.
PERTH	**G. R. E. Assurance Group
PIRAEUS	Miller, Ltd. E.P.E.
PORT ELIZABETH	**G. R. E. Assurance Group
PORT LOUIS	Ireland Blyth, Ltd.
PORT MORESBY	**G. R. E. Assurance Group
PORT OF SPAIN	Alstons Marketing Co. Ltd.
PORT SAID	El Menia Shipping Agency
PORT SUDAN	May Working People Corporation
PORT VILLA	Les Comptoirs Francais
PUERTO RICO	See San Juan
PUSAN	Hyopsung Shipping Corporation
QUEBEC	Guardian Insurance Co., of Canada
RABAUL	**G. R. E. Assurance Group
REUNION	*Mancini & Cie
RIJEKA	Edgar H. Greenham & Co. Ltd.
RIO de JANEIRO	**G. R. E. Assurance Group
RIYADH	Aljabre Trading Company
ROSARIO	S. A. Mar Com e Indus y de Rep
ROSEAU	Da Costa & Musson Ltd.
ROTTERDAM	Blom & Van der Aa
SAIGON	*Denis Freres S.A.
SASKATCHEWAN	Guardian Insurance Co., of Canada
ST. GEORGES	W. E. Julien & Co. Ltd.
ST. JOHN'S	John Francis Anjo
ST. KITTS	Delisle Walwyn & Co. Ltd.
ST. LOUIS	†General Adjustment Bureau
ST. VINCENT	Hazells, Ltd.
SALISBURY	**G. R. E. Assurance Group
SANDAKAN	Harrisons & Crosfield
SAN FRANCISCO	Deans & Homer
SAN JUAN	Alvaro R. Calderon Inc.
SAN SALVADOR	F. D. Gibson & Co.
SANTIAGO	*Sociedad Comercial Cominsa Limitada
SANTO DOMINGO	Kettle, Sanchez & Co. C. por A.
SANTOS	Norton, Megaw, Hampshire & Co. Ltd.
SAO PAULO	**G. R. E. Assurance Group
SEATTLE	Albany Insurance Company
SEYCHELLES IS	See Mahe
SIBU	The Borneo Co. (Malaysia)
SINGAPORE	**G. R. E. Assurance Group
SLIEMA	Walter Camilieri Successors, Ltd.
STOCKHOLM	Emil R. Boman A/B
SUEZ	†El Menia Shipping Agency
SUVA	**G. R. E. Assurance Group
SYDNEY	**G. R. E. Assurance Group
TAIPEI	Tait & Co.
TAMATAVE	Paul & Roger Duponsel & Co.
TAMPA	†Toplis & Harding Inc.
TANGIER	A. Mortarotti
TAWAU	Harrisons & Crosfield (Sabah)
TEHERAN	N. Nahai Bros.
TENERIFFE	Hamilton & Co.
TOKYO	John Swire & Sons (Japan) Ltd.
TRIESTE	Edgar H. Greenham & Co.
TRIPOLI	Libyamar S.p.A.
VALENCIA	Guardian Assurance Company Limited
VALLETTA	Alfred Formosa & Sons Ltd.
VALPARAISO	*Sociedad Comercial Cominsa Ltda.
WELLINGTON	**G. R. E. Assurance Group
YOKOHAMA	John Swire & Sons (Japan) Ltd.
ZANZIBAR	Zanzibar Wharfage & Co. Ltd.

* Agents for payment of claims only.

** Guardian Royal Exchange Assurance Group

† Surveyor only

NOTICE

In the event of loss or damage on any shipment to the following Countries:

India

Bangladesh

Zambia   Lloyds agent at NDOLA

report same immediately to and arrange for a survey with either Lloyds Agent or ILU agent at the port of discharge or disaster.

8/79

to South Africa, you will go through many temperature changes and sweating of the cargo could develop. This would cause labels to come undone or condensation to build up within the cargo itself. Expansion and contraction can develop again from the temperature changes. In North America, most firms have equipment that can handle most types of packaging, but, when shipping to other areas of the world, the ports may not have the proper equipment to handle the goods in a safe manner.

Further, in this line of thinking you must consider the receiver's capabilities. Has he a rail siding, can he accept truck deliveries, is the cargo going to be stored indoors or out, has he the proper type of lift trucks or is he relying on an overhead crane, for example. Many times the receiver will indicate in the letter of credit, order or import license the type of packing, for example, 50 kilo bags or 45 gallon drums. Many times he may be indicating by this move, his handling ability at dockside or plant.

Pilferage: On the waterfront, pilferage is an art. When you package, be aware of it and make allowance for it. If you are shipping ball point pens or any other article easily sold black market, try to avoid putting a description on what the goods are on the outside of the package. People shipping these types of articles have gone to colour coding and other masking type of description. Aside from damage, it is safe to say pilferage comes a very close second in insurance claims. Don't be lured into thinking "Aw, they won't pinch that, what good is it to them?" These men are professionals. While working in Montreal, I saw two truckloads of wet salted cattlehides disappear on a Sunday. When I say two truck loads, I mean they came on the pier with a lift truck and two trucks and carted them off. It is obvious they had a pre-arranged sale made as this is not the commodity you would want to hide in your cellar or garage. I tell this little story as I think it underlines just how far these people will go. If you are shipping a machine, remove and crate any piece that could be removed. Ports around the world spend millions as do the terminal operators, but this problem is far from being beat so be aware of it and pack accordingly.

Labeling and Tagging: If you are shipping canned goods or bottled goods, it is a good idea to arrange to have the labeling done at destination if possible. The sweating feature I mentioned is one reason but language is another. The cost of printing these types of labels can sometimes be a lot cheaper at destination and, you have the language problem beat. The outer markings of the crates or boxes should be complete without becoming a half hour's reading. The receiver's address should be complete and large enough to be readable. The gross and net weights should appear, along with the length, width and height. This aids the many people who may have to handle the goods enroute. In the case of dangerous cargos, regulations are set out internationally which are coloured labels with designs on them showing what the cargo will do. For example, goods that explode will show a firecracker with a wick exploding or a picture of flame is shown on flamable cargo. These labels are evidence to those people who cannot read what the dangerous cargo will do if not given special handling. As you can see, these labels are taking much the same form international road signs take now. When tagging cargo, waterproof inks must be used and the tags must be affixed with wire or very strong cord.

The Pallet or Unit Load: With rising labour costs, shippers have always to be looking at ways to avoid any handling that uses manpower instead of machine power. The pallet you decide on should have four-way entry. This benefits you in your warehousing in that you do not need to leave space to get at the cargo and it facilitates faster handling in transit. When shipping export you must remember that while you may not stack palletized goods, the carriers in transit may. Know it and provide for it in your package.

When shipping bagged commodities, triotex bags are very popular because they are made of laminated plastic sheets that have a ribbed texture to them which is designed to keep bags from slipping off one another when stacked on a pallet. The asbestos people have gone with a pressure packed bag; it squares the bag off making the cubic lower and handling easier. Also, you use less bags with a much better stow. When buying pallets, have more than one supplier as they are very hard to come by in peak shipping periods.

Heavy Machinery Packing Problems: A problem that has come up with heavy machinery moving by rail has been when the railways hump cars. As you have no doubt seen when the car starts its decline on the hump, grabbers slow it down. That is providing all grabbers are operating all the way down the hump. If everything works the car should be moving at about 3-4 mph but sometimes, particularly in winter, they slip and can hit at 7-10 mph. The result is obvious. The goods shift on impact and damage can result. If you insist, when making shipment, that the cars are not to be humped, the rails will oblige but it may take a little longer to get to destination.

In an effort to reduce the cubic size of the units, shippers do some dismantling. You must be sure that facilities exist at destination to reassemble. It is wise when designing large machinery to engineer lifting hooks or eyes on the machine itself. This eliminates poor handling by stevedores.

The subject of nesting comes up but it is limited to products that can be nested within one another without damage. If you use metal strapping, you must be careful that the guage of strap is correct for your product. We see many cases of metal strap chaffing and cutting packages. Another area in metal strapping is when people use it to strap piles of cans or small drums to pallets. If too heavy a strap is used it may cause the cans to collapse under pressure or actually nest down into another.

In Australia, they have rules that say only kiln dried wood can be used in packaging. The reason we are told is that the types of insects that inhabit wood multiply at an alarming rate in their climate. They actually burn wood on the dock that shows any signs of infestation.

The Container's Effect on Packaging: The shipping business did not change much from sailing ships to motor ships but containers have had a resounding effect on shipping, particularly in the area of packaging. About five years ago we had seven lines servicing the U.K. and continent with breakbulk vessels. Today we only have two main lines. There are a few others but I am staying with regular liner services. Now, most available services to these areas are containers vessels.

The most common error is when a shipper thinks of a container as 8 ft. x 8 ft. x 20 ft. Those are the outside dimensions. The inside dimensions vary slightly but a good rule of thumb would be 7'6" x 7'6" x 19'6". It is not safe to say that a forty foot can hold twice as much weight as a twenty because of road load limitations in various countries. Most people look at 40,000 lbs. in a twenty.

but when using forties the weight allowable is ruled by the road limitations of the countries of reception. Packaging can be somewhat reduced with the use of containers since it is better protected and there is less handling but avoid reducing it too much as this will result in claims. We have seen people revert to straight domestic pack and the results have been heavy damage. Securing inside the container is of prime importance since the container could move on many modes of transport en route. Exporters must stay abreast of all new developments in the container field as many types of containers serve many commodities.

The inner securing rails or hooks are not always the same in every container. Properly equipped, the securing devices can save you a lot of dunnage and blocking. The steamship lines will send representatives to your plant to show you proper stowage and it is well to take advantage of this advice because it serves you for years. If you have a liquid commodity it sometimes is worth your while to own your own containers, but this is a very expensive way of shipping unless you get full utilization of the equipment. This is not unlike owning tank cars in rail. Rental of standard type containers is popular but only for very specific commodities moving on regular trade routes on a steady basis. Rental fees are per day and since you do not control the movements of the carriers you leave yourself wide open to expensive delays. In an effort to get maximum utilization of equipment, lines are starting to insist that a shipper use a maximum amount of the container or they are charged a minimum per container. This in the long run helps all exporters as maximum use is being employed. Your facilities may mean that it is easier for you to use an open top container which can be loaded by an overhead crane. This is fine but can your receiver discharge at destination? The containers like rail cars are subject to demurrage. While the liners do not adhere to the time limits as close as rail demurrage right now, there is a strong move in that direction. Lift trucks and other lifting devices must have dimensions that allow them to enter and more important manipulate within the container.

You may feel I have spent a lot of time on this matter but we are in the container boom right now and you must educate yourselves to the problems. Too often people think of the container as the end all but no matter how you look at it, it is only a box.

<u>Airline Packaging</u>: When shipping by air the object is to keep the weight and cubic to a minimum because of the very high rates. I.A.T.A., the International body governing air shipments, have I.A.T.A. pallets which are lighter than the standard pallet. These pallets come with a cardboard sleeve that fits over the cargo and can be stapled to the pallet. These are used for people who consolidate but you as an independent shipper can purchase them for a shipment. The need for extensive packaging is not the same as ocean because airlines have the most up to date handling methods simply because they are such a new mode of transport compared to ocean.

Cargo is placed into an aircraft container which has many names but the most popular is an igloo. The igloo is shaped to fit into the aircraft with hardly any loss of cubic. These igloos provide the airline with the favourable ability to pre-stow their cargo in advance. The actual loading of the craft is the easiest. The igloos are standard size meaning they can be handled mechanically at basically any airport in the world.

<u>Shipping</u>

<u>Introduction</u>: I have spent time discussing containers in the proceeding section and packaging, but they could fit in this section as well. I hope by now you are starting to see how close all our subjects are related.

<u>How to Choose the Carrier</u>: In reaching a decision on what route is best for your goods, many things must enter into the picture. The following is a check list of which all or some will apply depending on the move.

1. Do the loading and sailing dates coincide with your planned production?

2. What is the regularity of sailing dates offered by the line being considered and what has their past performance been like?

3. If you are a member of a freight conference, are they a conference carrier?

4. What are the ETA's (estimated times of arrival) of the vessels? The first to sail is not always the first to arrive due to rotation of discharge ports.

5. Is the line exact and speedy in returning documents to you or will you have to tie up your money waiting for ocean bills?

6. What type of vessel do they employ, has it heavy lift capabilities, oversized tween decks, is it a cellular or breakbulk vessel, what is their availability of containers?

7. Is the service a direct service or is it an extention of a service that could cause delays?

8. How financially stable is the carrier? This is most important when planning long term quotations or arrangments.

9. How are they at settling claims?

10. Is the service a direct service or will the cargo be transhipped, meaning many handlings and possible damage?

11. What are their terminal or dock facilities like?

12. What is their main line of endeavour? Are they in business to carry some long term charter cargos which may mean they would give your cargo second class attention.

13. What is the labour situation at the ports they use to load?

14. Has the receiver in his letter of credit or order insisted on a flag carrier?

15. Do import licences insist on any particular line?

16. How old are the vessels? Vessels past a certain age means they are not the right class and insurance rates are higher.

17. What type of back up service does the line have over his competitors in case you fail to connect with one vessel or they leave your cargo behind?

18. Does the line show or has it ever shown any favouring of other ports of countries at the same time forsaking the Canadian cargo?

19. What currency do they quote their rates in? It seems small but on large volume shipments it can add up.

20. Does the line have feeder services to other areas at their main ports of discharge or must they hand cargo over to other carriers?

21. Is direct always the cheapest route? We have a case where we truck cargo to Miami and it goes on a ship to Panama with a savings of about 40% against the Montreal/Panama ocean rate.

22. Does the line have RO/RO vessels? This is very important on wheeled vehicles. You can save on heavy lift charges since the units are towed on and off the vessel instead of the line having to hire shore cranes, the cost of which reflects in your freight bill.

23. Does the letter of credit allow transhipment or part shipment - does it have an expiry date dangerously close to the sailing date?

These factors and more will go into your choosing of a carrier.

Conference vs Non Conference: To start I think it important to explain what a freight conference is and what they try to achieve. In very general terms they are a group of lines servicing the same area who establish the rates and rules to be applied. They ask exporters to contract with them as members of the conference. By doing so the shipper agrees to ship all his cargo to that area by a conference carrier and the lines agree to provide regular sailings to that area. I have in the foregoing given you a very general description of conference carriers.

Non Conference carriers, on the other hand, offer rates slightly less than the conference rates (about 10%) but they are bound to nothing. They can move their ships on any trade route and have been known to jack rates up during peak periods. Please understand the non conference carrier plays a very important role. They can and will lower rates in some cases. They tend to keep the conference honest in their rate making talks. In a way the conference is a cartel. A tolerated cartel with a sense of responsibility but nevertheless still a cartel. The conference have rules as to how rates are to be assessed. They can penalize you for misdeclaring goods and can even charge you dead freight if they can prove it. Dead freight is if you have 2,000 tons of cargo booked and shortly before the vessel was to sail you cancelled it, you could be charged dead freight which means you would pay the freight even though you did not use the space. This is rarely assessed as the lines must prove that they turned down other cargo to protect the space for you, but there are cases on record where they have charged it and won their case in court. If you find yourself in a position where you have a chance of obtaining good regular export orders but the freight rate is just too high, you can appeal to the conference who can take your volume into consideration and possibly bring the rate into a more realistic category. You can apply for and get project rates for specific movements. In this area, again, you must prove that unless the rate is modified there will be no sale. Conference lines usually check the export B-13 declaration description against the description shown on the bill of lading to avoid misrepresentation in an effort to get a lower rate. With money being as tight as it is, the member lines in some conferences have credit agreements whereby you or your forwarder must pay the freight within a certain time or your firm is put on a blacklist that is circulated among the conference lines. Armed with this they can refuse to release your ocean bills of lading until you pay the freight on the last shipment, even if the last shipment moved with one of the other lines.

Inland Shipping: Truck and rail are two main services employed but on bulk commodities inland water transportation can be used. When dealing with railways you must be aware of the rules. You must know the connections, location of loading points and delivery stations. Piggy back is very popular now as well. Containers again show their power in the type of equipment the railways are building now. Many years ago the railways had only a few types of cars like the box car, the open gondola car and tank cars. They then went through a stage of developing specialized cars. Since container has bolted on the scene, they are working at break neck speeds to acquire flat bed cars that can handle containers. They feel that the container will one day be completely intermodal and that nearly all cargo, domestic as well as export, will move in this method. The truckers are doing the same. They too have switched and are concentrating on equipment geared towards the container.

Demurrage is a key factor in inland. The idea is to penalize people who hold up equipment. They feel if they do so there will be more equipment available to everyone. It is evident that they do not make any real money on demurrage, it is more a deterrent to people using their equipment as a storage area. Their rates are fairly standard and sell service above all. They are licenced to various towns and cities and, while they may take cargo to New York for example, they end up having to transfer it to another carrier enroute. Owning your own fleet of trucks again is very expensive and it relies on volume and specific problems to make it worthwhile. Water transportation in Canada is a good bargain but you do not get the quick transit time. With our weather the service is seasonal. There has been talk of developing a way to keep the St. Lawrence Seaway open year round but because of the move by ocean vessels to east coast ports and the decline in overseas carriers that service the lakes, there may not be enough interest left. The day of the ship coming to the cargo is over; now it's bring the cargo to the ship. Again our friends the container and rising costs caused this swing.

Truck vs Rail: Canadian rails are subsidized which is much different than in most countries. Because of this rather unique situation we have a very uncomplicated rail system. Truck lines on the other hand are only licenced to specific areas meaning you have to be dealing with many more people. Trucks are much more susceptible to weather than rails and in Canada that has to be considered. The rates are comparable but it is important to examine the advantages of both. You may encounter multiple handlings with truck that may not occur with rail. All factors should be examined before a decision is reached.

Shipping by Air: It is a common misconception that air is too expensive. True, rates are infinitely higher but when using air what are your reasons? I will give a few examples that I have experienced.

Conditions sometimes indicate air and the cost versus other costs amount to next to nothing. We have seen a large electrical control company we represent where they have air freighted large pieces of electrical apparatus to an overseas customer. Many times when an intricate piece of electrical equipment is purchased a service guarantee or service contract is included. The penalties built in to the contract are high because with the right stock control the problem should never arise. But they do. When you consider what penalties you are faced with together with the cost of the plant or machine being down for weeks, the cost of air freight is peanuts. Laboratory equipment and instrumentation of all sorts are certainly worth the extra. It's like buying a $8,000 automobile and not including a $75 radio.

There are commodities that lend themselves to air, like fresh flowers. KLM do a big business in tulips and tulip bulbs.

Livestock is a big commodity now for airlines. It just makes sense to air freight instead of ocean where you take a risk of less. A cow can endure a 6 hour flight but a 7 day voyage is different.

When air freighting you are wise to look for the airline with the direct flight. Transferring at airports is well done and quick but it still is an extra handling.

Documentation

Introduction: There is no possible way to make this subject glamorous. All I can do is point out the importance of the documents to the export move. Let us assume the engineer has developed a fine product, the sales people have gone out and obtained the order, the credit people have done their work and the production or shipping department have shipped it. All that remains is to prepare the paperwork. All the hard work done by the aforementioned people can go straight down the drain if the documents are made wrong. To countries like Peru there are fines levied of up to 40% of the F.O.B. value for improper documentation. In Venezuela customs people are paid a commission on the fines they apply so they are checking very close. Again, no glamour but all important. There is very often confusion as to title of the goods, for example, F.O.B. plant, C & F, CIF, etc. On page 79 is a graphic example which we feel should have these terms easier to understand.

In this section, we will take the matter from after the order has been accepted, the letter of credit has been received and the

284

import licence has been obtained by the receiver. We have chosen Brazil. Because Brazil is one country that asks that insurance be placed in their country, we have a C & F sale. At the end of this article are included one copy of each of the documents required.

Steps to Follow When Preparing the Documentation:

1. We need the order to ascertain the prices, terms of sale and exact description of the goods, reference numbers, customer's delivery instructions.
2. The import licence from which we will extract information in Portuguese that is required on the bills of lading and commercial invoices.

3. The letter of credit provides us with the description, (which is usually the same as the import licence description), the terms, the shipping route (for example, Canadian or U.S. port to Santos, Brazil.)

The Ocean Bill of Lading: Each line has its own printed form but they all have much the same format. As you can see it is almost like filling in a questionnaire. We direct your attention to the letter of credit description which is inserted under the description of the goods. This must show. To Brazil it is a rule that you must show the import licence number, date of issue, place of issue, validity date and tariff number that the goods are covered by. As you will see, all this information is available on the credit or import licence, it is just a matter of picking it out.

You will also note we have shown "loaded on board" because most bills of lading are considered received for shipment unless there is the on board notation. If you have a situation where you did not need an on board bill - let us say you were exporting to a parent company abroad - you can demand and get a bill of lading before the vessel sails, that is to say as soon as the steamship line accepts delivery of the goods. If you need an on board bill you have to wait until the vessel sails to get your bill. There is another clause on this bill that is applicable for Brazil and that is the "not an endorsement - signed for customs purposes only" section. Also to Brazil you must indicate the freight payable both in figures and in words. These are rules that apply to Brazil. We have picked this country as it is one of the countries with many regulations.

SELECTED TRADE TERMS

Note: This diagram gives an approximate idea only of the meaning of the selected trade terms.

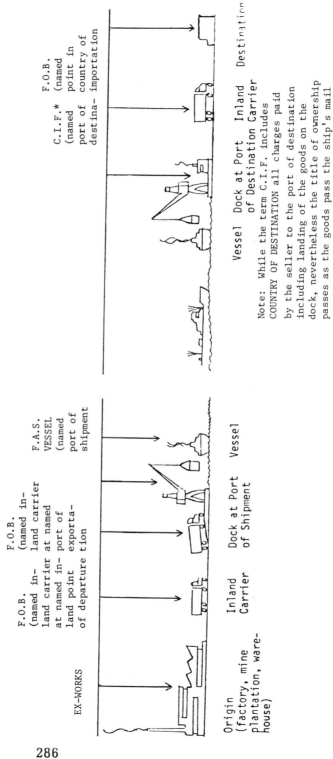

Note: While the term C.I.F. includes COUNTRY OF DESTINATION all charges paid by the seller to the port of destination including landing of the goods on the dock, nevertheless the title of ownership passes as the goods pass the ship's mail at the port of shipment.

Having prepared this bill of lading on a spirit master, you would lodge it with the steamship line who, after loading of the cargo and sailing of the vessel, would return to you three signed originals and five nonnegotiable copies signed and other copies nonnegotiable. The reason for three originals signed goes back to the days of sailing ships when they were not sure if the carrying vessel would actually make it to destination so they put one on the carrying vessel, one on another vessel consigned to the receiver and, one was retained at point of shipment in case both vessels went down. Once one of the three originals has been endorsed and surrendered to the steamship line, the other two are deemed null and void. The five signed copies of the bill is a rule just for Brazil. It goes back to about five years ago when we had to have documents legalized by the Brazilian consuls. The consuls no longer legalize the papers but the customs and import control people still require them so when you get them make sure they are sent to Brazil with all other papers. The steamship line assigns the bill of lading number and dates it. So as not to confuse you, bills of lading to other areas are not as complex. Usually they are acceptable in English and customers usually indicate any special notations required.

The Export Invoice: A big mistake made by exporters is to try to use their domestic invoice as an export invoice. This should be avoided. There are some cases where the two are interchangeable but not many. Avoid making the invoice into a story book. Use it to collect money, do not use it as a stock control feature or anything else. It's fine to have references indicated but watch that you are not getting into multiple references.

To construct the export invoice in this case you need the letter of credit, the licence and a copy of the bill from which you get the ocean freight. You will note on the commercial invoice we have shown the complete import licence description, date of issue of the licence, the licence number, the place of issue, the validity, the tariff item, the country of origin, the country of shipment, the port of loading, the port of discharge, the manufacturer, and exporter, the vessel and its flag. All this is in Portuguese and is required for Brazil. We break the price down by showing the F.O.B., freight and C & F prices. The freight shown on the ocean bill must agree with that shown on the invoice. The invoice should be signed as well.

The Certificate of Origin: You will note again we have shown the
licence description, the licence details and we have had it stamped
by the Toronto Board of Trade. The credit asks that the documents be stamped by the Chamber of Commerce but the Board of
Trade will suffice. Documentation requirements vary by country.
Advice is available from the Department of Industry, Trade and
Commerce and The Canadian Manufacturers' Association, to mention
a few, and it is well that you look into the documentation procedures to avoid heavy fines. Some countries charge consular fees.
The one we just covered did not but Argentina, for example,
charges $1^1/2$ of the selling price.

Consular blanks are obtained from the various consuls and are
usually charged for per set. It is in this area that many firms
revert to a forwarder. It is difficult for firms to maintain trained
people, particularly those trained to know documentation to all
parts of the world. Mistakes can be very expensive so the fee
charged by the freight forwarder is a very minimal expense.

Airway Bills: The airway bill is quite straight forward. It
doubles as a certificate of insurance if insurance is required. It
is a through document that covers the goods from origin to destination. Shippers can advance such charges as inland freight or
forwarder's fees and the airline will collect these at destination.
You will note we include here an airway bill that is charged on a
weight different than the actual gross weight. What this means is
the cargo is moving volume metric. The steamship lines charge on
volume when they charge per 40 cubic feet. The airlines are doing
much the same because if you multiply the measurements out and
divide by 194 you establish the volume metric weight.

The Packing List: The document is usually prepared by the plant
or mill. It shows the weights net and gross, marks and numbers
and product codes.

The Export B-13: All shipments being exported require an export
B-13 form. Like many other forms it is a matter of answering the
questions and filling in the slots. Failure to provide customs with
a B-13 would result in a fine of $400. Usually this document goes
with the goods to the terminal, airport or dock. We draw your
attention to the section "subject to drawback". If the goods in
whole or in part originated in the U.S.A., for example, you may

have paid duty on them crossing the border, in which case if you export them out of Canada you are entitled to a drawback of these duties.

The Draft or Bill of Exchange: We think of a draft like a cheque. When honoured you receive payments. Drafts should be endorsed and the terms should be indicated. On your draft you should make reference to the letter of credit as we have done on the bottom of the order acknowledgement on the next page.

stelco

The Steel Company
of Canada Limited

General Office
Hamilton, Ontario
L8N 3T1
(416) 528-2511

ORDER ACKNOWLEDGEMENT

JUNE 5,1974

TO: A.B.C. TINPLATE CO. DO BRASIL S.A.
SAO PAULO,BRASIL

RE: YOUR ORDER NO. N-1230
OUR ORDER NO. 1234

DEAR SIRS:

WE ACKNOWLEDGE WITH THANKS YOUR ABOVE REFERRED TO ORDER AND ARE PLEASED TO CONFIRM THIS ORDER AS FOLLOWS:

ITEM 1)   APPROX. 110,000 KILOS
833mm X 587mm X 0,22mm
CANADIAN MADE ELECTROLYTIC TINPLATE, U/A,BRIGHT FINISH,EXPORT WRAPPED IN PACKAGES OF 100 SHEETS

PRICES: $647.10 PER 1000 KILOS U.S. FUNDS,F.O.B. PORT OF SHIPMENT,TO BE SHIPPED TO SANTOS,BRASIL.

DELIVERY: EX. MILL HAMILTON,CANADA, END SEPTEMBER EARLY OCTOBER 1974

OCEAN
FREIGHT &
SURCHARGES:PREVAILING AT TIME OF SHIPMENT WILL BE PREPAID AND ADDED ON THE FACE OF THE COMMERCIAL INVOICE AT COST AS PER BILL OF LADING

TERMS: LETTER OF CREDIT SHIPMENT AT 60 DAYS FROM DATE OF BILL OF LADING

YOURS SINCERELY
THE STEEL COMPANY OF CANADA LIMITED.

PER: *J. Smith*
        J. SMITH.

290

Netumar International Inc.
NY BROADWAY—STE A
NEW YORK, N.Y. 10004
TEL. (212) 344-4920

COMPANHIA de NAVEGAÇÃO MARITIMA NETUMAR
Headquarters: Rua Guilherme Moreira, 194, Manaus—Amazonas—Brazil
Rio de Janeiro Offices: Ave. Presidente Vargas, 482, Rio de Janeiro—Brazil
(SPACES IMMEDIATELY BELOW FOR SHIPPERS MEMORANDA—NOT PART OF BILL OF LADING)

SAGUENAY SHIPPING LTD.
GENERAL AGENTS CANADA
1060 UNIVERSITY STREET
MONTREAL, CANADA H3B 3A3

DELIVERING CARRIER TO STEAMER: **TRUCK**
CAR NUMBER—REFERENCE

FORWARDING AGENT - REFERENCES
EXPORT DEC. NO.

MINSHALL FORWARDING LIMITED, 66 YONGE STREET, TORONTO, ONTARIO

BILL OF LADING (Continued From Reverse Side)

SHIPPER
THE STEEL COMPANY OF CANADA LIMITED, HAMILTON, ONTARIO, CANADA

CONSIGNED TO
~~NOTIFY~~ **A.B.C. TINPLATE CO. DO BRASIL S.A., SAO PAULO, BRASIL**

ADDRESS ARRIVAL NOTICE TO / ALSO NOTIFY
A.B.C. TINPLATE CO. DO BRASIL S.A.
SAO PAULO, BRASIL

(Without Liability To Carrier See Clause 17)

VESSEL	FLAG	PIER	PORT OF LOADING
A VEGA	**BRASILIAN FLAG**		**HAMILTON**

FOR PORT OF DISCHARGE (Where goods are to be delivered to consignee or on carrier) / FOR TRANSSHIPMENT TO (If goods are to be transshipped or forwarded at port of discharge)
SANTOS, BRASIL

PARTICULARS FURNISHED BY SHIPPER OF GOODS

MARKS AND NUMBERS	NO. OF PKGS.	DESCRIPTION OF PACKAGES AND GOODS	GROSS WEIGHT IN KILOS	GROSS WEIGHT POUNDS
A.B.C. TINPLATE N 4310 SAO PAULO VIA SANTOS 802/1-81	81	BUNDLES ELECTROLYTIC TINPLATE (FOLHAS DE FLANDRES ELECTROLITICA) "FREIGHT PREPAID" "LOADED ON BOARD" DATE: OCTOBER 1, 1974. PER: _____ GUIA DE IMPORTACAO: 18-74/071902	111,010	244,733
NOT AN ENDORSEMENT SIGNED FOR BRASILIAN CUSTOM PURPOSES ONLY: THE STEEL COMPANY OF CANADA LIMITED PER:		DATE DA EMISSAO: 7 JUN 74 PRACA DA EMISSAO: SAO PAULO (SP) VALID PARA EMBARQUE ATE: 4 DEZ 74 ITEM DA TARIFA: 73.13.04.99 STEAMSHIP CONTRACT NO: TN 15-15		

The Brazilian Merchant Marine Renewal Tax on freights and charges excluding taxes, as stipulated in Brazil Law No. 790 effective August 27, 1969 shall be collected in Brazil from consignee.

Fast - Regular Service

between

U. S. Atlantic - U. S. Great Lakes

Canadian Ports

and

Brazil, Uruguay, Paraguay

and Argentina

FREIGHT RATES AND CHARGES		*PREPAID	COLLECT
244,733 Lbs. @ 60.00 2240 Lbs.	$	6,555. 35	$
BUNKER S.C. @ 15.00 "		1,638. 84	
" @ "		$8,194.19	
Cu. Ft. @ 40 Cu. Ft.		U.S. FUNDS	
" @ "			
(EIGHT THOUSAND ONE HUNDRED AND NINETY FOUR DOLLARS AND NINETEEN CENTS U.S. FUNDS)			
SURCHARGE			
Consulate Bill of Lading Fee Payable at Port of Discharge			
TOTAL		$	$

Voy. No. 1-GB

DATED AT MONTREAL

B/L No.	Month	Day	Year
15	OCT.	1	74

In Witness Whereof, the Master, his representative has signed 3 Bills of Lading (exclusive of copies) all of the same tenor and date, one of which being accomplished the others shall be void.

FOR AND ON BEHALF OF THE MASTER
By Saguenay Shipping Limited, as Agent for the Master

CERTIFICATE OF ORIGIN

The undersigned M.S. PHILIP, AGENT FOR ....
(Owner or Agent, or &c.)

for THE STEEL COMPANY OF CANADA LIMITED, HAMILTON, ONTARIO, CANADA .... declares
(Name and Address of Shipper)

that the following mentioned goods shipped OCTOBER 1, 1974 .... on S/S A VESSEL
(Date) (Name of Ship)

under Invoice No 9-12 .... dated .... OCTOBER 1, 1974 ....

consigned to A.B.C. TINPLATE CO. DO BRASIL S.A., SAO PAULO, BRASIL

.... are the product of the DOMINION OF CANADA ....

NUMBER OF PACKAGES BOXES OR CASES	MARKS AND NUMBERS	WEIGHT IN KILOS GROSS	NET	DESCRIPTION
81 BUNDLES	A.B.C. TINPLATE N 4310 SAO PAULO VIA SANTOS 802/1-81	111,010 244,733#	109,633 241,696#	FOLHAS DE FLANDRES, ELETROLITICAS, QUALIDADE U/A ACABAMENTO BRILHANTE, TEMPERA 2, TIPO "D", ESTANHAGEM 0.75 LIBRAS (ALUMINUM KILLED - DUREZA PERMANETE) EMBALAGEM: CAIXAS CON 100 FOLHAS CADA, EM FARDOS PESANDO APROXIMA-DAMENTE 1.200 QUILOS LIQUIDOS. MEDIDAS: 833 MM X 587 X 0,22 MM ELECTROLYTIC TINPLATE U/A WATERPROOF PAPER AND METAL WRAPPED .75# COATING T2 Al KILL 22 MM 833 MM X 587 MM (79# BW 32-13/16 X 23-1/8) GUIA DE IMPORTACAO: 18-74/071902 ITEM DA TARIFA: 73.13.04.99 DATA DA EMISSAO: 7 JUN 74 VALIDA PARA EMBARQUE ATE: 4 DEX 74

Dated at TORONTO, CANADA .... on the 1st .... day of OCTOBER 19 74

Sworn to before me

this 1st day of OCTOBER 74 Notary Public, Judicial District of York
for MINSHALL FORWARDING LIMITED.
My Commission expires Feb. 8th, 1975.
(Signature of Owner or Agent)

The TORONTO BOARD OF TRADE, II ADELAIDE STREET WEST, TORONTO, ONTARIO, CANADA .... has
(Name and Address of Authorized Trade Organization)

examined the manufacturer's invoice or shipper's affidavit concerning the origin of the merchandise, and, according to the best of its knowledge and belief, finds that the products named originated in CANADA ....

(Signature)
THE BOARD OF TRADE OF METROPOLITAN TORONTO

292

IRREVOCABLE COMMERCIAL LETTER OF CREDIT

FORM 1018 12-641
PRINTED IN CANADA

No. 54321

BANCO DO BRASIL S.A. SAO PAULO
(BRANCH)

SEPTEMBER 1, 1974
(DATE)

To THE STEEL COMPANY OF CANADA LIMITED,
HAMILTON, ONTARIO, CANADA

ATTENTION: EXPORT CREDIT DEPARTMENT

WE HEREBY AUTHORIZE YOU TO DRAW ON A.B.C. TINPLATE CO. DO BRASIL S.A.

UP TO AN AGGREGATE AMOUNT OF $80,000.00 U.S. FUNDS

AVAILABLE BY DRAFTS AT 60 DAYS FROM DATE   FOR 100 % OF INVOICE VALUE
BILL OF LADING

ACCOMPANIED BY THE FOLLOWING DOCUMENTS.

1. COMMERCIAL INVOICE IN 10 COPIES ORIGINAL OF WHICH HAS BEEN CERTIFIED
BY THE CHAMBER OF COMMERCE

2. COMPLETE SET CLEAN ON BOARD OCEAN BILLS OF LADING CONSIGNED TO A.B.C.
TINPLATE CO. DO BRASIL S.A., NOTIFY: SAME AND MARKED FREIGHT PREPAID
SHOWING AMOUNT OF FREIGHT PAID IN FIGURES AND WORDS, WHICH MUST
COINCIDE WITH THAT ON INVOICES

3. CERTIFICATE OF ORIGIN AND ORIGINAL AND 5 COPIES CERTIFIED BY CHAMBER
OF COMMERCE.

4. PACKING LIST IN THREE COPIES

COVERING SHIPMENT OF: FOLHAS DE FLANDRES ELETROLITICAS
AS PER IMPORT PERMIT NO 18-74/07/902
C&F SANTOS BRASIL NOT LATER THAN OCTOBER 5, 1974
TRANSHIPMENT PROHIBITED

FROM ANY CANADIAN AND/OR U.S. PORT TO SANTOS, BRASIL

PARTIAL SHIPMENTS ARE   PERMITTED.
(Insert "are" or "are not")

DRAFTS MUST BE DRAWN AND NEGOTIATED NOT LATER THAN OCTOBER 15, 1974

THE DRAFTS DRAWN UNDER THIS CREDIT ARE TO BE ENDORSED HEREON AND SHALL STATE ON THEIR FACE THAT THEY ARE

DRAWN UNDER BANCO DO BRASIL S.A.   BRANCH

LETTER OF CREDIT NO. 54321   DATED SEPTEMBER 1   '74

WE HEREBY AGREE WITH THE DRAWERS, ENDORSERS AND BONA FIDE HOLDERS OF THE BILLS DRAWN IN COMPLIANCE WITH THE
TERMS OF THIS CREDIT THAT THE BILLS SHALL BE DULY HONORED UPON PRESENTATION AT THE DRAWEE BANK.

_____   _____
Accountant   Manager

BILL OF EXCHANGE

XW288

DRAFT NO.

9-12

THE STEEL COMPANY OF CANADA, LIMITED

PROTEST IMMEDIATELY FOR NON PAYMENT

SIGNATURE

DUE DATE

NOVEMBER 30, 1974

DATE

TORONTO, CANADA

OCTOBER 1 19 74

FORWARDING BANK'S NUMBER

RECEIVING BANK'S NUMBER

TO: A.M.C. TINPLATE CO. DO BRASIL S.A.
SAO PAULO
BRASIL

(DRAWEE)

AT 60 DAYS FROM BILL OF LADING DATE

of the same tenor and date unpaid) for value received.

OF THIS FIRST/SECOND OF EXCHANGE (SECOND/FIRST

Pay to the order of THE STEEL COMPANY OF CANADA LIMITED, HAMILTON, ONTARIO, CANADA

the sum of SEVENTY-NINE THOUSAND
ONE HUNDRED THIRTY-SEVEN------ .70
U.S. FUNDS

.70
100 Dollars. $ 79,137.70
U.S. FUNDS

IN CASE OF NEED NOTIFY .

THE STEEL COMPANY OF CANADA LIMITED,
EXPORT CREDIT DEPARTMENT,
HAMILTON, CANADA

THE STEEL COMPANY OF CANADA, LIMITED

PER:

DRAWER

DRAWN UNDER BANCO DO BRASIL S.A. LETTER OF CREDIT NO. 54321 DATED SEPTEMBER 1, 1974

Para preenchimento pela CACEX

[1] Numero 18-74/07/902	[2] Data da emissao 7 JUN 74	[3] Praca da emissao SAO PAULO (SP)	[4] Valid para embarque ate 4 DEZ 74	Cod.ag 26.9

[6] IMPORTADOR: ABC TINPLATE DO BRASIL S.A.
ENDERECO: SAO PAULO, BRASIL

[7] INSCRICAO NO C.G.C.C.P.P. 611461487
04257 Cx.Int. 1608

[8] CONSIGNATARIO:
ENDERECO: O mesmo.

[9] INSCRICAO NO C.G.C./C.P.F.

[10] FABRICANTE: THE STEEL COMPANY OF CANADA LTD.
ENDERECO: HAMILTON - ONTARIO - CANADA.

[11] EXPORTADOR: THE STEEL COMPANY OF CANADA
ENDERECO: LTD., HAMILTON - ONTARIO - CANADA

[12] CODIGO [13] APLICACAO DA MERCADORIA
Para uso proprio

[14] REPRESENTANTE, NO BRASIL, DO FABRICANTE E/OU EXPORTADOR:
ENDERECO: Nao ha.

[15] FORMA DE PAGAMENTO
Saque a Vista.

[16] 038

[17] PAIS DE ORIGEM Canada	[18] CODIGO 149	[19] PAIS DE PROCEDENCIA Canada	[20] CODIGO 149	[21] PORTO DE DESCARGA Santos

MERCADORIA — Preco F.O.B. em moeda estrangeira

[23] Item da tarifa	[24] Peso liq. Kgs.	[25] Quant.	[26] Discriminacao	[27] Unitario US$p/1000 Kgs.	[28] Total U.S.$
73.13.04.99	200.000		Folhas de flandres, eletroliticas, qualidade U/A, acabamento brilhante, tempera 2, tipo "D", estanhagem 0,75 libras. (Aluminun Killed - Dureza permanente)	647,10	129.420,00

EMBALAGEM: Caixas com 100 folhas cada, em fardos pesando aproxima damente 1.200 quilos liqui dos.

Medidas: 833 mm X 587 mm X 0,22 mm

"Enquadramemo na Resolucao no 1.993, de 31.12.73, do Conselho de Politica Aduaneira (D.O.U. de 9.1.74), sujeito a manifestacao do mesmo Orgao, tendo em vista a existencia de producao nacional."

Consular Administration

[29] TOTAL 200.000	[30] CODIGO DA MOEDA 26	[31] VALOR TOTAL F.O.B. 129.420,00

[32] VALOR TOTAL F.O.B. POR EXTENSO:
(Cento e vinte e nove mil, quatrocentos e vinte dolares).

[33] SALVO INDICACAO EM CONTRARIO, O VALOR F.O.B. ACIMA INDICADO, SEM DESCONTOS PORVENTURA CONSIGNADOS, E VALIDO PARA OS FINS PREVISTOS NA PORTARIA GB-355, de 5-6-69 DO MINISTERIO DA FAZENDA.

[34] Pretende o importador seja a operacao enquadrada.................

Na resolucao do C.P.A. de 09 de janeiro de 1974, numero 1.993, com isencao do imposto de importacao

[35] A CARTEIRA DE COMERCIO EXTERIOR DO BANCO DO BRASIL S.A., concede a presente guia de importacao para as mercadonas acima especificadas.

THE STEEL COMPANY OF CANADA, LIMITED
EXPORT PACKING LIST
LISTA DE EMPAQUE PARA EXPORTACION

A1012A (REV.7-73)

stelco

DATE SHIPPED
FECHA DE EMBARQUE
SEPTEMBER 25, 1974

SOLD TO / VENDIDO A	SHIP TO / EMBARQUE A
ABC TINPLATE CO. DO BRASIL S.A.	M.V. "A VESSEL"
SAO PAULO,	C/O SAGUENAY SHIPPING,
BRASIL	WELLINGTON STREET DOCK,
	HAMILTON

ROUTE/RUTA
TRUCK/CAMION [X]   STELCO   CNR [ ]   CPR [ ]   CSL [ ]

OCEAN CONTRACT
CONTRATO MARITIMO   **TN 15-15**

SHIPPING INSTRUCTIONS
INSTRUCCIONES DE EMBARQUE
RECEIVING UNTIL SEPT. 26/74

FREIGHT
FLETE   PPD [X]   COLL [ ]

CAR NO.
CARRO NO.

B/L NO. **158085 to 94**
CONOC/EMBRQ.NO.

SEAL NO.
SELLO NO.

INVOICE HEADING
ENCABEZAMIENTO DE FACTURA   **ELECT.25#, MRT 3, MELT, OIL**

PRODUCT ACCOUNT		MILL / MOLINO			CUST. ORDER PEDIDO CLIENTE	B.W./G.A. GROSOR	SIZE / TAMANO		TOTAL		BASE BOXES CAJAS BASE
	PRE.	ORDER / PEDIDO	ITEM RENGL.				WIDTH ANCHO	LENGTH LARGO	PKGS PAQUE.	SHEETS/LAM	
012-**111.65**	TE	8881-A	802	765	.22	587	833	1,286	84	3114

BUNDLE NUMBERS NUMERACIÓN DE BULTOS	TOTAL BDLS. BLTS.	SHEETS PER BUNDLE LAMINAS POR BLT.	TOTAL SHEETS LAMINAS	GROSS WEIGHT/PESO BRUTO		NET WEIGHT / PESO NETO	
				POUNDS LIBRAS	KILOS	POUNDS LIBRAS	KILOS
802/1 to 802/78 802/80 to 802/81	80	1,600	128,000		110,425		109,065
802/79	1	684	684		5		566
	81		128,684	244,733	111,010	241,696	109,633

SPECIMEN

MARKS / MARCAS
ABC TINPLATE
N 4310
SAO PAULO
VIA SANTOS
802/1-81

296

XX167B (REV.9-67)

THE STEEL COMPANY OF CANADA, LIMITED
WILCOX STREET, HAMILTON 23, ONTARIO, CANADA

stelco

CABLE ADDRESS:
HAMSTELCO - HAMILTON
TORSTELCO - TORONTO
MONSTELCO - MONTREAL

EXPORT INVOICE

WORKS	OUR ORDER NO.	INVOICE NO.	NO. PAGES	PLACE	DATE
HAMILTON	1234	9-12	1	TORONTO CANADA	OCT I /74

SOLD TO:
A.B.C. TINPLATE CO. DO BRASIL S.A.
SAO PAULO,
BRASIL

SHIPPED TO:
SAME

CODE NO.

ROUTE   EX. HAMILTON CANADA VIA "A VESSEL" BRASILIAN FLAG VESSEL

B/L NO.	CAR NO.	FREIGHT
		C & F SANTOS, BRASIL

TERMS
LETTER OF CREDIT NUMBER 54321

CUSTOMER'S ORDER NO.
N-1230

MARKS AND NUMBERS ON PACKAGES	COUNTRY OF ORIGIN - CANADA / DESCRIPTION OF GOODS	QUANTITY	CURRENT DOMESTIC VALUE IN CURRENCY OF EXPORTING COUNTRY, SEE PAR. 3-4 OF CERTIFICATE @	AMOUNT	SELLING PRICE TO PURCHASER @	AMOUNT
BDLES	FOLHAS DE FLANDRES, ELETROLITICAS, QUALIDADE U/A, ACABAMENTO BRILHANTE, TEMPERA 2, TIPO "D", ESTANHAGEM 0.75 LIBRAS (ALUMINUM KILLED - DUREZA PERMANENTE) EMBALAGEM: CAIXAS COM 100 FOLHAS CADA, EM FARDOS PESANDO APROXIMA-DAMENTE 1.200 QUILOS LIQUIDS. MEDIDAS: 833 MM X 587 MM X 0,22MM	POUNDS	KILOS		PRICE PER 1000 KILOS	
81	.75# COATING T2 A1 KILL .22 MM 833 MM X 587 MM (79#BW 32-13/16 X 23-1/8)	241,696	109,633		$647.10	$70,943.51
	GUIA DE IMPORTAÇÃO: 18-74/071902 DATA DA EMISSAO: 7 JUN 74 PRACA DA EMISSAO: SAO PAULO (SP) VALIDA PARA EMBARQUE ATE: 4 DEZ 74 ITEM DA TARIFA: 73-13.04.99 PAIS DE ORIGEM: CANADA PAIS DE PROCEDENCIA: CANADA PORTO DE EMBARQUE: HAMILTON, CANADA PORTO DE DESCARGA: SANTOS, BRASIL FABRICANTE: THE STEEL COMPANY OF CANADA LIMITED HAMILTON, ONTARIO, CANADA EXPORTADOR: THE STEEL COMPANY OF CANADA LIMITED HAMIL HAMILTON, ONTARIO, CANADA VESSEL: A VESSEL FLAG: BRASILIAN FLAG		F.O.B. HAMILTON VALOR FLETE MARITIMO VALOR TOTAL C & F SANTOS	70,943.51 8,194.19 $79,137.70 EE.UU		THE STEEL COMPANY OF CANADA LIMITED PER: _____

OS PRECOS AQUI CONSIGADOS SAO OS CORRENTES NO MERCADO
DE EXPORTACAO PARA QUALQUER PAIS. NO PRECO SUPRA NAO
ESTAO INCLUIDAS OUTRAS DESPESAS. TRANSACAO EFETUADA
DIRETAMENTE COM O IMPORTADOR NO BRASIL. NAO MERCADORIA
NAO PUBLICAMOS CATALOGOS E/OU LISTAS DE PRECO PARA ESTA MERCADORIA.

PACKING DETAIL		MARKS
109,633 NET KILOS 111,010 GROSS KILOS		A.B.C. TINPLATE
81 BUNDLES 241,696# NET 244,733# GROSS		N 4310 SAO PAULO VIA SANTOS 802/1-81

ENUMERATE THE FOLLOWING CHARGES AND STATE WHETHER EACH AMOUNT HAD BEEN INCLUDED IN, OR EXCLUDED FROM, THE ABOVE VALUE		AMT. IN CUR-RENCY OF EX-PORTING COUNTRY	STATE IF INCLUDED OR EXCLUDED
1. CARTAGE TO RAIL AND/OR TO DOCKS			
2. INLAND FREIGHT AND ANY OTHER CHARGES TO DOCK INCL. INLAND INS.			
3. LABOR PACKING GOODS INTO OUTSIDE PACKAGES	HAD SIMILAR GOODS BEEN SOLD FOR CON-SUMPTION IN CANADA		
4. VALUE OF OUTSIDE PACKAGES			
5. WHARFAGE			
6. OCEAN FREIGHT			
7. INSURANCE			
8. IF GOODS ARE SUBJECT TO ANY CHARGES BY WAY OF ROYALTIES			
9. OTHER CHARGES OR EXPENSES			

CANADA CUSTOMS — EXPORT ENTRY

						REPORT NO	
SEE CUSTOMS MEMORANDUM D22-1 AND STATISTICS CANADA EXPORT COMMODITY CLASSIFICATION	PLACE OF LADING TORONTO, ONTARIO						

CARRIER FROM PLACE OF LADING
TRUCK

EXPORTING CARRIER (IF KNOWN)
A VESSEL

OUTPORT

ENTRY NO.

PORT

MODE OF TRANSPORT FROM PORT OF EXIT	HIGHWAY ☐	RAIL ☐	WATER ☒	AIR ☐	PARCEL POST ☐	OTHER (SPECIFY)

NAME OF EXPORTER/OWNER
THE STEEL COMPANY OF CANADA LIMITED

ADDRESS OF EXPORTER
HAMILTON, ONTARIO, CANADA

COUNTRY OF FINAL DESTINATION
BRASIL

NAME OF CONSIGNEE
A.B.C. TINPLATE CO. DO BRASIL S.A.

CURRENCY IN WHICH VALUE IS SHOWN
U.S. DOLLARS

ADDRESS OF CONSIGNEE
SAO PAULO, BRASIL

MARKS ON PACKAGES	NO. OF PACKAGES	DESCRIPTION OF GOODS GIVE SUFFICIENT DETAIL TO PERMIT CODING ACCORDING TO STATISTICS CANADA EXPORT COMMODITY CLASSIFICATION	SHIPPING WEIGHT	QUANTITY USE UNIT REQUIRED FOR EXPORT COMMODITY CLASSIFICATION	VALUE F.O.B. PLACE OF LADING	IF FOREIGN GOODS IN SAME CONDITION AS IMPORTED, GIVE COUNTRY OF ORIGIN
A.B.C.	81	BUNDLES ELECTROLYTIC TINPLATE	244,733#		$70,943.51	
TINPLATE			111,010			
N 4310			KILOS			
SAO PAULO						
VIA SANTOS						
02/1-81						

SPECIMEN

(INDICATE IF APPLICABLE) ARE / WERE THE GOODS	SUBJECT TO DRAWBACK ☐	IMPORTED ON 1/60TH BASIS ☐	IMPORTED UNDER LICENCE ☐	Estimated inland freight charges from place of lading to port of exit	$400.00

PORT OF ENTRY AND ENTRY NO. (IF KNOWN)

IF GOODS NOT SOLD, STATE REASON FOR EXPORT. (LOAN, REPAIR, PROCESSING, ETC.)

EXPORT PERMIT NO.

I hereby certify that the information given above is true and complete in every respect.

Firm MINSHALL FORWARDING LIMITED   Address 68 YONGE STREET, TORONTO, ONTARIO

Signature .... Date SEPTEMBER 25, 1974   Indicate status

OWNER ☐   AGENT ☒

STAMP OF CHIEF PORT

THE STEEL COMPANY OF CANADA LIMITED

HAMILTON ONTARIO CANADA

USE SPACE ABOVE FOR RETURN ADDRESS

014-5 46 **YYZ**
014-5 46

TORONTO INTERNATIONAL AIRPORT | PANAMA

MIA   AC   PTY BN

AIR CANADA

IATA

A. B. C. HOTELERO EL PANAMA S.A.
APARTADO 4444
PANAMA 1 REPUBLICA DE PANAMA.

Shipper's name and address
Nom et adresse de l'expéditeur

A. B. C. UPHOLSTERY COMPANY
4444 DYKE STREET
TORONTO ONTARIO.

Issuing carrier's agent, name and city
Nom et adresse de cet agent

SEA AIR INTERNATIONAL FORWARDERS LTD.
MALTON P.O. BOX 101 MISSISSAUGA ONTARIO.

SEPTEMBER 30th 1974 | MALTON ONTARIO.
EXECUTED ON - ETABLIE LE (Date) AT A (Place Lieu)

Agent's IATA code
60-1-7400

Currency			Declared value for customs	Amount of insurance
CDN M	MTR B	$95.00 E	$266.00

Accounting information - Renseignements comptables

Ins. Value $266.00 @ .15¢ per $100.00 = .40¢

No. of pieces RCP	Actual gross weight	Kg Lb	Rate class	Commodity item No.	Chargeable weight Poids Taxation	Rate Charge Tarif / Montant	Nature and quantity of goods (incl. dimensions or volume)
1	71	L	V		237	.61	OFFICE CHAIR
							32" x 30" x 48"
1	71	L					

PRE PAID PORT PAYE	Prepaid weight charge	Prepaid valuation charge	Total other prepaid charges	Due carrier	Due agent	Total prepaid
	$144.67 V	C		A	P	$ 145.07

FOR CARRIER'S USE ONLY AT DESTINATION
RESERVE AU TRANSPORTEUR A DESTINATION

R	PUP	DEL	INS .40

COLLECT CHARGES IN DESTINATION CURRENCY
A ENCAISSER EN MONNAIE DU PAYS DE DESTINATION

| S | | | |
COD amount - Montant C.R.

| T | PUP | DEL | |
Total charges - Total des frais

COLLECT PORT DU		V	C Due carrier	A Due agent	Z	COD amount - Montant C.R.	Total collect - Total dû

B13's HEREWITH........EXPORT PAPERS ATTACHED:
NOTIFY CONSIGNEE UPON ARRIVAL AT DESTINATION....

Handling information - Précisions pour la manutention

Pricing, Quotations and Credit
by
F. Irvine Ryckman
Export Consultant

Tendered Prices:

As in domestic trade, this approach to pricing is usually associated with government business at all levels, large contracts, or installations of capital goods or works. In most countires there are agencies that specialize in the processing of tenders originating within their home country, and Canadian exporters are well advised to make use of these specialized services. The translation of an invitation to tender, into English, and the clarification of technical details, require expertise that is not common to most Canadian firms. For the beginner the Canadian Trade Commissioner operating in the importer country, is a good source to approach for information agencies specializing in tender calls.

A tendered price usually has to be extremely competitive, unless the offered goods or services have features that give the exporter a distinct advantage. The more aggressive exporters are alert to the impact of warranties, post-delivery servicing, personnel training, provision of consulting services, and similar extras which are offered free of charge as part of the tender. Exotic financing terms are frequently offered as part of the price.

Since specific classes of trade cannot be examined in detail, it should be sufficient to point out that a tendered price based on manufacturing cost plus a modest profit is most likely to be competitive. If the price contains a wide range of administration and selling and other expenses, it will probably be non-competitive.

Negotiated Prices:

When a Canadian exporter has located a foreign importer interested in his goods or services and is determined to make a sale, he must proceed on the basis that his price is negotiable. The importer is interested solely in his laid down cost and the exporter is interested in profit on the sale, so there has to be some compromise.

Customarily the exporter quotes a price with all costs included plus his desired profit. This price will include insurance and freight. If the customer response is negative, freight can be excluded if the customer thinks he can get a better rate, or the exporter can reduce the freight charge if he feels he can get a better rate. The same applies with insurance. If there are import licences, surcharges or prior deposits, perhaps these can be financed by the exporter to reduce the laid down cost to the importer. More advantageous credit terms will also affect the customer in the same way. If negotiation in these areas fails, then the normal approach is to reduce the base price. Under no circumstances should an exporter be in a hurry to reduce his base price. It is much easier to reduce or curtail the concessions made in financing, insurance, or freight than to reduce the base price. It is not unreasonable to ask for a greater volume of business from the customer in return for concessions made on price, or in the alternative, a reduction in quality or some other feature commensurate with the price reduction.

Whenever possible, prices should be negotiated on a principal to principal basis, rather than through agents. This approach is especially desirable where a long term relationship is anticipated.

Pre-Set Prices:

When an exporter wishes to penetrate or probe a foreign market, a preset price is often a good approach. There is a need for skill in assessing the current price levels in the target market. The pre-set price ordinarily must be commensurate with the quality offered and the ability of the exporter to meet demand. If a market is controlled by competitors and an exporter wishes to penetrate it, a low price should only be offered on an introductory basis, otherwise a price war could result. In such circumstances the price may fall below the breakeven level for the Canadian exporter. In some cases, the exporter should continue to sell because the competition may be trying to protect a lucrative market against newcomers. Once established, the exporter can start raising prices either independently or in consultation with his foreign competitors. No seller enjoys seeing money left on the table.

In probing the market, the technique is much the same. Goods are offered at a pre-set price just to gauge reaction at that level. This is a good technique if supply capability is limited, as when disposing of surplus production to prevent a fall in domestic prices, or when disposing of seconds and goods that are out of style.

The concept of setting a share of a market as a goal and using pre-set pricing as a means to achieve that goal, is usually linked up with a marketing policy of achieving profit goals by the large volume, low mark-up technique. The credit risks inherent in trying to gain volume too quickly, are rather great, especially in the underdeveloped countries.

Determination of Prices

USE OF BUDGETED COSTS - this is a dangerous approach because of the probability of under estimating some factors such as volume, legal costs, insurance, shipping costs, etc. Generally, it is the only way to get started, making use of existing personnel, plant, equipment, and administrative techniques.

USE OF ACTUAL COSTS - this technique tends to be more realistic if the existing pattern of business will not be upset by export sales and no significant change in overhead will be involved. The weakness is that it does not take into account the unique costs of export business. Generally overlooked are such things as special packaging, extra documentation, additional legal costs, additional insurance costs, additional communication expense, and bank charges over and above those incurred in domestic activity.

USE OF KNOWN MARKET PRICES - this is perhaps the most sure-fire way of establishing initial prices. The technique provides the opportunity to sell at a profit if you know your costs. It offers a great potential for cost recovery. The exporter selects markets offering the best profit potential. The danger lies in assessing the accuracy of the prices available, as they may be based on high or low volume, good or bad payment conditions, or special marketing relationships established between historical exporters and importers.

TRANSFER PRICING - Some exporters set up a foreign corporation to which they sell at a price just above cost. This minimizes the tax impact. The foreign corporation makes the profit which can be brought home at will.

The Influence of Incremental Costs in Price Setting

There are many areas of cost that will vary substantially as between export and domestic business. You will find, for example, that your sales costs will tend to peak up rather quickly if your export selling program is successful. Usually, this is due to the hiring of more people and the hiring of specialized people.

Invoicing can often become a source of cost that will distort your profitability. In export, more forms are required, and if you generate a significant export volume, you will find that you will have to have specialized people undertaking the invoicing function.

Accounting is not quite as difficult as sales and invoicing, but here again, you will find that you will tend to strain your existing accounting organization when your start asking for more details concerning production costs and administration and selling expenses. You will also find that you will be relying on your accounting people to provide you with answers on tax matters, and as a consequence, your accounting staff will have to grow with the development of your export business.

Advertising in connection with the development of export sales can be quite costly as it involves the use of specialized people to avoid using offensive terminology when coverting English to some foreign language and in avoiding the use of slogans or pictures which might also be offensive. Unless your company is particularly large and has need of a large volume of advertising, this is an area that could best be left to outside agencies.

Legal costs, whether due to greater use of your own legal department or your own lawyers if you engage outside personnel, will tend to rise rather sharply when you first enter the export field. By and large, this is because of our tendency to be overly cautious in the beginning. The fear of the unknown almost forces us to seek legal guidance covering the impact of regulations and so forth.

If significant sales in foreign market are anticipated, the exporter is well advised to establish contact with a law firm in that market. Advice on the proper wording of drafts, collection procedures stemming from non-acceptance or non-payment, and import regulations affecting the product being exported, are matters requiring special attention. The local Canadian Trade Commission, local banks, and other Canadian exporters can help in the selection of a suitable law firm. Legal expense should be taken into account when considering the cost of export business, especially where complex sales are involved or where the exporter is selling to foreign government entities.

Shipping

The need for special packaging for protection against the elements and for protection against rough handling will force your shipping costs up. Greater handling in getting goods to ports and long ocean voyages also will raise costs.

Brokers & Forwarders

The fees charged by brokers and forwarders are generally not out of line considering the expertise involved. For the beginning exporter, these additional costs may cause some concern, but as time goes on, it should become apparent that they are well justified. It should be kept in mind that some forwarders and brokers have more experience in some markets than others and a new exporter should feel free to engage the services of those brokers or forwarders that are best equipped to handle specific sections of his business. Some exporters make it a practice to recover some of the costs involved in this area by assessing a special charge for special documentation. Caution is advised in dealing with some of the large international agencies. Shop around among the large and small forwarders. Always ask if you will get a bill of lading issued by the carrier. It often pays to get the opinions of other exporters.

Agents

Unless an exporter has considerable knowledge about a market or has sufficient business to justify a staff in that market, he will almost always have to rely on the activities of commission agents. The commission paid should be no more or no less than what is generally acceptable in the trade and this can be determined quite easily from trade associations both domestic and foreign and from the Trade Commissioner involved. These commissions are direct charges against profitability and consequently should be considered carefully. Depending on the nature of your business, you may find that you will have to negotiate with a prospective agent on matters of cost sharing regarding communications. Some exporters expect agents to send them unlimited quantities of telexes and cables covering trivial details without any regard for the cost to the agent of such communications. Normally, agents expect to bear a certain amount of expense to keep their principals informed. If you expect that you will require a great deal of your agent's time and that his communications cost will be high, then you should negotiate these matters at the very outset.

A final note of caution is in order. The cost of an agent's commission should not be the deciding factor in setting policy. In many export markets it is very difficult and costly to terminate the services of an agent or to switch agents, even if no formal agreement has been signed. Local legal advice should be obtained before making use of an agent or accepting business referred by an agent.

Bank Charges

These are generally associated with the handling of bills of exchange or drafts. Depending on the markets, they can be incidental items or they can be quite onerous. Generally, you can get some insight into the costs involved by discussing this matter with your bankers and with the Trade Commissioners abroad. If you feel that the charges are too steep to be absorbed, then you should negotiate these with your customer.

Insurance

This can be quite an important element of cost attributable solely to your export operations. The extra cost of protecting your goods while in transit from your factory to your customer's plant in some foreign land can be rather extensive. If you are a prudent exporter, you will be careful to protect yourself against expected risks and will cover yourself warehouse to warehouse. The impact of these expenses will of course depend upon how your goods are sold. If insurance is for the buyer's account and you are satisfied that his insurance is complete in every detail, then your insurance costs will not have a very serious affect on your profits; however, if the insurance is for your own account, you will have to take this cost into consideration when setting your export price.

A great deal of discussion of incremental cost is of little value in this presentation, as the best we can hope for is to point out their existence and the fact that they can have an impact on your profitability. If your export volume becomes important, you will have to begin isolating export and domestic costs in order to gauge the acceptability of your export business.

Moral Aspects of Pricing

Whether you are in the field of selling goods or services, you will inevitably encounter situations where business is obtained for considerations other than price.

In heavy construction projects, it is not uncommon to see great international engineerng firms building dams and hydro electric projets all over the world. In the case of capital goods, there are some types of machinery that are known world-wide and for many years some of the great European producers of machinery and equipment were known universally as the best sources of such goods. In the case of consumer goods, the same also can be said. Certainly in the last few years we have become quite familiar with the activities of some of the offshore automobile makers, tire producers and camera producers. Many of these well recognized products sell on their own merits. In the case of the Canadian exporter going abroad to sell his goods, in a market where they are relatively unknown, he will undoubtedly face many new and interesting challenges.

Perhaps one of the most difficult situations to resolve is that arising from the necessity to literally buy your own business. Some offshore importers think nothing of asking suppliers to furnish them with some monetary inducement to place business. Similarly, some offshore importers find it necessary to accumulate foreign currency abroad and therefore request suppliers to undertake over-invoicing and other practices in order to generate foreign credits for such importers.

It is well known that in some industries there are established groups of manufacturers who are deeply involved in the export markets of the world and who meet regularly to set prices and quotas for different market areas. It is not the purpose of this paper to deal with the moral issues involved in such activities. The sole purpose of mentioning them at all, is to simply indicate that such practices do exist and that these moral considerations must be dealt with when engaging in export activity. In some cases, the practices referred to are more deeply entrenched than one might suspect and you must recognize their existence if you are going to do business in the accepted fashion. If you recognize that these practices do exist, and wish to avoid them, you will have to make certain allowances in your pricing techniques in order to surmount the obstacles which are obviously there to be faced.

Pricing Objectives

There are no precise rules for effective pricing of a product. Presumably, the financial plan of a company will indicate whether or not export activity is to be examined as a means of fulfilling the financial plan.

Once the decision is made to undertake export activity, then the objective of the pricing policies must be considered. There are many alternatives to be considered, but primarily the basic decision will involve the direction of the marketing activity. A single country may be selected as a target for export activity and then a pricing technique adopted which will either gain one single large importer as a customer, or several large importers as customers or will achieve a small amount of sales to a number of importers in that one country. The other alternative is to set a pricing policy aimed at the penetration of a number of countries followed up by the secondary considerations of whether the price in each country is to be directed toward the successful selling of one or more large customers or many small customers.

.In most instances, one would be tempted to say that the selling of many customers in many countries would be the ideal objective, as this would involve the spreading of risks and the protection of your business against bad influences on a large scale. If a particular country or a particular customer encountered difficulties and you were unable to export to that particular country or customer, your total business would not be unduly affected. Unfortunately, it is very difficult to rationalize when discussing export activity because one must consider the nature of the product involved and the state of development of your potential markets and your potential customers. If you must achieve high volume, the usual course is to pick out the major consumers in each market and set your prices so as to maximize your penetration and obtain the greatest possible volume. Some companies seek a great diversity of markets and then adjust their prices upwards or downwards to give them optimum production.

The secret of the whole exercise is to know your costs.

QUOTATIONS

As a means of entering the export markets of the world, quotations are undoubtedly the most effective. Considering only the Canadian situation, it is quite obvious that through the Trade Commissioner Service of our government, Chambers of Commerce in Canada and abroad, Trade associations in Canada and abroad, it is possible for the Canadian exporter to quote on his goods in just about any major market in the world. The quotation must, of necessity, offer quantities, qualities and deliveries in terminology that is known and accepted in the marketplace. A survey of any market will easily yield the names of principal users of your product. In the beginning, a quotation that is vague on acutal price details can be sent to such potential users in the hope that your quality and quantity and delivery will encourage the potential customer to ask for more information. At this stage, the quotation becomes a very important tool. Depending upon the nature of the competition, the nature of the market and the nature of the goods involved, you can either bare your soul in a complete quotation or pay a personal visit to your potential customer and explain your prices in detail. At this stage, it is customary to determine the severity of your competition if your potential customer suggests that you are not competitive. Here you are faced with the difficult situation of appraising the realism of the prices offered by your competitors. If you are talking to large importers, it is quite likely that they will enjoy preferential treatment with respect to freight rates, credit terms, insurance, and possibly financing. Generally speaking it is best to maintain a fixed price on your own goods and become competitive by absorbing freight charges or insurance costs. In the area of credit terms, if the customer is a good one, then you can offer financing facilities that will enable your customer to buy the foreign exchange necessary to purchase your goods. Usually, you are able to offer him local currency at rates better than those available to him as a local industry. Often, by making use of the customer's own bankers, you will offer him an incentive to buy from you rather than from your competitors, although you should always remain alert to the fact that in the export field, your competition will undoubtedly have a long history of activity in export affairs and consequently, will frequently know many of the tricks of the game. This should not discourage you, however, because often a fresh approach as opposed to traditional patterns, will work wonders. You should also cash in on the fact that in many instances, Canadian goods are considered to be on a par with those from the United States, and consequently, in some markets for some goods, Canadian quotations are looked upon with interest. The danger in quoting is often the rigid approach. Flexibility is required in export trade to a far greater degree than in domestic trade and consequently your initial quotation should allow for negotiation. If you know your costs, you can make your offer based on maximizing your return in line with the prices in the market you are intending to enter. During the subsequent exchanges of correspondence, or in meetings with your potential customers, you will rapidly determine the real situation, and at this point you fall back on the old device of reducing cost factors in order to bring your price more into line. Here again, you must remember that you should try to keep your price per article on a fairly firm basis and adjust such things as freight, insurance, and credit items in order to reduce the laid-down cost of your product to your potential customer. In this way, you can later increase your profit by adjusting the freight absorption or the credit terms being offered, without changing the price of the goods.

You will find that after your quotation has been accepted by your customer, a pro-forma invoice will normally be asked for. This is an invoice without official status, purporting to cover a specific quantity of goods, with a specific description and including all of the elements that go to make up the final price to your customer. It will show your customer the final cost to him, laid down, of a specific quantity of your goods. Quite often, the customer will sign a pro-forma invoice and return it as an order to deliver goods as described. A pro-forma invoice should be accurate as it may be the basis for a letter of credit, an exchange permit or an import licence.

Once you have made offerings in a market, it is likely that word of your activities will spread throughout the trade. When your first shipment enters a market, you will find that most potential buyers will be aware of the fact that you are now an exporter, and opportunities will likely arise. The initial quotations (and pro formas) must reflect the psychology of your approach to that particular market. In the long run, it is best to avoid becoming identified as a low-priced supplier. In the long run, it is best to become identified as a high priced, high quality source of supply, then if you adjust your price downwards, your customers will feel that they are getting a bargain.

CREDIT

When an enquiry is received from a foreign land there are all sorts of items to be dealt with, including price, delivery, freight, packaging, insurance and, of course, payment. After these points are settled and the shipment has gone, everyone heaves a sigh of relief except the credit man, as he still has to collect. His job may be complicated by receipt of a cable from the agent stating something like this -- "Vessel Robin Keeting arrived with heavy weather damage to cargo and vessel". The problem of protecting such a receivable and obtaining payment is not always readily resolved, but, of course, it could be worse if a news bulletin announced, at the same time, that a revolution had occurred and the country of destination was in a state of siege.

The purpose of the foregoing illustration is to establish the goal of the credit function, as payment for the goods or services sold. The attainment of this goal is not always easy, nor is the path always clear and direct.

In order to obtain some idea of the scope of credit, let us consider the steps involved in developing, executing and completing an order.

(A) Market Analysis

When an order is received, some attempt must be made to evaluate the risks involved in selling into the country from which the order is received. Some of the factors to be considered are as follows:

> Customary Credit Terms
> Government
> Economy
> Foreign Exchange
> Banking

Customary Credit Terms

The customary credit terms may be obtained from the Department of Trade and Commerce, Ottawa, from banks, or from your agent, if you have one. The terms requested by your customer are considered in the light of the information you have gained from your other sources and may be double-checked by consulting other firms selling in the same market. This is a simple operation, but is important in obtaining an initial impression of the market.

Government

Appraisal of a government is a difficult task. Historical data is readily available from banking and government sources, but the problem is to interpret the data, keeping in mind that you are interested in current and anticipated attitudes to trade and commerce. Political doctrine in some countries may be strange, but you should try to avoid making comparisons and stick to your object of evaluation of the government with respect to trade. The stability of past governments is some basis for confidence, but you must be alert for the winds of change. The situation in Britain is a case in point. Traditional trading attitudes can become history overnight. Non-tariff barriers to trade can be instituted on short notice by any government, hence the need for careful appraisal. To meet the need for current information, it is advisable to subscribe to the bank circulars which are made available as a public service. Some of the large United States banks send out excellent bulletins intended for those interested in foreign trade. Any agent worth his salt should also be in a position to supply valuable information relating to the current and anticipated situation in his country. It is not my intention here to single out specific countries that have unstable governments, but rather to stress the importance of vigilance in connection with the appraisal of the government in the country in which you are going to sell.

Economy

The economy of a country is obviously a matter of concern to the credit man because of its direct relation to the availability of the means of payment. It may not be acceptable academic practice to treat such a broad subject in a general way, however, I must do so in order to complete my outline of the credit function. A few danger signals should suffice to demonstrate the problems in this area. Some of the emerging nations are markets for Canadian products, but they are risky because of their economy. There may be dependence on a single major exportable good, which may be an agricultural product such as coffee. In such a case, a drought or a fall in world market prices can have grave consequences on the economy and your customer may not be able to sell your product or may not be able to pay for it. Strikes by labour in a major industry can affect the balance of payments position of a country and cause delays in the payment of debts expressed in foreign currency. It may be difficult to separate economic and government factors when appraising a market, but in reality it is not necessary to do so as long as you take a careful look at both. In this area, the banks and government officials are able to furnish excellent data. You will find it easy to assess the status of industry, commerce and labour in a general way and establish a basis of confidence (or otherwise) in the market being considered.

Foreign Exchange

Foreign exchange availability is a matter of great importance to everyone involved in foreign trade. Most exports are made with the understanding that payment will be received in United States dollars, pounds sterling, or Canadian dollars. If your customer cannot get such foreign exchange, you are in trouble, but you are probably not alone. The normal approach is to consider the present and past foreign exchange situation in your market and then try to estimate what the future situation will be. Your banks and government agencies can be of considerable help, but they cannot make the judgement for you. If you are selling on terms calling for payment in six months, you are at the mercy of countless factors that affect the availability of exchange. International influences could affect your market at any time and with startling rapidity. When this happens, remittances of foreign exchange may be placed under government control, which usually results in a slowness of payments, or imports may be regulated through licensing. In some instances, importers are called upon to deposit local currency in order to obtain a licence to import and this deposit requirement may affect the importer's ability to pay for the goods being imported. Under such circumstances it sometimes becomes necessary for a supplier to arrange a loan of local currency to his customer, which adds to the risk appraisal problem of the credit man. It has become standard practice for the leading countries of the world to offer assistance to those countries with exchange difficulties and when this happens, you may find yourself in the fortunate position of receiving payment just when you had given up hope. It may be your own money going from one pocket to another, but that is another story and hardly pertinent to this discussion.

Banking

On the subject of banking, it should be sufficient to point out that some care must be excercised in dealing with foreign banks that are not well-known. When a customer insists that you present your draft through a specific bank, make sure by checking with your own banker that the foreign bank is reputable and skilled in foreign transactions. You will find that the Canadian banks are well represented, either directly or through foreign correspondents, in virtually every market of the world so there is no need to take unnecessary risks in this respect.

As you may have noted, market analysis is substantially a matter of using common sense in studying and assessing the environment in which your customer operates. The status of your customer is another matter entirely.

(B) Credit Appraisal of the Customer

As was mentioned earlier, the general idea of business activity is to sell something and get paid. The job of the credit man is to assess the probability of the customer paying when the bill is due. The point to remember about the appraisal of a customer is that the total information obtained about the customer must create

313

confidence in the customer's willingness and ability to honour his obligations. Essentially, the following points should provide sufficient background for a decision to be reached:

Status:
   make sure your customer enjoys a good reputation for reliability and ir respected in his business community.

Financial Position:
   assets should be sufficient to enable your customer to withstand the normal ups and downs of business. He should be making a profit and enjoy the confidence of his banker. Be cautious in considering balance sheet data because in some countries taxation is based on declared capital, so naturally there is a tendency in such instances toward undervaluation of assets. The major international accounting firms provide analyses of the accounting procedures in most trading countries.

Cost of Money:
   quite often your customer may be reported as slow in meeting commitments, however, if interest rates are high in the country involved, your customer may find it more advantageous to operate on suppliers' money and pay them nominal interest than to borrow locally at high rates in order to pay his obligations as they mature.

Experience of Others:
   most credit reports will make some comment in this regard. When a report states that your customer pays local and foreign suppliers in a satisfactory manner, you can be reasonably sure that you will be paid.

Importing Experience:
   this is quite an important factor. Credit reports on foreign buyers usually will comment on importing experience and will name internationally known suppliers. If your customer has been importing for years, you can rest assured that he is aware of the regulations and documentary requirements, and is conscious of his reputation. You also have other suppliers to turn to for comment.

It should be stated here that Dun and Bradstreet Inc., New York, International Division, offer an excellent credit investigation service. Details of costs and services available can be obtained easily through your nearest office of Dun and Bradstreet of Canada Ltd. To supplement their reports, you will find that the Trade Commissioner Service, Department of Industry, Trade and Commerce can furnish you with supporting data. Bank reports are also obtainable, but these are frequently rather short and lacking in detail. Some foreign banks provide detailed credit reports, usually in anticipation of handling the collection paper if export business is developed.

(C) Acceptance of the Order

When you have dealt with the country and customer risks as outlined above and have decided to accept an order, there may still be a credit factor involved relating to the actual order. As you know, price is an important element in foreign trade. Your customer, of course, looks at his laid down cost. If your price is acceptable but other expenses add to the laid down cost, longer credit terms may have to be granted in order to reduce the laid down costs to your customer. By way of illustration, consider this simplified transaction. Assume your account is faced with a cost of $1,000 for your product on sight draft terms, and he must borrow at 24% to pay your invoice. Assume it takes 5 months for the customer to receive your goods and convert them to cash.

His cost is $1,000 for the product
plus   100 interest (24% - 2% per month for 5 months)
Total Cost $1,100

If your customer is given credit terms which will allow him to sell the article and obtain payment so he can in turn pay you, his cost changes as follows:

$1,000 for the article
nil interest
$1,000 Total Cost

While this may be an oversimplification of actual circumstances, you will note that credit terms may be invoked to lower your effective price. Export credit men are constantly faced with this situation. The same result may be achieved by making local currency available to your customer via your bank in Canada or elsewhere, to pay prior deposits, surcharges, or other importation expenses. The mechanics of such operations are peculiar to individual cases so there is no point in going into detail. It should be obvious that the credit man is involved in these techniques of price reduction and must be quite confident that the risks undertaken are fully justified. The credit terms employed must be governed by the individual situation, hence it is sufficient to state that you will grant open account, draft, or letter of credit terms, depending on the impact of all factors. When actually setting terms for an order, a realistic approach is necessary. If a foreign customer is reluctant to accept a draft or pay for goods before they arrive and clear customs, then you will usually have to comply. Letter of credit terms, while still in common usage, are not as acceptable as they once were because of cost, stringent requirements and other considerations. However, such terms are often the only solution in high risk situations.

(D) Documentation

In general, the credit function does not usually embrace all phases of documentation, but it is an extremely important element to the export credit man. When an export order has been filled, that is to say, the goods have been packed and shipped, the credit man requires all the documents necessary to meet the import regulations of the country to which the goods are consigned. While the preparation of the proper documents may appear to be a simple, routine chore, this is not necessarily the case. The importance of good work in this area cannot be stressed enough. If the papers relating to a shipment do not comply exactly with the regulations of the foreign country to which shipment has been made, the goods in question may be subject to seizure and fines may be levied against either the importer or the exporter. Where import licences are involved, terminology, quantities and values shown on the invoice usually have to coincide precisely with the import licence. If packaging has not been executed properly and goods going aboard a vessel show signs of damage, the exporter may receive a "noted" or "claused" bill of lading making reference to the damage. Most banks, indeed virtually all banks, demand a clean bill of lading when receiving documents for collection either against a draft or against a letter of credit. When invoices must be visaed by a foreign consulate, the subsequent discovery of an error may create great difficulties together with expense and embarrassment for the exporter. If you remember that the export documents covering a shipment, represent the goods, then you should understand the necessity for careful preparation of such documents. If your customer does not receive valid documents, he may simply abandon the goods and refuse to have anything to do with the shipment. When payment is refused, you will find yourself in a most awkward situation. You may allege that title has passed, but it will not do you a bit of good. If you sue, it will be costly, or if you take possession of the goods, it will be an expensive move. No matter what you do, you will pay dearly for your carelessness in not executing precisely correct documents. In the field of export trade, there are people known as forwarding agents who specialize in the arranging of ocean shipments and the preparing of export documents. Forwarders make it their business to keep current on the documentary requirements of foreign markets, hence, knowledgeable people recommend the use of forwarding agents, if you are not thoroughly familiar with export documentation. Since it is common practice for export credit men to use bills of exchange or drafts as a collection device, you can understand why credit men insist on the accurate preparation of export documents.

As a final point, it should be remembered that speed is also a necessity. If documents do not arrive at the destination until after the shipment, the goods may have been impounded by customs authorities and fines may have to be paid before the goods are released. In such cases, the exporter usually has to pay. Added to complications at the destination, there may be problems in originating a collection through a bank, if presentation of documents is delayed. A bill of lading may become "stale dated" if it is not negotiated promptly. Generally, banks are realistic in this respect, and if they are reasonably sure they can get the documents to the destination before the carrying vessel, they will accept them. The concern shown by banks over late presentation, and faulty documents, is most evident where a letter of credit transaction is involved.

The exporter is advised to make sure that adequate insurance coverage is in force on all export shipments, to protect his interests in the event of damage or loss while his goods are in the hands of customs authorities at the destination.

The remarks made in this section apply to all export documents, including the bill of lading, commercial invoice, consular invoice, insurance certificate, certificate of origin, import licence, and the test certificate.

(E) Collection

Where collection is made under a letter of credit, there are no problems if all conditions are met, as payment is made immediately the specified papers are presented. If a letter of credit fails, or if you have granted open account terms, or if you have issued a draft, payment depends primarily on the ability and integrity of the customer. If the customer refuses payment, then you, as an exporter, must take the initiative, and act promptly. No matter how carefully you have selected a collecting bank, you must remember that such a bank can only follow your instructions relating to the handling of your collections. This means that you must be prepared to act independently. If you are selling in a market constantly, it is advisable to make contact with a lawyer and perhaps give him power of attorney to act on your behalf. A lawyer should be selected with great care and investigated in the same manner as a customer. A lawyer who represents large international concerns may be more costly to retain, but may save you money in the long run because of his skill in dealing with export-import problems.

Assuming you have obtained a lawyer in your foreign market, you should notify him immediately by telephone, telex, or cable of a serious default in payment and give him clear instructions on the course you wish him to take. If possible, all drafts issued by you, as an exporter, should carry protest instructions at least for non-payment. In simple terms, protest means that your draft is presented for payment by a public official and notice is published if payment is refused. The advantage of protest lies in the fact that the draft itself becomes evidence of debt, and does not require other documentary supporting evidence, such as a signed purchase order and receipted delivery papers. Immediately the collecting bank notifies you that payment has been refused and the draft protested, you should instruct the collecting bank to surrender all the documents to your lawyer and at the same time advise your lawyer of the action to be taken. In essence, you should strive for prompt action and capable on-the-spot representation in order to safeguard your interests and obtain collection. A wait-and-see attitude may prove costly.

In the event that you have sold on open account or have not issued protest instructions, collection may be more difficult. You must determine quickly but judiciously if non-payment is due to a situation that threatens the collectibility of your account, such as insolvency. In such a case, make sure your legal representative gains possession of a signed purchase order, and the receipted delivery papers, as quickly as possible and again give instructions on the action to be taken. If you have faith in your legal representative, it is often wise to advise him simply to take whatever action is necessary to collect your account. Naturally, you will be guided in all circumstances by the amount of money involved.

Perhaps one of the most trying situations is that resulting from government intervention. If your customer has paid but the transfer of exchange is stopped by the local government, about all you can do is have your local agent, or legal representative, constantly try to obtain a release of your money. In every case of difficulty in collection, it is advisable to keep your local agent informed of your thoughts and actions, and conversely you should insist that your agent keep you abreast of all developments. Although he may not be able to assist you immediately or directly, the Canadian Government Trade Commissioner should be given full details of any serious collection problem. Where failure to collect is due to interference of the local government, the Trade Commissioner can sometimes render assistance by making representations on your behalf.

The financial effects of non-payment may be minimized by credit insurance. The Export Development Corporation, Ottawa, is a Crown Corporation that is in the business of insuring export transactions. Coverage and cost are governed by the type of policy. It is a protective measure that exporters should at least examine.

Credit costs are variable. As you engage in more export activity, expenses directly attributable to credit will rise, in a series of plateaus, largely due to the necessity of adding to staff as volume increases. In relation to the volume of sales, it is generally true that the expenses associated with credit investigation, collection and communication are not too great. Credit personnel should visit foreign customers regularly in order to develop first hand knowledge of the customers, banks, lawyers, accountants, and government officials. The cost of this activity is easily offset by the advantages gained through improved sales and receivables.

EXPORT ITEMS

Instruments and Terms Used in Foreign Trade

Draft: A written order, in which the person drawing the draft (drawer), instructs another person (the drawee), to pay a certain sum of money, on a definite date, to a third person (the payee), or to his order, or to bearer.

A draft is sometimes referred to as a "Bill of Exchange". This term is usually confined to foreign transactions. Bills of exchange are frequently issued in duplicate as a protective device. The original documents controlling title to the shipment accompany the "First of Exchange" and the "Second of Exchange" is sent under separate cover with duplicate documents. The second set becomes void upon arrival of the first, or vice versa.

Drafts are usually employed in transactions involving shipments of merchandise, but they may also serve as a demand to collect a past due debt, to secure payment on securities shipped from one point to another, etc.

A draft may be payable at sight, or on demand, or a certain number of days thereafter, or upon arrival of the goods for which the draft is to cover settlement.

Sight Draft (S/D): A draft that is payable on presentation; also known as a demand draft.

Time Draft: A draft that is payable a given number of days after date of the instrument (date draft) or after initial presentation to the drawee, such as 30 days after sight. Abbreviated 30 d/d or 30 d/s. The time may also commence with the date of the invoice, or of the bill of lading, but the time must be readily determined. It should preferably be within the control of the exporter or the collecting bank.

Arrival Draft: A modified sight draft which does not require payment when the draft itself arrives but is payable upon arrival of the goods covered by the draft. Problems arise if the goods do

320

not arrive, or are damaged, or delayed because of a sinking, diversion, or strike.

Bank Draft: A cheque drawn by a bank on another bank. Such drafts are customarily used where it is necessary for the customer to provide funds which are payable at a bank in some distant location.

Clean Draft: A draft to which there are no documents attached.   The documents, if any, are sent directly to the buyer. In such cases, the seller has confidence in the buyer that the draft will be paid and permits him to have the goods before payment or acceptance of the draft.

Documentary Draft: A draft to which documents are attached which usually control possession of the goods covered by the draft (bills of lading, insurance certificates, etc.).   Such drafts are customarily accompanied by instructions regarding the conditions upon which the documents may be surrendered usually payment or acceptance of the draft.

Letter of Credit (L/C):   A formal letter issued by a bank which authorizes the drawing of drafts against the bank up to a fixed limit and under terms specified in the letter.   Through the issuance of such letters, a bank pledges its credit on behalf of its customers and thereby facilitates the transaction of business between parties who may not be otherwise acquainted with each other.

Letters of credit are issued in a variety of forms and with terms which vary according to the particular transaction involved.

Commercial Letter of Credit: A letter issued in favour of the seller of goods authorizing the drawing of drafts covering the value of goods shipped to the purchaser.   Usually, the drafts must be accompanied by shipping documents conveying title to the goods.   The drafts may be payable upon presentation to the bank which issued the credit or at some later time as fixed by the terms of the credit.

The letter of credit may be sent directly by the issuing bank, or its customer, to the beneficiary, or the terms of the credit may be transmitted through a corresponding bank.   In the latter event, the correspondent bank may add its guarantee to that of the issuing bank, depending on the arrangements made between the seller and the purchaser. When such a guarantee is added, the letter is described as a <u>confirmed</u> credit.

Letters of credit may be <u>revocable</u> or <u>irrevocable</u> depending on whether the issuing bank reserved the right to cancel the credit prior to its expiration date.

<u>Authority to Purchase (A/P)</u>: A letter similar to a Commercial Letter of Credit, except that the drafts are drawn on the buyer and not a bank. The seller of goods is informed that the advising bank will purchase his drafts within a fixed dollar amount and under such conditions as are stated in the letter of authority. The advising bank obtains funds for the purchase of the drafts by debiting the account of the foreign correspondent on whose behalf it is acting, or it may collect directly from the foreign buyer. These instruments are not in general use, but are still sometimes used by multinational trading companies.

<u>Travelers Letter of Credit</u>: A letter addressed to all of the bank's correspondents, generally, authorizing them to negotiate drafts drawn by the beneficiary named in the credit, upon presentation of proper identification and up to a total limit specified in the credit. Such credits are also known as Circular Letters of Credit because they may be presented for negotiation to a number of banks in the course of use.

In addition to the letter of credit itself, the beneficiary is furnished with a separate list of the bank's correspondents which includes a special form known as a Letter of Identification containing a specimen of the beneficiary's signature, certified by the bank issuing the credit, to serve as a basis of identification for the beneficiary. Payments are endorsed on the reverse side of the letter of credit by the correspondent banks when they negotiate drafts. Not common now as travellers cheques, credit cards, and direct bank transfers are much easier to use.

<u>Open Account (O/A)</u>: Open Account, no draft drawn. Transaction payable when specified, e.g., R/M, return mail; E.O.M., end of month; 30 days, 30 days from date of invoice; 2/10/60, 2% discount for payment in 10 days, net if paid 60 days from date of invoice. If no term is specified, O/A usually implies payment by return mail.

BILL OF LADING (B/L):   A document issued by a carrier (railroad, steamship, express company, or forwarding agent) which serves as a receipt for the goods to be delivered to a designated person or to his order.   The bill of lading describes the conditions under which the goods are accepted by the carrier and details of the nature and quantity of the goods, name of vessel (if shipped by sea), identifying marks and numbers, destination, etc. The person sending the goods is the "shipper" or "consignor", the company or agent transporting the goods is the "carrier", and the person to whom the goods are destined is the "consignee".   Bills of lading may be negotiable or non-negotiable.   Caution is advised concerning the use of bills of lading issued by a forwarding agent instead of a carrier.   Consult your insurance company, lawyer, and bank.

Straight Bill of Lading: One in which the goods are consigned directly to a named consignee and not to his order.   Delivery can be made only to that person.   Such a bill of lading is non-negotiable.

Order Bill of Lading: One in which the goods are consigned to the order of any person or to the person acting as consignor (the shipper).   In the latter case, it must carry the consignor's endorsement in blank on the reverse side.   This is a negotiable bill of lading and the form required when given as collateral to a loan.   It is customarily used when payment depends upon a letter of credit or a draft.

Clean Bill of Lading: One in which the goods are described as having been received by the carrier in "apparent good order and condition" and without qualification.

Unclean Bill of Lading: One in which a notation has been made by the carrier of any defects found in the goods when they are received for transporting.   For example, such phrases as "3 crates broken" or "4 sacks torn" may be inserted.

Stale Bill of Lading: One which has not been presented under a L/C to the issuing bank within a reasonable time after its date, thus precluding its arrival at port of discharge by the time the steamer carrying the related shipment has arrived.   Usually 10 days is maximum but length of voyage governs.

Certificate of Origin: A document in which the exporter certifies to the place of origin (manufacture) of the merchandise to be exported. Sometimes these certificates must be legalized by the consul of country of destination, but more often they may be legalized by a commercial organization, such as a Chamber of Commerce, in the country of manufacture. Such information is needed primarily to comply with tariff laws which may extend more favourable treatment to products of certain countries. Where the goods exported contain foreign components, it is usually advisable to show the principal elements. Example: 85% Canada - 15% U.S.A.

EXTENDING CREDIT IN INTERNATIONAL TRADE

Payment Terms and Instruments:

Not all export transactions involve actual credit risk. In some markets the importer finances his purchases by arranging for payment to the supplier against presentation of invoice and shipping documents to the buyer's U.S. banking connection or to his confirming house or purchasing agent. Many large firms in Europe and some other markets regularly pay their trade bills by confirmed, irrevocable letters of credit, thereby relieving the exporter of virtually all risk by providing for dollar payment at time of shipment. In such cases the exporter need be little concerned with the credit status of either the customer or the destination country. Here, however, it should be mentioned that the exporter does, or may, incur a potential credit risk when he accepts a letter of credit which is revocable or which is not confirmed by a U.S. or Canadian bank; or, in Far Eastern trade, a payment instrument known as an "Authority to Purchase" or an "Authority to Pay". Before agreeing to these forms of payment, he should familarize himself with their conditions and clearly understand his possible liability thereunder.

To an ever-increasing extent, however, overseas buyers now expect their foreign suppliers to grant terms which permit them to pay for their purchases on or after receipt of the goods. In today's highly competitive world market, the exporter who demands payment by bank letter of credit stands a good chance of losing desirable business. One major reason for this is that, in many parts of the world, local bank and similar credit facilities are so restricted that payment through letter of credit is unduly expensive and burdensome. It ties up working capital and curtails business expansion. In these credit markets, of which all the Latin American countries are prime examples, imports are usually financed by means of documentary drafts. The payment terms vary, according to the customer, the trade and the market, but on consumer goods they usually range from Sight Draft, Documents against Payment (SD/DP) (which is the equivalent of cash on delivery), to 30, 60, 90, 180 days, or longer, evidenced by a Time Draft. Such terms give the buyer the approximate number of days specified in the draft, either (a) from date of invoice or shipment (Date Draft), or (b) from the date of his signed "acceptance" of the draft (Time Sight Draft), in which to pay the bill. In either case the collecting bank requires the buyer's "acceptance" of the draft before it turns over to him the title-bearing documents which enable him to clear the goods through Customs. Upon its acceptance, the draft then becomes a negotiable instrument with a fixed maturity date. On capital goods -- heavy machinery, plant equipment, etc. -- the payment terms may run from six months to five years, often subject to an initial cash payment, the balance evidenced by a series of drafts or notes, interest-bearing and payable in monthly, quarterly or semi-annual instalments, perhaps secured by a title-retention instrument, chattel mortgage, or other lien on the equipment, or by a bank guarantee or other collateral.

In the Far East it is quite common for credit terms to be arranged on the basis of a time draft with documents to be surrendered on payment. Under these terms, the buyer is not entitled to the documents which give him possession of the shipment until he pays the draft. In customary practice though, the collecting bank may release the shipment against the buyer's trust receipt, the bank thereby making itself responsible for payment of the draft at maturity. Such payment terms minimize the exporter's credit risk. Canadians selling to Far Eastern trading companies often encounter these terms.

Open account, or "clean" (i.e. non-documentary) draft, terms are often granted to selected customers in all markets, but only to those of proved responsibility and integrity. These open account customers remit payment on the pre-arranged due date directly to their suppliers, thus saving bank collection charges.

Incidentally, it is always well for the exporter to have an advance understanding with his customer regarding payment of bank collection charges and other incidental expenses. Though some exporters are willing to assume these items, they are generally for the customer's account.

With occasional variations, to meet specific customer and market conditions, these are the standard terms under which most export business is transacted.

Risk Analysis:

There is an element of risk in every credit sale, and in some overseas markets the risk is more complex and not as readily measurable as in domestic trade. Yet, the credit losses sustained on export business are generally lower than in the home market. One reason for this is that firms abroad who qualify as direct importers are usually more substantial and more anxious to preserve their established supply sources, than the run of the mill domestic account. The experienced exporter will grant credit only after close analysis of the current status of each customer and market, and will endeavor to keep his total risk exposure, especially in questionable markets, within a predetermined ceiling. Above all, he will make sure that his export credit management is in competent hands.

The major export credit risks are:

(a) commercial;
(b) political;
(c) catastrophe.

Sometimes non-payment is attributable to a combination of these.

The commercial risk relates to the buyer's financial capacity and his moral integrity. Does the customer have the means and ability to pay, and is he likely to honor his obligation even though conditions turn against him; or does his record indicate that he may seek to evade payment by rejecting or not picking up the shipment, by making unjustified claims, or by some other subterfuge? The commercial credit risk includes the possibility of loss by reason of the debtor's insolvency, or protracted default. Under good credit management, fortified with reliable information, it represents no more than a normal business hazard.

The risks usually classified as "political" are peculiar to the export trade. They are not as easy to assess, or to provide against, as the commercial credit risk, because they involve possible causes of non-payment which arise from the more or less arbitrary and unpredictable actions of governments. They are beyond the control of either the seller or the buyer. That political hazard which is most feared by exporters is the exchange transfer risk. On several occasions within the recent past, delays in transferring dollars have seriously affected the liquidity of export receivables. Even when credit had been extended to solvent, reliable customers who paid their bills when due, these export receivables in certain less stable countries have been frozen for lengthy periods pending the conversion of the customers' local currency payments into dollars and the remittance of those dollars to Canada. Such payments delays occur when the central bank or other exchange control authority in the debtor's country becomes so short of dollars and of other freely convertible currencies that it suspends payments to commercial creditors abroad until its reserves are replenished either by new export earnings or by borrowing from government institutions abroad.

The activities of the World Bank (International Monetary Fund) have reduced the area of danger with respect to exchange transfer risk, but it remains an ever-present hazard in doing credit business with the lesser-developed countries whose currency stability is closely tied to world prices of their commodity and raw material exports.

Other risks generally classified as "political" include the possible imposition of new import licensing or other restrictions after acceptance of the order; war, revolution, civil disturbance; and added transportation, insurance or other charges occasioned by interruption or diversion of voyage and not recoverable from the buyer. In some cases the credit grantor must also weigh such imponderables as devaluation, excessive fluctuations in currency value, or in labor and material costs, especially in undertaking long term contracts for specially manufactured goods.

Catastrophe type risks which can affect ultimate payment include such natural disasters as earthquakes, floods, hurricanes, general conflagrations, large-scale looting or defalcations and other major unforeseen developments.

Protection against credit loss due to the customer's insolvency or protracted default, as well as against prolonged exchange transfer delay and most of the other political risks cited, is now available to Canadian exporters through the Export Development Corporation, Ottawa. This is a Crown Corporation that offers insurance coverage to exporters to encourage the financing and expansion of export trade.

Customer Information:

With an initial order from a new account, the exporter's resident or traveling representative is encouraged to include bank and trade references furnished by the customer, perhaps augmented by background data gleaned from local informants, such as other businessmen who know the background of the new customer.

The export credit manager must be sure that each field representative knows the corporate credit policy, and is aware that no sale is completed until the bill is paid. Recognizing that it is in his interest to do advance screening and to suggest deferred payment terms only to accounts believed to be credit-worthy, and finding that attention to these details usually expedites approval and shipment of his order, the sales agent is apt to become a close and valued colleague of the credit manager. He aids in smoothing out and minimizing the effects of claims and disputes, in following up and explaining the causes of delayed payments, and in keeping his principals informed of significant developments, favourable or adverse, which bear on the credit status of his clients. However, not even the most competent representative is necessarily a good judge of credit risk, nor does he always have access to adequate information. His true function is to make sales. Hence the final authority and responsibility for credit granting must always rest with management, and, at best, the representative's information is but the foundation upon which the master credit file is built. It is from the sum-total of the data assembled in this customer file that credit approvals, credit limits and payment terms are decided. Into the master file goes information from many sources -- for example:

(a) individual reports on the customer, prepared by qualified and reliable credit information agencies;

(b) financial and operating statements - from the customer himself or from financial publications or other sources;

(c) ledger experience as supplied by the customer's trade references;

(d) reports from local bank references and from other banks maintaining international credit files;

(e) information supplied by the Canadian Government Trade Commissioner Service.

Though it often has value, the data from trade and local banking references is not always as impartial as could be desired. Obviously, no credit seeker will refer to those whose experience with his account has been unfavourable. Moreover, it is not usual for banks abroad to be financially interested, as part owners or as heavy creditors, in the firms they report upon. Banks also tend to be ultracautious and reserved when supplying written information, especially of an unfavourable tenor, either because of their confidential relationship to their clients, or from a natural desire to avoid possible legal involvement.

These are among the reasons why the experienced credit executive supplements his data from other sources, with reports prepared by specialized international credit reporting agencies. These credit agency reports are based primarily on field investigations by trained reporters -- men skilled in appraising the financial strength, integrity and business competence of firms in their communities. Each subject of a report is invited to file with the credit agency, its current operating and financial statements, plus other pertinent data. Though not all firms abroad will respond, an ever increasing number now recognize the advantages derived through their being accurately reported on, and rated, by agencies serving the international trading community. This aids in broadening their supply sources, in their search for new product lines, in securing profitable distributorships, and in general it facilitates their overseas commercial relations. Besides antecedent and other background and financial data, the credit agency report includes the ledger and sales experience of all suppliers and principals known to be dealing with the subject, plus information, verified and cross-checked, from banking and commercial sources. Though they make no claim to infallibility, these credit agencies render essential services to the export trade. They keep subscribers informed of vital changes in the status of their overseas customers. Often their warnings of impending difficulties permit timely protective action, saving costly collection steps and sometimes bad debt write-offs. An upgraded rating may be the green light for liberalized credit facilities, leading to increased sales and profit.

The information in the master credit file, regardless of source, is highly perishable and must be regularly revised. Not even the oldest, best-paying customer is immune to the effects of changing market conditions or other major developments. To get the most value from their services, the credit manager will share with his information agencies, his own experience with his customers. When submitting an inquiry, he will indicate the amount and terms of the proposed credit, present outstandings, and payment record of the customer. He reports payment delays, abandoned shipments, unjust claims, trade disputes and other significant happenings. His credit service agencies are thereby better able to serve him and his trade. The credit manager encourages his trade colleagues to also make active use of these service agencies, thereby enhancing their general effectiveness.

Country Information:

To keep abreast of the economic, exchange, political and other conditions and trends which may influence his risks, the credit executive also maintains a file for each of his active and potential markets. His notes made from attending group meetings, his exchanges with his bankers and with other traders, reports from his field representatives, excerpts from publications and from services subscribed to, all contribute to these country files. Trade publications specializing in the international field are especially helpful. A good example is International Trade Review (a Dun & Bradstreet publication), a monthly magazine for firms that sell, ship or otherwise operate abroad. Significant developments in principal world markets are regularly summarized in its pages, besides frequent surveys of individual countries. One page of each issue presents in chart form a resume of current World Market Conditions. This shows the currency values, exchange rates of today as compared with a year ago, exchange restrictions, recent collection experience, trade payments and internal business conditions, in some seventy countries. Among the many other highly valued periodicals are <u>International Commerce</u>, published by the U.S. Department of Commerce, the Federal Reserve Bank of New York's monthly tabulation of the Latin American Credit and Collection experience of leading U.S. banks, the publications of the International Monetary Fund and the World Bank, and the many bulletins and booklets issued by leading commercial banks with international departments, and by the regional and national export associations.

Setting Limits:

His analysis of the contents of his country information files guides the credit executive in adjusting his credit terms and market exposure limits. Keeping the exchange transfer risk foremost in mind, he is especially watchful for each development which may bear on the ability of customer countries to meet their dollar obligations. When he recognizes the signs of a developing foreign exchange shortage, he may find it necessary to shorten terms and cut his commitments in that market and may eventually arrange for his customers to establish letters of credit to cover their new orders until the situation clears.

Adjustments and Collections:

Maximum export sales volume can seldom be attained without the customer list including a percentage of firms that do not measure up to the highest credit standards, hence the maturity of each bill and its prompt settlement must be closely followed. Past-due accounts can sometimes be collected by close direct mail follow-up, perhaps with the intervention of the local representative. Differences in business pyschology and practice overseas must be taken into account, and judgment and skill exercised in the collection of accounts. Often what appears to be a deliquency is found to be attributable to some error in the exporter's shipping department, or the fault may lie with the carrier, the collecting bank, or other intermediary. Settlement of an actual past-due item can sometimes be achieved by the exporter accepting an immediate part payment and agreeing to an extended maturity for the balance. It then becomes advisable to have the debtor accept a new draft to cover this unpaid balance, showing the new maturity date, this to retain the exporter's legal rights. When the amount involved is substantial, and especially if the debtor's solvency or integrity is in question, the draft may be made subject to protest, for non-payment at maturity. Protest often brings immediate settlement, and, even when it does not, it usually simplifies and expedites subsequent legal action. Non-legal measures are generally preferred as they are the most economical means of collecting deliquent bills. The collection services offered by international credit service agencies are widely used by exporters in this connection, especially if there are many accounts involved for modest amounts, in developed countries.

With a view to simplification and economy of time and money in the adjustment of trade disputes, it is well to have properly worded arbitration clauses in all sales contracts and other commercial agreements. The International Chamber of Commerce is widely accepted as an arbitrator. Arbitration in Switzerland or most major cities can be arranged.

The Role of Credit:

Though the export business will always be subject to change in its make-up and direction, it is an essential part of Canada's economy and a plus factor in the profitable operation of our industry, agriculture, and work-force, with increasingly favourable long term growth prospects. The mounting competition and all present or future road-blocks merely spur the capable exporter to greater effort and more resourcefulness. Commercial credit, wisely administered and controlled, is and will continue to be a vital factor in this overseas trade, and, while the risks and problems involved sometimes differ from domestic practice, the experience of thousands of seasoned traders, large, medium and small, proves that they can be met. The key to success in export, as in all credit granting, is competent, experienced management.

Terms of Sale Affecting Ownership, Credit and the Placing of Insurance

There are various terms of sale such as: F.O.B. (Free on Board), F.A.S. (Free Along Side), C&F (Cost and Freight), which are common to foreign trade and yet are frequently misunderstood. These foreign trade terms of sale are of interest to the export credit man as well as other export personnel. Unfortunately these foreign trade terms are not interpreted in the same manner in all countries with the result that disputes often arise when there is damage in transit and ownership is open to question.

In North America, the Revised American Foreign Trade Definitions -1941 - are perhaps the best known, but they do not necessarily apply to all trade into or out of North America. The
precise meaning of the terms of sale is a matter that must be
agreed upon by the seller and the buyer in the contract of sale.
This point is especially important in view of the fact that courts of
various countries interpret foreign trade terms of sale in different
ways.

Precision of meaning is also important when using terms relating to quantity, volume, length and so forth in conjunction with
contracts of sale. The necessity for agreement is perhaps most
easily illustrated by the word "ton" which can mean -- a metric ton
(2204.6 pounds, a long ton (2240 pounds), or a short ton (2000
pounds).

Agreement as to costs is also an important element to be considered as a part of the terms of sale. For example, if inspection
certificates are required, there must be prior agreement between
the seller and the buyer regarding the payment of the expenses of
such certificates. Normally, all expenses are for the account of
the seller up to the point at which the buyer must handle the
subsequent movement of the goods. There are many elements in a
contract which cannot be covered here. My object in enumerating
a few of the common terms of sale is to emphasize the importance
of prior negotiation of such terms, and the absolute necessity of
avoiding the pitfall of believing that there are "customary" practices which are universally acceptable.

Ownership Situations:

At what point does the title to property actually pass from
seller to buyer? Determination of the ownership of goods moving
in foreign or domestic trade is not always a simple matter.

The terms of sale govern this relationship of property to
owner. An understanding of the different types of terms of sale
is essential if we are to know when insurance should be placed.

As classified in the Revised American Foreign Trade Definitions -1941, there are six groups of terms of sale:

1) <u>Ex Point of Origin</u> (as "Ex Factory", "Ex Warehouse", etc.)

These terms require the seller to place the goods at the disposal of the buyer at the specified point of origin on the date, and within the period fixed. The buyer must then take delivery at the agreed place and must bear all future costs and risks.

It should be emphasized that the goods are at the risk of the buyer from the time he is obligated to take delivery, even though he may not actually take delivery at that time. The buyer acquires an insurable interest as of that time and should protect his interest accordingly. The seller should consider contingency insurance in case the goods are abandoned.

2) <u>F.O.B.</u> (Free on Board)

Here the seller is required to bear costs and charges and to assume risks until the goods are loaded on board a <u>named</u> carrier at a <u>named</u> point. This might be on board a railroad car at an inland point of departure or on board an ocean vessel at a port of shipment.

Loss or damage to the shipment is borne by the seller until loaded at the point named and by the buyer after loading at that point, and insurance protection should be arranged accordingly. Actual transfer of interest is evidenced by the carrier furnishing a clean bill of lading or other transportation receipt.

It should be noted that F.O.B. sales terms, specifying named points beyond the seller's premises (for example F.O.B. vessel), place upon the seller the risks of transit until the title passes to the buyer at the point specified. In actual practice, however, F.O.B. terms are often so loosely specified that it is not easily resolved whether the seller or the buyer should bear the risk of physical loss or damage.

The seller is better advised to provide his own insurance protection through the use of an F.O.B. Sales Endorsement to his policy rather than rely on the warehouse-to-warehouse coverage contained in the buyer's insurance policy. The suggested coverage protects the seller from transit risks from the point of origin to the point at which title passes to the buyer.

334

When sales are made under letters of credit, the letters of credit normally cannot be used until an on-board bill of lading has been issued. If a loss or damage occurs before goods are loaded on board the ocean vessel, a clean on-board bill of lading will be not available and letters of credit cannot be used. This places a financial risk on the seller since he may not then be able to get the benefit of any insurance that the buyer may have arranged. Here again the seller should arrange for insurance to give him full protection.

At times, and particularly in certain trades, the seller on F.O.B. terms may provide marine insurance on behalf of the buyer. However, this involves a non-ownership situation and is discussed later.

Caution is advised when payment terms involve a draft calling for acceptance or payment before the documents are surrendered. The seller should employ the shipping terms consistent with the retention of title and insurance should also be controlled by the seller until the goods are taken over to the buyer.

3) F.A.S. (Free Along Side) as "F.A.S. Vessel, named port of shipment"

These sales terms require the seller to place goods along side the vessel or on the dock designated by the buyer, and to be responsible for loss or damage up to that point. Insurance under these terms is ordinarily placed by the buyer, but the seller should protect himself with an F.O.B. Sales Endorsement, as described above, for risks prior to the transfer of title. As in the F.O.B. discussion, the non-ownership situation is discussed later.

4) C&F (Cost & Freight) Named Point of Destination

Under these terms, the seller's price includes the cost of transportation to the named point but does not include the cost of insurance. Insurance under these terms is the responsibility of the buyer. The seller is responsible for loss or damage until the goods enter the custody of the ocean carrier or, if an on-board bill of lading is required, when the goods are actually delivered on board. Here again the seller needs insurance protection to that point at which his responsibilty for loss or damage ceases.

5) <u>C.I.F.</u> (Cost, Insurance and Freight) Named Point of Destination

Under these terms the selling price includes the cost of the goods, marine insurance, and transportation charges, to the named point of destination. The seller is responsible for loss or damage until the goods have been delivered into the custody of the buyer.

In C.I.F. sales, the seller is obligated to provide and pay for marine insurance, and to provide war risk insurance as obtainable in his market at the time of shipment. War risk insurance is at the buyer's expense. The seller and buyer should be in clear agreement on this point since in time of war or crisis the cost of war risk insurance may change rapidly.

It is desirable that the goods be insured against both marine and war risk with the same underwriter so that there can be the least possibility of dispute arising as to the cause of loss, as in the case of missing vessels and, to lesser degree, wartime collisions.

The character of the marine insurance should be agreed upon insofar as being W.A. (With Average) or F.P.A. (Free of Particular Average), as well as any other special risks that are covered in specific trades, or against which the buyer may wish individual protection. Among the special risks that should be considered and agreed upon between seller and buyer are theft, pilferage, leakage, breakage, sweat, contact with other cargoes, and other risks peculiar to any particular trade. It is important that contingent or collect freight and customs duty should be insured to cover Particular Average losses, as well as total loss after arrival and entry but before delivery.

In all cases, there should be a clear understanding as to the value for which the goods are to be insured. This may be of importance in case of assessment in general average. Full insurance to value will avoid difficulty should a general average situation arise.

In C.I.F. sales the seller must use ordinary care in selecting a financially sound underwriter. Should claims arise from a shipment, it is the buyer's responsibility to secure settlement. With the good will of the customer in mind, the exporter should select an underwriter providing fair, prompt and covenient loss service.

6) Ex Dock, Named Port of Importation

This term is more common to U.S. import than to export practice where it is seldom used. Under these terms the seller's price includes the cost of the goods and all additional charges necessary to put them on the dock at the named port of importation, with import duty paid. The seller is then obligated to provide and pay for marine insurance and, in the absence of specific agreement otherwise, war risk insurance.

The seller is responsible for any loss or damage, or both, until the expiration of the free time allowed on the dock at the named port of importation. Otherwise the comments under C.I.F. terms above apply here as well.

Non-Ownership Situations:

In certain situations the seller has an insurable interest, even though title has passed to the buyer and he is therefore a non-owner. In these situations the seller sells on terms F.O.B. inland point, he transfers the title to the buyer before the commencement of the ocean voyage. In this case the obligation to place marine and war risk insurance rests, strictly speaking, with the buyer.

However, it is customary in many trades for the seller on F.O.B. terms (or similar terms), by arrangement, to obtain insurance, as well as ocean freight space, for account of the buyer.

This is, in effect, an agency relationship. It can be provided for by a policy clause reading:

"to cover all shipment made by or to the assured for their own account as principals, or as agents for others and in which they have an insurable interest, or for the account of others from which written instructions to insure them have been received prior to any known or reported loss, damage, or accident, or prior to sailing of vessel."

Moreover, the seller on F.O.B. or other terms, under which the title passes to the buyer at some inland point of departure, will have a financial interest in the goods until payment has been received. This situation arises when the terms of payment call for sight draft against documents, or for acceptance at 30-60-90 days sight, or for open book account.

Under such circumstances, the seller will be well advised to place his own insurance to protect himself in the event that the loss or damage to the shipment impairs the buyer's desire to make payment as originally contemplated. For example, the buyer may be uninsured or the buyer's coverage may be inadequate because of under-insurance or restricted conditions. The buyer's insurance company may be less liberal in loss adjustments than the insurer of the seller or, because of currency restrictions, a foreign company may be hampered in its ability to transmit funds.

When claims are paid by a foreign insurance company, devaluation of foreign currencies may cause loss in exchange when the insurance is not expressed in United States dollars.

Insolvency of the foreign insurance carrier, while unlikely, could also occur to the embarrassment of the buyer.

In the event of the buyer's own insolvency, any claims collected under his own open policy might be recoverable in favour of his insolvent estate and not, in the first instance at least, in favour of the seller in this country.

At times the total loss of a shipment has prevented the payment for the goods. This has occurred in countries which would not allocate foreign exchange unless the goods are actually landed and cleared through customs.

Some of these contingencies may seem remote. However, they do point up the fact that a seller does in fact bear a financial risk until such time as payment from the foreign buyer is actually in hand.

The seller will be able to meet such a situation at moderate cost by placing insurance with his own underwriters in this country on a "contingency" or "difference in conditions" basis. The foreign insurance will then be primary in its attachment. However, to the extent that it may fall short in a given situation, it will be supplemented by the seller's coverage. The seller is then protected.

The foregoing considers the situation from the standpoint of the exporter who sells on F.O.B. terms. A sale on terms requiring the seller to arrange insurance will frequently simplify the problem. This enables the seller to place his own primary insurance and thus to deal throughout with his own underwriters in this country.

When there are world currency dislocations this is a distinct advantage. In the event of a loss, the seller who has placed insurance in this country may be able to make replacement shipments without becoming involved in foreign exchange or import control difficulties. At the buyer's request, he can credit himself with the insurance proceeds following the loss or damage to the original shipment and apply such credit to future shipments.

The foreign trader will need to consult his insurance specialists freely, in working out the insurance coverage which will protect his financial interests.

Formerly it was the practice to arrange specific marine insurance policies only when they were needed. This method is still used by those not regularly engaged in foreign trade.

However, by far the greater volume of ocean marine insurance is now written under what is known as open policies. These are insurance contracts which remain in force until cancelled and under which individual successive shipments are reported or declared. The open policy saves time and expense for all concerned and is important in the protection of receivables.

Commercial Bank Export Financing
by
Eric D. Ferguson
Vice President
Trade Finance - Canada
World Trade and Merchant Banking Division
The Royal Bank of Canada

1. INTRODUCTION

Export trade is a rewarding area of business. It has many things in common with business here in Canada. Foreign buyers, like those on the other side of town, are keenly interested in the price, quality, and availability of the goods you are offering. They also want to know how the goods will be shipped, who will cover the transportation and insurance costs, and when payment will have to be made.

You will, however, face a larger number of different decisions when involved in exporting. Many of these decisions are not complex, but their variety makes exporting more interesting than doing business exclusively in Canada. Exporting becomes profitable when the right options are chosen.

I don't want to give the impression that you must make a vast number of decisions with every export sale. In many cases, industry practice, competitive pressure, and common sense will narrow the range of options available. You won't have difficulty deciding whether to:

- Use a U.S. flag vessel to ship goods to Iran

- Agree to deliver goods F.O.B. vessel, Churchill, Manitoba in January, or

- Require a confirmed letter of credit before selling to IBM.

While these examples illustrate some of the obvious pitfalls of export trade, they are also meant to point out the needs for you to know your <u>customer</u>, your <u>competition</u>, and the <u>environment</u>. Probably no one person will have all the information that you may need in order to start exporting, or to move into a new market. However, many of the people you will be meeting during this course will have some of the answers.

For my own part, I will try to shed some light on the mysteries of trade finance, including:

- Short term export finance,
- Seller credit,
- Buyer credit,
- Trade guarantee schemes.

You must have a good understanding of these topics because your customer may want financing, and your competitors may be offering it. Before beginning commercial negotiations, you should try to anticipate what type of financing your customer may want, and have a good idea what will be possible. After all, why should the financing component of your proprosal be any different than your sales price, technical specifications, or delivery schedules?

There are many exciting success stories of Canadian companies growing spectacularly through exporting.

To be successful yourself, you will have to be a step ahead of your competition. You will have to satisfy your customer's needs technically and financially. I am sure that you already have the ability and resources to do that, but we all have to make sure that we persist and push ourselves to meet these challenges.

2. SHORT TERM EXPORT FINANCING

In order to make a sale, it may be necessary for you to offer your customer some form of credit. This can be done in a number of ways, and the method you choose will depend upon how well you know your customer, and what financing is being offered by your competition.

Before we examine the major tyes of short term credit (i.e. less than one year), I think it is important that we focus briefly on your customer. If you, or the bank, are going to extend credit to the customer, it will be necessary for someone to assess whether that buyer is good for the money.

Unfortunately, credit evaluation takes time, and information. Financial statements and bankers' reports are the main sources of this information, and buyers realize that it will be needed if they are to receive credit. Unfortunately, salesmen are usually too shy to ask for it.

Bankers, on the other hand, are usually described as being a rather sour bunch. I suspect that we acquired that reputation after receiving one too many last minute credit requests with no supporting information. You will keep your banker much happier, and have greater success, if you give us as much lead time as possible, and provide:

-- Complete name and address of the buyer

-- Complete name and address of the bank branch with which the buyer deals.

-- Financial statements of the buyer where available.

It doesn't seem like much, does it?

Well now, let's move on to the various types of short term trade financing.

A) OPEN ACCOUNT

This is the most common and simple method of financing export sales. Most of our exports to the U.S.A. are financed under open account, and the method is used frequently for sales to a number of European countries.

The process of selling under open account, internationally or domestically, is virtually identical, i.e. you:

-- asses the credit-worthiness of the buyer
-- ship the goods
-- send an invoice, which may be payable in, say, 30, 60, or 90 days
-- hope that you get paid.

In such cases, a bank may provide financing for your receivable, but only as part of your overall credit line. The risk of non-payment remains exclusively yours, although insurance protection in the event of non-payment may be provided by the Export Development Corporation, or other private insurers.

B) COLLECTIONS

Instead of sending an invoice, you may decide to obtain payment by drawing a Draft on the foreign buyer, and arranging for a bank to collect the funds on your behalf.

Drafts (or Trade Bills) are usually described as being either clean or documentary. Most Trade Bills are documentary, i.e., they are accompanied by a series of shipping documents. The documents are important because they usually give the holder title to the goods.

There are two basic types of documentary collections, both of which afford somewhat more protection than an open account transaction.

I) Documents on Payment (DOP)

Using the DOP method, you ship the goods and bring to the bank a draft drawn on the buyer, together with the shipping documents. At your request, we will forward the draft and documents for collection to our correspondent bank (or our own branch) in the buyer's city. The foreign bank will be instructed not to release the documents until payment is received. When this occurs, the funds will be sent back to us, and credited to your account, while the buyer will be able to obtain the goods from the customs warehouse.

This system is simple, but it is not absolutely foolproof. There have been instances where the documents have been re-leased prior to payment, taking away any protection you may have had; or, if payment is not received, you must decide whether to warehouse, or reload the goods.

II) Documents on Acceptance (DOA)

In some cases, you may wish to provide a period of credit to your customer. Under the DOA system, you will draw a draft on the importer for the appropriate amount and trade term (i.e., a time draft).

Documents will be released to the buyer against signed acceptance of the draft. At maturity, the buyer pays the collecting bank the amount due under the bill. The funds will then be remitted back to your bank in Canada, and will be credited to your account.

The advantages of using documentary collections are readily apparent:

-- Some control over the goods is maintained through control of the documents,

-- When trade credit is offered using the documents on acceptance process, the buyer acknowledges his debt to you. Of course, acknowledging a debt doesn't guarantee that it will be paid, but my lawyer friends tell me that it is better to have an accepted Trade Bill in court, than a purchase order and invoice. On the other hand, litigation in most foreign countries is even less pleasant than it is here in Canada.

C) LETTERS OF CREDIT (L/C)

Letters of Credit are widely used instruments of international trade. They give you, the exporter, the benefit of being able to transfer your credit risk away from your customer, to a bank.

A commercial Letter of Credit is simply an instrument or letter, issued by bank for account of an importer, in favour of an exporter, for the purpose of financing the purchase of goods or services. In other words, it is a written undertaking by your customer's bank, that drafts drawn by you on the importer, will be paid on presentation on the due dates. The Letter of Credit does contain a number of conditions however, which must be strictly adhered to, or the drafts will not be paid. If, for example, the L/C calls for 12 copies of the commercial invoice, and only 11 are provided, then the opening bank will not pay.

During the commercial negotiations, you and your customer will agree on all aspects of the transaction, including those documents that must accompany the L/C. The importer will know, for example, what documents are required to get goods through customs in his country. Those documents will almost certainly be listed in the Letter of Credit.

Letters of Credit can be amended after they are opened, provided that the parties agree. They cannot, however, be cancelled by the opening bank unless they are revocable. Obviously, you should only accept Letters of Credit that irrevocable.

As I mentioned previously, if an L/C is used, your credit risk is transferred from your customer to his bank. If that bank is financially sound, and is located in a prosperous country, then your risk may be quite small. On the other hand, you may not feel too secure with an L/C opened by a bank in Upper Volta or Angola. If this is the case, you could ask us to confirm the Letter of Credit. In other words, if the foreign bank doesn't pay, we will (provided, of course, that we had agreed to accept the risk initially). I would, however, caution you that even confirmed Letters of Credit are not absolutely iron-clad. They will not protect you against not being able to deliver the documents required -- ports closed (Iran), bottoms not available (Cuba*), or foreign exhchange blockage (Jamaica).

I have treid to cover the highlights of Letter of Credit, but would caution you that there are many technical aspects that must not be overlooked. Many books have been written on Letters of Credit and I would suggest that you examine one or two in order to become more familiar with the subject. Your best source of information and advice, however, is the Letter of Credit specialist, and you should contact him for assistance.

D) EXPORT CREDIT INSURANCE

One of the services provided by the Canadian Government's Export Development Corporation is export credit insurance. Several forms of insurance are provided, and I am sure Don Keill will have something to say about them.

---

* Cuban Letters of Credit often specified that goods were to be shipped in Cuban vessels. If the Cubans happened to be short of money, the ships wouldn't arrive.

I will say, however, that having EDC insurance often makes it easier, and less expensive to obtain bank financing for your foreign receivables. If those receivables are being financed on a recourse basis (i.e., loans or recourse purchase of Trade Bills), it is possible to instruct EDC to pay any losses to a bank. While this is ot an assignment of the policy, it does offer a bank some degree of security.

If foreign receivables are purchased without recourse, your EDC insurance policy may be assigned to a bank. This provides the bank with 90% protection, but the remaining 10% will be at the bank's own risk.

I suggest that you familiarize yourselves with EDC's insurance programs. The corporation publishes a number of useful brochures, and has representatives in the major cities across Canada with whom you can discuss your requirements.

3. SUPPLIER CREDIT

There may be occasions when you have extended credit to your customer, and you in turn would like to obtain some form of financing for your own foreign receivables.

A) Discount of Term Drafts

As mentioned earlier, one of the most common methods of extending credit to your customers is through the use of term or time drafts. Term drafts are used either with collections (documents on acceptance), and Letters of Credit. Unlike those receivables arising out of sales made on open account, drafts may be purchased by a bank with or without recourse to you, i.e.:

i) With recourse: When a bank purchases a draft from you with recourse, any non-payment by the buyer will be charged directly to you. This differs very little from a loan, except that a loan appears as a direct liability on your balance sheet, while a draft that is purchased with recourse is only a contingent liability.

If you anticipate a reasonable volume of such transactions, a line of credit may be established for you by the bank for discounting trade acceptances. These lines are normally revolving, and would form part of your overall line of credit. Drafts are usually purchased at a discount, and the rate charged would be similar, if not identical, to that charged on your other borrowings.

ii) <u>Without recourse</u>: If you would prefer to obtain financing that is completely off your balance sheet, the bank will consider purchasing (discounting) a draft <u>without</u> recourse to you. In other words, if a loss is incurred, it will be for the bank's account.

In order for the bank to assume this risk, it will be necessary to assess the buyer's financial condition (your assistance may be sought in obtaining such information). If it is acceptable, the draft will be discontinued at a rate that reflects the risk of non-payment by the buyer.

The risk may be substantially improved by the addition of a guarantee or aval from your customer's local bank. (This is quite common in many countries). The rate that would be charged in this case would refelect the risk of non-payment by the bank rather than the buyer.

If you anticipate regular dealings with a particular buyer, it is often useful to arrange for a revolving non-recourse discount line to be established. The line would not form part of your own credit facilities.

B) <u>Discount of Commercial Invoices</u>

While the practice of discounting term drafts is well established, it unfortunately is not applicable in those cases where goods are sold on an open account basis. More than 60% of Canada's exports are sold in this way, and as you know, when sales are made on open account, the accounts receivable remain on the exporter's books, and are financed as part of its normal domestic credit line. In many cases, exporters prefer to obtain immediate cash for their receivables, but have not been able to do so if the sale is made on open account.

The Royal Bank has recently devised a method of financing open account sales in the same way that Trade Bills are financed. This is accomplished by having the foreign buyer acknowledge their acceptance of the amount and term of an invoice, and agree to remit the funds on the due date. While the accepted invoice is

347

not a negotiable instrument like a Trade Bill, we are prepared to treat such invoices as if they were.

This form of off-balance sheet financing (which may be recourse or non-recourse), has not previously been available in Canada, but we feel that it will have a significant impact on the ability of exporters to finance their foreign sales.

We will be providing this financing through a wholly-owned subsidiary of the bank, Royal Bank Export Finance Co. Ltd., for REFCO for short. REFCO will not have its own branch network, but will operate out of our international centres across the country. (REFCO will also be the financing vehicle for the discounting of Trade Bills).

We are very excited about this new service, and are confident that it will meet a very real need of the Canadian exporting community.

C) A Forfait Financing

Another type of supplier credit is a Forfait Financing which is a medium term financing technique that the Royal Bank has just introduced to Canada although Forfait Financing has been used in Europe for some time. However, I have no idea why it hasn't been used in Canada until now.

Forfaiting is a term generally used to denote the purchase of obligations falling due at some future date, arising from the sale of goods and services, without any recourse to any previous holders of the obligations.

In a typical transaction, you will receive a cash downpayment of 10-20% of the contract, and trade receivables, such as Bills of Exchange or Promissory Notes guaranteed by a bank in the importer's country, for the rest. The receivables normally bear interest at a fixed rate, which can be either incorporated in the face value of the receivables, or expressed in a separate set of receivables having maturity dates coinciding with the principal payments.

The Royal Bank will purchase the receivables from you at a discount from their face value. The amount of the discount represents our interest charge, and is fixed at the time of purchase even though the receivables may not be payable for several years.

The transaction can be completed in just a few days, and involves a minimum of paperwork. We are very excited about the program, and hope that it will become widely used in this country.

4. BUYER CREDIT

Medium/long term financing is often offered by exporters to enable foreign buyers to purchase capital goods or other fixed assets. In other words, you and/or the bank and the Export Development Corporation lend money to your customer to buy the goods in question. Such financing is usually called "buyer credit".

Because of the very great economic and political importance of the export sector to the economies of industrialized countries, it is not surprising that governments are frequently directly involved in providing financial assistance. This assistance takes many forms, including insurance and offering subsidized loans for foreign buyers.

EDC will, for example, make loans that:

- are usually at a fixed rate of interest (but a portion of the financing may be floating at commercial bank rates),

- may be for terms of up to 12 years, and more

- may be dominated in one or more of the major international currencies. The loan documentation will make provision for disbursing Canadian dollars to you in accordance with a pre-arranged schedule.

Canadian banks can usually provide complimentary financing at floating rates for the 15% downpayment on Canadian goods and services, as well as 100% financing for non-Canadian (e.g., local or foreign) costs.

The financing that I have described generally applies to transactions of at least $1 million. EDC has also established lines of credit with financial institutions in a number of countries that can be utilized to finance smaller sales.

You should also be aware that there is a fierce competition in most aspects of exporting "big ticket" items. For example, British manufacturers are able to offer fixed rate financing in a number of currencies at rates as low as 8-12%, while the Japanese are making export loan in yen available at even lower rates. Several other countries are equally aggressive, and we mustn't fool ourselves -- this is very tough competition indeed. Canada is prepared to match financing terms offered by other countries, but we must expect to lose some sales partially as a result of subsidized export financing.

5. FINANCIAL GUARANTEES

There are a number of types of guarantees which are used in certain export transactions. I will describe briefly the more important types.

I) Bid Bonds

Very often an exporter may wish to bid on a specific offshore contract and is required to submit a Bid Bond with the tender documents. This can range from 1% to 5% of the bid amount. The purpose is to provide some protection to the buyer in the event that the successful bidder does not enter into the contract after being selected. Often these bonds are issued by the local banks in the buyer's country at the request of the exporter's bank and against a counter guarantee of the exporter's bank. Instructions covering issuance are usually conveyed to the opening bank via a telex. As each country uses it own type of Bid Bond there is no real standard format prevailing for all countries. Simple drawing instructions are usually required.

II) Advance Payment Bonds

These bonds are normally used to secure advance or down-payment provided by the buyer, often reducing as down-payment is earned. As in the case of Bid Bonds, simple drawing instructions permitting easy call to the buyer are normal practice.

III) Performance Bonds

These may be called during the duration of a contract and utilized to provide compensation to the buyer in the event that the exporter for any reason fails to perform under the terms and conditions of the contract. The amount normally is reduced pro-rata with the value of the work undertaken for the contract. We would add that it is not uncommon for a Performance Bond to be issued in excess of the required figure or for a longer period to serve as a warranty.

IV) Warranty Bonds

These are issued to provide a compensation to a buyer in the event that product is faulty or does not work. It may be issued for up to 10% of the contract amount and essentially replace the hold back. These are commonly used in the Middle Eastern and Far Eastern countries and often in the U.S.A.

6. CONCLUSION

In conclusion, I would like to repeat that in order for you to be successful in exporting you will have to be:

- Very sensitive to the needs of your customers,

- Aware of what your competition is doing, and

- In tune to what's happening in the marketplace.

In today's environment, offering the right combination of price, quality, delivery and financing will be critical to your success. If you make a commitment to exporting, and are prepared to do what the marketplace demands, I am sure that you will find exporting to be a very interesting and profitable endeavour.

The Role of the Export Development Corporation in Export Financing

Donald Keill
Senior Vice-President - Export Insurance Group
Export Development Corporation
Ottawa, Ontario

The Export Development Corporation (EDC) is a commercially self-sustaining enterprise, owned by the Government of Canada, that provides financial services to facilitate and expand Canadian export trade and create employment at home. It does this by providing insurance, guarantees, direct financing and other services necessary for exporters and/or investors to compete in international markets. Similar facilities are provided by every major exporting country in support of its exporters.

EDC is a body corporate, having the capacity to sue and be sued.

Its Head Office is in Ottawa and Region Offices are located in Montreal, Toronto, Vancouver, and Halifax.

Direction of the affairs of EDC is vested in a 12-member Board. To reflect the nature of a publicly-owned corporation involved with the Canadian business and banking community, the Board of which the President of the Corporation is chairman, consists of senior representatives of Government and the Canadian financial and private business sectors.

Operating Capacity

EDC has authority to undertake maximum outstanding financial liabilities of $26 billion.

Insurance and Guarantees

The ceiling for liabilities of export credits insurance and guarantees issued under the authority of the EDC's management or Board of Directors is $10 billion.

liability of a proposed transaction is in excess of that which EDC would normally undertake, and in the opinion of the Minister it is in the national interest that a contract be entered into, the Governor in Council may authorize the Corporation to insure, or guarantee, or both at the Government's risk. The ceiling for government account is $3.5 billion. Foreign Investment Insurance is issued exclusively for Government account.

Loans and Guarantees

The ceiling for financing export sales of capital equipment and services may total $12.5 billion. EDC may lend up to a maximum liability outstanding of $10 billion under the authority of its Board of Directors; and $2.5 billion under the authority of the Government of Canada for the government's own account where the EDC Board has declined to approve because of risks, size or any other reason.

Funding

EDC meets its funding requirements by borrowing in the private and public capital markets around the world. The Corporation issues its own paper and enjoys a high-rated credit standing which enables it to obtain funds at favourable interest rates. Thus, the Corporation can offer competitive commercial financing arrangements to support Canadian export endeavours.

EDC offers:

1. Credits Insurance to exporters and Guarantees to banks and other financial institutions that finance Canadian exporters.

2. Direct loans to foreign buyers of Canadian capital equipment and technical services and guarantees to financial institutions against losses incurred in financing the foreign buyer in an export transaction.

3. Foreign Investment Insurance, insuring Canadians against loss of, or in respect of, investment abroad by reason of political action.

4. Performance Security Insurance and Surety Bond Cover for Canadian exporters, banks and other financial institutions against wrongful calls on performance bonds and guarantees and rightful calls which are outside the control of the exporter.

EXPORT CREDITS INSURANCE

Export credits insurance offers Canadian exporters protection against non-payment by foreign buyers outside due to both commercial and political risks.

Types of Cover

EDC policies may be issued to cover goods and services sold on short-term credit -- normally up to 180 days; or on medium-term credit -- normally up to five years.

As well as sales of goods and services, EDC may insure payment for invisible exports including the sale or licensing to a foreign customer of any right in a patent, trademark or copyright and advertising consultant fees, etc. Policies may be endorsed to provide cover for such transactions as floorplan arrangements, sales to affiliates and sales of consignment stock.

Risks Insured

The main risks covered under an EDC Policy are:

1. Insolvency of the foreign buyer;

2. Default;

3. Repudiation;

4. Additional handling charges resulting from interruption or diversion of voyage outside North America;

5. Blockage of funds or transfer difficulties which prevent the Canadian exporter from receiving payments;

6. War between Canada and the buyer's country;

7. War or revolution in the buyer's country;

8. Cancellation or renewal of an export permit or the imposition of restrictions on the export of goods not previously subject to restriction;

9. Any other cause outside the control of both the exporter and the buyer which arises from events occurring outside Canada and the continental United States of America - for example, the cancellation of an import licence or the imposition of import restrictions on goods not previously subject to licence or restriction.

Co-insurance

EDC normally covers a maximum of 90 per cent of the amount of the loss, with the exporter required to assume the remaining 10 per cent.

Types of Policies

There are basically two types of EDC policies: a Global Comprehensive Policy which covers export credit sales to all countries for the period of one year; and a Specific Transaction Policy which covers a specific capital goods or major service transaction.

Global Comprehensive Policies

Global Comprehensive Policies are available to cover sales of consumer goods and general commodities, or services, sold on short-term credit. There is no minimum dollar value of exports required.

The principle of insuring all export sales to all countries under such a policy gives EDC a broad spread of risk, which enables it to quote favourable premium rates. EDC is prepared to consider the exclusion of certain countries as long as those countries remaining to be insured offer the Corporation an acceptable spread of risk. Sales to the United States may be excluded.

Premiums are based on the class or type of goods or services sold; the countries to which they are sold; the length of credit terms for each country and other factors.

Premium rates are set out by country in each Policy and are payable monthly, based on the invoice value of credit sales for the previous month. If there have been no shipments during the reporting period, no premium is due.

Specific Transaction Policies

A Specific Transaction Policy is issued to cover a specific sale of capital, semi-capital goods or services sold on medium-term credit. The premium rates for this type of policy are higher than for Global Comprehensive Policies, since they are charged in respect of a transaction for which the risk is carried over an extended period. The premium is payable on acceptance of EDC's offer to insure.

Protection for Lenders

To assist the exporters in financing exports, EDC will agree to pay any Canadian bank or financial institution the proceeds of any loss payable under a policy. In addition, EDC will agree to assign the exporter's rights under a policy to a financial institution in return for non-recourse financing to the exporter.

In the case of Specific Transaction Policies, EDC may issue unconditional guarantees to chartered banks or other financial institutions that agree to provide non-recourse financing to the Canadian supplier.

FINANCING SERVICES

Financing Sales Abroad

EDC makes medium and long-term loans to foreign buyers of Canadian capital goods and services, or guarantees bank loans to such buyers. The Corporation also establishes lines of credit with certain countries and foreign financial institutions where such arrangements will facilitate and stimulate the export of capital goods and services from Canada.

In addition, EDC provides a Forfaiting (Note Purchase) program where the corporation will purchase series of promissory notes drawn by foreign buyers of Canadian goods and services and made payable to the Canadian exporter. These notes will be guaranteed by an acceptable bank and endorsed over to EDC on a non-recourse basis.

EDC funds are disbursed directly to Canadian suppliers on behalf of the borrower, in effect providing the exporter with cash sales. EDC loans have ranged in amounts from less than $100,000 to multiples of millions.

The Terms

A transaction eligible for EDC financing is normally one for which credit terms beyond two years are necessary and justifiable, although in practice, loans are more applicable for transactions of a size in which the terms of repayment are normally more than five years.

Each export transaction must provide significant benefits to Canada and is reviewed in consideration of such factors as: the level of the Canadian participation in the project; its Canadian content; the type and number of Canadian jobs sustained and/or created; the effect on sub-contractors and the impact of the transaction in creating future export orders. Further, it has to be demonstrated that the project is commercially and technically viable and offers adequate security to the lenders.

Application for Financing

Either the Canadian exporter or the buyer may submit a loan application to EDC. The borrower need not be the importer in the transaction, as for example when a government might borrow on behalf of one of its agencies, or a bank on behalf of one of its clients.

An early approach to EDC shoud be made to determine the eligibility of a proposed transaction for financing.

Canadian Banks

EDC seeks the maximum possible involvement of Canadian banks and other financial institutions and works with them in a variety of ways, including arrangements for direct participation, down-payment, pre-shipment and local-cost financing.

PERFORMANCE SECURITY INSURANCE

EDC may provide insurance and guarantees for advance payment and preformance-type bonds required to be established by the exporter in respect of an export transaction.

North American and Forfeiture-type Bonds

Bonds required by buyers to guarantee performance are of two types:

1. A North American type bond, which requires proof of default by the contractor and provides that the surety company take the decision with respect to the course of action to be taken to remedy the default;

2. A forfeiture-type bond, which may be called unilaterally on demand by the buyer and no remedial action may be taken. When bonds are callable on demand the exporter faces the risk of a wrongful or frivolous call by the foreign buyer -- this means the loss of the amount of the bond which could be 10 per cent or more of the value of the cancelled contract. North American performance bonds are normally provided by surety companies while forfeiture-type bonds are normally provided by the exporter's bank in the form of a Letter of Credit in favour of the buyer. The bank normally reduces the exporter's line of credit by the amount of the bond which decreases the firm's working capital.

The Program

A comprehensive, five-tier insurance package for performance bonds and guarantees is available to Canadian exporters, banks, surety companies and other financial institutions through EDC.

1. Performance Security Insurance: Exporter's Policy - insuring the exporter, up to 90 percent, against a wrongful call of the exporter's bond by the foreign buyer.

2. Performance Security Insurance: Bank Policy - insuring a Canadian bank or other financial institution against a call on a bond usually in the form of a Letter of Credit issued by it to a foreign buyer on behalf of a Canadian exporter.

3. Consortium Insurance - providing cross consortium liability insurance to members of a limited liability exporting consortium to protect members against the possibility of non-performance by one or more members of the consortium.

4. Surety Bond Insurance - insuring a domestic surety company which provides a performance bond to a foreign buyer. EDC will share the risk of loss on the basis of a percentage of the insured risk.

5. Bid Security Guarantees - covering financial institutions against both rightful and wrongful calls on Letters of Credit they have issued in favour of buyers on behalf of exporters as security for bids.

Eligibility

Performance Security Insurance with respect to an export transaction is available to any organization doing business in Canada.

EDC's normal operating criteria will generally apply in determining the eligibility of a proposed transaction. In most instances an export transaction insurable for purposes of EDC's credits insurance would be eligible for performance security insurance.

FOREIGN INVESTMENT INSURANCE

The major criterion for Foreign Investment Insurance cover is that the proposed Canadian investment benefit both Canada and the host country. Benefits to Canada include royalties, sales of capital equipment and services abroad, and proceeds from continuing sales of replacement parts, components and raw materials. Benefits to the host country include the expansion of employment, gains in production techniques and skills, and an improvement in the standard of living.

Flexible Coverage

The program covers three broad political risks:

1. Inconvertibility, or inability to repatriate earnings or capital.

2. Expropriation.

3. War, revolution or insurrection.

Investors are normally required to take coverage for all three political risks. Under certain circumstances, some selection of the cover may be considered.

The contract is available for up to 15 years and, as long as the conditions of the policy are maintained, can be cancelled only by the exporter, and not EDC.

Co-insurance

EDC requires the investor to carry a percentage of the risk, normally 15 per cent.

Eligibility

Almost any right that an individual or firm might acquire in a foreign enterprise is eligible -- including equity, loans, management or technical services contracts, royalty and licensing agreements.

Investment may be in the form of cash, contribution in kind, or a financial guarantee to a party investing in the foreign country.

Only new investments are accepted by EDC. They may include a significant expansion, modernization or development of an existing enterprise. Investments in oil and mineral exploration are also eligible.

Host Government Approval

The Canadian investor should obtain a statement from the host government signifying its approval both of the project or activity, and of the Canadian investment in that project or activity.

Export Financing - The Role of the Canadian International Development Agency

by
Malcolm Sutherland-Brown, P. Eng,
Director, Consultant and Industrial Relations
Canadian International Development Agency

BACKGROUND

Like so much of Canadian life and Canadian development, Canadian participation in international development or external aid has been evolutionary rather than revolutionary. We have increased our contributions in the 31 years since the start with the Columbo Plan (1950) with only $25 million to over $1.4 billion this year (1981-2). One thing which becomes clearer each year is that a tremendous cooperative world effort is necesary to improve the economic and social conditions in the poorer countries. I shall not dwell on this but get on with what Canada is doing and how Canadians and Canadian Industry, in particular, can and really must play a part.

CIDA'S AIM AND CANADIAN INDUSTRY

The aim of Canadian development assistance is to support the efforts of the Developing Countries in fostering their economic growth and the evolution of their social systems. That is rather a formal statement but put in other words: Canada has undertaken to transfer its experience, both in goods and services, to the Developing Countries. To do this it requires the help of Canadian Industry in the broadest sense of that expression. Again, put another way: the Developing Country is the client of CIDA while Canadian Industry provides the means of doing the work.

CIDA is often criticized for not fostering in some way, a particular section of Canadian Industry. However, there are others whose particular duty that is, particularly in encouraging export, such as the Export Development Corporation and the Department of Industry, Trade & Commerce. On the other hand, if a Canadian company can secure a contract in the CIDA programs or CIDA supported programs, it has one of the worries of doing business abroad removed. It is guaranteed payment, in Canadian dollars, in Canada.

Perhaps at this point I should describe the different programs and ways in which CIDA works.

MULTILATERAL PROGRAMS

There are many international acronyms or names that one hears such as: HABITAT, UNCTAD, UNIDO, UNDP, World Food Program, FAO, WHO, World Weather Watch and so on. Canada, mainly through CIDA, contributes to or takes part in these and others such as the various development banks. These programs are generally referred to as multilateral. About 37% of CIDA's funds are given to multilateral agencies and these funds are essentially untied. However, this operation buys the right for Canadian Industry to take part in or compete for the work of these agencies. This means that this year a contribution of $600 million opens a potential market of $25 billion.

BILATERAL PROGRAMS

These programs are where there is a direct relationship between Canada and the country which it is working with or helping (generally known as the Recipient). The funds may be provided as a grant or loan depending on the foreign exchange condition of the country and the type of work to be done. If a loan is involved it may be at 0%, with 10 years of grace and 50 years to repay, or with the more economically advanced countries at 3%, 7 years of grace and 30 years to repay. These bilateral programs are worked out after a request from the country concerned and after the CIDA planners have thoroughly studied it or worked it out with the country's planners or responsible agency. Bilateral work may take the form of the supply of goods or services. It may be food or commodities such as fertilizers or semi-processed materials like pulp in direct support of industry, or it may be projects in energy, telecommunications, transportation or the development of resources. It may be education from the construction of schools, colleges or universities, to equipping them and providing teachers or training for teachers. It is now recognized that the training of managers at all levels and of technicians is of the utmost importance.

One of the most interesting of the bilateral programs is the "Line of Credit". In this case a loan is made to the developing country to purchase under normal commercial arrangements, goods or services from Canada. Usually the lines of credit (LOC) operate under normal sales arrangements which CIDA merely monitors and then pays the bills.

The Bilateral Programs Branch has about 49% of the funds and this year that represents almost $700 million (see data sheet at end of text).

GUIDELINES AND RESTRICTIONS

I have already said that the multilateral programs are essentially untied. This means, broadly speaking, that the funds can be spent anywhere and for the aid of any country in the programs of the multilateral agencies.

In the bilateral programs, however, there are some restrictions or guidelines which must be followed. 80% of the bilaterial funds are tied to supply of goods or services from Canada. This requires that a company supplying services must be beneficially owned by Canadians, based in Canada, and employing Canadians. On the other hand if goods (rather than services) are being purchased, then the goods must have a "Canadian Content" of 66 2/3%. This figure has evolved over about 18 years, being reduced from firstly 100% and then 80% to take note of conditions which exist in Canadian Industry. Very simply the 66 2/3% "Canadian Content" will permit you to put an engine and possible a gear train in a piece of machinery. This is, of course, because very few IC engines and gear trains are made in Canada. In certain sophisticated machines it may allow you to install an imported computer or controls. The untied portion of the bilateral funds (20%) also permits the spending of funds in the recipient country for local costs. Generally the country itself (except in the case of the poorest) contributes to some part of the project such as local costs.

Very briefly I have explained the difference between "tied funds" (must mainly be spent in Canada) and "untied funds".

The latter may be spent almost anywhere and are usually allocated to multilateral agencies.

SPECIAL PROGRAMS

Another program which CIDA has been trying to encourage is that done under our Business and Industry Division in an effort to encourage the formation of businesses or industries in the Developing Countries. Provision is made for up to $10,000 in travelling expenses for a Canadian company to go to a Developing Country to see whether it can start a branch office or plant or other form of subsidiary. If a study or report is required CIDA will pay half its cost up to $100,000. An important consideration is that the recipient must have financial control, i.e. 51% but the Canadian company may also have a management contract. Several Canadian companies have been successful in this program and we hope more will take advantage of it. Two more recent programs of industrial cooperation for which CIDA will contribute up to $250,000 are:

a) The Canadian Project Preparation Facility (CPPF). This is mainly for consultants who can see a needed project in a developing country and receive agreement to their ideas by the country and CIDA.

b) The Canadian Technology Transfer Facility (CTTF). This involves ideas to improve working conditions and technology in a country and again requires approval by the country and CIDA.

CIDA will also support non-Canadian government organizations (or NGOs as we call them) if they are working in the poorer countries. Normally we will provide dollar for dollar to a Canadian group or service club such as churches, the Red Cross, Rotary Club and so on if they start an educational or health project such as schools or clinics. It is interesting to note that if the NGO is located in any of the four western provinces, their governments also contribute a dollar so that the original $1 becomes $4 when it gets to the project.

RESEARCH

I am often asked about research. This is mainly done by the

364

International Development Research Centre which this year received $37 million from CIDA (see data sheet). It is based in Ottawa but has an international board and staff and 3 offices overseas.

INTERNATIONAL EMERGENCY RELIEF

CIDA is the federal agency responsible for helping in international disasters such as earthquake, flood, drought, war aftermath and so on. This is generally done by a grant of funds through the Canadian Red Cross or direct dispatch of emergency food, medicaments, clothing or shelter. Funds required are always more than provided by the budget (see data sheet).

STARTING INTO EXPORT OR AID WORK

May I offer a few words of advice to anyone or any company considering a move towards overseas work. Whatever you do, start by contacting the Canadian Trade Commissioner in the country or region concerned. He will tell you whom to see and will "open doors for you". Further, he will tell you whether CIDA, EDC or any of the multilateral agencies are operating in the area. As far as CIDA is concerned he will tell you about any lines of credit it may have and whether it has a Field Representative in the area.

There are four factors in working abroad which must be stressed. It is difficult to put them in priority but I think the first one I have listed is really first. They are:

1. Management must be the very best because you are a long way from home and probably in difficult and strange surroundings.

2. Technical ability must be of the best because it is for this ability that you are there and you want follow-on business and the rest of us want business for Canada. These first two require that you put your best and most experienced people on the job.

3. Make sure you have financial capability or in other words be sure your credit is good. Your bankers at home may have to carry you for a while before the progress payments start to arrive.

A Case Study of Markets for Canadian Exporters in Michigan and Indiana

by
T. Frank Harris
Consul General of Canada
Consulate General
Detroit, Michigan

MARKETS FOR CANADIAN EXPORTERS
MICHIGAN AND INDIANA

Canadian Consulate
* 1920 First Federal Building
1001 Woodward Avenue
Detroit, MI 48226

4. Make sure you have gathered all the local knowledge you can. Though the trade commissioner can help you with the business community you must know as much as possible about the country and the people. Normally we in CIDA will help with briefings, you can get information from the foreign embassy or high commission in Ottawa or the Canadian embassy in the country will help. There are of course books to be read and possibly other Canadians who have visited the country.

TRENDS

A new Canadian strategy for aid will probably be published soon and it will stress development in three sectors as follows:

a) <u>Agriculture</u>, and this, broadly speaking, will cover all food production including fisheries and will include forestry work and rural development.

b) <u>Energy</u>, and this, in the broadest terms, will be to assist countries in overcoming the tremendous cost of petroleum.

c) <u>Social development</u>, which must include the training of all kinds of managers and technicians.

The budget this year amounts to about 0.43% of Canadian Gross National Product (GNP). It has been stated by the Government that it intends to raise this to 0.5% by 1985, requiring an increase each year in the budget of about 15%. The Government has also stated it hopes to increase the aid budget to the desired United Nations target of 0.7% of GNP by 1990.

CONCLUSION

I have run over the work of CIDA rather quickly when you consider the budget is about $1.5 billion but I think I will be able to fill in any gaps in our later discussion. I shall try to answer questions not only on the CIDA programs but the different parts of the world where they are operating.

ADDENDA

CIDA PUBLICATIONS

There are a few publications which might interest some of you. I have listed them so that you can decide whether you would like copies:

Strategy 1975-80
Lines of Credit (list)
Active Contracts (computer print-out)
Industrial Development Co-operation (brochure)
Directions in Development (magazine)

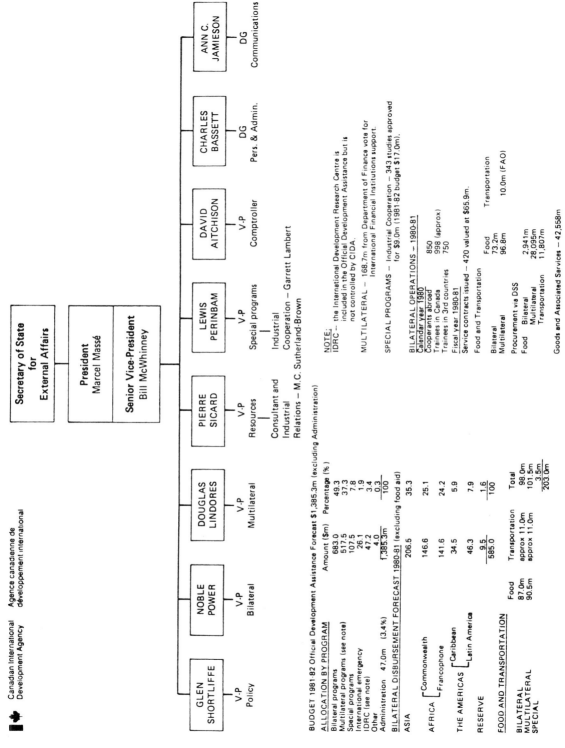

Canadian International Development Agency / Agence canadienne de développement international

Secretary of State for External Affairs

President Marcel Massé

Senior Vice-President Bill McWhinney

| GLEN SHORTLIFFE V-P Policy | NOBLE POWER V-P Bilateral | DOUGLAS LINDORES V-P Multilateral | PIERRE SICARD V-P Resources | LEWIS PERINBAM V-P Special programs | DAVID AITCHISON V-P Comptroller | CHARLES BASSETT DG Pers. & Admin. | ANN C. JAMIESON DG Communications |

Consultant and Industrial Relations — M.C. Sutherland-Brown

Industrial Cooperation — Garrett Lambert

BUDGET 1981-82 Official Development Assistance Forecast $1,385.3m (excluding Administration)

ALLOCATION BY PROGRAM

	Amount ($m)	Percentage (%)
Bilateral programs	683.0	49.3
Multilateral programs (see note)	517.5	37.3
Special programs	107.5	7.8
International emergency	26.1	1.9
IDRC (see note)	47.2	3.4
Other	4.0	0.3
	1,385.3m	100
Administration 47.0m (3.4%)		

BILATERAL DISBURSEMENT FORECAST 1980-81 (excluding food aid)

	Food	Transportation	Total
ASIA	206.5		35.3
AFRICA ⌈ Commonwealth	146.6		25.1
⌊ Francophone	141.6		24.2
THE AMERICAS ⌈ Caribbean	34.5		5.9
⌊ Latin America	46.3		7.9
RESERVE	9.5		1.6
	585.0		100

FOOD AND TRANSPORTATION

	Food	Transportation	Total
BILATERAL	87.0m	approx 11.0m	98.0m
MULTILATERAL	90.5m	approx 11.0m	101.5m
SPECIAL			3.5m
			203.0m

NOTE:
IDRC — the International Development Research Centre is included in the Official Development Assistance but is not controlled by CIDA.

MULTILATERAL — 168.7m from Department of Finance vote for International Financial Institutions support.

SPECIAL PROGRAMS — Industrial Cooperation — 343 studies approved for $9.0m (1981-82 budget $17.0m).

BILATERAL OPERATIONS — 1980-81

Calendar year 1980	
Cooperants abroad	850
Trainees in Canada	998 (approx)
Trainees in 3rd countries	750

Fiscal year 1980-81
Service contracts issued — 420 valued at $65.9m.

Food and Transportation

	Food	Transportation
Bilateral	73.2m	
Multilateral	96.8m	10.0m (FAO)

Procurement via DSS

Food	Bilateral	2,941m
	Multilateral	28,095m
	Transportation	11,807m

Goods and Associated Services — 42,558m

MCSB June 1981

THE MARKET

MICHIGAN
- 9.1 million population (est. 1976)
- total personal income $64 billion
- ranks sixth as a state in value added by manufacture
- metal products and automotive transport equipment are the chief industries
- if a nation, would rank as Canada's second largest customer, following only the rest of the United States

DETROIT
- potential market of five million highly paid consumers situated alongside the Canadian border
- ideal test market
- closer than many of your Canadian customers

INDIANA
- 5.3 million population (est. 1976)
- ranks eighth as a state in value added by manufacture
- total personal income of $37 billion
- leading industries include electrical machinery, transportation equipment and mobile homes

I. GENERAL

Area and Population

The trade territory covered by the Canadian Consulate in Detroit includes the State of Michigan 147,687 km² (57,022 sq. mi.), Metropolitan Toledo, Ohio and the State of Indiana 93,994 km² (36,291 sq. mi.) with the exception of the five northwestern Indiana counties. The 1976 population estimates are:

	Population
Michigan	9,163,100
Indiana	5,334,900
Metropolitan Toledo	791,600

370

Population of Principal Metropolitan Areas (1970 Census)

		Population
Michigan:	Detroit	4,389,900
	Grand Rapids	568,100
	Flint	514,700
	Lansing(Capital)	398,800
	Ann Arbor	248,100
	Saginaw	226,100
Indiana:	Indianapolis(Capital)	1,157,200
	Fort Wayne	373,700
	South Bend	275,600
	Evansville	248,300

Climate

The climate is typical of the northern United States - varied and changeable with moderately heavy snowfalls in winter and some days of great heat and humidity, with thunderstorms, in summer. In Detroit wide seasonal swings are tempered by proximity to the Great Lakes.

Local Time

Michigan and Toledo, Ohio - Eastern Standard and Daylight Saving Time (as in Ontario and Quebec)

Indiana - Maintains Eastern Standard Time year round.

Weights and Measures; Electricity

United States measures that differ from those used in Canada are:

1 U.S. pint	16 fluid ounces	473.12 millilitres
1 U.S. quart	32 fluid ounces	946.24 millilitres
1 U.S. gallon	128 fluid ounces	3,784.96 millilitres
1 Imperial proof gallon	1.36 U.S. proof gallons	5.15 litres

Electricity for domestic use is supplied at 115 volts, 60 cycles AC.

Public Holidays

New Year's Day	January 1
Lincoln's Birthday	February 12
Washington's Birthday	February (third Monday)
Good Friday	
Memorial Day	May (last Monday)
Independence Day	July 4
Labor Day	September (first Monday)
Columbus Day	October (second Monday)
Veterans Day	October (last Monday)
Election Day	November
Thanksgiving	November (fourth Thursday)
Christmas Day	December 25

The Canadian Consulate observes the more important U.S. holidays together with Canada Day (July 1), Canadian Thanksgiving (October, second Monday), and Queen Victoria's Birthday (May).

Historical Background

Michigan

Detroit was founded in 1701 by Antoine de la Mothe Cadillac as a fur trade post strategically located on the Great Lakes water route. In 1760 it was occupied by the British and held until 1796, the last significant place in the United States occupied by Britain. Michigan was admitted as a state in 1837.

Indiana

The "Hoosier" State was first visited by the French explorer Robert Cavelier de La Salle, who established numerous trading posts. England won control of the territory in 1763 following the French and Indian war and left in 1779. Indiana was admitted as a state to the Union in 1816.

II. ECONOMY AND INDUSTRY

Industry

Michigan

This state ranks 6th in the nation in terms of value added by manufacture with a total of $26.3 billion in 1974. Being the automotive capital of the world, transportation equipment accounts for about 40 percent of this total. One of the prime resources of Michigan is its pool of technological skills.

Michigan industry is highly diversified with 87 per cent of all manufacturing categories represented. Other major industries are machine tools, foundry products, metal stampings, drugs and chemicals.

The Detroit area represents roughly half the State of Michigan in population and production. It is a major banking centre and its port ranks second in collection of all United States customs districts.

Indiana

In 1977 Indiana ranked 8th in value added by manufacture at $15.8 billion. Machinery, particularly electrical and transportation equipment, accounted for about 32 per cent of this total. Important steel mills are concentrated in the northern region; major electronic firms and vehicle manufacturers are also established in this state. Other major industries are mobile homes and fabricated metal products.

Toledo

One of the ten largest ports in the United States, Toledo ranks number one among shippers of soft coal. It is conveniently located on Lake Erie, 96 kilometres (60 miles) from Detroit. In 1972 its value added by manufacture amounted to $1.9 billion. Its major industries are auto parts, transportation equipment and plate glass. It is also an important distribution centre for farm produce.

Agriculture

Michigan

In 1977 the number of farms totaled 78,000 with a value of products sold estimated at $1.7 billion. The state is a leading producer of dry beans, wheat, cherries and apples.

Hogs and corn are the two major farm income producers. In 1976 the 105,000 Indiana farms reported $3.4 billion of products sold. The state is known as the number one popcorn producer in the nation. Other major crops are soya beans, winter wheat and burley tobacco.

Natural Resources

Michigan

Michigan has the most abundant water resource of any state with four Great Lakes plus 11,000 inland lakes and 57,900 kilometres (36,000 miles) of rivers and streams. Mineral production was estimated at $1.6 billion in 1976. The southern part of the peninsula is connected to the world's largest salt deposit which extends to southern Ontario. Michigan is also an important producer of iron ore, cement, copper and magnesium.

Oil and gas reserves are modest, hydro potential nil. Once bountiful, timber reserves have diminished drastically in the south due to industrial development and are now chiefly concentrated in the northern area of the state.

Indiana

The state leads the nation in production of building stone, supplying approximately 80 per cent of the building limestone used in the United States. Coal production is also substantial. Important deposits of sand, gravel, sandstone and clay are among Indiana's major natural resources. In 1975, the value of mineral production was $1 billion with coal, petroleum and natural gas responsible for about 47 per cent of this total.

Trade with Canada

Rail

There are 10,678 kilometres (6,635 miles) of mainland track in Michigan and six rail ferries across Lake Michigan bypassing Chicago, whereas Indiana has a total of 10,592 kilometres (6,582 miles).

Canadian National Railways and the Canadian Pacific Railway have connecting services with affiliated lines in the two states together with terminal facilities and pool arrangements with other lines.

The names and addresses of the major railroad companies operating in Michigan and Indiana are as follows:

Michigan

Ann Arbor Railroad Co.	1348 Buhl Building Detroit, Michigan	(313) 964-3767
Canadian National Railways	131 West Lafayette Detroit, Michigan	(313) 962-2260
Canadian Pacific Railway Co.	2243 First National Building Detroit, Michigan	(313) 963-7820
Detroit, Toledo & Ironton Railroad Company	1 Parklane Boulevard Dearborn, Michigan	(313) 336-9600
Norfolk and Western Railway	115 Twelfth Detroit, Michigan	(313) 496-1850
Chessie System	One Northland Plaza Southfield, Michigan	(313) 552-5000

Indiana

Chicago, South Shore & South Bend	Michigan City, Indiana	(219) 874-4221
Ferdinand Railroad Company	Ferdinand, Indiana	(812) 367-1120
Illinois Central Gulf Railroad	428 Merchants Bank Building Indianapolis, Indiana	(317) 632-5361
Seaboard Coastline Louisville & Nashville Railroad	1103 East 28th Indianapolis, Indiana	(317) 923-2511

| Southern Indiana Railway Inc. | Chamber of Commerce Building Indianapolis, Indiana | (317) 634-2515 |
| Southern Railroad System | 505 Merchants Bank Building Indianapolis, Indiana | (317) 639-1424 |

Road

Michigan and Indiana have respectively 1,770 and 1,850 kilometres (1,100 and 1,150 miles) of designated interstate freeways. Additionally, Michigan maintains 14,800 kilometres (9,200 miles) of state highways and Indiana 18,185 kilometres (11,300 miles).

Commercial Canadian vehicles operating on United States highways are subject to local regulations which may vary according to state as well as province of vehicle registration. The Michigan Public Service Commission requires commission plates on all commercial carriers entering Michigan. These can be obtained from Secretary of State offices, scale stations or the Office of Motor Transportation, Lansing. Ontario trucks are allowed a single trip permit only, good for a single trip into the state at a cost of $20. Trucks from all other provinces are allowed 10 day permits at the same cost of $20.

Canadian trucks may purchase Michigan licence plates at costs based on GVW rating. In addition, the state collects a diesel fuel tax, calculated on the basis of miles driven in state and flat mile per gallon average. This is recorded voluntarily, but subject to random audit by state authorities.

For detailed information on up-to-date requirements in Michigan, Indiana, or Ohio, Canadian commercial vehicle operators should contact:

Title and Registration Division,
Department of State,
Lansing, Michigan.

or

Registration of Vehicles,
Bureau of Motor Vehicles,
325 State Office Building,
Indianapolis, IN 46204
Telephone: (317) 633-4828

Michigan Department of State,
Secretary of State Office,
312 Michigan Avenue,
Detroit, MI 48226
Telephone: (313) 963-8250

Department of Highway Safety
Bureau of Motor Vehicles,
4300 Kimberley Parkway,
Columbus, OH 43227
Telephone: (614) 466-2130

Waterways

Michigan relies more heavily on water transport than most states. The Detroit River is one of the world's busiest waterways and in 1975 the Port of Detroit handled 27 million short tons, 2.6 million of which constituted general cargo. Other Michigan ports are Muskegon, Port Huron, Sault Ste. Marie and Bay City.

Indiana has only a limited waterfront on the shore of Lake Michigan. The Port of Indiana, Burns Waterway Harbor, was completed in 1969 and provides berth for the largest ships engaged in Great Lakes and overseas shipping. Transit from the port of Indiana to the inland waterways is facilitated by barges operating on the Ohio and Mississippi Rivers.

Toledo is a major port specializing in the loading of bulk commodities.

Airways

Major airline companies such as American, Delta, Trans World, United, North Central, Pan Am and Eastern service the larger cities located in Michigan and Indiana together with the City of Toledo. They operate from Detroit's Metro Airport. Wright Airlines is the only airline using Detroit City Airport.

Air Canada and Nordair have excellent daily Canadian connections from nearby Windsor, Ontario.

III. SELLING TO DETROIT TERRITORY

Opportunities for Canadian Products

Despite already substantial sales of Canadian goods, tremendous potential exists for new Canadian exporters and new

Canadian Products. Buyers are interested in almost any item that can compete in quality, distinctiveness and laid-down price. Many existing U.S. supply sources are more distant than potentially competitive Canadian ones.

Michigan is the heart of the Great Lakes megalopolis, the heartland of North America. Detroit, fifth largest metropolitan area in the U.S., is far above average in income and below average in unemployment. It is one of the most logical markets for new Canadian exporters.

An Ideal Test Market

Average weekly income in Michigan, in U.S. dollar terms, is 10 per cent more than the Canadian average. Consumption patterns are generally similar. Canadian goods will not sell merely because they are Canadian; they must compete in all respects with U.S. goods and require merchandising techniques.

The Canadian Image

Many American businessmen are not aware of the high level of development of Canadian industry and have misconceptions about Canadian design and quality. U.S. firms often do not regard Canada as "foreign" and Canadian merchandise consequently is bought and invoiced through domestic purchasing departments - which can work to your advantage. Proximity to Canada and personal and corporate connections results in receptivity and a willingness to buy on the same basis as from domestic U.S. sources.

Positive Sales Psychology

Canadian exporters may face a double challenge: to sell as an American vendor does and overcome misconceptions about Canadian capabilities. The buyer must be assured that there is nothing risky about doing business with Canada or with a new supplier.

Before selling in the United States, Canadian companies should commit themselves to:

1. aggressively seeking out and pursuing business opportunities on a continuing basis;

2. making your first impression a positive one by coming prepared with a detailed listing of your capabilities, interests
   and past experience;

3. quoting, delivering and following up reliably and aggressively.

The Initial Approach

The best introduction is by a personal visit. Some type of
representative or distributor may be appointed later, but large
volume buyers usually want to meet their prospective suppliers
personally.

In planning the first sales trip, selection of calls and routing
are important and the Commercial Division of the Consulate can
provide guidance and introductions. Almost half of the purchasing locations in Michigan are outside of Detroit. If a number of
calls are planned it is usually most practical to make them by car.

Appointments often aren't necessary with individual buyers,
but as a matter of good form it is usually advisable to start with
the Director of Purchasing, or his equivalent, and through him
meet the proper buyer. An advance notification in this case is
suggested.

A complete presentation on the first call is most important.
This should include literature, specifications, samples if possible
and all the price, delivery and quality-control information a
buyer needs to evaluate your capabilities against his current
sources. Many buyers keep up-to-date vendor records. A favourable impression is made if a resume including the following can
be supplied at the time of the first visit:

- vendor's name, address and telephone number
- name address and telephone of local representative
  (if applicable)
- date established
- size of plant
- number of employees
- principal products

- location of plants
- description of production facilities and equipment
- description of quality-control facilities and procedures (becoming increasingly important to automotive buyers)
- transportation facilities
- approximate yearly sales volume
- list of three representative customers
- financial and credit rating.

Reciprocal Visits

Many buying organizations check out new vendors' facilities personally before placing continuing business. If they do not come as a matter of course, it is good sales strategy to invite them.

Following Up the Initial Call

Buyers, particularly in the motor vehicle field, expect to be called upon more frequently than their Canadian counterparts. This may be as often as every two weeks at some periods of the buying year. Most Canadian firms lack the sales force to accomplish this; however, the problem can be solved by appointing a manufacturers' representative or selling through brokers, jobbers or distributors as the situation warrants.

Price Quotations

Quotations should be submitted in both a laid-down basis, buyer's warehouse or factory, and f.o.b. Canadian plant basis exclusive of Canadian sales or excise tax. Always quote in United States funds unless specifically requested otherwise. The landed price should include transportation charges, U.S. customs duties if applicable, brokerage fees and insurance. The quotation should be comparable in format to quotations from U.S. sources. Buyers can't be expected to understand or be sympathetic to customs duties or other matters peculiar to international transactions. This is solely the responsibility of the Canadian exporter and a "cost" of international business.

Canadian exporters may not be granted the same opportunities for re-negotiating initial quotations as they have been accustomed to in Canada. Because U.S. buyers are often able to work to tighter purchasing deadlines and target prices, they may have to accept the first bid as final.

The Manufacturers' Representative

The commission agent or salesman is more commonly used as a sales channel in the United States than in Canada, and in the Detroit area this is especially true in the automotive industry. The better reps are highly qualified by education, training and experience. They know their customers and call regularly - not only on the buying level, but on engineering, design and quality control levels as well; thus they work in advance of model year buys and follow up on use of their principal's product.

Potential advantages of the rep include economy, closer contact with buyers - sometimes social - and nearness of the scene of possible problems. The Detroit office maintains information on the majority of manufacturers' representatives operating in Michigan, Indiana and Toledo, Ohio and can make suitable suggestions for Canadian manufacturers.

IV. SERVICES FOR EXPORTERS

Banking

There are no Canadian banks with representatives in Michigan, Indiana, or Metropolitan Toledo, Ohio, but the branches of Canadian banks in Windsor, Ontario are in constant contact with their counterparts on the American side of the border. In addition, the international divisions of the Canadian banks in Montreal and Toronto are in a position to assist exporters.

Please refer to "Useful Addresses" for a listing of prominent banks and customs brokers serving this market territory.

Patents, Trademarks and Copyrights

General

An informative booklet entitled "General Information Concerning Patents" is available from the Superintendent of Documents, U.S. Government Printing Office, Washington, DC 20302 at a cost of 20 cents.

Patents

All business with the Patent Office should be transacted in writing and all letteres addressed to the Commissioner of Patents, Washington, DC 20231.

U.S. patent laws make no discrimination with respect to the citizenship of the inventor. However, it is the inventor who must make application for patent and sign related papers (with certain exceptions).

Most inventors employ the services of patent attorneys or patent agents. The Patent Office cannot recommend any particular attorney or agent but does publish a list of all registered patent attorneys and agents who are willing to accept new clients and lists them by states, cities and foreign countries.

Trademarks

A trademark relates to the name or symbol used in trade to indicate the source or origin of goods. Trademark rights will prevent others from using the same trademark on identical goods but do not prevent others from making these goods without the trademarks.

The procedure relating to the registration of trademarks and some general information on trademarks is given in a pamphlet called "General Information Concerning Trademarks" which can be obtained from the Patent Office.

Copyright

Copyright protects the writings of an author against copying. Literary, dramatic, musical and artistic works are included within the protection of the copyright law which in some instances also confers performing and recording rights. The copyright goes to the form of expression rather than the subject matter.

Note: copyrights are registered in the Copyright Office in the Library of Congress and the <u>Patent Office has nothing whatever to do with copyrights</u>. Information concerning copyrights may be obtained from Register of Copyrights, Library of Congress, Washington, DC 20540.

Licensing and Joint Ventures

If you wish to market a patented invention or product in the United States, either under a joint-licensing agreement or some other arrangement, there are a number of firms specializing in patent and marketing services. The Canadian Consulate in Detroit can help in choosing such firms.

The Canadian-American Commercial Arbitration Commission

Reference to the above Commission is often made in standard commercial contracts between Canadian and American companies. In the event of disputes the Canadian firm simply refers to the Canadian Chamber of Commerce, 1080 Beaver Hall Hill, Montreal, Quebec, H2Z 1T2, and the American firm refers to the American Arbitration Commission, 140 West 51st Street, New York, N.Y. 10020.

V. CUSTOMS REGULATIONS AND DOCUMENTATION

U.S. Exports to Canada

Enquiries concerning the importation of U.S. products into Canada should be referred to the United States Embassy, 100 Wellington Street, Ottawa or the U.S. Consulate or Consulate-General in Vancouver, Calgary, Winnipeg, Toronto, Montreal, Quebec, Saint John, Halifax or St. John's.

Canadian Export Documents

All Canadian exports to the United States, even when accompanying returned American merchandise, must be accompanied by Canada customs export form B-13. Canada customs requires three copies at the same time of exportation, but it is wise to prepare at least five. Two numbered copies will then be returned to the exporter unless otherwise specified on the B-13. By doing this, the exporter avoids having to submit a form C-6 for additional certified copies of the B-13 should the goods be returned to Canada for any reason. Two numbered copies of the B-13 must always accompany the Canada customer entry as proof of export. B-13 forms may be obtained from Canada customs.

U.S. Customs and Market Access Information

To enjoy success in the United States market, a Canadian exporter requires market access information which falls into two basic categories: customs and non-customs. The former covers subjects such as documentation, tariff classification, value for duty and rates of duty, while the latter related to the many other U.S. laws affecting imports such as food and drugs, consumer product safety, environmental protection and so on. Exporters are strongly urged to obtain all market access information on new products to be marketed in the U.S. from the U.S. Division of the Department of Industry, Trade and Commerce, in Ottawa. The Division is constantly liaisoning with U.S. customs and other agencies on behalf of Canadian exporters, and over the years has developed an in-depth knowledge of the interpretation and implementation of regulations governing access for imports into the U.S. market.

The address is:

> United States Division
> Western Hemisphere Bureau
> Department of Industry, Trade and Commerce
> 235 Queen Street
> Ottawa, Ontario
> K1A 0H5
>
> Tel: (613) 996-5471

U.S. Customs Regulations and Documentation Tariff Classification and Value For Duty

Request for Prospective Rulings

The U.S. Division can obtain a PROSPECTIVE CUSTOMS RULING from Washington on behalf of a Canadian exporter for articles which have not yet been exported and are not at present under consideration by the U.S. Customs Service, provided that the following information is supplied. Failure to supply all of this information will only result in delays and confusion for the exporter.

General

a)   We require a written request signed by a person who has a direct and demonstrable interest in the question, also indicating that the merchandise or subject of the request has not previously, or is not now, under consideration by any U.S. Customs Service field office.

b)   Also, include a statement of all facts relating to the transaction such as names and addresses and other identifying information of all interested parties (if known), the probable port of arrival in the United States and a description of the transaction appropriate in detail to the ruling requested.

Tariff Classification Ruling

In addition to a) and b) above, the following information is required for a tariff classification ruling:

1)   A full and complete description of the article.

2)   The chief use of the article in the United States.

3)   The commercial, common or technical description.

4)   Metal, wood and mineral objects and combinations thereof should include a statement of the relative quantity (by weight and volume) and the value of each in order to determine the material in chief value and weight.

5)   Textile materials and articles should be identified as in (4) and include the method of construction such as knit or woven, the fibres present in percentage by value and if wearing apparel, for whom it is designed to be worn.

6)   Chemical products should be identified by their specifications and chemical analysis including a sample for U.S. customs use. Particular reference should be made if any part of the

formula consists of a benzenoid chemical or its derivative stating the function of such chemical in the product.

7) Photographs, drawings or other pictorial representations of the articles should be submitted when samples are not sent.

Valuation Ruling

In addition to a) and b) above, the following information is required for a Valuation Ruling:

1) All information required on a U.S. special customs invoice form 5515.

2) The nature of the transaction, whether f.o.b./c.i.f., ex factory or some other arrangement.

3) Relationship of parties (if any), whether the transaction is at arms length (i.e. between unrelated parties) and whether there have been other sales of the same or similar merchandise in the country of exportation, whether an agency situation exists and an explanation or copy of any agreement, contract or other relevant document.

4) A full description of the merchandise in order to determine if section 402 or 402(a) of the Tariff Act of 1930 applies and other relevant information required under the appropriate section.

Note: Privileged or confidential information should be clearly marked with an explanation as to why it is considered confidential.

Request for Internal Advice Rulings

Part 177.1(a)(2) of the Customs Regulations of the United States requires that questions arising in connection with current or completed transactions should be resolved by means of the INTERNAL ADVICE PROCEDURE at the port where entry was made. The request for an internal advice ruling can be filed by either the importer or his customs broker. The field office personnel all review the request and notify the importer of any points with which they do not agree.

The U.S. Division can provide valuable assistance and suggestions regarding points of law and previous customs practice which may support the importer's case.

Requests for advice from the U.S. Division should contain:

1) Copies of <u>all</u> documents related to the entry of the merchandise to which the request refers including those issued by U.S. customs.

2) A statement of <u>all</u> facts relative to the transaction from a commercial point of view such as domestic and foreign billing practices, price-list terms, end use of the goods, literature, drawings, pictures, method of shipment and all other pertinent facts.

3) A statement generally following the outline under "Request for Prospective Ruling". The U.S. Customs Service may, at its discretion refuse to consider a request for internal advice if, in its opinion, there is a clear and definite precedent that supports its position. If the importer is not in agreement with this position, he may request a "Protest Review Decision".

Request for Protest Review

When an importer does not agree with a decision of the U.S. Customs Service, he may request a PROTEST REVIEW within 90 days from the date of liquidation. The U.S. Division can assist the importer and his broker by providing advice and suggestions on what information can be used to support the importer's case.

Entry at Customs

Goods may be "entered for consumption" at the port of arrival in the United States, whether at seaboard or on a land border, or the goods may be transported in bond to an inland port of entry and there entered for consumption.

For such transportation in bond to an interior port, an immediate transportation entry (I.T.) must be filled out at the port of arrival by either the consignee, the carrier, the U.S. customs broker or any other person having a sufficient interest in the goods for that purpose. In cases where the Canadian exporter assumes responsibility for entering the goods through U.S. customs, he may find that there are advantages in having shipments entered for consumption at the nearest or most convenient port of arrival. In this way he can remain in close touch with the broker and U.S. customs at that port of entry. However, where the U.S. purchaser intends making his own entries, it may be more convenient to have the goods transported in bond from the port of arrival to the interior port nearest the importer.

Who May Enter Goods

Goods may be entered by the consignee, his authorized employees or his agent. The only agents who can act for importers in customs matters are licensed U.S. customhouse brokers. They prepare and file the necessary customs entries, arrange for payments of duties and release of goods.

The railway express companies or other transport companies may be prepared in certain cases to enter packages through customs for the account of the exporter. If there is some difficulty or special problem connected with a shipment, the carriers may turn the matter over to a U.S. customs broker at the exporter's expense.

Goods may be entered by the consignee named on the bill of lading under which they are shipped or by the holder of the bill of lading duly endorsed by the consignee. When the goods are consigned "to order" they may be entered by the holder of the bill of lading duly endorsed by the consignor. In most instances entry is made by a person or firm certified by the carrier to be the owner of the goods for customs purposes. When goods are not imported by a common carrier, possession of the goods at the time of arrival in the United States is sufficient evidence of the right to make entry.

A non-resident of the United States may make entry of his own goods as may a non-resident partnership or a foreign corporation. But the surety on any customs bond required from a non-resident individual, partnership or corporation must be incorporated in the United States. When merchandise is entered in the name of a Canadian corporation, that corporation must have a resident agent in the state of entry who is authorized to accept service of process on the corporation's behalf.

388

Documentation

Normally the only documents required when shipping to the United States are a bill of lading as well as a special U.S. customs invoice 5515 and/or commercial invoice (preferably both). The use of a typewriter in preparing documents is preferred; in any case, they should be legible.

Note: Do not use red ink to fill out documents.

Bill of Lading

Normally a bill of lading for Canadian shipments is required by U.S. customs authorities. In lieu of the bill of lading the shipping receipt may be accepted if customs is satisfied that no bill of lading has been issued. Entry and release of merchandise may be permitted without the bill of lading if satisfactory bond is given in a sum equal to one and one-half times the invoice value of the merchandise. A carrier's certificate or duplicate bill of lading may, in certain circumstances, be acceptable.

Invoice

Shipments in excess of $500 and subject to an ad valorem rate of duty, conditionally free of duty or subject to duty depending in some manner upon its value, should be accompanied at entry by a U.S. special customs invoice form 5515. However, copies of the commercial invoice are sufficient for shipments with an aggregate value of less than $500, duty-free shipments or shipments of articles subject to specific rates of duty.

Completion of Form 5515

U.S. customs forms 5515 are available free of charge from U.S. consular offices in Canada or can be obtained from commercial stationers. While only one copy is required by U.S. customs, it is usual to forward three: one for the use of U.S. customs when the goods are examined, one to accompany the entry and one for the U.S. customs broker's file. District directors of U.S. customs are authorized to waive production of special and commercial invoices if satisfied that the importer, because of conditions beyond his control, cannot furnish a complete and accurate invoice; or that a classification, appraisement and liquidation can properly be made without the production of such an invoice. In these cases, the importer must file the following with the entry:

1) any invoice received from the seller or shipper

2) a statement pointing out in exact detail any inaccuracies or omissions in such invoice

3) an executed pro forma invoice

4) any other information required for classification or appraisement.

Special information with respect to certain classes of goods is sometimes required when either the customs or commercial invoice does not give sufficient information to permit classification and appraisal.

Packing List

U.S. customs authorities require three copies of a detailed packing list. This should indicate what is in each box, barrel or package in the shipment. If the shipment is uniformly packed, this can be stated on the invoice indicating how many items are in each container.

Payment of Duties

There is no provision for prepayment of duties in Canada before exportation to the United States but it is feasible for the Canadian exporter to arrange for payment by a U.S. customs broker or other agent and thus be able to offer his goods to U.S. buyers at a duty-paid price.

Liability for payment of duty usually becomes fixed at the time an entry (either for consumption or warehouse) is filed with U.S. customs. The liability is fixed, but not the amount of duty which is only estimated at the time of the original entry. When the entry is liquidated, the final rate and amount of duty is ascertained. Obligation for payment is upon the person or firm in whose name the entry is filed.

Temporary Free Importation

Certain articles not imported for sale may be admitted into the United States under bond without the payment of duty.

Such articles must in most cases be exported within one year of the date of importation. Upon application to the district director, this period may be extended for a period not to exceed a total of three years.

Such articles may include the following:

-- articles for repair, alterations or processing (not manufacture)

-- models of women's wearing apparel by manufacturers

-- not for sale samples for order-taking (not to include photo-engraved printing plates for reproduction)

-- motion picture advertising films

-- articles for testing, experimental or review purposes (plans, blueprints, photographs for use in study or for experimental purposes may be included). In the case of such articles, satisfactory proof of destruction as a result of the tests with the production of a proper affidavit of destruction will relieve the obligation of exportation

-- containers for merchandise during transportation

-- models imported by illustrators and photographers for use solely in illustrating

-- professional equipment, tools of trade, repair components for equipment or tools admitted under this item and camping equipment; all the foregoing imported by or for non-residents sojourning temporarily in the United States and for use by such non-residents

-- articles of special design for temporary use exclusively in the production of articles for export

-- works of art, photographs, philosophical and scientific apparatus brought into the U.S. by professional artists, lecturers or scientists for use in exhibition and promotion of art, science and industry

-- automobiles, automobile chassis, automobile bodies - finished, unfinished or cutaway when intended solely for show purposes. The temporary importation bond in the case of these articles is limited to six months with no right of extension.

Commercial Travellers - Samples

Samples accompanying a commercial traveller may be admitted and entered on the importer's baggage declaration. In such cases, an adequate descriptive list or a U.S. special customs invoice must be provided. The personal bond of the commercial traveller is usually accepted to guarantee the timely exportation of the samples under U.S. customs supervision. Penalty for failure to export the samples entails loss of the privilege on future trips.

U.S. Anti-Dumping And Countervail Statutes

Due to the complexity of these statutes, exporters are encouraged to contact the U.S. Division of the Department of Industry, Trade and Commerce for answers to any specific questions.

Anti-Dumping

If a U.S. company has reason to believe that a product is being sold in the U.S. at a price lower than the price at which it is sold in its home market, an anti-dumping complaint may be filed with the U.S. Treasury Department. The anti-dumping petition must contain information to support the dumping allegations along with evidence of injury suffered by the U.S. industry affected.

A U.S. anti-dumping investigation must be conducted within specified time frames:

1. Within 30 days of receipt of an anti-dumping petition, the Secretary of the Treasury must decide whether or not to initiate an investigation.

2. Within six months (nine months in complicated cases) of the initiation of an investigation, the Secretary of the Treasury must issue a preliminary determination on whether or not there are sales at less than fair value, i.e. dumped prices.

3. If sales were made at less than fair value, the matter would be referred to the U.S. International Trade Commission (ITC) for an injury determination which must be made within three months of the date of referral to the commission.

4. If the International Trade Commission (ITC) finds injury to a U.S. industry, an anti-dumping finding would be issued.

Countervail

Under the U.S. Countervailing Duty Statute, an additional duty may be imposed upon dutiable articles imported into the United States if any bounty or grant upon their manufacture production or export has been made. The U.S. Trade Act of 1974 enlarged the scope of the U.S. Countervailing Duty Statute to include duty-free goods. This amendment brings within the purview of the law the 70 per cent of Canadian exports to the U.S. which were previously exempt. Application for countervailing duty against free merchandise will in most cases be subject to an injury determination by the U.S. International Trade Commission.

Marking of Goods
Country of Origin Marking

All goods must be legibly and conspicuously marked in English to show country of origin.

The use of stickers or tags is permitted if used in such a manner as to be permanent, unless deliberately removed, until receipt by the final purchaser.

Certain small instruments and utensils must be marked by die-stamping or cast-in-the-mould lettering, engraving or by means of metal plates securely attached to this article.

The U.S. Customs Service may exempt certain articles from this marking. In such cases the container must be suitably marked.

Composition Marking

Any product containing woollen fibre (except carpets, rugs, mats and upholsteries, or articles made more than 20 years before importation) must be clearly marked with the name of the manufacturer or the person marketing the product together with a statement of the fibre content of the product. If not suitably marked, an opportunity to mark under U.S. customs supervision is granted.

When the fabric contained in any product is imported, it is necessary to state the fabric's country of origin.

Fur products must be marked as to type (particular animal), country of origin and manufacturer's name; in addition they must be marked if they are used, bleached or artifically coloured, composed substantially of paws, tails, bellies or waste.

Food Labelling

All imported foods, drugs and cosmetics are subject to inspection by the Food and Drug Administration of the United States at the time of entry. The Food and Drug Administration is not authorized to pass upon the legality of specific consignments before they arrive and are offered for entry. However, the administration may offer comment on proposed labels or answer other enquiries from importers and exporters.

Advice on prospective food labels may also be obtained from the U.S. Division of the Department of Industry, Trade and Commerce in Ottawa.

Import Prohibitions and Restrictions

In addition to goods prohibited entry by most countries in the world, such as obscene or seditious literature, narcotics, counterfeit currency or coins, certain commercial goods are also prohibited or restricted. Moreover, various types of merchandise must conform to laws enforced by government agencies other than the United States Customs Service. Fur products are also subject to the Endangered Species Act and importation of certain fur skins would be prohibited.

Animals

Cattle, sheep, goats, swine and poultry should be accompanied by a certificate from a salaried veterinarian of the Canadian government to avoid delays in quarantine.

Wild animals and birds, or products thereof are prohibited if captured, taken, shipped, possessed or exported contrary to laws of the country of origin. In addition, the purchase, sale or possession of such animals is prohibited if contrary to the laws of any part of the United States.

Plants and Plant Products

Permits issued by the Department of Agriculture are required.

Regulations may restrict or prohibit importation.

Shipments of agriculture and vegetable seeds and screenings are detained pending the drawing and testing of samples and are governed by the regulations of the U.S. Federal Seed Act.

Postal Shipments

Parcels of aggregate value not exceeding one dollar (U.S. value) may be entered free of duty.

Commercial shipments of more than one dollar value must include a commercial invoice and a customs declaration on the form provided by the Canadian Post Office and give an accurate description and value of the contents. The customs declaration must be securely attached to the package.

If the shipment comprises two or more packages the one containing the commercial invoice should be marked "Invoice Enclosed"; other packages of the same shipment may be marked as "No. 2 of 3, Invoice Enclosed in Package No. 1".

A shipment in excess of $500 aggregate value must include a U.S. special customs invoice (form 5515) and any additional invoice information required. A shipment under $250 aggregate value will be delivered to the addressee. Duties and delivery fees for each package are collected by the postman. Parcels containing bona fide gifts exluding alcoholic beverages, tobacco products and perfumes to persons in the United States will be passed free of duty provided the aggregate value received by one person on one day does not exceed $10. No postal delivery fee will be charged. Such parcels should be marked as a gift and the value and contents indicated on the parcel.

American Goods Returned

U.S. products returned without any evidence of advanced value or improved condition may be entered duty free.

Articles exported from the United States for repair or alteration shall be subject to duty upon the value of the repairs or alterations. The term "repairs or alterations" means restoration, change, addition, renovation, cleaning or other treatment which does not destroy the identity of the articles exported or create a new or different article. Any article of metal (except precious metal) manufactured in the United States and exported for processing and again returned to the United States for additional processing is subject to a duty upon the value of the processing outside the United States provided the material which has been processed in Canada is returned to the original exporter for the further processing of the goods.

The cost or value of U.S. origin component parts used in the production of goods imported into the U.S. may be deducted from the value for duty provided the parts have not been subject to any change except operations incidental to the assembly process such as cleaning, lubricating and painting.

Special U.S. customs procedural requirements must be followed upon the exportation and return of American goods. Details may be obtained from the United States Import Specialists at border points or from the U.S. Division, Western Hemisphere Bureau, Department of Industry, Trade and Commerce, Ottawa.

Duty on Containers

If used in shuttle service, the following types of containers may enter free of duty:

1) U.S. containers and holders including shooks and staves of U.S. production when returned as boxes or barrels containing merchandise.

2) foreign containers previously imported and duty paid if any.

3) containers of a type specified by the Secretary of the Treasury as instruments of international traffic.

One-trip containers are included in the dutiable value of goods.

VI. YOUR BUSINESS VISIT TO THIS TERRITORY

There is no substitute for the personal visit. Correspondence, while better than nothing, does not excite the American businessman. In a few words, <u>he wants to be shown</u>.

When to Go

The best time to visit Detroit and Indianapolis is during spring and fall. Avoid the Christmas-New Year holiday period when most automotive offices are closed and the July-August vacation period.

How to Get There

Air

North Central has direct non-stop flights from Toronto to Detroit. Air Canada has several daily flights to Windsor from a number of Canadian cities. Nordair flies Montreal-Hamilton-Windsor twice daily.

Railways

Canadian National offers passengers service from Montreal and Toronto to Windsor, Ontario.

Buses

Greyhound Bus Lines maintains routes to the major cities in Michigan and Indiana.

Where to Stay

The Consulate will be pleased to suggest suitable hotels or motels in the territory. Please refer to Part VII, "Useful Addresses", for the names and addresses of some of the better known hotels and motels.

Routing of Business Calls

At least half of the buying locations in Michigan are outside the greater Detroit area and buyers are receptive to Canadian callers. In Michigan calls generally lie along the following three routes with kilometres and miles from Detroit indicated.

MICHIGAN 1-94	Kilometres from Detroit	Miles from Detroit	1-96	Kilometres from Detroit	Miles from Detroit
Ann Arbor	64	40	Lansing	134	83
Jackson	122	76	Grand Rapids	251	156
Battle Creek	190	118	Muskegon	301	187
Kalamazoo	225	140			
Benton Harbor	298	185			
Chicago, Ill.	462	287			

MICHIGAN 1-75	Kilometres from Detroit	Miles from Detroit	INDIANA	Kilometres from Detroit	Miles from Detroit
Pontiac	53	33	Fort Wayne	254	158
Flint	111	69	South Bend	386	240
Saginaw	159	99	Elkhart	362	225
Bay City	182	113	Indianapolis	444	276
Toledo, Ohio	97	60			

VII. USEFUL ADDRESSES

Canadian Consulate
1920 First Federal Building
1001 Woodward Avenue
Detroit, MI 48226
Tel: (313) 965-2811
Telex: 23-0715

Canadian Defence Liaison Officer
Attention: CDDPL-DT
Michigan Army Missile Plant
38111 Van Dyke Avenue
Warren, MI 48090
Tel: (313) 264-1100, ext. 2527/2528

Banks with International Departments
Michigan

Bank of Commonwealth
719 Griswold Street
Detroit, MI 48231
Tel: (313) 496-5800

City National Bank
P.O. Box 2659
City National Bank Building
Detroit, MI 48226
Tel: (313) 965-1900 Ext. 310/613

Detroit Bank & Trust
P.O. Box 59
Fort at Washington
Detroit, MI 48231
Tel: (313) 222-3300

Manufacturers National Bank of
  Detroit
100 Renaissance Center
Detroit, MI 48243
Tel: (313) 222-4000

Michigan National Bank of
  Detroit
500 Griswold Street,
Detroit, MI 48226
Tel: (313) 961-5300

National Bank of Detroit
611 Woodward Avenue
P.O. Box 116-A
Detroit, MI 48232
Tel: (313) 225-1000

Indiana

American Fletcher National Bank
  & Trust Co.
108 North Pennsylvania Street
Indianapolis, IN 46204
Tel: (317) 633-2345

Indiana National Bank
1 Indiana Square
Indianapolis, IN 46204
Tel: (317) 266-5111

Toledo, Ohio

Toledo Trust Company
245 Summit,
Toledo, OH 43603
Tel: (419) 259-8150

First National Bank of Toledo
Madison at Huron
Toledo, OH 43603
Tel: (419) 259-6895

Customs Brokers
Michigan

(313)

Altromsco Customs Brokers	461 West Jefferson, Detroit	554-0200
A.F. Burstrom & Son Inc.	15400 West Lincoln, Oak Park	968-1400
John V. Carr & Son Inc.	1600 West Lafayette, Detroit	965-1540
F.X. Coughlin Company	28451 Wick, Romulus	946-9510
Dorf International Inc.	1234 1st National Bldg.Detroit	961-6524
Duty Drawback Services Inc.	22120 Grand River, Detroit	537-7670
Export-Import Service Co.	28265 Beverly, Romulus	292-3440
W.R. Filbin & Co. Inc.	2436 Bagley, Detroit	964-1144
I.C. Harris & Co.	660 Woodward, Detroit	961-4130
S.H. Moulton & Co.	28055 Wick, Romulus	946-5400
F.W. Myers & Co. Inc.	1300 West Fort, Detroit	964-5665
V.G. Nahrgang Co.	155 West Congress, Detroit	962-4681
Wm. R. Neal, Inc.	645 Griswold, Detroit	961-7121
Pacific Customs Brokerage Co.	243 West Congress, Detroit	964-2540
Rea Express	2500 Newark, Detroit	962-2345
J.D. Richardson Company	1225 Lafayette Bldg. Detroit	962-0693
Gerry Schmidt & Co.	28111 Hoover, Warren	574-1200
C.J. Tower & Sons Inc.	645 Griswold, Detroit	961-1124
S.J. Watt	20258 Woodland, Harper Woods	881-7840
W.F. Whelan Co.	Detroit Metro Airport, Romulus	942-9450

Indianapolis, Indiana

Kenneth Williams & Assoc.	P.O. Box 41607, Indianapolis Int'l Airport	(317) 243-7577
Quast & Co., Inc.	P.O. Box 41594, Indianapolis Int'l Airport	243-8361

Toledo, Ohio

R.G. Hobelmann & Co. Inc.	Edward Lamb Bldg. Toledo	(419) 243-3247
Seaway Forwarding Corp.	National Bank Bldg. Rm.725	242-7318
Trans-World Shipping Service	Board of Trade Bldg. Toledo	-

Bonded Warehouses
Michigan

Ammex Warehouse Co. Inc.
Corner 21st and Porter
Detroit, Michigan
(313) 496-0630

Corrigan Systems
2000 Westwood
Dearborn, Michigan
(313) 274-4100

Detroit Harbor Terminals Inc.
4461 West Jefferson Avenue
Detroit, Michigan
(313) 825-3200

Detroit Marine Terminals Inc.
9401 West Jefferson Avenue
Detroit, Michigan
(313) 843-7575

O.H. Frisbie Moving & Storage Co.
14225 Schaefer
Detroit, Michigan
(313) 837-0808

International Great Lakes Shipping
4461 West Jefferson Avenue
Detroit, Michigan
(313) 554-2600

Michigan Liquor Control Commission
2251 Dix Highway
Lincoln Park, Michigan
(313) 383-4000

U.S. Equipment Co.
20580 Hoover
Detroit, Michigan
(313) 526-8300

F.X. Coughlin Co.
28451 Wick Road
Romulus, Michigan
(313) 946-9510

Central Detroit Warehouse
18765 Seaway Drive
Melvindale, Michigan
(313) 388-3200

Grand Trunk Warehouse &
Cold Storage Co.
1921 East Ferry
Detroit, Michigan
(313) 921-8380

P. Leiner & Sons America Inc.
20101 Nine Mile Road
St. Clair Shores, Michigan
(313) 772-2600

Mowhawk Liqueur Corp.
1965 Porter Street
Detroit, Michigan
(313) 962-4545

Palmer Moving & Storage Co.
7740 Gratiot
Detroit, Michigan
(313) 921-1035

Riverside Storage & Cartage
Co.
547 Cass Avenue
Detroit, Michigan
(313) 961-0606

Walker International
2101 West Lafayette
Detroit, Michigan
(313) 496-1171

Viviana Wine Importers Inc.
15100 Second Boulevard
Highland Park, Michigan
(313) 883-1600

Wolverine Storage
38160 Amrhein
Livonia, Michigan
(313) 537-8850

Toledo, Ohio

Great Lakes Terminal Warehouse Co.
355 Morris
Toledo, Ohio
(419) 241-4231

Toledo Foreign Trade Zone
Operators Inc.
3332 Saint Lawrence
Toledo, Ohio
(419) 729-3704

Hotels

Detroit Plaza Hotel
Renaissance Center
Detroit, Michigan
(313) 568-8000

Holiday Inn
22900 Michigan Avenue
Dearborn, Michigan
(313) 278-4800

Pontchartrain Hotel
2 Washington Boulevard
Detroit, Michigan
(313) 965-0200

Howard Johnson's
Washington Boulevard &
Michigan Ave.
Detroit, Michigan
(313) 965-1050

Northfield Hilton Inn
5500 Crooks Road
Troy, Michigan
(313) 879-2100

Troy Hilton
1455 Stephenson Highway
Troy, Michigan
(313) 583-9000

Book-Cadillac Hotel
Washington Boulevard &
Michigan Ave.
Detroit, Michigan
(313) 256-8000

Hyatt Regency Dearborn
Fairline Town Centre
Dearborn, Michigan
(313) 593-1234

Windsor, Ontario

Richelieu Inn
430 Ouelette Avenue
Windsor, Ontario
(519) 253-7281

Holiday Inn
480 Riverisde Drive W.
Windsor, Ontario
(519) 253-4411

Wandlyn Viscount Motor Inn
1150 Ouelette Avenue
Windsor, Ontario
(519) 252-2741

The major hotel chains are well represented in Toledo and in other major centres in Michigan and Indiana.

Regional Offices

IF YOU HAVE NOT PREVIOUSLY MARKETED ABROAD, CONTACT ANY OF THE CANADIAN TRADE OFFICERS OF THE DEPARTMENT OF INDUSTRY, TRADE AND COMMERCE AT THE ADDRESSES LISTED BELOW.

NEWFOUNDLAND LABRADOR	P.O. Box 6148 127 Water Street (2nd Floor) St. John's, Newfoundland A1C 5X8	Tel: (709) 737-5511 Telex: 016-4749
NOVA SCOTIA	Suite 1124, Duke Tower 5251 Duke Street Scotia Square Halifax, Nova Scotia B3J 1N9	Tel: (902) 426-7540 Telex: 019-21829
NEW BRUNSWICK	Suite 642, 440 King Street Fredericton, New Brunswick E3B 5H8	Tel: (506) 452-3190 Telex: 014-46140
PRINCE EDWARD ISLAND	P.O. Box 2289 Dominion Building 97 Queen Street Charlottetown Prince Edward Island C1A 8C1	Tel: (902) 892-1211 Telex: 014-44129
QUEBEC	C.P. 1270, Station B Suite 600 685, rue Cathcart Montreal, Quebec N3B 3K9	Tel: (514) 283-6254 Telex: 055-60768

	Suite 620, Place Quebec Quebec, Quebec G1R 2B5	Tel: (418) 694-4726 Telex: 051-3312
ONTARIO	1 First Canadian Place Suite 4840, P.O. Box 98 Toronto, Ontario M5X 1B1	Tel: (416) 369-4951 Telex: 065-24378
MANITOBA	507 Manulife House 386 Broadway Avenue Winnipeg, Manitoba R3C 3R6	Tel: (204) 949-2381 Telex: 075-7624
SASKATCHEWAN	Room 980 2002 Victoria Avenue Regina, Saskatchewan S4P 0R7	Tel: (306) 569-5020 Telex: 071-2745
ALBERTA NORTHWEST TERRITORIES	500 Macdonald Place 9939 Jasper Avenue Edmonton, Alberta T5J 2W8	Tel: (403) 720-2944 Telex: 037-2762
BRITISH COLUMBIA YUKON	P.O.Box 49178 Suite 2743 Bentall Centre, Tower III 595 Burrard Street Vancouver, British Columbia V7X 1K8	Tel: (604) 666-1434 Telex: 04-51191

V
Canadian
Market
Penetration
Strategy

Penetration of the United States Market
by
Peter Tower
President
C.J. Tower & Sons

Considerable credit is due to Wilfrid Laurier University because it was among the first to formalize discussion of export trade in this course in International Marketing. This effort coupled with ongoing programs of the Canadian Department of Industry, Trade & Commerce, of the Ontario Department of Industry & Tourism, of the Canadian Manufacturers' Association and of Canadian Export Association --- all of these working together, and separately, have to be given great credit for the dynamic growth in total exports and exports to the U.S.A. in particular.

I doubt if there is any comparable situation where so much help --practical step by step, hand fashioned help -- is available to anyone who wishes to seek expanded sales through export. This is probably why Canada -- though she ranks only 30th among the countries of the world in terms of population is 5th among them in terms of trade which is carried on in significant amounts with 130 other countries. Canada accounts for almost 5% of total world exports. To support your economy, and to finance the imports of necessities not found here or not efficiently produced, Canada must export an astounding 20% of gross national product. This is a unique and formidable task. Comparable figure in the United States is about 10%.

What is exporting anyway? Exporting merchandise is merely sending it beyond certain confines. In a sense, selling Toronto-made goods to Peterborough is exporting them. Exporting to another country really has only one additional characteristic. The internationality of the transaction exposes the goods to a different set of laws, chief of which is usually a tariff.

Certainly the prime target for Canada exports has been and will continue to be the U.S.A. Here literally, at your feet is an expanding market of over 220 million persons vested with the world's largest disposable income. In the decade to come, personal spending alone is projected to double from the present 617 billion per year to 1200 billion. Industrial and government spending will have corresponding growth as U.S. gross national product goes from the present 1 trillion to 2 trillion dollars by 1980. And there is no other market in the world where it is more possible for a Canadian to say that export selling is almost like selling in the home market. Selling Toronto goods to Pittsburgh is almost exactly the same as selling to Peterborough. The same languge, same terms, same currency, and same method of delivery can be employed. The sole difference between these two transactions is that the U.S. Tariff confronts the Pittsburgh delivery. My work in the business world is as a United States Customhouse Broker. A Customhouse Broker is the specialist who assists owners of merchandise to secure the most favorable legal admission of those goods to the U.S. commerce. I am very much involved with that single factor which distinguishes home market transactions from sales for export to the U.S.A., the U.S. Tariff. Last year my company was responsible for the U.S. Customs entry of very nearly 2.5 billion dollars of Canadian material and products -- just about 22% of the total goods shipped to the U.S.A. from Canada.

The first main point I wish to emphasize is that although there are many common terms and situations, it is best to consider that there are virtually no analogies between U.S. Tariff and U.S. Customs procedures and those of any other country. A knowledge of Canadian Tariff and Canadian Customs procedures is often a handicap to persons trying to understand U.S. affairs, and it is necessary to divorce your thinking on them completely. The entire legal structure, purposes and objectives, the self-interest, and the administrative procedures are as different as the administrators themselves are different people. The second point to make clear is that there is no high degree of precision surrounding the U.S. Tariff. Though extremely complex, it has many broad provisions which leave much discretion and decision in the hands of Customs officials administering it. Dealing with U.S. Customs matters is as much an art as a science.

Obviously the first thing which needs to be done with any product is to ascertain if there are potential customers for it. When their location is known an idea of the available transportation becomes desirable. This will identify the gateway or gateways you must employ. Under ideal circumstances the use of a single port of entry has much to recommend it.

I imagine you have already heard that your marketing prospects will be greatly enhanced if you arrange to sell at duty paid prices -- you assume responsibility for Customs clearance and duty expense, if any. This is certainly so in case of any product similar to or competitive with articles already produced or available in the U.S.A. Under U.S. law the Customhouse Broker can act for the Canadian exporter and at his expense just as simply as when he is acting for the U.S. importer. And taking responsibility for duty has some beneficial side-effects. Inasmuch as U.S. Tariff classification and valuation are all predicated on facts -- i.e. formulas, costs, prices, -- which only the Canadian exporter can furnish, he cannot escape involvement to this extent. If duties are the responsibility of the U.S. buyer, he will generally learn these details of your business.

If you are responsible, only your Customhouse Broker and the Customs people will know of them and your customer will have no chance of learning them. Equally important, the U.S. buyer is not apt to challenge or seek improvement in decisions by U.S. Customs, which, if adverse, may discourage him from purchase of your product especially if he has alternative domestic sources. You, on the other hand, have the incentive and the information which may enable you and your Customhouse Broker to seek and obtain better results. Finally, by being responsible for the clearance and duties, if any, you can select the port(s) of entry instead of having goods cleared at numbers of destinations which is not only expensive in time as well as money, but undesirable for other reasons. Apart from the fact that many large inland points are not Customs ports of entry -- several whole states lack any such facility --- U.S. procedure encourages use of as few ports as possible, preferably one, and preferably a border port of arrival conveniently close to you. U.S. law requires Customs officials at each port to independently investigate and conclude the Tariff applicable to each article entered there. Where several ports are employed you become involved in furnishing information to each of them. If one or more of them arrives at a different conclusion from the others, you will suffer from uncertainty while they resolve their differences under a time-consuming procedure. If they are unable to reach a common decision, or if you disagree with that decision, the matter must then be referred to the Bureau of Customs, Washington, for resolution, and uncertainty and delay continues that much longer. So it is best if you assume responsibility for Customs clearance and use a Customhouse Broker at a border port which is near you. This way Customs' decisions can be accelerated and if you are in disagreement an approach to the Bureau of Customs for review can be had at the earliest date.

Let's go back a little. After you select a port of entry you should carefully select a Customhouse Broker. These people are licensed by the United States Treasury Department which means that they are roughly equivalent to certain basic knowledge. Beyond that, however, they can differ enormously in competence and resources. You should use as much care and deliberation in this selection of a U.S. Customhouse Broker as you do in choosing your lawyers, bankers and other agents. The knowledge and service of your Customhouse Broker can have a profound effect on your U.S. export program. Many persons are entirely too casual in this area and leave the selection to carriers and others or simply choose the broker who offers the lowest price. (Incidentally, I'm not here imposing on your time simply to make a pitch for myself or the use of Customhouse Brokers. Because border clearance is so predominant and because procedures are complex, over 95% of all commercial importations into the U.S.A. are processed by Customhouse Brokers and very few importers -- even when located to do so -- arrange their own clearances. Almost all engage brokers to do it or in the case of Canadian trade prefer that the Canadian seller do so.)

I have mentioned uncertainty. Most uncertainty about U.S. Tariff applicable to a product can be minimized if not eliminated. When you have determined your port of entry and Customhouse Broker you should meet with him to discuss your entire export program. To be meaningful, people completely familiar with your product and its sale should be present. The success of the venture depends upon the mutual exploration of all the facts surrounding the product and the Tariff consequences of each of those facts. Holding this conference at the port of entry enables a number of your people to become acquainted with the people and facilities with which they may be concerned from time to time later. Because U.S. Tariff classification and value for duty is so extremely complex, it is important to discuss whether minor changes in product or sales procedure may be beneficial. If your product incorporates, or could be made with, any components which are of U.S. origin, this important fact should be brought to light. Possible interest in and regulation of imports by other U.S. Government Agencies --- Food & Drug Administration -- Meat Inspection Division -- Agricultural Marketing Service -- Federal Trade Commission, and the like will be considered. A full discussion of charges and payments and required documentation will occur. You should be able to leave this meeting with an understanding of your obligations, with an assurance that your traffic will be given prompt and proper attention, and with a reasonably accurate idea of the rate of duty or range of rates of duty applicable, plus a reasonable estimate of the ultimte appraised value. As a rule, it is useful at this point to determine the best rate of duty you can hope to obtain, as well as the worst which might be held applicable. This will dictate what steps should next follow. It may seem wise or necessary to obtain a Bureau of Customs ruling as to Tariff classification. Such rulings can be obtained. Ordinarily, this classification ruling will not be changed to impose higher duties unless it should later prove to be clearly wrong. In most cases, in that event, the ruling imposing higher duties will be effected only as to merchandise entered 90 days after notice of the change.

A similar ruling as to value is not available. Another procedure available to Canadian exporters with respect to present or proposed transactions is the Canadian Query Program. This was set up to provide persons in Canada an opportunity to discuss matters relating to appraisement, classification, marking, and other related topics pertaining to the importation of merchandise. At present, five Customs officials are assigned to this activity according to the geographic location of the persons making inquiry. One at Buffalo handles such inquiries from persons in Ontario, east of London. When request is made, an interview is arranged and the officer secures as much information as possible regarding the product and its sale. Based on this he prepares a report containing his conclusions, which is then circulated and is reviewed at the Bureau of Customs in Washington. They issue a ruling as to classification which is binding to the same extent as the rulings obtained by you and your broker if you apply to Washington directly. They issue non-binding advice regarding probable valuation.

I'd like to go on to describe our entry procedure. It commences with the actual arrival of merchandise. Copies of your invoice should accompany the goods. At most Canadian border ports immediate release procedures are employed, meaning that your broker will request Customs to inspect the merchandise on the basis of your invoice. For this reason it is important to select a broker who has personnel stationed at actual merchandise arrival points at all times when Customs clearance is available. If the merchandise is found to agree with the documents and is otherwise admissable, the carrier is allowed to proceed. Inspection occurs right in railcars and in trucks without unloading, and whole trains can be processed in an hour or so and average clearance of a truckload requires less than 20 minutes. The important thing is to have good documents present.

Underlying this procedure is a bond -- a bond furnished by the broker, or in certain cases it may be appropriate for you or your customer to give the bond. This bond is conditioned that in consideration of the release of the merchandise prior to entry, and prior to ascertainment of duties, the principal undertakes to file entry promptly and to pay any and all duties, taxes, or other charges ultimately assessed as a result of the importation. A short time is allowed for entry papers to be prepared and filed with Customs. Where duty is indicated the necessary amount is tendered. Entry is made on the basis of the best information available, which may range from nothing more than what appears on your invoice to a well-settled classification or value basis arrived at in connection with previous identical importations or by ruling or otherwise. When entries are presented, Customs review them for timeliness, completeness and accuracy. They can reject the entry and require it to be made differently. When accepted, any duties paid are termed estimated duties. Subsequent to entry Customs must ascertain all the needed information which will permit final determination of classification and value and the calculation of liquidated duties. If none of the information is present at time of entry, as is generally the case on original shipments, much time can elapse while Customs gather and consider the details. You can assist by insuring that all inquiries are given prompt and thorough attention. At some point whether immediately after entry or a much later date, Customs arrive at what are termed liquidated duties. Whenever liquidated duties differ from estimated duties, an adjustment is made at that time, either a refund or a collection. These are sometimes referred to as retroactive assessments but that is not accurate. It occurs simply because Customs will release goods prior to determination of actual duties provided we agree to pay those duties when they are fixed.

When we disagree with Customs' decisions, we can submit our counter-argument to the port and seek reviews at higher levels including the Bureau of Customs. Where no change is accomplished and we continue to disagree, a formal protest can be filed and customs again must consider but different personnel handle the case. If no change is accomplished, the matter may then be summoned to the United States Customs Court for judicial decision.

The point here is not to frighten or confuse but to illustrate how much latitude exists and to show the importance of exploring every aspect of a Customs matter with a qualified expert and not to assume that there is so much precision in these things that Customs decisions are apt to be infallible or that you can deal with them without specialized assistance.

I believe that too much attention has been focused on difficulties that a few have had, or thought they were having, with U.S. Customs. Against this, statistics show that vast quantities of goods are moving south unhindered. My belief and my experience is that any Canadian businessman willing to involve himself can find satisfaction and profit in export trade to the United States. All that is necessary is to learn what is expected and what to expect.

You who are taking this course are exhibiting just such an involvement and I'm sure that many of you are already, or will be, highly successful in International Marketing for that very reason. Congratulations to you.

Penetrating the U.S. Market

by

T. Frank Harris
Consul General of Canada
Consulate General
Detroit, Michigan

Almost every paper that has been written, almost every speech that has been spoken on Canadian trade is wrapped around our dependence on export markets. We are a trading nation -- almost 25 percent of our income is derived from exports. In 1980, we imported $68.9 billion worth of goods and exported $74.2 billion worth. The United States absorbed about sixty-three percent of our exports and supplied about seventy percent of our imports. The story has been told so often, with only a variation in figures, that those who read and hear it tend to "tune out". But businessmen shouldn't, for within the story is a message to individual Canadian manufacturers on how to realize additional profits.

In the beginning, almost every businessman has rather limited horizons. He usually aspires to a business of modest size that caters to customers in a restricted geographical area. Once he has realized his original goal, however, his horizon broadens and eventually he comes to the point where it appears it can broaden no farther. If he has saturated the domestic market or even his regional domestic market, I suggest a look at the United States.

From a cursory glance at statistics on trade between Canada and the United States, it is obvious many Canadian exporters have not only looked, but are actively selling to our neighbours to the South. In 1980, Canadian exports to the U.S.A. amounted to $46.8 billion and imports reached $48.4 billion. There is a disparity in the relative importance of this trade in that Canadian exports to the U.S.A. represent nearly 16.5% of Gross National Product compared to Canada importing less than 2% of U.S. total production.

The composition of Canada/United States trade reflects a significant imbalance in the degree of manufacture of products exchanged. A considerably larger amount of U.S. exports to Canada contain high technology or a greater degree of processing than is the case for Canadian exports to the U.S.A. Nevertheless, the U.S.A. is by far the largest market for Canadian manufacturers. Fully manufactured products exported to the U.S.A. amounted to $16.7 billion and accounted for approximately 37% of total exports to that country in 1980. In comparison fully manufactured products accounted for approximately 30% of total exports to all markets, only about 16% of exports to the E.E.C. and less than 3% of exports to Japan in the same year.

And what encouraged the Canadian manufacturers of these products to sell and ship to the U.S.? The many benefits that result from penetrating the largest and most affluent market in the world!

Rather than discuss those benefits in general terms, let us take a look at an imaginary, but typical, manufacturer in Waterloo who decides to export. What benefits can he hope to realize?

Increased Throughput

No matter what comes out of his factory, there is an upper limit to the number of Canadians who will buy his products. And that upper limit determines the throughput of his factory. Our Waterloo manufacturer, in order to lower his unit production costs and make more profit, needs more throughput. If he can achieve more throughput by developing outlets in the U.S., he not only realizes a profit on his export sales, but a better margin of profit on his domestic sales as well.

Marketing Stability

As an exporter to the United States, the manufacturer in Waterloo is less vulnerable than the non-exporter to fluctuations in the Canadian economy. Although it has often been said, and is generally true, that the Canadian economy follows any dips or rises of the U.S. economy, there is a time-lag that's advantageous to Canadian exporters. Usually while business is picking up in the U.S., several months elapse before the Canadian economy is affected. During this period, the Waterloo manufacturer will write a growing number of orders with his U.S. customers while the non-exporter is waiting for business to improve in Canada. By the time that happens, demand in the U.S. is apt to have slackened off and the Waterloo manufacturer can keep his factory occupied with the increasing number of orders he, too, is receiving from domestic customers as the Canadian market picks up. This pattern tends to repeat itself enabling the Waterloo manufacturer to operate his factory at peak efficiency while the non-exporter struggles with fluctuations in domestic demand.

Enhanced Prestige

Because the American market is so big, it is the most desirable -- and sought after -- in the world. Whether the Waterloo businessman wants to expand his sales to still other countries or is content to limit his exports to the U.S., proven saleability in the U.S. market gives his product prestige.

Export Experience

Should the Waterloo businessman decide later on to expand his sales to "foreign" countries, the experience he has gained in export documentation, packaging goods for export, arranging for export financing and foreign collections will make it easier for him to enter overseas markets. Although competition in the U.S. is fierce and buyers are demanding, it is easier for Canadians to do business there than anywhere else in the world. American buyers speak the same language as most Canadians and follow the same business practices. Many of them have Canadian relatives and friends and have holidayed in Canada. They don't think of Canadians as "foreign", but as neighbours for whom they have a high regard. In this atmosphere, the Waterloo businessman is on equal footing with competing U.S. suppliers -- a situation that does not exist for Canadians in any other country in the world, with the possible exception of Britain.

A Thumbnail Sketch of Uncle Sam's Marketplace

For the exporter in Waterloo, the proximity of the U.S. marketplace is a great advantage -- one he has over those trying to penetrate the market from more distant lands. It takes the Waterloo manufacturer 10 hours to drive to Chicago; less than 2 hours to fly. He can drive to Detroit in 4 hours. He can make delivery to his American customer as quickly as he can to most of his customers in Canada. And although he is not really close to "all" the American market, anymore than he is close to "all" the Canadian market, he doen't have to be. He can establish warehouse facilities in strategic centers of the U.S. just as he may already have done in Canada. For the U.S., like Canada, IS A COHESIVE MARKET AREA. Shipping procedures, customs regulations, etc., are the same whether you are shipping to the West Coast of the United States, the Deep South or to the East Coast.

Cohesiveness is not restricted to the technical aspects of buying and selling either; advertising and promotion through American media (TV, radio, magazines, and newspapers) build up a cross-country demand. But now that I have mentioned the market's cohesiveness, I must also mention its variables.

It would be erroneous to suggest that the New Yorker buys exactly the same product in the same quantity as someone in the Mid West, or that he can be "sold" in exactly the same way. Tastes in consumer goods, for example, differ appreciably in various parts of the country. Hazardous though it is to generalize, many have labelled the U.S. West Coast susceptible to fadish and flamboyant styles; the Mid West as conservative and Easterners as sophisticated and demanding. Each supplier must determine for himself whether or not the labels apply to his product.

In discussing the benefits that accrue to the exporting Waterloo manufacturer, I mentioned the competitiveness of the U.S. market. It would be impossible to over-emphasize the degree of competition in this marketplace, for the American buyer has not only his own countrymen constantly knocking at his door, but salesmen from Japan, Germany, Italy and South America, etc., as well.

Special Sales Effort Required

In all sections of the U.S., buyers expect to be "sold" on a product or service. They are conscious of their position as customers and expect a salesman to tell them why they should buy his product rather than someone elses! They also expect follow-up. If they don't get it from one supplier, there are plenty of others to provide it. It is, therefore, not unusual for salesmen of such relatively slow-moving items as car tires to contact their customers two or three times a month to insure that their needs are met. After a sale has been made and terms and delivery agreed upon, U.S. buyers assume suppliers will live up to their agreements. If something happens to slow down delivery (and Canadian suppliers should go out of their way to see this doesn't happen), the U.S. buyer expects to be informed of the circumstances immediately. If he isn't informed, and the reasons for the delay are not acceptable to him, a competitor will get the next order.

Although U.S. buyers expect a lot, they are also highly receptive to new products and unique promotional ideas -- more so than buyers in Canada or other countries. Receptiveness may be just a dominant characteristic of the American temperment, but I suspect U.S. buyers are so receptive because they realize that if they pass up something new their competitors may buy it and make a fortune. Friendly and receptive though they may be, the U.S. buyers' demands include insistance that the supplier (Canadian or otherwise) take care of any administrative details connected with delivery of goods ordered. They want the transaction to be handled as if they were buying from an American supplier.

Watch the Trends

It is worth mentioning that the U.S. market is highly susceptible to political and economic trends, and those who watch the trends can capitalize on the demands they create. Those continuing to making headlines in the U.S. are:

(1) Conservation of energy, which has stimulated demand for products such as mass transportation equipment and down sized, fuel efficient motor vehicles, heat pumps, solar heating systems and insulating material.

(2) Similarly, the concern of Americans for the safety of nuclear power plants has opened up markets for safety equipment in this field and may make the CANDU nuclear generating stations developed in Canada more attractive to U.S. power companies.

(3) Concern over the environment, which has expanded the demand for environmental protection devices.

Earmark a Portion of Your Plant Capacity for Exports

Earlier, I spoke of the U.S. buyers' insistance that he receive the same service from Canadian suppliers as he does from his supplier in the United States. This maxim applies, not only in regard to service but also prompt delivery. The U.S. buyer must be treated as a valued, regular customer whose requirements will be met to the fullest extent possible no matter how tight supplies get.

Canadian manufacturers unable to meet peak domestic demand have no future in the export business and certainly none in the U.S. market. In short, a Canadian manufacturer can only penetrate and hold onto the U.S. market if he has sufficient plant capacity to accommodate his American as well as his Canadian customers in good times and bad.

U.S. Tariffs and Other Barriers

Of all markets open to Canadian exporters, the U.S. is one of the most accessible. Aside from quotas on dairy products, there are virtually no restrictions on the importation of Canadian products. It is true that some government agencies are obliged, under the "Buy American Act", to purchase their requirements from domestic sources only. But in times of shortage, even these restrictions are sometimes waived.

Duties levied on products entering the U.S. from Canada are seldom prohibitive. They weren't prohibitive for the $46.8 billion worth of Canadian goods that crossed the border into the U.S. in 1980.

Selling in the Mid-West

Because of the enormity of the U.S. market as a whole, most Canadian exporters decide to tackle one section at a time. Since part of the Mid-West happens to be the territory covered by the Canadian Consulate in Detroit, it is the area I know best. I'll briefly sketch its special characteristics.

For trade purposes the Detroit Consulate covers Michigan, most of Indiana and the City of Toledo, Ohio ... an area of 94,000 square miles containing a population of 15 million with an annual disposable income (after taxes) over $100 billion. Its two principal marketing and distribution centers are Detroit and Indianapolis, but Chicago influences the western portion of the territory. Detroit, of course, is right on Ontario's doorstep. It is closer to us here in Waterloo than many of your Canadian customers. There are good facilities for handling bulk and general cargo as well as warehousing. It also offers easy access to the entire United States heartland and is, of course, the world capital for the automotive industry. Customs brokers and forwarding agents are available, as they are in other major ports in the country.

Probably the most interesting fact about Michigan is that if it were a nation, it would rank as the destination for more Canadian goods than any other country in the world except for the United States itself. Of the $46.8 billion exported to the U.S.A. last year, nearly $9 billion was sent to Michigan. And it wasn't just a market for cars and parts. Food, lumber, newsprint, winter clothing, metalworking and plastic moulding machinery, chemicals, and furniture all figure importantly in our exports. Exports to Indiana were approximately $957.5 million and also included a wide variety of products.

How to Sell In the U.S.A.

Assuming you have decided to expand your sales in the United States, how do you go about it?

First you have to determine your export price. If you have never exported before, you probably are unaware that Canadian sales and excise taxes do not apply on goods exported from Canada. By subtracting such taxes from your domestic prices, you can determine your price at the factory -- usually referred to as free on board factory price, or FOB factory.

Door to Door Transportation

Since American buyers are accustomed to receiving merchandise they order at their doorsteps, you must work out the cost of transporting your products to the nearest U.S. Customs port(s) of entry and onward from there to the larger centers in the U.S. Fortunately, excellent transportation facilities are available between our two countries. You can ship by rail, air, highway, or barge to your U.S. customers.

Should you decide to ship by truck from the Toronto area, for example, all you need to do is ask Thibodeau-Finch Express Ltd., Canadian Freight-ways or Smith Transport how much it costs to ship to points in the U.S.A. For names of international trucking firms operating out of Waterloo and other Canadian centers, consult the yellow pages of the phone book.

For information on the cost of shipping by rail, contact Canadian National Railways or Canadian Pacific Railway Co. in Toronto or Montreal. If your products are light and of high value, the major air carriers operating between your community and the U.S.A. can tell you how much it will cost to ship by air.

By consulting these various sources, you can determine the exact cost of shipping each of your products to customers in major centers of the U.S.A. As most shipments are also insured, the phrase used to describe **delivered prices** is CIF, meaning cost of product plus insurance and freight to the destination. With the help of the transportation companies, you can calculate the price of your products CIF Detroit, Indianapolis or other U.S. cities.

U.S. Tariffs

Having determined your export prices, FOB factory, and the cost of moving your products to major cities in the United States, your next step is to determine the U.S. duties that will apply on your products. You can do this by:

(1) Enlisting the help of the U.S. Division, Western Hemisphere Bureau, of the Department of Industry, Trade and Commerce in Ottawa which will assist you in obtaining the best possible tariff treatment for your products under existing U.S. laws.

(2) Applying directly to the District Director of Customs at the nearest U.S. port of entry.

(3) Employing a U.S. Customs broker at the port of entry nearest your factory who will assist you in obtaining a ruling on the classification of your product and its valuation for duty purposes.

Whichever route you follow, a detailed description of your product will be needed (illustrated sales literature will sometimes suffice) as well as a listing of the components of chief value of each of your products. If some of the components you use come from the U.S.A., be sure to draw this to the attention of U.S. Customs.

Also remember that in making shipments of over $500 in value to the U.S., you must complete a Canadian Customs B13 form (five copies) and a U.S. Special Customs Invoice form 5515 in three copies. For fuller details, consult the Department of Industry, Trade and Commerce booklets on U.S.A. Markets for Canadian Exporters such as the one on Michigan and Indiana. For neophytes in the export business, the employment of a U.S. Customs Broker is probably the simplest and easiest approach. Such brokers know what shipping documents are required and U.S. Customs procedures. They can guide newcomers in the business past the many pitfalls that await the unwary.

An example of one such pitfall is the U.S. Court decision which reversed the previous U.S. Customs policy of accepting FOB factory prices as the basis for determining value for duty on sales made at duty paid prices in cases where actual sales at FOB prices have been made previously, or where the customer had been offered FOB prices but chose instead to purchase at duty paid delivered prices. Canadian exporters offering their products on a CIF basis only have their goods valued on a CIF basis and end up paying duty on a portion of the freight cost in addition to the factory price of their product. Remember this and make a point of quoting FOB factory prices to your U.S. customers and list the transportation, brokerage fees, and insurance fees separately on your invoice.

Focusing On the Most Promising Market Area

Once you've worked out delivered (duty-paid) prices to the larger cities in the United States, your next step is to determine what area of the U.S. offers the best prospects for your line.

Canadian trade Commissioners stationed at Consulates throughout the United States can help you identify the more promising market areas for your products. If you tell them how you are marketing your products in Canada and provide them with descriptive literature and prices on your line, they will place you in touch with potential agents, or import/distributors. If you produce consumer goods and wish to sell directly to department stores, the Trade Commissioner will provide you with the names and addresses of buyers in the larger stores and retail chains in his territory.

Personal Visits A Must

After deciding what portion of the U.S. market you should tackle first, make plans to visit that area to select a suitable representative and call on buyers. Inform the Trade Commissioner in the center you plan to visit of your intentions and ask him to set up appointments for you. Prior to your departure for the U.S., determine how much of your plant production can be earmarked for export. It would also be a good idea to decide on the amount of time and money you are prepared to spend on developing outlets in the U.S. By approaching American buyers with a clear idea of the quantities you are able to supply and the amount of advertising and other support you can give to promote the sale of your product, your chances of success are substantially increased.

Bear in mind that many of the larger U.S. firms keep detailed information on companies with whom they do business. Therefore, you should prepare a short profile on your company along the following lines, for such customers:

- Name and address of your company and telephone and telex number
- Date established
- Number of employees
- Yearly sales volume
- Principal products
- Size of plant and production capabilities
- Location of branch plants, if any
- Quality control procedures
- Transportation facilities
- Representative customers
- Current credit rating.

Purchasers of more sophisticated equipment also want to inspect the manufacturing facilities of prospective suppliers. If your products fall into this category, it is a good idea to let prospective buyers know that a visit to your plant would be welcome.

Like most businessmen, U.S. buyers are keenly interested in meeting prospective suppliers face to face. They will be impressed by your taking the trouble (and expense) of travelling south to meet with them, (North from Windsor to Detroit), especially if you have arranged an appointment beforehand through the trade Commissioner's office. Such appointments are normally made for you with the Director of Purchasing who will sometimes call in one or more specialists on his staff to participate in the initial interview. The larger and more complex the enterprise, the more specialized its buyers are likely to be.

In the course of your conversation with prospective customers, you will probably discern the big difference between selling in Canada and selling in the U.S. is the intensity with which salesmen in the U.S. woo their customers. As mentioned earlier, it is not uncommon for salesmen of even relatively slow-moving items to call on their important customers every week or ten days. The salesman who keeps his company's products uppermost in the mind of the buyer, and makes a point of being on hand when orders are likely to be placed, usually gets the business.

The cost of maintaining such close contact with buyers is reflected in commissions paid to manufacturers' representatives which range from 5% to as high as 20% depending on the product. Every manufacturing/agency relationship is individually tailored to create the desired results. Commissions are established by several variables including pioneering, engineering, servicing, and requirements of an individual product in any given territory. Complete agreement, preferably in writing, by the manufacturer and the agent as to the expected goals and results is the best possible assurance of success. Some Canadian firms have balked at paying such commissions but they forget the representative has to meet competition from other salesmen and does not make money unless his principal does. Of course, a representative or distributor is only as strong as the support he gets from his principals. To enable the representative of your choice to market your products successfully, you must provide him with full information on your merchandising methods in Canada and warn him in advance of changes contemplated in your product line. Make a point of accompanying him on initial calls to larger customers and plan to join him on his rounds regularly.

Sales Promotion

After having appointed an agent or obtained orders from some of the larger department stores, start thinking about ways in which you can promote the sale of your products in the U.S. market. One very effective way of bringing your products to the attention of prospective buyers is to participate in U.S. trade shows and expositions. Thousands of such shows are held each year. The more important ones are listed in the <u>Directory of Trade Shows and Expositions</u> published by the OFFICE OF EXPOSITIONS AND SPECIAL PROJECTS, United States Travel Service, U.S. Department of Commerce, Washington, D.C. 20230. You should find a copy at the U.S. Consulate nearest you but, if not, you can obtain one by writing directly to the U.S. Department of Commerce in Washington, D.C.

Some U.S. trade shows such as the Society of Automotive Engineers and the Society of Mechanical Engineers Shows in Detroit attract buyers from all over the world and are recommended for participation by the Department of Industry, Trade and Commerce in Ottawa. When this happens, Canadian firms planning on participating can apply to the Department for financial assistance under the **Program for Export Market Development.** Such assistance could cover 50 percent of the costs of the space and design and construction of your booth plus airfare and a $100 per diem for company personnel manning the booth. These contributions by the Department are recoverable at the rate of 1 percent of sales resulting from participation in the show during an agreed period, normally three years. If little or no sales result from your participation in the show, repayment is not required.

Another way of promoting your sales in the U.S. is to participate in Trade Missions organized by the Federal and Provincial governments. There are both incoming and outgoing missions. The incoming bring customers to your door and the outgoing take you to prospective customers. Either type can yield dividends. Make a point of informing the Department of Industry, Trade and Commerce in Ottawa of your interest in such missions.

To Summarize

Earmark a portion of your plant capacity for customers in the U.S. Calculate your export prices in U.S. dollars FOB factory as well as duty-paid to U.S. destination. Quote on FOB factory basis and list separately on your invoice the transportation, insurance and customs brokerage charges. Work closely with the commission agent of your choice and remain alert to opportunities for promoting your sales in the U.S. through participation in trade shows and missions. Stick to the delivery schedules agreed upon with each customer and follow-up with them directly or through your agent every few weeks. Enjoy the added profits and satisfaction of selling your products in the largest and most competitive market in the world.

Opportunities in the European Common Market
by
J.E.G. Gibson
Director General
Bureau of European Affairs
Trade Development, Department of External Affairs
Government of Canada

When I first took part in this course two years ago, Professor
Overgaard indicated that he would be glad to have someone like
me who, in his words, "had just returned from the trenches". I
suppose that this was a fair description, although I cannot say
that I ever thought that I was fighting a battle in the country to
which it was accredited, which was the Netherlands. In fact, I
had the good fortune to be located in the European country that
today is probably the most favourably inclined towards Canada
and, indeed, has become one of our major international economic
partners. This friendly attitude, combined with the traditionally
international outlook of the Dutch, made my job, in fact, a relatively straightforward one, albeit a most stimulating experience.
This is not the case in all countires of the European Economic
Community which in reality represents a wide variety of very different marketing situations, but after two years of dealing with
all EEC markets from Ottawa, I am totally convinced of the
strength of that overall market and of the excellent long term
prospects there for Canadian exports and as a source of new
technology.

In planning a global marketing strategy we see the EEC as a
major outlet for Canadian exports and, at the same time, a market
which has rapidly expanded for us even in the face of today's
world-wide economic slowdown. The figures speak for themselves
insofar as in 1980 our exports to the EEC collectively amounted to
$9.43 billion representing nearly 13% of our exports on a world-
wide basis and over 42% of our exports to the world with the exception of the United States of America. Significantly, to date in
1981 our exports to the EEC are running slightly behind those of
1980 and, indeed, the EEC's share of Canada's total exports has
fallen to 12%. These figures will come as no major surprise to
those of you who follow exchange rate movements and are aware

of the increasing strength of North American dollars vis-a-vis most European currencies. Therefore, when I speak about the European Economic Community, I am speaking about an area of extremely high prosperity and one that has a remarkably high propensity to consume.

I am also, however, speaking about a community of countries that has banded itself together with a view towards enhancing its collective economic development and in the process protecting itself to some extent against imports from outside the Community. Thus it is that most non-EEC nations including Canada are faced with a common external tariff whether selling to France, Italy or Luxembourg and, indeed, we are also faced with a variety of other factors some of which I hope to deal with in this article. I hope in the process, however, to point out a few ways and means of approaching the European Common Market generally and some individual markets specifically.

The Bilateral Relationship

It became evident to our government some twelve years ago that, as the EEC went through its early years of operating as a unit, it would be necessary for us to not only maintain our bilateral activities with the governments of member states but also to develop relations with the secretariat of the Community with a view towards ensuring that Canadian interests were not overlooked when Community decisions were being taken. This coincided with the third option strategy that resulted from a foreign policy review carried out at the beginning of this decade, and inevitably the two factors were put together with the result that, in 1976, an economic cooperation agreement was signed between the Government of Canada and the Council of the European Economic Community. Several factors contributed to the conclusion of this agreement including the desire on both parts to maintain and expand business prospects in each other's marketplaces and the recognized need for dialogue between two trading units. This economic cooperation agreement, more properly known as the framework agreement and sometimes inaccurately called the contractual link, provides a vehicle for both parties to take into account each other's interests, capabilities and requirements in developing economic policies and to identify the potential for trade and industrial cooperation between the two parties. The agreement stipulates reciprocal most favoured nation (MFN) tariff treatment and also provides a regular vehicle for consultation between the two parties with respect to the development of trade, the identification and resolution of problems impinging upon the development of trade and consultations on virtually all aspects of economic relations between the two parties. The agreement also sets out in some detail the types of business agreements that the parties to the agreement are trying to foster including investment flows, intercorporate links particularly joint ventures, scientific and technical exchange as well as, of course, direct trade.

The agreement also established a formal means for working together. This machinery includes a joint cooperation committee which normally meets annually at the ministerial level and under that committee are two major sub-committees, namely the general and preparatory sub-committee and the industrial cooperation sub-committee. The general and preparatory sub-committee deals with general trade policy subjects, fact finding on items of mutual interest and the development of ideas for cooperation in mutually agreed fields. The industrial cooperation sub-committee is the one which is of more direct interest to the business community in that it deals with all aspects of industrial cooperation which broadly defined includes joint ventures in production and foreign commerce. The objective of both parties, however, is to expand intercorporate links and, therefore, to the extent possible, activities are aimed at consolidating existing business relationships and trying to promote new business arrangements. This sub-committee has established several working groups to explore in detail sectors that have been mutually agreed as offering potential to both parties. The sectors include telecommunications, forest products, aerospace, non-ferrous metals and nuclear materials and, at this time, the parties are also examining other possible sectors. Generally speaking, activities within these sectors have included the sending of missions to each others' countries for direct business-to-business meetings, as well as meetings at the level of government officials to identify specific opportunities.

From my observation in the field, the approach has worked reasonably well to this end insofar as I have seen the establishment of a number of new business arrangements between Canadian and Dutch companies as a result of these missions. Certainly there is a strong disposition on the part of the EC Commission and the Canadian Government to do all that they can to create a climate in which private enterprise can expand its commercial interests. The important point, however, is that governments are really only able to undertake activities that are in fact aimed at creating the most favourable possible trading environment. It is up to the business concerns within the member states of the EEC as well as Canadian companies to capitalize upon the activities of their governments and thus the whole exercise of industrial cooperation will only work if the private and public sectors of both parties to the framework agreement work in closely agreed harmony. I would suggest to this point that this has been very much the case as seen from both sides. As a result of these activities Canada has, for example, received several industrial cooperation missions sponsored by governments or industry associations from almost all member states.

In turn, we have dispatched several vertically structured missions to Europe over recent years and we also sent one high level businessmen's mission, led by the then Minister of Industry, Trade and Commerce, in late 1977. In all cases, it was the observation of our posts in Europe that individual business members of the missions were very soon returning to Europe to follow up on opportunities that were uncovered during their participation in the officially sponsored missions.

I hope, therefore, you will realize that neither the EEC nor the Government of Canada have set out to create a bureaucratic structure that might impede direct business participation. This has not proved at all to be the case and indeed I think that the proof of the business/government cooperation can be amply pointed out by the statistical evidence in terms of improved exports to the EEC and indeed EEC exports to Canada.

The Market

The justification for industry and government involvement in developing commercial and economic links between Canada and the European Economic Community can be quickly found in the significant size of the community as a trading partner for Canada. The Common Market represents a total consuming population in excess of 270 million spread over ten nations of Western Europe. The present community accounts for no less than 20% of the world's output of goods and even more interesting at least 25% of total world trade. Its annual imports are in excess of $300 billion which on a value basis makes it nearly 20% larger than the total U.S. import market ($253 billion) and 40% of the imports into the Community are manufactured goods. These figures are even more interesting if you stop to recall that the EEC figures, of course, take no account of trade within the community, that is to say goods moving from France into Germany or to any other Community member state are no longer regarded as imports but as internal or domestic trade. In other words, there is a very large market being pursued by world exporting nations outside the Community. In reverse, the Community accounts for some 9% of Canadian imports most of which are in the form of fully or semi-manufactured products or consumables. The present balance of trade with the community as a whole is in Canada's favour largely due to our massive exports of industrial raw materials and semi-processed goods destined for upgrading into manufactured products inside the community. This need of the community's for regular supplies of production materials will undoubtedly continue to form the main basis of Canada's exports into Europe in the foreseeable future. But it is the hope and indeed the policy of the Canadian Government to seek access and promote exports of fully manufactured products into Europe thus increasing employment in our own country. To put this into context, one notes that manufactured goods account for 40% of total EEC imports but only 12% of imports from Canada. Indeed on a world-wide basis, 30% of our exports are fully-manufactured products.

Our other economic tie of significance with the Community is that of foreign investment. At least 15% of the total foreign investment in Canada has come from companies within the member states of the EEC and as you may have observed during the past few years, with very hard European currencies and a lower valued dollar, there has been a flurry of activity in our country on the part of European investors. As an example the Netherlands has now become the third largest source of foreign investment in Canada (after the U.S. and Britain) and even more startling, that same small nation is the largest single source of foreign investment in the United States.

In summary, what we are looking at in the European Economic Community is a highly prosperous economic bloc -- recent visitors to London and Paris can attest to the high cost of living compared to Canada, the differential being at least 30% and visitors to Germany cannot help but be impressed with the outward signs of prosperity ranging from hundred of thousands of high-speed Mercedes Benz to a generally bouyant atmosphere reflected in all aspects of life in that country. We are also looking at Canada's second largest trading partner and, as I have already indicated, one of our fastest growing trading outlets. When the Common Market was first conceived, outsiders predicted that the creation of a European Economic Community would result in diminished access to European markets as a consequence of the imposition of a common external tariff. The result some twenty-four years later is that thanks to the removal of internal tariffs within their Community, production units have been able to expand rapidly to take advantage of the vastly increased markets and this in turn has made those European suppliers more competitive on an international scale. At the same time, the increased European Prosperity has generated new import opportunities and this is where Canada and other outside nations have been able to move in. As I have already indicated, on a per capita basis the European Economic Community now represents a larger global import market than does the United States of America.

The common external tariff has over the years been progressively lowered and following the implementation of the multilateral tariff negotiations which were concluded over two years ago, one can anticipate further cuts in Community tariffs. These cuts will affect a wide range of industrial materials, agricultural products and finished goods of both a consumer and industrial nature. A wide range of existing Canadian exports will be favourably affected by these cuts which, as you know, are supposed to be implemented on a gradual basis during the 1980's. There are areas where we would have liked to have seen significant tariff cuts made and I include amongst these the areas affecting several forest products and non-ferrous metal products. Nonetheless, the overall approach to cutting is bound to be beneficial insofar as over the years the EEC has built up a series of duty free and other preferential trading arrangements with neighbouring states, such as those of the European Free Trade Association, and those cuts in the most favoured nation (MFN) rate, which applies to Canada, will help narrow the differential between the tariffs which we must face and the lower tariffs enjoyed by neighbouring European states.

One disappointment during the multilateral tariff negotiations (MTN) was that the Community was not prepared to countenance any fundamental changes in its common agricultural policy (CAP) and it is here that we get into the area of non-tariff barriers (NTB) which represent, in some cases, a significant obstacle to the development of markets within the EEC. The common agricultural policy and related policies provide a wide range of measures that benefit or protect domestic European producers. Included amongst these is the system of variable import levies applied to imports of many agricultural products into the Community. The effect of these levies is to make up the difference between world market prices and the EEC support price plus an additional amount to ensure that Community production receives preference in a competitive situation. Similarly, for other agricultural products the Community imposes a minimum import or reference price that is based on EEC market prices and thus ensures no advantage to imports over European products. Proceeds from import levies and customs duties largely underwrite the CAP which in turn provides for a system of production and export subsidies known as "restitutions" for Community products that effectively enable Community products to compete with lower world prices at home and in world markets.

In addition, member states within the Community employ various measures or practices that constitute NTB's and that can directly affect Canadian exports to those markets. Paramount amongst these are government procurement practices which vary from one state to another, but which frequently, in effect, direct business to domestic producers in the first instance, EEC suppliers in the second instance, and third countries in the last instance. Similarly, many countries apply national standards to various products that have the effect of adversely affecting imports insofar as the standards are always drawn up on the basis of domestic products. The DIN standards in Germany are a case in point, and these, for example, served for many years to preclude us from developing within Germany a market for Canadian timberframe constructed homes. Similarly, systems of road tax based on horsepower have in the past been discriminating against imports of standard North American model cars into the Community. I might add that the effect of this is less than it used to be due to the lower valued dollar and to the greatly increased prosperity in Europe which has to some extent been reflected in a tendency to drive flashy cars including those of a North American manufacture.

To give you further examples specific to the market in which I was working, you may be aware that Canada has developed a good production expertise for smoke sensors for use in homes. The Canadian products generally employ a very low radio active source as the unit powering the sensor and Dutch law does not allow for radio active sources to be used in the home. Curiously, the law makes no reference to luminous dials on wristwatches! Similarly, we frequently run into regulations prohibiting the use of artificial additives to foodstuffs. As an example, peanut butter lovers will find the Dutch product very different from ours insofar as the Dutch is absolutely pure foodstuff whereas the Canadian product contains artificial additives. While these may seem to be small examples, one must remember that they loom large in the minds of individual manufacturers who are trying to increase their production capacity through expanded markets.

I trust that you will not take from my foregoing remarks the impression that selling into the EEC is very difficult because this is certainly not the case. Non-tariff barriers are a regrettable fact of life in virtually all major markets of the world and people have long since learned to live with them even if they do not accept them.

The Marketing Approach

In approaching the whole question of doing business within the EEC it seems to be that there are three main ways in which business can be pursued and these are, albeit, in reverse order: (1) establishment of a branch manufacturing operation within the Community; (2) establishment of a joint venture with an existing European concern to manufacture under licence or assemble within Europe; and (3) direct export from Canada. I am not really here to speak to the first two considerations as these are normally the types of activity that are undertaken after an exporter has es-tablished his market position. I do, however, mention them because both offer one major benefit and that is that the company is then doing business inside the EEC and, therefore, is no longer subject to the measures on imports which I have discussed earlier. As I have also indicated, the Europeans rely upon imports of raw materials which they in turn upgrade inside their own markets and certainly local upgrading or assembly is one good way to reduce the impact of import tariffs and other measures but it, of course, requires a completely different risk undertaking than do direct exporters from Canada. Without wishing to belabour this subject, I would denote that joint ventures abroad and particularly in Europe is one of the main reasons for the Americans' successful penetration of overseas markets including those in Europe.

Turning to direct exports, these can be examined and developed using a wide variety of information sources. Before you commit yourself to any marketing decisions in Europe, I would strongly recommend that you speak with officials in our Department of External Affairs at Ottawa. There are at least two sections that you should contact at the outset. The first of these is the Industry Sector Branch of the Department of Regional Industrial Expansion that has responsibility for your product. Within the branch you will find an official who is generally knowledgeable about the Canadian manufacturing capability for your product area and who at the same time has some knowledge about export marketing prospects. The other section is the Bureau of European Affairs where I work. The Bureau's responsibilities include the maintenance of an overview of Canada's overseas export activities, which in this case would be the European Economic Community, and the development of marketing strategies to capitalize upon prospects abroad. Between the Bureau and the Industry Sector Branch we think that we can give you a good general appraisal of your sales prospects in a given part of the world and following that we would quickly pass you on into the hands of our Trade Commissioner Service Posts at our Embassies and Consulates abroad, who would be in a position to provide you with information specific to their marketplaces and your prospects for doing business in their areas. Thus between Ottawa and the posts abroad you would be in a position to gather together general marketing information and specific information on the countries that are of interest to you. Our posts abroad--and I might mention that 20% of our Trade Commissioner strength is located within the 13 posts of the European Economic Community--will be pleased, in addition to providing you with specific market information, to introduce you to customers, agents and other middlemen and government officials if required in their territories. The last category of government officials is, of course, important in the event that the government is a potential customer or in the event that regulatory approval of some description is required before your product can be imported into that market.

Once you have amassed the foregoing information you will want to decide whether or not you wish to proceed. I would urge you to give serious consideration towards the use of the government's program for export market development to help in underwriting the costs of your initial market exploration activity. Once you arrive in the same target market, I would ask you as a first point of departure to call on the local Canadian Trade Commissioner to finalize your plan and program of visits.

Speaking generally about marketing in Europe, I would say firstly that a knowlegeable and active local representative is not only desirable but absolutely essential if you are intending to establish a long term marketing position. The markets of Europe, as I have indicated earlier, are, in the main, very different from each other and they are certainly different in character from the domestic Canadian market. Therefore, you will require a person or persons to interpret the market for you and ensure that your bests interests are being pursued. In this same vein, Europeans are quality and service conscious and I would urge you to consider whether or not your product should be stocked and have available immediate servicing, from a European source. Naturally, some products do not lend themselves to this, but for those that do you should be in a position to react immediately within the context of the European marketplace. The Europeans are, of course, price conscious but quality and service are every bit as important. Naturally the follow-up requirement is important in the European market and your customers once committed to you will fully expect to hear from you or your representative on a regular basis. If they don't you probably will not see them again!

Lastly, I might mention the importance of trade fairs in Europe. While the use of trade fairs is very common in the United States and to some extent in Canada, it is almost a must in Europe. Vertically structured trade fairs are going on all the time in the major markets but Germany appears to be the main centre of activity for this, and indeed many German fairs are viewed as international marketplaces as customers come from all over the world to see what is on display. If it is any guide as to how important the Government of Canada views the use of particular trade fairs, I could tell you that fully 40% of the government's total budget for trade fairs abroad is directed into the European Economic Community.

In recent years it has become apparent that the European Economic Community can offer Canadian exporters avenues into third markets. The two main ways in which this has been achieved are jointly undertaken projects such as the Saudi Arabia telephone system contract being undertaken by Canadian, Dutch and Swedish firms and the use of European trading houses. In the latter category, I was greatly impressed by the opportunities that we had to sell through Dutch trading houses into other parts of Europe, the Middle and Far East. One must recall that many Europeans, and particularly the Dutch, have historically made their living from foreign trade and some of these countries must, therefore, trade in other peoples' merchandise as well. Thus if this opportunity arises and you wish to take advantage of European foreign trading expertise, your best course would be to consult with the local Canadian trade office with a view towards assessing the bona fides of the trading houses before committing yourself to a course of action.

The European Community has gradually expanded in terms of the number of member states over the years. It is expected that as many as two more nations will join the Community during the 1980's and the prime candidates are Spain and Portugal, both of whom represent significant middle-size export markets for Canada. Accession to the market will of course mean some changes in the traditional trading patterns of these prospective new member states and Canadian companies currently trading in these markets are well advised to take all possible steps to consolidate their existing positions before accession occurs. At this point in time, it is difficult to predict exactly when further Community enlargement will take place but negotiations are under way.

It is evident to anyone involved in international trade or international affairs that the European Economic Community is now well established as a major economic force. As an example, the EEC now negotiates in international forums, such as the multilateral tariff negotiations, as one unit. It is no great secret that in Europe there have been disputes between member states, but when the EEC speaks to the outside world it does so as a unit.

The Community as a whole has a large manufacturing base and foodstuffs production capability, and if there are any weaknesses in the chain, these can be ascribed to certain energy shortfalls and, of course, the need to import industrial raw materials from outside the Community. However, the Community has the means including the wealth available to overcome these and given good political and economic relations with its major trading partners, continuity of supply of materials and energy should be assured. It is for these reasons that we view with great optimism Canada's trading prospects with the European Economic Community.

We believe that a realistic and active trading framework has been established between Canada and the European Community and on a daily basis we see new opportunities being pursued by Canadian exporters.

Doing Business in the European Economic Community

Prepared by
The Western Europe I Division×
European Bureau
Department of Industry, Trade and Commerce
Ottawa

INTRODUCTION

CANADA AND THE EUROPEAN COMMUNITY

With the entry of Britain, Denmark and Ireland, the European Community (EC) has become by far Canada's biggest trading partner after the United States. The EC buys over 1/3 of Canada's overseas exports and 12% of Canada's total world exports. However, only 3% of EC imports come from Canada, compared with Canada's 21% share of the United States market. Moreover, only 11% of Canada's sales to the EC are fully-manufactured goods, although such items make up about 45% of EC imports from all sources and 34% of Canada's total world exports.

The Community supplies more than 1/4 of Canada's imports from overseas and 8% of Canada's total imports. Almost 2/3 of EC sales to Canada are fully-manufactured products.

The EC has a population of about 260 million and generates almost 1/5 of the world's output of goods and services. It is the world's largest trading entity, accounting for about 1/4 of world trade, excluding exchanges among EC member-countries. The EC represents by far the greatest concentration of economic wealth, industrial power and technological capability outside North America. It was with a view both to making decision-makers in this very important part of the world more aware of Canada's economic interests, and to facilitating the entry of Canadian business people to Europe, that in 1976 Canada and the Community concluded a Framework Agreement for Commercial and Economic Cooperation.

THE EUROPEAN ECONOMIC COMMUNITY

The European Community unites the economies of nine countries: Belgium, Britain, Denmark, France, Germany, Ireland, Italy, Luxembourg and the Netherlands. Its present membership was attained when Britain, Denmark and Ireland joined the Community in 1973.

Legally, there are three European communities, but they share the same institutions:

-- the European Coal and Steel Community (ECSC), created in 1951;

-- the European Atomic Energy Community (Euratom), created in 1957;

-- the European Economic Community (EEC), created by the First Treaty of Rome and which came into being on January 1, 1958.

In July 1968, the six original members achieved their customs union by completely removing customs duties and quotas on internal trade. Goods now move freely among all member states, and each member charges the same duty on a given importation from third countries. (As of July 1, 1977 Britain and Ireland had brought their external tariffs into accord with those of the other members of the Community. Thus, Canada no longer is granted preferential tariff access to either of these countries.)

As a result of a series of free trade agreements between the Community and its seven neighbours who are banded together as the European Free Trade Association (EFTA), industrial goods are traded duty-free between the sixteen member states, including the EEC nine, plus Austria, Finland, Iceland, Norway, Portugal, Sweden and Switzerland. For some products, such as aluminum, steel and paper, an extended period of tariff-dismantling has been granted extending until 1984. Only goods which originate in the free trade area enjoy such duty-free tariff treatment. Detailed rules of origin have been worked out to prevent exporters in non-member countries from shipping a pro-

439

duct to a participating country with a low duty rate and then re-exporting the same product to a fellow member state that has a higher national tariff. Similarly, regulations stipulate the percentage of third country value (components, material or labour) that may be incorporated into certain products for inter-EEC/-EFTA trade. Certificates of origin containing signed statements of value, describing contents in descending order of importance, by percentage, are required for each shipment. Canadian manufacturers and exporters of parts and components, should familiarize themselves with these rules of origin, as they pertain to their particular product.

Greece and Turkey are associate members of the Community, with an arrangement for the gradual establishment of a customs union with the EEC as a preparation for possible Community membership. The Community has preferential trade agreements with Spain, Lebanon, Egypt and Israel, and association agreements with Malta, Cyprus, Morocco and Tunisia.

In 1971 the EEC established a system of generalized preferences for developing countries. The system permits duty-free entry of manufactured and semi-finished products and some processed farm goods. Primary products are excluded. Duty-free treatment may be withdrawn if certain historical ceilings are exceeded. In addition, the Community under the terms of the Lome Convention of 1975 grants duty-free and quota-free entry to all manufactured goods and almost all agricultural products from 46 countries in Africa, the Caribbean and the Pacific areas which were formerly dependent territories of member-countries of the Community.

CUSTOMS TARIFF STRUCTURE

The Common Customs Tariff (CCT) of the EEC (which applies to goods imported into the Community from third countries, including Canada) is based on the internationally agreed system of classification of imports known as Customs Co-operation Council Nomenclature (commonly known as the Brussels Tariff Nomenclature) which is employed by approximately 75 countries throughout the world. Under this classification system, the correct tariff classification for most imports into the Community may quite readily be determined.

The CCT contains about 100 tariff classifications which are consolidated into 21 sections and 99 chapters as well as interpretive rules. The layout of the CCT is set out in four columns. The first column indicates the tariff heading number, the second provides a description of the goods, while the third and fourth columns provide for "Autonomous" and "Conventional" rates of customs duties. Customs duties applicable to imported goods originating in countries which are Contracting Parties to the General Agreement on Tariffs and Trade (GATT), including Canada, or with which the Community has concluded agreements containing the most-favoured-nation tariff clause are the "Conventional" duties as shown in column 4. Where no "conventional" duty is shown against a heading or sub-heading, or where the conventional rate is higher than the autonomous rate shown in column 3, duty will be charged at the autonomous rate.

Customs duties in the Community are levied as either "ad valorem" or "specific" charges. Ad valorem duties are used most widely throughout the tariff and are charged on a percentage of the declared value as defined by EC regulations (see "Value for Duty" section below). In the remaining classifications where specific rates are applicable, the charge is made at so much per unit of net weight or other measure of quantity as specified.

As of July 1, 1977 the customs tariffs of Britain, Ireland and Denmark became fully aligned with the Community's Common Customs Tariff which was already in existence throughout the original member countries of the EEC.

Under the terms of preferential trade agreements between the EEC and certain Mediterranean countries and developing countries, many goods imported into the EEC from these countries are granted preferential rates of duty, either at reduced rates or duty-free.

Canadian exports to the EEC, however, do not benefit from any such arrangement.

Information about the classification of Canadian goods in the CCT and the rates of customs charges applicable may be obtained by contacting Western Europe I Division.

VALUE FOR DUTY

The value to be declared on Customs entries (whether for goods free of/or exempted from duty, goods subject to a specific duty or goods subject to duty ad valorem), is the value as set out in the EC Regulations, which are based on the Customs Co-operation Councils' definition of value for customs purposes.

Briefly stated this value is the "normal" price which the goods would fetch, at the time when they are entered for home use, on sale in the open market between buyer and seller independent of each other, with delivery to the buyer at the port or place of importation, the seller bearing freight, insurance, commission and all other costs, charges and expenses incidental to the sale and delivery (except any duty or value added tax chargeable in the Community).

When goods are imported under a contract of sale negotiated under open market conditions between buyer and seller independent of each other, their value for the purpose of duty is normally taken to be the price payable under the contract, adjusted as may be necessary to take account of the costs, charges and expenses as above. Where an amount in foreign currency has to be converted to its EEC member-state equivalent, the rate of exchange to be used is that appropriate at the time of lodgement of the Customs entry.

Under these circumstances, the invoice value may be accepted as the basis for the "normal" price. However, special price arrangements between suppliers and importers who are agents, brokers, licensees, distributors, or concessionaires, or who are business associates of the supplier are considered by the customs authorities as a departure from the "normal" price concept. In this situation the customs officials may initiate inquiries for the purpose of establishing a proper dutiable value. Increasing the agreed-upon price for duty purposes could result from such investigations.

The value for the purpose of ad valorem duty is the value as previously mentioned at the time when the goods are entered for home use. When warehoused goods are entered for home use, the value may be different from the value at the time of entry for warehousing at importation.

ANTI-DUMPING DUTIES

The EC Council of Ministers and Commission are constitutionally responsible for the application of Community anti-dumping controls. They are, however, dependent upon individual member-states for the processing of applications for invoking the regulations, submission of relevant details, requests for immediate intervention in the market place (provisional anti-dumping duty), and enforcement of Council decisions.

Under the anti-dumping regulations, national authorities are empowered to impose anti-dumping duties on imports from any country if the imports are dumped or subsidized and it would be in the Community interest to take such action, provided that they are satisfied that the dumping or subsidization is causing or threatening material injury to a Community industry or to an established industry in another GATT country which exports like goods to the Community, or that it is retarding materially the establishment of an industry in the Community.

Goods are regarded as dumped if the export price from the country of origin or export is less than the fair market price there. The fair market price is the price at which identical or comparable goods are being sold in the ordinary course of trade in the country of origin or export, but subject to any adjustments necessary to ensure that the comparison between the fair market price and the export price is effectively a comparison between the prices on two similar sales.

If, however, identical or comparable goods are not sold in the country of origin or export, or are not sold in circumstances which enable the fair market price to be determined by reference to the domestic selling price of the goods, the fair market price is to be determined by reference either to any representative price obtained for the goods when exported to another country with appropriate adjustments, or to the cost of production of the goods, with appropriate additions for administrative, selling or other costs and profit. Finally, where the system of trading in the country or origin or export is such, as a result of government monoply and control, that the fair market price cannot appropriately be determined in any of these ways, it may be determined by reference to any price obtained for identical or comparable goods exported to the Community from another country, with adjustments to ensure that the comparison is between the prices on two similar sales.

Subsidies include any bounty or subsidy given by a government or other authority on the production or export of goods, whether directly or indirectly.

There is also power to impose provisional charges if the facts so far before the authorities indicate that dumping or subsidization is taking place and is causing or threatening material injury to a Community industry. No duty can actually be levied by virtue of a provisional charge order, but security (normally a cash deposit) may be required under the order for any may be imposed retrospectively, but only for any period during which the provisional charge was in force and its rate may not exceed that of the provisional charge. Provisional charge orders expire after three months, and as they can only be renewed for a further three months, their maximum period is six months. In the case of imports from countries which have signed the GATT Anti-Dumping Code (including Canada), the Commission will extend provisional charge orders for six months only if exporters and importers concerned request such an extension.

Where the Commission finds evidence requiring that measures against dumping be taken, they shall inform all interested parties by publication in the Official Journal of the European Communities indicating the product, country of origin and/or export, the member state affected, the names of the exporters and of the importers.

It is open to the overseas manufacturer and exporter, as well as to the importer of the product concerned, to offer the appropriate authorities any evidence relevant to anti-dumping application and to express objections to it. Similarly, consumers and users of the imported product may express their opinion, since the Commission finally has to determine whether the imposition of a duty is in the Community interest. The Community has no statutory power to compel any person to furnish information, but it points out that it is in the interest of all parties that a decision should only be reached in the light of a knowledge of all the relevant facts and considerations.

Representations may be made orally or in writing to the Commission. To facilitate these representations, a summary of the application is given on a confidential basis to all parties who have a _bona fide_ interest in the case. There are no public hearings and normally no confrontation of the opposing parties.

Under the terms of the GATT Anti-Dumping, the Canadian Government (and similarly any Canadian exporter concerned) is informed when an investigation into dumping duties is being considered. It is in the interest of a Canadian exporter, on receiving such notice, to contact the Western Europe I Division for consultation and guidance in the early stages of these developments.

VALUE ADDED TAXES

Most products sold in the EEC, whether imported from abroad or manufactured domestically, are subject to a value added tax. This tax is popularly known as the TVA from the French appellation, "taxe sur la valeur ajoutee", or VAT, the designation used in Britain. While all the countries in the Community have a standard method of application of VAT, the applicable rates are not harmonized and vary widely from country to country.

In most cases, there are two or three categories of rates: a standard rate, a lower rate or exemption applicable to foodstuffs or other essentials, and a higher or major rate applicable to luxury goods or non-essential articles. For example, the standard rate in Britain is 8%, exemption or nil rate is granted on certain essentials and a rate of 12.5% applies to a wide range of goods regarded as non-essential, including many household electrical appliances and cameras.

The standard rate in the other countries is as follows (as of August 1977):

Belgium	- 18%	Denmark	- 18%
France	- 20%	Germany	- 11%
Italy	- 14%	Ireland	- 20%
Luxembourg	- 10%	Netherlands	- 18%

Value added tax is assessed on the duty-paid value of imported goods. Information regarding the duty and value added tax rates charged by the member states of the community may be obtained from the Western Europe I Division. Inquiries should contain detailed product description, including the Brussels Tariff Nomenclature number or export commodity number, if known, and the country of destination should be cited.

NON-TARIFF BARRIERS

Non-tariff barriers (NTB's) may said to be measures and practices, public or private, other than a customs tariff, operated in a country, or by a common agreement in two or more countries, which have, directly or indirectly, the effect of hindering trade.

Now that tariff barriers are being lowered through trade negotiations and freer trade is being encouraged, NTB's take on much greater significance than before. For the most part outside the agricultural sector, these barriers are not imposed by the EEC but result from the application of national regulations of individual member states. However, some restrictive aspects of Community policies have the effect of distorting trade with third countries.

Some of the NTB's that affect Canadian exports into EEC Markets are as follows. Other are identified elsewhere in this publication under "National Regulations".

EUROPEAN ECONOMIC COMMUNITY

A) Variable Levies:

Variable import levies are applied to many agricultural products. Calculation of the levy differs from product to product, but it generally represents the difference between the world market price and the EEC support price, plus an additional amount to ensure that Community production receives preference.

B) Minimum Price Regulations:

A minimum import, or reference, price based on EEC market prices is applied to fresh apples, cherries, peaches, pears, plums, seed corn, tomatoes and other produce. Offsetting compensatory taxes are levied on imports selling below the reference price.

446

C) Production Subsidies:

Production subsidies are used for the manufacture of starch, beer, casein, chemicals and pharmaceuticals, made from sugar, and olive oil used in canning. Denaturing subsidies encourage the feed use of domestic wheat and sugar. A subsidy is provided for converting skim milk powder to feed. Subsidies are paid to EEC crushers of _domestic_ rapeseed and sunflower seed receive premiums to offset the higher cost rather than use cheaper imports. Support payments are also made to producers of flax, hemp, cottonseed, hops, herbage seed and silk.

BELGIUM

A) Government Procurement:

Foreign bids may be rejected if, for economic reasons, it is essential that the contract should go to domestic industry, subject to price differentials generally not exceeding 10%.

B) Standards:
Special health and sanitary requirements govern imports of pork and products containing pork, beef cuts, veal and horse-meat.

Road taxes on cars are based on horesepower, which discriminates against standard North American models.

DENMARK

Import calendars restrict third country imports of agricultural produce during periods of the year when domestic production is being marketed. Canadian exports affected include apples, pears, cherries, plums, berries and some vegetables.

Denmark employs a milling mixture regulation for wheat, rye, meslin, flours, groats and meals. If domestic production is sufficient to meet domestic consumption, a 100% domestic grain milling mixture is enforced, which precludes the use of imported grains.

A licensing requirement is imposed on virtually all imports that compete with domestic products, including meat, dairy products, cereals, animal fats and oils, etc. This licensing is discretionary and restricts the quantity of imports.

FRANCE

A) Government Procurement:

First administrative preference in government purchases is given to French goods, second preference to EEC suppliers, and third country purveyors are considered when supplies from the first two sources are not available. There is an almost exclusive "Buy French" policy for telecommunications equipment.

B) Standards:

Stringent health and sanitary regulations govern many products. Live poultry and processed poultry imports, for example, are not admitted from any country that does not, by law, forbid the feeding of estrogens, arsenicals, and antimonials to poultry. Poultry vaccine produced in the Community is subsidized to French poultry producers.

C) Discretionary Licensing:

Discretionary licensing on a wide variety of goods, including petroleum products, textile goods, electronic components and other products covered by quantitative restrictions, distorts regular trade patterns in that delays in granting import licenses on seasonal or perishable items induce importers to source these materials within the community.

GERMANY

All food and agricultural products entering Germany are subject to a rigid food law, which is more restrictive than EEC requirements. Foods to which anti-oxidents, such as BHA and BHT, have been added are prohibited, and products made of flour containing bleaching agents and/or baking quality improvers, such as bromates, that are not specifically permitted by the Food Law, are also prohibited. Inspection requirements hamper foreign imports of pork and variety meats by increasing importer costs.

Specified packaged food and beverages are subject to mandatory container standards. Those goods not subject to the mandatory container standards are subject to a unit price labelling requirement.

Distilled spirits which compete with the neutral spirits produced by the German Spirits Monopoly Administration, are not permitted to be imported. Discretionary licensing on certain other alcoholic beverages and vinegar also act as a deterrent to imports.

ITALY

A) Discriminatory Taxes on Automobiles:

Road taxes on standard size North American automobiles are much heavier than on small European models, being based on cylinder displacement.

B) Government Procurement:

Government purchasing is normally reserved to Italian suppliers, as Government departments, in principle, do not have relations with foreign firms or suppliers and buy only from companies legally established in Italy.

C) Motion Picture Restrictions:

Foreign films are limited by a time quota measured against the running time of domestically produced films. There are also local work requirements which necessitate the employment of Italian nationals in foreign produced films, and discriminatory admission taxes on film houses or theatres showing foreign-made motion pictures.

NETHERLANDS

Marketing regulations prohibit corn syrup as an additive to certain foodstuffs. They effectively prohibit the sale of food products such as chocolate and similar food preparations, fruit purees, pastes, most jams, jellies, marmalades and other prepared or preserved fruits, and fruit juices, if they contain corn syrup. There is a ban also on many other additives, such as certain artificial colors, preservatives, vitamins, etc. in foods and drinks, effectively curbing imports.

In addition to these trade distorting barriers, the individual member states also apply those measures listed under the European Economic Community.

The items enumerated here are examples only. There are a number of other practices which may be described as non-tariff barriers which are minor in nature, but nevertheless are irritants to the free flow of trade. Exporters to the Community should be prepared to deviate from the norm in order to comply with specific instructions received from agents or importers, as some so-called "non-tariff barriers" may be temporary in nature, or imposed only during specified periods of the year.

DOCUMENTATION

There is no prescribed form of customs invoice required to clear Canadian goods through customs in the various member states of the EEC. Generally all that is required is the exporter's normal commercial invoice and the usual shipping documents covering the exported goods. The following notes may be helpful:

Commercial Invoice: Two copies of the commercial invoice, giving full particulars necessary to establish the c.i.f. value, are required. Although no special form or contents are prescribed for the commercial invoice, it is advisable to include the following: date and place of shipment; name and address of seller and buyer; mode of transport; number, kind and markings of of the packages and their numerical order; exact description of the goods, e.g., customary commercial description according to kind, quantity, grade, weight (gross and net, preferably in metric units), etc., with special emphasis on factors which may affect value; agreed-upon price of goods, including unit cost and total cost f.o.b. factory plus signature of a responsible official of the shipper's firm. Chamber of Commerce certification and consular legalization are not usually required.

Certificate of Origin: A certificate of origin is not usually required for imports from Canada, but when requested by the importer for "in-quota" imports of certain goods such as wines, textiles, etc., copies should be provided on the general form sold by commercial printers. Certificates of origin, when required, usually must be certified by a recognized Chamber of Commerce, Board of Trade or similar organization.

Bill of Lading: There are no regulations specifying the form or number of bills of lading required for any particular shipment. A bill of lading customarily shows the name of the shipper, the name and address of the consignee, port of destination, description of goods, listing of the freight and other charges, number of bills of lading in the complete set, and the date and signature of the carrier's official acknowledging receipt on board of the goods for shipment. The information given should correspond with that shown on the invoices and packages. Bills of lading direct or "to order" are accepted. The airway bill replaces the bill of lading on air cargo shipments.

Packing List: Although not required, a packing list is useful in expediting and in clearing goods at the port of entry. Such a list should describe accurately and in detail the contents of each case or container included in the shipment and give the net and gross weights, together with c.i.f. value of each commodity.

Health Certificates (Plant and Animal Products): When exporting plants, plant products, animals or animal products to the Community, it is often necessary to have such shipments accompanied by a health certificate issued by Agriculture Canada. If you are planning to enter such markets, it is advisable to contact the Health of Animals Branch (for animals and animal products) or the Plant Protection Division (for plants and plant products) of Agriculture Canada - either in Ottawa or at the agriculture office in your region to determine the conditions that must be met when shipping these products to the European Community.

Additional Notes: Wherever possible, the required documentation should be forwarded separately to the consignee, prior to the departure of the goods for submission to Customs with the entry documents. Enclosing them in the package being shipped will cause delay.

In addition, when possible, designations and descriptions on documents should be in terms of the Common Customs Tariff or the national tariff of the country of destination, and when feasible, in the language of the member state to which the goods are consigned. English or French documents are, however, acceptable throughout the Community.

TEMPORARY ENTRY (CARNET)

(1) What is Carnet?

The "Carnet (Admission Temporaire - Temporary Admission)", commonly known as the ATA Carnet, is a special customs document that simplifies customs procedures for business and professional people wishing to take commercial samples and related materials into most major countries for a temporary period.

The Carnet consists of a green folder into which are incorporated a number of coloured customs sheets. There is a pair of white sheets for each country to be visited -- one sheet for entering the country, the other for leaving the country. Perforations separate these sheets into counter foils (top) and customs clearance vouchers (bottom). The vouchers are stamped, signed and held by customs authorities at the points of entry and of departure. The counterfoils, also stamped and signed by customs, remain in the Carnet folder. There is also a pair of yellow sheets (both counterfoils and vouchers) for leaving and returning to Canada. When goods are to make a straight border-to-border transit of a country, pairs of blue sheets will also be included.

Your Carnet will be prepared specifically to meet your requirements. (2) Why Use a Carnet?

The Carnet is a valuable aid toward the rapid and convenient movement of temporarily imported goods from one country to another. It eliminates customs procedures which include the preparation of national entry forms or the purchase of a bond for security purposes at every customs station. These details involve time, effort and expense.

Thus, the Carnet allows the business traveller to:

• use a single Carnet for goods which will pass through the customs of several countries in one trip;

• make customs arrangements in advance for the countries he wants to visit;

• make these arrangements quickly at a pre-determined cost;

- make as many trips as desired within the one-year period of validity of the Carnet.

(3) Who Can Use a Carnet?

Canadian companies will find the Carnet system of value to many of its representatives travelling abroad:-

- salesmen
- technicians
- licensing representatives
- professional teams.

(4) How Did Carnets Begin?

Under the auspices of the Customs Cooperation Council, and in conjunction with the General Agreement of Tariffs and Trade, several countries adopted, in 1961, general rules on the temporary duty-free importation of commercial samples, professional and other equipment. Their purpose was to facilitate international commerce as well as the international exchange of specialized skills and techniques. Several customs conventions were adopted, among which was the Customs Convention on the ATA Carnet for the Temporary Admission of Goods (1961).

Canada acceded to the ATA Carnet Convention on July 10, 1972. The government designated The Canadian Chamber of Commerce as the agency which will issue, administer and guarantee ATA Carnets in Canada.

(5) What Goods are Excluded from the Carnet System?

Consumable or other disposable goods such as leaflets, brochures, etc., cleaning materials, paints, oils, etc. and foods, which are either given away, disposed of or used abroad, are excluded from the Carnet system.

Also excluded, because they are not considered samples:

- unmounted gem stones, one-of-a-kind mounted gems or pieces of jewellery; handmade one-of-a-kind articles, such as carpets, certain pieces of furniture, paintings, sculptures, etc.

Any matter of doubt as to whether an item can be covered by a Carnet should be referred to the Canadian Chamber of Commerce. The Canadian Chamber reserves the right to refuse to issue a Carnet to any applicant.

(6) <u>For How Long is a Carnet Valid?</u>

A Carnet is valid for one year from the date of issuance. This period cannot be extended, and all items covered by a Carnet should be returned to Canada by the time a Carnet expires.

(7) <u>How Long Does it Take to Obtain a Carnet?</u>

Four days, from the time an application arrives at the Canadian Chamber, should be allowed for the application to be processed. This period could be shorter or longer depending on the volume of applications at any given time.

(8) <u>For What Countries May Carnets be Used?</u>

Carnets may be issued for al EEC countries.

(9) Further information and application forms may be obtained from:

> Carnet Canada
> The Canadian Chamber of Commerce
> 1080 Beaver Hall Hill
> Montreal 128, Quebec
>
> Tel: (514) 866-4334

LABELLING, PACKING AND ADVERTISING FOODSTUFFS FOR SALE TO CONSUMER

The EC Commission presented a draft directive on the labelling, packaging and advertising of pre-packaged foodstuffs for retail sale to the Council of Ministers in May, 1976.

It is anticipated that the directive will recieve approval by the end of 1977, with each member state required to amend its national legislation to comply with the directive within the year following approval. Products will be required to meet the labelling standards 24 months after approval of the directive, and trade in products which do not comply with the provisions of the regulations will be prohibited 3 years after the date of publication.

The following particulars should be noted by exporters of pre-packaged food products to the Community.

The label will be required to indicate:

a) Name under which the product is sold.
b) List of ingredients.
c) The net quantity in the package, in metric terms.
d) Date of minimum durability (shelf life).
e) Special storage conditions or methods of preparation.
f) Name and address of manufacturer or packer, or seller established in the Community.
g) Country of origin.
h) Instructions for use when purchaser would be unable to prepare contents without such instructions.

If the foodstuff has been prepared for consumption, the label must also indicate whether the contents have been steamed, boiled, smoked, freeze-dried, powdered, deep-frozen or prepared in some other manner.

If this directive is adopted as presented to Council, labelling which is considered to mislead purchasers as to the origin, composition, quantity, identity, characteristics, method of manufacture or production, will be banned and the goods will not be eligible for trade.

The language used in labelling or advertising may be that of the member state to which the goods are consigned for sale, and/or any other recognized language of the community. The Commission proposes that the characters be not less than 1.5 millimetres high, and not less than 1/10th the size of the largest characters used on the label, with a maximum size of 5 millimetres high.

Until this regulation has the force of law, national labelling laws remain in effect (See "National Regulations" section of this publication).

COMPETITION POLICY OF THE EEC

The Community has a vigorous competition policy. Restrictive agreements, such as market sharing, are outlawed, and dominant positions may not be abused. The Commission has considerable authority to implement the policy, namely investigative and enforcement power, including court action and fines for infringements.

The basic Commission authority lies in the Treaty of Rome, which prohibits restrictive training arrangements including those which fix prices, limit production, and delineate markets without benefiting the consumer. These regulations apply to domestic agreements between two or more national companies, and to arrangements between EEC firms and those in third countries. The Treaty of Rome prohibits any "abuse of a dominant position" within the EEC insofar as it affects trade between member states. However, the article does not define "dominant position".

Community law on restrictive and abusive practices exists side-by-side with national regulations in this field, which has lead to misunderstandings in the past. Where conflicts occur, the matter may be resolved according to guiding principles established by the Court of Justice. Community law has primacy and must be fully and uniformly applied throughout the Common Market.

HARMONIZATION OF INDUSTRIAL STANDARDS

The Community regards the diverse standards that apply in the member countries as technical obstacles to trade and has an ongoing program for harmonizing standards based on the Treaty of Rome providing for the "approximation of laws".

To date, 58 directives have been issued in the industrial sector, with an additional 50 already submitted by the Commission to the Council for approval. In most cases, a directive is a statuatory instrument of Council which becomes binding on the member states, eighteen months after publication. Enforcing EEC standards are the responsibility of each member state.

Of the standards that have been harmonized, to this date, the major portion relate to highway truck carriers, automobiles, agricultural tractors, and meteorological equipment. It is generally accepted that until a directive has been approved by Council and published in the EC Official Journal as a regulation, national standards will remain in effect.

Exporters to the EEC of industrial goods or equipment may continue to rely on their customers for guidance as to the standards that must be complied with on shipments to Europe. If advise is received of alterations or modifications to be made to goods for export to the Community, interested parties may contact the Western Europe I Division or the relevant Industry Sector Branch for verification of the EC regulation, or clarification of the specific directive.

THE EC COMMON AGRICULTURAL POLICY

Although the European Community is Canada's largest export market for agricultural products, in many instances it is a difficult market as a result of the Common Agricultural Policy (CAP). Since its introduction in 1962, the CAP has had a major influence on agricultural production and trade in the member states of the European Community and worldwide. The fundamental elements of this policy involve: (1) the abolition of barriers to intra-Community trade; (2) the provision of internal support for market prices; and (3) the establishment of common border regulations for both imports and exports. Through the use of intervention agencies, which buy up agricultural commodities at predetermined price levels, the EC has supported domestic market prices for most agricultural commodities at levels that are generally well above world market prices. This is made possible by protecting the domestic market from foreign competition through the use of variable import levies, which prevent foreign goods from being sold in the EC at prices below those charged locally and ensure that imports are made only to the extent of filling gaps which cannot be covered by Community production.

The maintenance of high domestic prices has stimulated agricultural production in the Community, and surpluses have been accumulated for products such as beef, milk powder, butter and others. To enable Community exporters to sell competitively on world markets, a restitution (subsidy) is paid to bridge the gap between high Community price levels and lower world prices. In some instances, this has given EC agricultural exports a competitive advantage in third markets over those from other countries.

The Common Agricultural Policy is financed through the European Agricultural Guidance and Guarantee Fund which derives about two-thirds of its revenue from customs duties and agricultural import levies and the remaining one-third from contributions assessed on the nine Member States.

Marketing in the Peoples Republic of China×

by
Herman O.J. Overgaard
Professor of International Business
Wilfrid Laurier University

The People's Republic of China constitutes a market the size of which, in terms of population, boggles one's imagination. In this country live almost one-quarter of the world's population, but for most of us, China is virtually an unknown entity "... shrouded by a haze of preconceived ideas and worn-out cliches."[1] In an age when Shanghai, Canton, and Peking can be reached within a matter of hours by 'plane from Vancouver, Rudyard Kipling's famous lines "East is East and West is West and never the twain shall meet" have become obsolete as far as Canadian trade in China is concerned.

After nearly two decades of isolationalism, the Chinese market has once again become accessible to many countries around the globe. Canada was the first major Pacific nation to officially recognize the People's Republic of China (October 1970), and took the opportunity to send a trade mission to that country in August, 1971. Subsequently, Canada was invited to put a solo Trade Fair in Peking from August 21 to September 2, 1972, in which some 200 firms and 500 Canadian businessmen participated. During the past year or so, Peking (the capital of China) has become the mecca of several countries, including among others Sweden, Japan, Italy and the United Kingdom. Now the governments of the People's Republic of China and the U.S.A. have agreed to establish missions in each other's capital. All of these countries are keenly interested in developing the Chinese market.

---

[1]Rene Goldman, "China Among the Nations", in Ray Wylie, China: An Introduction for Canadians, Toronto: Peter Martin Associates Limited, 1973, p. 105.

However, while China is the most tantalizing market in the Far East, it is also one of the most difficult for Western businessmen to penetrate. If trade between China and Canada is to be developed, certain factors have to be kept in mind. The Chinese do not separate the trade from politics. Therefore, before one tries to develop trade with the People's Republic of China, one is well advised to acquire a knowledge of the social, economic and political side of its history. Its policies and much of its behaviour today have their roots in the country's past experience. If one is going to penetrate the Chinese market, one has to be aware of and sensitive to the many problems that the Chinese have had in the past which have contributed to the present milieu in China.

First, China has a four-thousand year history, which makes it one of the oldest nations in the world. In addition, China has been invaded numerous times, and the fact that Mao Tse-tung has been able finally to unite China and establish peace on the home-front has made him revered by his countrymen. However, the fact that he is now 80 years of age and that the Prime Minister, Chou En-lai, is 76, suggest that in a country with such a large population, one should watch the political scene very carefully in the event of a change of leadership.

It is also well to recall that, when the present Communist regime took over the government of mainland China in 1949, it introduced ideological and educational reforms into the school system to make education a political instrument to serve the proletrariat.[2] The Great Cultural Revolution (1966 to 1969) served to bring matters to a head and resulted in the purge of numerous teachers and government officials. Consequently, it is necessary to have some appreciation of what took place during the Great Cultural Revolution if one is to comprehend the pyschological motivation behind the attitudes of the Chinese today.

---

[2]In 1958, Chairman Mao advanced the principle "Education must combine with politics and be productive." Subsequently, in 1966 Mao issued his "May 7 instructions" on education in which he said of the students: "While their main task is to study, they should, in addition to their studies, learn other things; that is, industrial work, farming and military affairs ... The period of schooling should be revolutionized, and the domination of our schools by bourgeois intellectuals should by no means be allowed to continue."

The size and the geography of the country is also of interest to anyone hoping to develop markets in the People's Republic of China. In terms of land mass, China has an area of some 3.7 million square miles, making it the third largest country in the world next to the Soviet Union and Canada. But, unlike the latter two countries where much of the land is too far north to be very productive, China is located in a wide and more productive climate range. China is roughly 3,000 miles long and 2,000 miles wide, lying approximately between 50 degrees latitude in the north and 22 degrees latitude in the south (see Figure 1). Figure 2 gives some idea of the relative sizes of China, Canada, and the United States. Thus, Peking which is located on the 40 degree latitude, is on the same latitude as Columbus, Ohio. Canton, on the other hand, which is some 1,200 miles south of Peking, is on the tropic of cancer as is Havana, Cuba. The average monthly temperatures in Peking for January and July are 24° and 78°F respectively compared with 56° and 84°F respectively for Canton. As one travels from north to south in China, the rainfall increases from an average annual precipitation of almost 25 inches in Peking to over 70 inches in Canton. Thus, China has quite a wide range of climate.

While China is primarily an agricultural country - over 80 percent of its people are directly or indirectly involved in farming - China is rapidly becoming industrialized. China's industrial output is already the highest among the emerging nations. Historically, the major industries in China have been food processing and textiles. Today, China is the world's largest producer of cotton and cotton products. Since 1959, however, metal processing has become the country's largest industry.

In addition to producing most basic commodities, Chinese industry is producing an increasing variety of modern technological products such as power generating equipment, large diesel-electric locomotives, ocean-going ships, electronic computers, numerically controlled machine tools, and synthetic fibres as well as complete plants for the chemical and petroleum industries, all of which China is interested in selling to other countries. Recently, China exploded a thermo-nuclear bomb and placed a comparatively large satellite into orbit.[3] When the People's Republic

[3]The People's Republic of China, Department of Industry, Trade and Commerce, Government of Canada, Ottawa, November 1971, pp. 4-5.

FIGURE 1

People's Republic of China

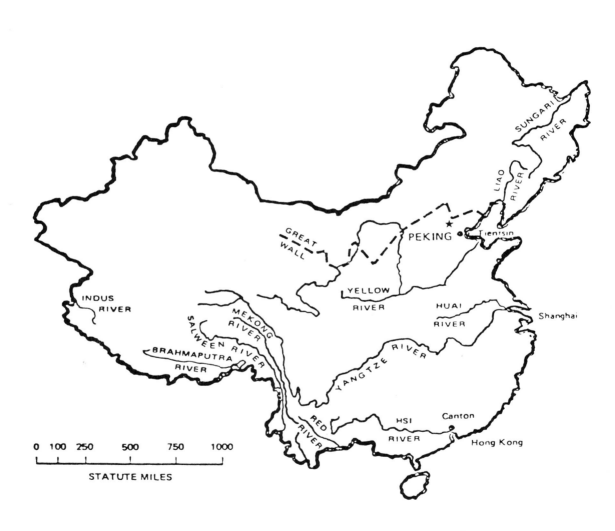

Source: "Trade With China", An AMA Research Report,
American Management Association, Inc., February 1973.

FIGURE 2

Map of China Superimposed on Map of North America

Source: Wylie, R., "Canada's Relations With China: A Brief Survey", China - An
Introduction For Canadians, Edited by R. Wylie, Toronto: Peter Martin
Associates Limited, 1973, p.148.

of China first participated in the Canadian National Exhibition in Toronto in August, 1972, the products exhibited there included not only some heavy industrial equipment but also some very sophisticated consumer goods. From this, it may be assumed that China is very keen to develop international trade, although the emphasis seems to be on exports.

The foregoing constitute quite an impressive list of products. It is obvious that China has a certain amount of technological know-how and expertise which allow it to produce a wide range of products. However, because China has only a limited number of technically trained people, the country has to establish certain priorities. Thus, while it is currently the policy of the Chinese Government to try to be self-sufficient, China does not have the technical know-how to produce everything it needs. Therefore, it has to import certain goods and services.

Another basic problem facing China in its effort to industrialize on a massive scale is that the country does not as yet produce much savings nor does it seem to have a sufficient supply of raw materials. In order to break out of the vicious circle of poverty and under-development, capital formation is needed which in turn requires capital savings which presupposes a surplus. But to date, China has had very little to offer for sale in international markets. Chinese agriculture, for example, so far tends to operate at the subsistence level, producing enough to feed everyone in China in good years but not enough in bad years.

China produces a few surplus items such as tea, soy beans, mushrooms, tung oil, silk, antimony and tungsten. These are exported to earn badly needed foreign exchange but are not adequate to finance a sizeable industrial program. China has the world's largest known coal reserves which are considered to be of high quality. But these are still largely untapped due to the lack of adequate transportation facilities. Nevertheless, China is the second largest producer of coal, after the Soviet Union.

But the goods offered for export sale at their Canton Fairs and at their August, 1972 Toronto exhibit, give some indication of China's determination to industrialize. To date, however, China has followed a policy of self-reliance and has attempted to pull herself up by her own boot straps. But technological change and capital investment do go hand in hand; often they are inseparable. If China is to pursue its industrialization program effectively, it must try to develop or buy the latest type of technology which in turn will enable her to produce goods on a scale that will help the country to earn large amounts of foreign exchange. Although China has up to now dealt on a pay-as-you-go basis, there are some indications that China is considering recognizing the credit system and even accepting certain forms of assistance from other countries in order to accelerate her rate of industrialization.[4]

It has been estimated that the total foreign trade of China in 1970 was $4.3 billion. This is some 20 percent less than that of Hong Kong with its four million population. Thus, although China has the largest population of any country in the world, her share of world trade is only about one percent of the total.[5]

China's exports and imports tend to be about equally balanced as is the country's policy to pay for imports from export earnings. Perhaps this policy reflects the fact that in Maoist ideology, reliance on imports is "bourgeois" thinking. In 1970, China's exports and imports each amounted to roughly $2 billion or $2.50 per capita. By comparison, Canada's total exports in 1972 were $23 billion or $1,000 per capita.

A study of China's trade patterns reflects some interesting information. Exports are chiefly raw and processed agricultural products such as tea, peanuts, rice, vegetable oils and seeds, and livestock, textiles, metals, hog bristles and feathers. On the other hand, imports are mainly wheat, chemicals, fertilizers, iron and steel, other base metals, transport equipment, machinery and various types of key raw materials such as rubber and copper.

A review of China's foreign trade patterns over the years reveals a complete reversal of trading partners. In the past,

---

[4]In 1974, China purchased some heavy industrial machinery from Japan for 20 percent cash and the balance spread over 5 years at 6 percent. This was the first time China has purchased industrial goods on credit.

[5]Trade With China, An AMA Research Report, "China Trade: An Overview - Dale Tarnowieski", p. 3, American Management Association, Inc., Feb. 1973.

China's major trading partner was the U.S.S.R. For example, in 1959, China's foreign trade with the Soviet Union amounted to $2 billion but by 1970 it had declined to $55 million. Formerly, 60 percent of China's foreign trade was with Communist countries, but today almost 80 percent of it involves trade with non-Communist countries.[6] In 1969, Canada ranked as China's seventh most important trading partner as indicated in Table 1.

Table 2 indicates the major items which Canada imported from China in 1970, largely walnuts, peanuts and cotton textiles, amounting to a total of $19 million.

Table 3 lists the principal Canadian exports to China in 1970. The total value of Canada's exports to China in 1970 was $141,994,000 of which wheat accounted for 84 percent and another 15 percent was derived from sales of aluminium, zinc, iron and steel, nickel and assorted semifabricated products of these metals.

As can be seen from these trade figures in 1970, China purchased seven times as much from Canada as Canada bought from China. From a political as well as an economic point of view, if Canada hopes to establish a firm foothold in the China market, it is absolutely essential that Canada pursue a policy of actively stimulating imports from China. One of China's problems here is its shortage of hard foreign exchange. It would be in Canada's best interests if she could somehow arrange, directly or indirectly, to extend long-term credit to China. By such means, Canada could effectively penetrate the progressively expanding Chinese market.

However, in order for a Canadian businessman to be able to sell successfully in the China market, he must understand that the methods of introducing products to the People's Republic of China and of negotiating business with that country are quite different from those used in doing business with Western countries. Because China is a socialist country, all its foreign trade, both import and export, is controlled and managed exclusively by

---

[6]N.D. Modak, Executive, "China - and the Pacific Rim Community", Southam Business Publications, Limited, Don Mills, Ontario, April, 1973, p. 22.

TABLE 1

CHINA'S FOREIGN TRADE*

(Unit: US $Million)

Country	Imports from 1968	Imports from 1969	Exports to 1968	Exports to 1969	Total Trade 1968	Total Trade 1969
Japan	325.4	391.1	224.2	234.5	549.6	625.6
Hong Kong	1.4	1.1	310.2	327.3	311.6	328.4
West Germany	167.2	150.9	82.1	84.2	249.3	275.1
Britain	68.3	124.6	82.3	90.6	150.6	215.2
Singapore	26.8	58.9	151.8	139.8	178.6	198.7
Australia	89.5	117.2	30.6	39.5	120.1	156.7
Canada	151.2	113.8	21.7	25.5	172.9	139.3
Italy	61.1	56.3	48.0	64.1	109.1	120.4
France	86.4	43.2	52.8	69.6	139.2	112.8

*Source: Markets for Canadian Exporters - People's Republic
of China, Department of Industry, Trade and Commerce, Ottawa, Canada.

TABLE 2

PRINCIPAL CANADIAN EXPORTS TO CHINA*

(Unit of Value: Cdn. $'000)

	1969	1970	Jan.-July 1971
Wheat, except seed	19,775.8	119,497.2	102,795
Durum wheat	-	-	12,603
Alberta Winter Wheat	-	2,064.6	-
Scrap Iron and Steel	1,985.8	2,041.2	2,600
Nickel and Nickel alloy scrap	296.2	-	-
Nickel anodes, cathodes, ingots and rods	274.8	12,853.0	743
Aluminum pigs, ingots, shot and slabs	-	2,879.2	2,198
Woodpulp (total)	-	-	1,551
Tallow	-	356.4	942
Nickel and alloy fabricated material	-	1,015.0	-
Zinc blocks, pigs and slabs	-	1,127.4	-
Insulated wire and cable	-	54.5	-
Tire Fabrics, Rubber Coated	-	-	457
Ships and Boats NES	-	-	248
Laboratory optical instruments, equipment and parts	-	50.5	-
X-ray and Related Equipment	-	-	236
Special Construction Fabrics NES	-	-	78
Total, including all others	122,417.6	141,994.7	124,480

Note: Only those items of total value in excess of $50,000 are shown separately.

*Source: Statistics Canada.

TABLE 3

PRINCIPAL CANADIAN IMPORTS FROM CHINA*

(Unit of Value: Cdn. $'000)

	1970	Jan.-July 1971
Walnuts, shelled or roasted	2,481.3	2,098
Gloves, all types	1,619.1	1,111
Pants, men's and boys' cotton	1,213.9	1,073
Sweaters, knit	747.5	705
Pillow cases, cotton	680.7	459
Shirts, cotton, except knitted	616.2	789
Print cloth and sheeting cotton	511.4	757
Mushrooms, canned	446.6	670
Pyjamas and sleepwear	-	400
Peanuts, green	557.6	-
Tablewear, ceramic	376.9	-
Towels, cotton	371.5	-
Outerwear, except knitted	334.9	-
Blankets of cotton	313.5	-
Washcloths, bath mats and sets	304.8	-
Total, including all others	19,027.8	13,595

Note: Only those items in excess of $300,000 are shown separately.

*Source: Statistics Canada.

the Government. All foreign trade in China is conducted through nine state trading corporations. The head offices of these corporations are all located in Peking, with branch offices in certain main industrial centres. Each corporation is responsible for a certain category of items and the export and import of such goods.[7]

Furthermore, each of the Corporations has an agent in Hong Kong. These agents are an important liaison between Western countries and the Trading Corporations, and are primarily responsible for Chinese trade and interests in Hong Kong and Southeast Asia. Even though the Trading Corporations prefer to deal direct with exporters from other countries, these agents can be helpful in discussing business prospects in China, especially since appointments with them may be easily arranged. Furthermore, the agents in Hong Kong are not only a good source of commercial intelligence for the Canadian businessman, but they also provide an excellent channel of communication with their principals in China. However, if possible, it is best if one can make the initial approach to the head office of the appropriate Corporation in Peking.

Incidentally, any correspondence addressed to someone in the People's Republic of China should refer to the country by that name or as China, preferably the former. Also the correct and only name to use for China's capital is Peking. Otherwise the mail will not be delivered.

China operates on a planned economy which is the responsibility of the Trading Corporations together with the Bank of China and economic and planning authorities, to allocate priorities and to import materials and equipment accordingly, based on the Government's five year plan. Normally, details of such plans are not made public. However, one can gain some information by examining trends and patterns of trade.

In order to discover whether or not the Chinese have an import requirement for a particular product, it is advisable for a

---

[7]A list of the names and addresses of these corporations may be obtained by writing to the Canadian Department of Industry, Trade and Commerce, Ottawa.

Canadian businessman to make a specific offer. It is very important, particularly in making the initial approach, to submit a fairly detailed proposal in six copies.

The most important business event for anyone wanting to trade with the People's Republic of China is the Canton Export Commodities Fair. It is held twice a year in the City of Canton (now officially known as Kwangchow) in the spring from April 15 to May 15, and in the fall from October 15 to November 15. In the fall of 1972, the Canton Trade Fair attracted some 16,000 visitors from all over the world. The Chinese negotiate as much as 30 to 50 percent of their total foreign trade during these fairs. Interestingly, the Chinese prefer to meet you in Canton because the Canton Fairs are where the Chinese exhibit their products available for exports. It is a unique opportunity for Canadian exporters to meet face to face with representatives of China's Trading Corporations and conduct business negotiations. On the other hand, it is also an excellent opportunity for Canadian importers to have a first-hand look at Chinese products.

Admittance to China is by invitation only. Thus, in order to attend the Canton Trade Fair, a businessman must be invited by one of the nine Trading Corporations. A request for such an invitation is normally only successful if the businessman concerned has already had some correspondence with the appropriate Trading Corporation, unless, of course, his product is of special interest to the Chinese, such as the Boeing 707. Once an invitation has been issued, both an entry and an exit visa will be granted upon application to the Embassy of the People's Republic of China, P.O. Box 8935, Ottawa, Ontario, K1G 3J2.

In dealing with a socialist country such as China, which uses the state Trading Corporations to negotiate all the country's exports and imports, the Western businessman is faced with a different purchasing situation than that normally found on the North American continent or in Western Europe. First of all, if your product is not included in its five year plan, it is usually a waste of time pursuing trade enquiries any further.

However, if a firm is interested in exporting to China and the Chinese are interested in its product, it is the responsibility of the Chinese Trading Corporation to contact the appropriate end users and insure that details of your proposals and samples are studied and considered by them. In China, direct dealing with an end user by an exporter can be difficult, first because it is not easy to arrange meetings with an end user, and second, because the decision to purchase is not made by the end user.

Another problem in dealing with the Trading Corporation is the length of time required to obtain an order. In domestic trade particularly, and usually in trading with Western Europe, the marketing plan is developed for a twelve month cycle, and the salesman is expected to produce some orders in that period of time, sometimes even on a daily basis. In North America there seems to be something magic about a twelve month accounting period, and management has great difficulty understanding that in dealing with countries like China, the sales effort may take from three to five years to obtain the first order. However, when an order is obtained, the size of the market is usually such that it is well worth the effort. Consequently, developing business with the Chinese usually requires a great deal of time, effort, persistence and patience.

When quoting prices, it is best to quote them in Canadian dollars or pounds sterling, but not in U.S. dollars. Contrary to what the advertisements claim, the American Express card was useless in China at the time of the Peking Fair. Furthermore, no quotations should be made C.I.F. or C and F unless specified by the buyer. Normally, the Chinese desire quotations to be stated in terms of "F.A.S. the vessel" or "F.O.B. and stowed the vessel". The reason for this practice is that, in the majority of cases, the Chinese arrange their own shipping for both bulk and general cargo, using their own ships as much as possible. In addition, insurance is handled either by the China Insurance Company or the People's Insurance Company of China.

The usual method of payment is made by irrevocable letter of credit opened by the buyers or their principals through the Bank of China, in favour of the seller and payable on presentation of documents at the Bank of China. The Trading Corporations and the Bank of China are scrupulous in meeting their commitments. China's reputation for honouring its financial obligations is among

---

[8]The People's Republic of China, Department of Industry, Trade and Commerce, Government of Canada, Ottawa, November, 1971, p. 15.

the highest in the world. A number of Canadian banks have now made arrangements with the Bank of China to handle accounts of their customers engaged in trade with China.

As far as patents and trade marks are concerned, it is possible to register trade marks in China but there is no patent protection.[9] One should be prepared that the Chinese may wish to buy only one of a firm's products for purposes of study and knowledge. In our tours through various factories in Peking, we discovered that the Chinese do study foreign products and through domestic manufacturers they adapt them to local needs. For example, one day we were on a tour of a plywood manufacturing centre and we noticed an electric drying oven manufactured in Germany and immediately next to it was a similar model manufactured in China. While some of the castings were not as well machined as those on the oven manufactured in Germany, both machines seemed to be operating equally well.

Communication is not a problem as far as language is concerned in doing business in China. Up until 1970, the Russian language was the most popular foreign language in China, but today English is the most popular. At the Peking Fair, there was at least one interpreter for each booth, and there were over two hundred booths. Many of the interpreters were teachers and professors who taught English in the universities. During our stay in China, I met only one professor who spoke English and who had ever been out of China. In speaking with the Chinese, we were told many times that there is a keen interest in China to learn English because it is the most popular business language throughout the world.

It is usual for business persons dealing with the Chinese to exchange business cards, and it is helpful if one side of the card is printed in Chinese.

Another point of interest is that when travelling in China, never tip anyone, anywhere. Tipping is strictly forbidden throughout the country. The Chinese people want to be friends with the Canadians and therefore, it is customary to express

---

[9]<u>The People's Republic of China</u>, Department of Industry, Trade and Commerce, Government of Canada, Ottawa, November, 1971, p. 16.

one's appreciation verbally instead of tipping. As a matter of fact, the Chinese will not accept gifts, so one should not embarass them by offering gifts. The only occasion when I saw the Chinese accept a gift was when one of the Canadian businessmen offered two Chinese each a coloured picture of the birthplace in Gravenhurst of Dr. Norman Bethune, which were enthusiastically accepted.

It should be recognized that the Chinese do not do business with firms but rather with people, and such people have to be considered by the Chinese to be "friends". Several times during the Peking Fair, I was asked by Chinese Professors why Canada wanted to trade with China. When I replied that it would be profitable for both our countries, I was told that this answer was not good enough. After giving five or six other reasons, each one of which was considered to be inadequate by the Chinese, I asked why China wanted to trade with Canada. The answer was that "China wanted to be friends with Canada". Just as the word "agape" in the Bible has a much broader meaning of the word "love" than the English terminology, so the word "friend" in Mandarin has a much deeper significance than it has in the English language. We found that the fact that Dr. Norman Bethune, who was a Canadian, was considered by the Chinese to be a great friend of China was very much in Canada's favour.

If your proposal to buy or to sell is of interest to the Trading Corporation to which you have been writing, you will probably receive an invitation to attend the Canton Fair. Such an invitation should be accepted if you wish to do business in China. When you arrive there, you should contact the appropriate Trading Corporation for an appointment. When you come to the meeting, you should bring all your correspondence and other pertinent information with you. The Trading Corporation will provide the interpreter through whom you will discuss details with the Corporation officials. Whenever you meet with the Corporation representatives, you will be served vast quantities of tea, along with a touch of Mao's philosophy. During the first visit, you will likely be told, in a very polite manner, that your proposal is very interesting and that the People's Republic of China are very grateful that you have come to visit them, but they are unable to give you an answer immediately. You may be told that they have to talk to end users to determine the product requirements. It may even be suggested to you that you make a tour of the fair and bring back any helpful criticism. Usually, the meeting ends with the suggestion that they will let you know when they can continue the discussion.

Your liaison person will contact you when the next appointment is arranged. You will find that the Chinese are interested in obtaining as much information as possible, while on the other hand you may find it very difficult to obtain information from them. You have to be able to prove through technical presentations why the Chinese need your particular product. In this regard, North American "hot" sales talk does not bring results in China. One doesn't sell to the Chinese; rather they buy from you. It is most helpful to have copies of your sales literature printed in Mandarin. The Chinese have a great appetite for any kind of sales literature. If your firm sends a representative to China, the importance to the Chinese of being able to talk with someone from your firm who has a good technical knowledge of its product should be kept in mind. Furthermore, the older your representative, the more respect he is accorded in China. It is interesting to note that when the United States appointed the head of its Mission in Peking recently, they selected a diplomatic veteran of seventy-five years of age for that very reason.

As the Chinese wish to trade with friends, it is absolutely imperative that you establish with them personal confidence in yourself and thus in your firm. Normally, this will require several meetings during which time you may feel that not much is being accomplished compared with the results you would receive if you had put in the same time with a North American customer. Selling in the Chinese market requires a vast amount of patience. On the other hand, the Trading Corporation representatives are professional traders, and are very hard bargainers.[10]

You may feel very frustrated because it is very difficult to distinguish the clerks from the decision makers. For example, when we first arrived in China, we found it most difficult to differentiate the managers from the workers because everyone seemed dressed alike. We were constantly told that everyone in China is equal, but it soon became apparent that some people were more equal than others. Gradually we learned to examine a

---

[10] For example, in bargaining about the price the Chinese may ask you for a "friendship discount".

475

person's dress and this would give you some clues as to his approximate status. We would look at such things as whether he had cuffs on his trousers, whether he wore a Mao jacket, the number of pockets on his jacket, and the quality of cloth in his clothing. In addition, the higher officials drove around in larger automobiles. Thus it was obvious that market segmentation does exist in China just as it exists everywhere else.

A few of the firms discovered much to their surprise that during the negotiations at the Fair, the pretty Chinese girl serving the tea was actually the head of the team and the top decision maker on behalf of the Corporation.

After you have successfully concluded your negotiations, you do not have to be concerned about any hanky-panky. The contract states precise standards and specifications. As long as your firm fulfills the terms of the contract, the Chinese will carry out their obligations. We found the Chinese to be honest and reliable. For example, in one of our booths we left some Chinese money on the counter the first day of the Fair, and it was still there two weeks later after a quarter million visitors.

Generally speaking the Chinese are not interested in buying machines and equipment with labour saving devices. China has plenty of labour and no unemployment so this point of view is understandable. However, the fact remains that in certain cases where priorities have been allocated, the Chinese are interested in buying the latest technology in order to reach a certain goal that they have set, even though such equipment may be capital intensive and do away with many jobs.

As far as China's future import needs in the near future are concerned, it would appear that these will focus on medical equipment and drugs, particularly anti-biotics, transport equipment for transportation and road building, electronic equipment, airfield equipment and commercial aircraft, certain types of foodstuffs, crude rubber, synthetic fibres, organic and inorganic chemicals, chemical fertilizers, machine tools and electric machinery, plastics, trucks and appliances. Copper, nickel, lead, aluminium, zinc, iron and steel, diamonds and platinum, as well as paper and paperboard and certain types of prefabricated buildings also may be in demand.

From the consumer point of view, the department stores in Peking for example, were always full of people who seemed to be waiting in lines to buy various things. Although clothing is still rationed - a person may buy a set of summer clothing one year and a set of winter clothes the next year - the shops in Peking seemed to have large amounts of inexpensive fish, meat, vegetables and fruit. We never saw any beggars or people starving in Peking.

Although private autos are apparently not owned by the Chinese, bicycles are quite common. One estimate is that there are 1.7 million bicycles in Peking. A bicycle costs an average Chinese worker three months' pay. After they purchase a bicycle, the next thing they usually save for is a transistor radio or a watch.

As more Chinese travel abroad, the demand for a limited amount of certain household consumer goods could begin to rise. However, at present, these items have little or no political, economic or cultural value in China.

This brings me to another observation, namely that while capitalist and Maoist processes of economic development have several common factors, nevertheless the difference between the two approaches are many and profound. From our brief experience in China, it was obvious that there was a profound disagreement between Mao's philosophy and the private enterprise point of view. It appears that their emphases, values and aspirations are quite different from those of our economy. In China, the state has monopoly on everything, including foreign trade.

There are no private companies in China. The Government there is the only employer so everyone who works is paid by the Government regardless of whether he is operating a barber shop or working in the fields. The salaries range normally from $18 to $90 a month. The communes and factories all produce according to a national productivity plan, and they in turn sell everything to the Government. Consequently, it is difficult for the Chinese to understand the term "profit" because the relationship between production costs and the selling price really does not have the same relevance in China as it does in our economy.

Another thing we found in China was that there was no un-employment and no waste. In one furniture factory, for example, all the little end pieces of lumber left over from cutting the lumber to produce the furniture were glued together to make new boards. Therefore, when we mentioned productivity to them, the Chinese did not seem to understand the term, or if they did, they did not consider it very important because of their huge labour force.

Perhaps the most striking difference between our economy and that of China concerns goals. In Mao's philosophy one goal is to raise the level of material welfare to the population on an egal-iterian basis, so that everyone rises together. This requires the country to operate at the level of the lowest common denominator, and thus the transformation of man is being accomplished seem-ingly at the expense of economic growth. Thus we cannot meas-ure China's development solely by our standards. The fact is that over the past several years, China has made very remarkable economic advances on most fronts. The country is now able to feed, clothe and house everybody, and is trying to provide health and education for all its people.

While all these gains were being made, the Chinese have been devoting an unusually large amount of their resources to their industrialization program. Some experts have estimated that China's industrial production has risen on the average by at least eleven percent annually since 1950.[11] This is an exceptionally high rate of growth for an emerging nation, and suggests the possibility of a rapidly growing Chinese foreign trade. The Can-adian Government has helped Canadian firms to open the door to the China market, but it cannot carry them across the threshold. The Canadian businessman has to walk across it himself. He has to be there personally where the action is.

In conclusion, whenever a firm contacts a China Trading Corporation it should notify the Canadian Embassy in Peking accordingly. The Canadian Embassy in Peking is the eye, nose and ears of the China scene for the Canadian businessman. It is also recommended to keep in constant contact with the appropriate

---

[11] Gurley, John W., "The New Man in the New China", The Center Magazine, Vol. III, No. 3, May, 1970.

Commercial Officers in the Department of Industry, Trade and Commerce in Ottawa. It is distressing how many Canadian businessmen tend to overlook this valuable resource whose professional assistance is free for the asking.

Six Steps in Penetration of the Market in the People's Republic of China

by
Hans A. Baehr
Manager, Trading Development
Canada Wire and Cable (International) Ltd.

<u>Six Steps That Are Helping to Enter the Market of China</u>

<u>Step One</u> was for our Government to prove to the People's Republic of China that we Canadians are the right people to buy from.

As China already was a good customer of our wheat, it was time anyway to open diplomatic relations with them and this happened about two years ago.

<u>Step Two</u> is for our Industry to convince China that the <u>quality</u> of our <u>finished goods</u> is in line with the highest International standards. They do not like to buy second quality.

Step Two is where our Canada Solo Fair came in very handy. The fair was also useful in accomplishing Step Three.

<u>Step Three</u> where the individual company must prove through technical presentations facing a professional audience, why the Chinese need <u>their specific products</u>. Please realize that North American hot sales talk does not work in China. You do not sell to them. They buy from you. If, at this stage, interest in <u>your product</u> is indicated, you may proceed to:

<u>Step Four</u> where you have to establish personal confidence in you and your Company. This may be a long-time process and the Canada Solo Fair was also an excellent opportunity to at least start with Step Four.

Repeated visits at their Spring and Fall fair times and follow-up correspondence in sending new product information will keep their interest alive. For certain products you may be able to use a 'bird dog' or an Agent in Hong Kong. He will keep your product steadily in front of the Chinese State Trade Corporation involved with your product.

For this type of service an Agent Company may charge you with a nominal fee and a performance bonus. __Naturally, you could try__ to work directly without a Hong Kong Agent, but with the help of our Commercial Officers at the Canadian Embassy in Peking. It is a question of how much time you can or wish to spend waiting for an interview in Canton or in Peking, under adverse conditions. These Hong Kong Traders usually by experience know their way to the heart of the Chinese much better than we do.

All these efforts may then be rewarded through an invitation to exhibit your product at one of their Fairs. Such an invitation is usually a sign for their interest in buying your product... if the price is right... This is getting us to:

__Step Five__ where you have to be prepared to face the Chinese State Trade Corporation involved.

Please note that they will have done their homework. You will be astonished about their knowledge of your competitors' products and prices from all over the world. Please do not forget that at present the industrial Nations of the world are eager and trying to place samples with these huge customers of tomorrow. They hope for substantial orders in the time to come. Your negotiating partners will be "professional Traders" on the other side. They may not know too much about your specific product and its application. But, they are very hard bargainers and good psychologists. Your "professional" sales talk and substantiating technical argument will be acknowledged with a very polite smile. At the end you feel they are now on your side and you are prepared to relax only to discover their argument, that your points were well made - however, your price per horsepower is too high!

Please also be prepared that they may wish to buy one of your products only for study and knowledge. They will call this "your contribution to the friendship of our two Countries" and they may mean it, being not too familiar with our free enterprise profit motivations.

481

After the negotiations have been successfully concluded, please do not worry about any shady after-deals. The <u>people of the Republic of China are honest</u> and will confirm the exact content of your oral agreements in a protocol to be signed by both partners. And, by the way --- <u>you do not need</u> a credit reference. Just fulfill the contract as signed and the payment will be on the way.

Now comes the last, but most important:

<u>Step Six</u>, that is the after-sales follow-up.

In case your first products sold prove of value for the Chinese, you may be in for considerable opportunities. This warrants exceptional efforts and investments in time and money for you and/or a possible Agent or Trading Company representing you in Peking. It is recommended to keep contact with our Federal Government's Commercial Officers in Peking and also with your Commodity Officers in Ottawa.

VI
Canadian Management and International Business

Managing in other Cultures: Some Do's and Some Don'ts

by

Joseph J. Distefano
Professor
University of Western Ontario

NEW "PEOPLE PROBLEMS"

"People problems" top the list of most managers who are asked about the difficulties they encounter in their work. But if "normal" troubles weren't enough, now a new kind of human problem faces an increasing number of managers ... those who operate in other countries or cultures.

The magnitude of business done by such managers is already significant. Studies done for the Gray Report point out that $300 to $450 billion, 15% of the output of non-Communist countries, is produced by multinational firms. Estimates show a dramatic growth in these figures to $1 trillion in 1980 and over $2 trillion by 1990 (1/2 the free-world output). Futurists Kahn and Wiener predict that by the year 2000 approximately 2/3 of the non-communist output will be produced by only 300 to 500 multinational firms.

Clearly, men involved in such work need special abilities. They need conceptual understanding of the multi-cultural situations in which they are immersed. And they need new operating skills.

---

* This article was adapted from a presentation to the Associates' Research Day, School of Business Administration, The University of Western Ontario in May 1972. The author gratefully acknowledges the help of the following: Mr. Peter Green who collaborated in writing several of the cases cited, numerous businessmen and government officials who cooperated with us, and the Corporate Associates of Western's School of Business Administration who funded the research through the Plan for Excellence.

Consider this true-to-life case:

You're an area administrator in an Eastern Arctic settlement hit with an epidemic of rabies among the Eskimo dogs.[1] As the government representative and one of the 30 whites in this community of some 500 Eskimos it is your responsibility to insure the public safety. Therefore at your initiative the community council composed of young bilingual Eskimos and some whites passes a resolution that all of the 600 dogs be chained. But some of the Eskimos either refuse to chain their dogs or ignore those that break loose. What should you do?

You plead with those who aren't cooperating and ask your Eskimo friends to intervene. The response? Inaction. You ask help from a local missionary who is influential. He tries, but still nothing happens. As the rabies spread you show frightening movies about the effects of the disease on humans and fly in the area's top doctor to reinforce the films through lectures. Several Eskimos still appear indifferent to your efforts and the community solidarity which you worked so hard to obtain starts to disintegrate. Soon some of the whites are openly hostile to the uncooperative Eskimos who they view as stupid or malevolent and begin to shoot loose dogs on sight. What should you do now?

If you're smarter than most, you'll try to find out why the Eskimos aren't chaining their dogs. And you'll discover that those involved believe that there is a fixed amount of sickness in the world. Therefore, it is to their advantage for dogs to be sick, for they believe when another species is suffering, humans will be spared. Most of us would never imagine such a view of the world given our notions of man's control of and mastery over his environment. This dramatically true case illustrates both the importance and hidden nature of our culture (the general beliefs, traditions, assumptions and values that we accept as defining man and his world and which guide our behavior). The story also demonstrates how important it is for a manager or an administrator operating outside his own culture to understand both his own and other cultures and to act on his understanding in order to operate effectively. Success on these dimensions depends on two factors ... firstly, an appreciation that one's values and traditions are neither absolute nor universal, and secondly, the sensitivity to adapt to diverse cultural surroundings.

485

Cultural differences increasingly emphasized within countries also highlight the fact that the need for these skills is not limited to jet-set executives travelling to exotic foreign lands. A very successful electronics firm operating in New England illustrates this point.[2] Over a period of 18 months three top salesmen were transferred from New York to Houston to develop that expanding market. They not only failed to produce sales, but also successively requested transfers and, when refused, left the company. Only through a chance encounter with a Texas president did company executives learn that the problems were rooted in cultural differences. For the very qualities that guaranteed success in Manhattan - promptness for appointments, concise sales presentations with minimal casual chatter, and a focus on business and product issues - where anethema to the Texan who complained that the salesmen never had time to become his friend. And without friendship he refused to do business, a response that the salesmen took as a polite way of expressing disinterest in their products!

FREQUENT PROBLEMS AND SUGGESTED SOLUTIONS

This case again points to the under-the-surface nature of the problems that face the manager operating in a cross-cultural setting.[3] Of course, a host of highly visible problems such as volatile exchange rates, protective tariffs, legal barriers, etc. face the multicultural manager. In limiting our discussion only to human problems rooted in cultural differences, there is no intended implication that these other problems are non-existent or easily solved. But expert advice is already acknowledged as necessary for such highly publicized problems. In contrast, cultural issues affecting firms are more often misread or dismissed as indigenous "oddities". Neither a systematic body of knowledge nor pool of experts exists on a parallel with the resources available for legal and economic problems.

To date the collective experience of managers and educator-researchers suggests that certain problems recur as both companies and governments initiate or expand their cross-cultural operations. Common problems together with some "do's and don'ts" for their prevention or solution are presented below under five headings of:

1. Making the Decision
2. Conducting Operations
3. Selecting Personnel
4. Training Personnel
5. Experiencing Cultural Shock

While the generalizations at first glance seem so obvious as to be dismissed as common sense, it is appropriate to warn that the knotty cases from which these abstractions emerged were peopled by highly intelligent and experienced executives. And almost all of them made costly errors in spite of these apparently common sense guidelines. At the same time be cautioned that the guidelines are not simple solutions in themselves, but are only suggestive of the painstaking analysis required to deal with any specific situation.

MAKING THE DECISION

DON'T assume away the problem. Most case studies reveal the same pattern. Managers are so attracted by the potential of the cross-cultural venture that they are blind to the problems. A good example comes from the Canadian rail system in their efforts to build a line in the North.[4] The company had total command of the technology; it knew the demanding environmental conditions and put a well-intentioned and sensitive manager in charge of the project to hire Eskimos to help build and subsequently maintain the line. Undoubtedly motivated by expected mutual advantages to both the company and the Eskimos, the firm failed to consider culturally related problems which quickly surfaced when the Eskimos and their families were brought to the training center and then put to work on the line. When hunting season arrived, men disappeared into the bush. Trained as engineers, the Eskimos found it difficult to keep the trains on schedule. When they got tired, they simply stopped the long trains on the single track and slept. This was their view of normal behavior which didn't take into account delaying other trains. When the company sought remedies, Eskimos misinformed their supervisors (when their friends were present, but corrected the information when their friends left the employ of the firm). The results of these and other problems were increased costs, hostility from other minority groups working on location, and the eventual loss of all but 3 of the 80 Eskimos that the company hoped to retain as permanent employees.

DO include cultural problems in estimating costs and developing preventive measures. Companies used to operating cross-culturally are often prone to being seduced by their previous expertise into ignoring this warning, especially when introducing a change in a situation where they have long experience. A firm with experience in the Arctic predating Confederation provides an illustration.[5] Based on their excellent experience in hiring Eskimo clerks and identifying significant potential savings (for example, in transportation), the company decided to employ the Eskimos in retail managerial positions in their home communities. Soon the pressures of strong family relationships were in evidence. One manager, bowing to this pressure, extended credit to customers in excess of their earnings for several years in the future. With a sense of futility after realizing his plight, he permitted customers to purchase whatever and whenever they wanted and kept sketchy records on cigarette packs, old envelopes, etc. Other managers responded in the other extreme by inflating prices, extending no credit and being miserly in their fur pricing. One man was reported to be incredibly tight. There was a file for sale in his store priced at two fox skins. When the customer only had one skin to offer, the manager broke the file in half! In order to insulate himself from family pressures, he over-protected his store, and his relatives and neighbours lived in fear of him.

Albeit extreme examples, these incidents highlight the need to anticipate cultural problems. But, as this case shows, experience doesn't necessarily provide precognition. An ad hoc inventory of past problems isn't the same as a conceptual scheme or framework which by itself suggests, in advance, problems that are likely to occur.[6] For example, in the case just cited the policy change might have been examined for the effects of the Eskimo's notions of family values and their interplay with the economic system.

CONDUCTING OPERATIONS

Several problems emerge when a company actually starts operations with or in other cultures. Relocating workers for training or for employment, often taken for granted in North America, is one example. In the 60's the Department of Indian Affairs and Northern Development relocated several Eskimo families when the mine where the men had become skilled workers, closed.[7] As part of the assistance provided a loan fund was set up to cover costs of purchasing homes and furnishings. After remaining at the new location for verying periods of time, seven of the eight purchasers abandoned their homes (and mortgages) to return to the old community. The complex legal and financial problems resulting for the Department were rooted in the Eskimo's very different conceptions of property ownership, time perspective, legal agreements, etc. So a well-intentioned program of assistance back-fired partly because of assumptions made by government men (who were most probably unaware that they were making such assumptions) that the Eskimo shared white values and perspectives.

Other problems occur because the ways of doing business are different in different cultures. Often interrelations between political, ethical and economic systems vary from our own as is true in several countries where Canadians are deeply involved in commerce. If your comapny has a subsidiary in South Africa whose key man is suddenly reclassified from "White" to "Colored", your options for redress are considerably different because of the different relations between government and business there.[8] And if you act as you might in response to an administrative error in Canada - e.g., request aid from your Parliamentary representative in expediting a correction - you are likely to add to the problem rather than solve it.

Another sensitive area of operations is in hiring, firing and promotion practices which in North America are strongly related to a person's achievement. But in Japan these policies are guided by age, seniority, education and family background to a much greater extent. So if you are the personnel director of the Canadian based multinational firm, Javitt Industries, what do you do to solve a personal conflict between two key Japanese executives whose vying for influence with headquarters threatens the effectiveness of your whole operation in Japan.[9] If you follow your own cultural norms by rewarding achievement and accomplishment, you may offend and therefore lose the entire sales force in Japan. But can you decide on action that may run counter not only to company policies established in North American, but also to your own ideas of fairness?

Or, put yourself in the place of an Indian who grew up in Africa as the youngest of three bothers and several cousins in the family business. You've just finished your M.B.A. at Western in

Canada and have forwarded an analysis of the African organization together with recommendations for rationalization of the management structure to the family firm.[10] Your cousin, who stands to benefit from implementation of the report, has hidden it from your uncle because he fears the uncle's anger at the report's contradicting the traditional norms guiding respect and status appropriate to relatives and elders. How do you apply your newly acquired analytic abilities without forfeiting your contribution to and rewards from the company?

One could report operating problems originating in cultural differences almost endlessly. But what should we do about them?

DON'T exclude yourself from being part of the problem. Too often in the cases cited above the principals defined the problem exclusively in terms of the "host" country nationals.[11] There is an even greater tendency to go beyond this potential error and blame the "foreigners" for the troubles. From there it is an easy step to assuming that people with traditions, values and orientation different from your own are inherently inferior. When you hear, "I was there a whole year and couldn't teach those dumb natives anything", a little probing will often reveal this hidden assumption operating.

DO try to adapt your management practices and systems to the other culture. As is the case with all truisms, it is easier to state than implement. It first of all requires that we be aware of the other culture and how our systems and practices match or clash with it. And the difficulty in just becoming aware of our own culture's influence on our managerial behavior has already been described. Secondly, there is the difficulty of overcoming the tendency to feel our way of doing thing is the one, right way. An aid to increasing our flexibility regarding means is attention to ends. If, for example, our goal really is to have a viable Japanese subsidiary, then attention to indicators of outcomes, like growth, should make it easier to allow and even encourage promotion policies based on Japanese values. In fact, if we really are open to other cultures, it is likely that we will find our own lives as well as company practices being broadened and enriched by the infusion of new ways of thinking and acting.

Inevitably, however, there will be areas where we are either unwilling or unable to adapt to local customs. For example, in the railroad case mentioned earlier the trains had to be kept running in order to protect men and property from injury. In these cases it is vital that the company be honest and complete about its inflexibility. Even more important is that it describe to those involved the consequences of the cultural differences so they can make a well-informed choice. As an Eskimo offered a job on an Arctic oil or gas well, if I know in advance about the psychological stress I face by working away from my family for specified periods of time without leaving by my own choice to hunt, it will be to my benefit and the company's. Of course, the company's ability to provide such information is again contingent on thorough knowledge and consideration of these issues. But in the cases described earlier it was not the willingness of the firm to deal with these issues that was a problem but their competence to do so. I am convinced that it is in the best interests of all parties for both businessmen and government administrators to develop this competence. For activities involving cross-cultural contact, the effective and profitable use of human and financial resources depends on it.

SELECTION OF PERSONNEL

One of the most critical decisions influencing the company's ability to perform effectively in other cultures is the selection of personnel from home office who work in other countries. These personnel who interpret and implement headquarters policies in the field are the key to whether the "Do's" and "Don'ts" listed above are followed. The guidelines emerging from research and experience are offered below.

DON'T rely exclusively on technical competence. While this may seem too naive a prescription, surveys on selection of personnel for overseas assignments currently being conducted at the University of Michigan show that a candidate' sheer technical ability to perform a specific job is a major (and almost sole) criterion for selection. As in many cases where the Peter Principle seems to operate, managerial error in omitting or ignoring important factors during selection or promotion is a more accurate view of the resulting problems.

Lest we forget the problems, remember the case of the electronics salesman noted earlier. The three men who quit had all been selected because they had performed so well in New York. A similar case occurred recently when a major international oil company panicked after losing several of their best men who had been selected for foreign postings. With the help of a consultant the company estimated that they had lost $15,000 per man, each of whom had lasted an average of only seven months before quitting the company or requesting immediate transfers back home.

DO make your selection decisions in stages using several criteria. The consultant's report for the previously mentioned oil company includes recommendations which have been confirmed by the case research conducted at the University of Western Ontario.[12] The first stage can be described as preselection and is characterized by the company's providing information to the candidates. As much information as is possible should be given about the specific requirements of the situation and not just the job. Here it is important to include date about language, food, housing, education facilities, and cultural and economic aspects of the region. This provides the context within which the job description takes on meaning. And it is absolutely vital that information which affects wife and children not be omitted. Given these data employees can better screen themselves in or out of the pool of candidates.[13]

Only when well-informed men have indicated a desire for the assignment abroad, should the company reverse the information flow and gather data about the candidates. There are some obvious criteria to consider like age and seniority. Middle-aged personnel are more likely to provide the optimum blend of physical vigor, openness, maturity, knowledge of and stature within the firm. But less obvious factors are equally important. In fact, in our studies the most pervasive reason for problems in cross-cultural situations could be traced to the family. Where wife and children are unahppy, breakdowns in the job, the family, or both inevitably follow. Yet preliminary results of the Michigan study show that only a small percentage of multi-national firms collect information about wives of candidates and their attitudes about going abroad. And only a fraction of this small percentage ever use this information in making a decision.

Another important factor is the reason the man gives for wanting the job. If he and his wife speak enthusiastically of enjoying change and variety and of learning and experiencing new languages, customs, etc., they are more likely to have the flex-

492

ibility and tolerance for ambiguity needed for the assignment (especially in contrast to those who give vague statements such as "I'd like a career overseas" or who haven't previous experience in successfully moving to several places within their own company and country).

TRAINING OF PERSONNEL

The "do's and dont's" of training complement the selection process. One of the most important rules is **DON'T omit the man's wife.** While the man has some familiar constants in the new location ... for example, he may be doing a similar kind of job such as improving a control system or balancing production lines ... his wife is often faced with an almost totally different environment for household activities. She is also less likely to have people around her who speak her own language.

An excellent example of effective incorporation of both wives and children in the training stage is the Public Service Commission's Bicultural Development Program.[14] This program is designed for senior civil servants and their families who spend a year in Quebec City learning about the total Francophone culture (French-speaking administrators go to Toronto for the Anglophone cultural experience). Prior to their year in the other culture the men and all their families receive up to six months intensive language training which equips them for effective learning as soon as they arrive in their new settings. In the early years of the program when such training was brief and less effective, participants found they spent most of the year away learning the language instead of meeting the program's bicultural objectives. They also found much more strain inside their families than when they, their wives and children were adequately prepared before leaving. The lesson is the same for business, though companies rarely give adequate notice for such ideal training. However, the point is that whatever time is available should be used for the wife's benefit as well as her husband's.

DO employ "emotional" training as well as cognitive training. The lack of factual information isn't what disorients most managers who go to other cultures. Rather it is the difference in the life styles and behavior of the people. Therefore, whenever possible experiential kinds of learning (modified kinds of "sensitivity" training) should be included with the more usual language training and factual data supplied by the company. CUSO and the Peace Corps have excellent descriptions of the techniques that they employ, and consultants can provide assistance in designing and implementing similar training especially tailored to a particular company's needs. In the absence of first-hand, "live" experiences of this kind, it is wise to approximate the learning. One approach is exemplified by a young manager for Brascan who was preparing for an extended period of work in Brazil.[15] Not only did he study Portuguese and digest factual data relevant to Brascan's operations and his particular job, but he also immersed himself in popular magazines and newspapers from Brazil, read about the history, literature, arts of the country and regularly conversed over the telephone with his Portuguese instructor to feel comfortable in that different experience. He tried to sensitize himself to subtle aspects of the culture that would affect his working relationships with people and attempted to learn about regional differences in the country as well. From recent correspondence it would appear that his careful preparation, designed and carried out largely in an informal way over several months before departure, has been successful in relatively "painless" acculturation and a much more rapid ability to operate effectively in his job.

CULTURE SHOCK

No matter how carefully personnel have been selected and trained, after an initial exposure to a new setting some degree of cultural shock is inevitable.[16]

DON'T neglect the warning sign of isolation. One of the most common signs of culture shock is withdrawal which may be manifested in many ways. A man may isolate himself in his office when his required activities take him into the new cultural milieu which he is avoiding. Or his absenteeism from the office may increase sharply while he takes refuge in the psychological comfort of his home. Still another form is his retreat (joined by his wife) into a sub-community of people from his home country.

DO provide support, especially in the early days. This prescription is the best "cure" for cultural shock, as well as an effective preventive step. Being met at the airport, having furnished accommodations ready upon arrival, and being assisted in orientation to the city and its services, and being accompanied in the first ventures into the new culture (such as his wife's shopping for food or child's first days in school) are all helpful forms of support which ease the period of transition. Bilingual locals are useful in performing these functions, although they may not be as aware (their culture is as hidden from them as ours is from us) of the wide potential sources of disorientation. Perhaps the best guides are people from the new arrival's home culture who have been in the country long enough to have acculturated themselves, but not so long as to be insensitive to the needs of the neophytes. The company can assist by gathering the collective experience of its "cross-cultural employees" and preparing a standard list of helpful activities to support new arrivals.

CONCLUSION

While it is a truism that our world is getting smaller and that the pace of change is accelerating, the hidden forces of culture and their determinants on our lives change very slowly. Perhaps the most vivid illustration of this point is Japan. Although many decades have passed since that country's exposure to the West, much of contemporary life in Japan is still guided by the traditional cultural principles. Although the external shape of her industrial and economic growth resembles (and surpasses) the West, the structures and processes inside the organization that have fed the successes are indelibly stamped with Japanese, not Western, culture.[17]

If this is true of Japan after such a long exposure, we should also consider the cases of South America, Africa and China where Canada has great opportunities for mutual economic development. The application of the principles outlined here are critical to Canada's successful dealings not only with these and other countries, but also with the multicultural environment inside Canada itself. In the long run the success of all nations, and perhaps even our survival, depends on our ability to share and adapt to each other's cultures.

As we venture into various multinational endeavors we would do well to listen to the cautious advice of Dostoevsky in The Brothers Karamazov. Speaking through the devil who appeared during Ivan's nightmare to lament the pressures from above for changes in Hell, he says, "Reforms, when the ground has not been

495

prepared for them, especially if they are institutions copied from abroad, do nothing but mischief."

FOOTNOTES

[1] See "The Sick Dogs" (A and B), case #31005, School of Business Administration, The University of Western Ontario, and "Stresses of Change and Mental Health Among the Canadian Eskimos" F.G. Vallee, Arch. Environ. Health, Vol. 17, October 1968, pp. 565-570 for fuller accounts of this situation.

[2] "Norse Electronics", Organization Behavior and Administration, P.R. Lawrence et. al., 1965 revised edition, Irwin-Dorsey Press, Homewood, Illinois.

[3] Note the distinction implied by the term "cross-cultural". I am not referring to the situation of Brazilians managing in Brazil and how that is different from Canadians managing in Canada, but to the situation of a manager from one culture, (e.g., Brazil) who operates in the other culture (e.g., Canada). Most business schools deal with the former through courses in Comparative Management which often fail to deal with the operating realities of multinational firms. In contrast, the latter situation requires a Cross-Cultural approach which is much more complex and difficult to treat adequately.

[4] See "Great Slave Lake Railway", case #WAP 169 School of Business Administration, University of Western Ontario.

[5] See "Hudson's Bay Company", case #31409, School of Business Administration, University of Western Ontario.

[6] Such conceptualizations exist in anthropological literature. The author has built a course on "Problems in Cross-Cultural Management" around one such formulation and is currently "translating" the scheme from the jargon of social science and developing its application to the problems summarized in this article.

[7] See "Eskimo Loan Fund", case #31043, and "Eskimo Potpourri: Some Notes and Some Poetry", case #WAP 178, School of Business Administration, University of Western Ontario.

[8] See "A Question of Colour", S.M. Davis, Comparative Management, 1971, Prentice-Hall, Englewood Cliffs, New Jersey.

[9] See the disguised case of "Javitt Industries", case #31048, School of Business Administration, University of Western Ontario.

[10] See "Bhiwar Enterprises", case in preparation, School of Business Administration, University of Western Ontario.

[11] For an illustration of the effects of a single man making this error, see "Compania Cruz de Sur", case #ICR 302, Intercollegiate Case Clearing House, Harvard Business School. He lost two years of his life and over $400,000 by always definig his problems as external to himself.

[12] Personal communication from Dr. Dennis Gallagher, Denver, Colorado.

[13] Note that this is the same point made earlier in the reverse situation... that of screening potential employers from other cultures to work with your company.

[14] See "Bicultural Development Program (A)", case #WAP 164, School of Business Administration, University of Western Ontario for an overview of the program and cases (B) and (D), WAP 165 and 167, respectively, for interviews with participants at two points in the program's history.

[15] See "John Moore, Jr.", case in preparation, School of Business Administration, University of Western Ontario.

[16] For a concise statement of the causes, symptoms and "treatment" of this phenomenon, see "Culture Shock and the Problem of Adjustment to New Environments", K. Oberg, Bobbs Merrill reprint series, Indianapolis, Indiana. The discussion in this section of the article draws on his insights as well as evidence from our case studies.

[17] For evidence of the pervasive truth of this assertion see Mannual of Employment Practices in Japan, 1970, American Chamber of Commerce in Japan, 701 Tosho Building 2-2, Marunouchi, 3-chome, Chiyoda-du, Tokyo.

Similarities Among Countries Based on Employee Work Values and Attitudes

by
Simcha Ronen and Allen I Kraut
Professors
Tel Aviv University

THE MUSHROOMING GROWTH of international commerce and multinational companies has drawn increasing attention to the effectiveness of managerial practices and the differences in employee attitudes from country to country. A better understanding of these issues, on a cross-national basis, could make management of international organizations more effective. For example, such understanding would improve the ability to transfer international assignees, establish workable regional policies, and introduce new management practices. In addition, management theories developed in a particular country could be tested in others, and the impact of social and cultural forces on management practice could be explored.

The universality of managerial practices and employee attitudes has been the focus of most cross-national research to date. Webber,[3] suggests that some forces are responsible for convergence of practices and attitudes while other forces are responsible for divergence. The forces of convergence stem from common economic orientation, manifested in technology, education and

Simcha Ronen is Visiting Professor at New York University's Graduate School of Business, and recently taught at Yale University, while on leave from Tel Aviv University's Recanati Graduate School of Business Administration. He has done research and lectured widely in the field of organizational behavior.

Allen Kraut has done international personnel research for some years and was recently Visiting Professor at the Recanati Graduate School of Business Administration at Tel Aviv University. He is on the adjunct staff of Pace University's Graduate Business School.

pragmatic philosophy. These forces dominate in the firm-environment relationship and in the men-work relationship. The forces of divergence rest on natural resources, time, demography and, most vital, culture. Such sources of diversity exert stronger influence on the interpersonal relationships and patterns of motivation and communications within the firm.

Webber's proposition implies degrees of similarity among employees from different countries. Thus, one might establish meaningful groups of countries based on similarity of employees' attitudinal and behavioral measures. Clustering could test the validity of Webber's proposition, and also have many practical implications for the administration of international enterprises. The investigation of such relationships is the major thrust of this research.

CROSS-NATIONAL COMPARISONS

Few comparative management studies deal with country clusters. Many which appear to be relevant at first have severe restrictions and limitations. As Ajiferuke and Boddewyn[4] point out, relatively few cross-national studies have presented quantitative results or have used common research tools and adequate methodologies. Only a few have attempted to investigate occupational groups other than managers. Most combine data from employees in various settings and fail to control variables such as level of technology and type of company.

An extreme limitation, stressed by Nath[5] is the small number of countries used for comparison, lessening possibilities of generalization and the chance to construct meaningful clusters. A few studies have reported cross-national comparisons involving a number of countries ([6],[7],[8],[9],[10],[11],[12]). These studies reported many similarities in practice and attitudes among certain countries but made no attempt to form clusters of nations based on these similarities.

Two major studies grouped countries into clusters according to employee atttitudes. Haire, Ghiselli, and Porter,[13] using 3,741 managers from 14 countries, investigated differences in need satisfaction, attitudes toward management practice, and cognitive descriptions of the managerial role. They found that 28 percent of the variance was associated with nationality; but the differences among individuals were about two and one-half times as great as the differences among countries. There was a strong and consistent tendency of managers to express similar beliefs about management practices.

It was found, however, that countries could be clustered into more or less homogeneous groups based on intercorrelations of standard scores obtained for each country from scales measuring leadership, role descriptions and motivation. As depicted in the left side of Exhibit 1, the clusters found were: Nordic-European countries, Latin-European countries, Anglo-American countries, Developing countries, and Independent (Japan). The clustering was explained on the basis of cultural influence (mainly religion and language) and level of industrialization.

EXHIBIT 1

Country Clusters Reported by Haire, et al., and Sirota & Greenwood.

Haire, et al.		Sirota & Greenwood	
Cluster	Countries	Cluster	Countries
Anglo-American	U.S.A. U.K.	Anglo	U.S.A. U.K. Canada South Africa New Zealand Australia Austria Switzerland India
Latin Europe	France Belgium Spain Italy	French	France Belgium
Nordic European	Denmark Norway Sweden Germany	Northern European	Denmark Norway Finland
Developing Countries	Argentina Chile India	South Latin American	Argentina Chile
		North Latin American	Coumbia Mexico Peru
Independent	Japan	Independent	Japan Brazil Germany Israel Sweden Venezuela

500

The process may be likened to cutting up a world globe and pressing it flat to get a two-dimensional picture of the earth. The description of the structure obtained is carried out by first interpreting the meaning of proximity between individual countries, and then proceeding to partition off the map into clusters which correspond to substantive concepts. Then, interpretations may be drawn on the basis of inter-country similarity within each cluster, as well as in the basis for distinguishing between clusters.

Data

The results presented below are based on three sets of data. We utilized two data sets that are based on secondary analyses of data from the studies by Haire et al. and Sirota and Greenwood. A new body of data, not reported elsewhere, is based on a 1968 study of 4,000 technical employees working in 15 countries for a European-based multinational electronic company. No country had less than 40 employees participating. Within a larger opinion survey questionnaire administered on company time, employees were asked to rate the importance of 22 work goals on a 5-point Likert-type scale. The questionnaire was written in English, translated into the various languages used, and then independently translated back into English as a check on accuracy. The work goals, designed to tap a broad array of work-related expectations, are shown in Exhibit 2.

EXHIBIT 2

List of Work Goals Rated by Technicians:

1. Opportunity for higher earnings
2. Security with company
3. Security in present position
4. Fringe benefits
5. Personal time
6. Co-workers
7. Autonomy
8. Effective department
9. Training opportunities
10. Contribution to company
11. Physical conditions
12. Recognition
13. Prestigious company
14. Company with advanced technology
15. Challenge
16. Organizational climate
17. Opportunity for promotion
18. Area
19. Supervisor
20. Keep (technologically) up-to-date
21. Use skills and abilities
22. Day to day learning

RESULTS

These data are displayed in the space diagram of Figure 1. The mapping represents the intercorrelations of ratings by the technical employees from 15 countries, based on rank order correlations across the 22 work goals for each pair of countries. (The coefficient of alienation is .07, corresponding to a rank order correlation of about .99 between the interpoint distances and the correlation coefficients computed in the monotonic transformation of the original matrix. This indicates a very satisfactory two-dimensional representation).

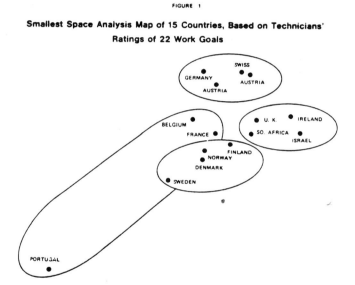

FIGURE 1

Smallest Space Analysis Map of 15 Countries, Based on Technicians'
Ratings of 22 Work Goals

Four clusters of countries can be observed from the space diagram: The Nordic cluster including Norway, Finland, Denmark, and Sweden; the Latin-European cluster, including France, Belgium and Portugal; the Germanic cluster, consisting of Germany, Switzerland, Austria I and Austria II (a spearate subsidiary in Austria serving much of the Eastern European bloc); and lastly the Anglo cluster, including the United Kingdom, South Africa, Ireland, and Israel (formerly an English mandate state and strongly under the Anglo-American industrial influence).

Our choice for clustering was consistent with popularly applied groupings based on language and cultural background, as well as geographic proximity. From the resulting clusters, it appears that none of these attributes individually can account for the relatively clear clusters. For example, Germany, Austria, Switzerland share the same language, and are similar in cultural background and geographic proximity. The United Kingdom, Ireland, South Africa, and Israel are not in the same geographic area but share some cultural and linguistic background. France, which is similar to Belgium in location, language, and cultural background (at least for the French-speaking population), is close in our diagram to other highly industrialized countries in the Nordic cluster as well as to the Anglo cluster. Portugal, which has been clustered with the Latin-European countries, seems to be quite dissimilar to her counterparts in the cluster, although she is even more dissimilar to the Germanic and Anglo countries.

Figure 4 depicts a space diagram of the intercorrelations based on managerial attitudes as reported by Haire et al ([13], p. 288). (The coefficient of alienation is .22 indicating a satisfactory solution for a two-dimensional representation).

FIGURE 2

Smallest Space Analysis Map of 14 Countries in Haire et al Study

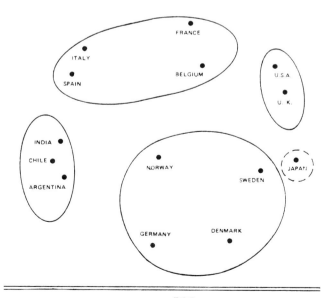

The clusters found by them are clearly differentiated in the space diagram. The clusters are: The North European (Norway, Germany, Denmark and Sweden), the Latin-European (Belgium, France, Italy and Spain), the Developing countries (Argentina, Chile and India), and the Anglo-American (United Kingdom and the United States). Japan was not included in any of the above clusters and was labeled Independent.

From our analysis, however, it is possible to observe both the interrelationship among the clusters as well as the relative positions of the individual countries within clusters and of the Independent country, Japan. The distribution of the countries from right to left seems to be based on their degree of industrialization. The Developing countries appear in the left-hand side (Argentina, Chile and India). Close by are the two least developed countries of the four in the Latin-American group, Spain and Italy. Moving right we find the most highly industrialized countries - Japan, United Kingdom, United States and Sweden.

FIGURE 3

Smallest Space Analysis Map of 25 Countries in Sirota and Greenwood Study

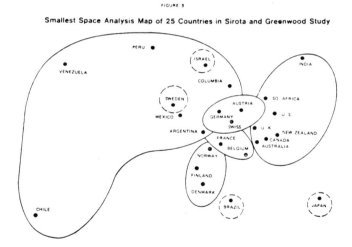

Although Japan was identified by Haire et al as an Independent country, not included in any of the other clusters, it can be easily observed that Sweden and the Anglo-American countries are most similar to Japan in managerial attitudes. We have identified the Latin-European countries in one cluster, as did Haire et al. Still, it is obvious that Belgium and France are more similar to one another (and closer to the Anglo-American countries) than they are to Italy and Spain.

504

An important difference between the results of our data on technicians (shown in Figure 1) and that of the secondary analysis of the managerial data from Haire et al shows up in the positioning of Germany. In the Haire et al study Germany appears in a North European cluster, probably because their sample lacked some of her neighboring countries. Our data from the previous study shows that Germany is distinctively part of a Germanic cluster, with Austria and Switzerland included.

The data collected by Sirota and Greenwood were also analyzed using the SSA. Employees in 25 countries belonging to three different occupations were surveyed about their desired work goals. These work goals were similar to the ones asked about in our study of technicians above, and were cast in an identical format. The findings for their three occupational groups were highly similar to one another and a good solution is provided by an SSA based on all three groups combined. The results are shown in Figure 3. (The coefficient of alienation is .14, again showing a good fit in a two-dimensional projection).

A broadly comprised Anglo-American cluster (United States, United Kingdom, New Zealand, Australia, Canada, South Africa, and India) appears clearly differentiated from the other clusters. The other clusters are: the Nordic, including Norway, Finland and Denmark (although Sweden seems to be independent of these); a broadly spread Latin-American cluster (although Sirota and Greenwood distinguished a Northern group made up of Mexico, Colombia and Peru and a Southern cluster comprised of Argentina and Chile); Latin-European, including France and Belgium; and Central European made up of Germany, Austria and Switzerland (which is a cluster not identified by Sirota and Greenwood).

The Independent countries seem to be: Sweden, Japan, Brazil, and Israel. Venezuela, which Sirota and Greenwood label as an Independent, is included in our results within the Latin-American cluster. Brazil, however, is out of this cluster and appears here too as an Independent country, closer to the Northern European countries (as does Argentina). Japan, as in the previous results, is an Independent country and appears to be most similar to the Anglo-American and Nordic clusters.

In this space diagram, the most complex of the three presented, the more highly industrialized nations tend to be in the center, while the Developing countries are distributed on the upper and left borders. Our clustering was directed largely by conventional wisdom, primarily our knowledge of language similarities, and secondarily, geographic proximity. These factors also helped to identify Independents from among countries which appeared to be in alien clusters. In addition, we were guided by the results of Sirota and Greenwood's groupings and those of Haire et al. The resulting space diagram is relatively close to the Sirota and Greenwood clustering, with two major exceptions: our map produces a distinct Germanic (or Central European) cluster and fails to support two Latin American clusters. In addition, the position of the Independent countries relative to the various clusters is greatly clarified.

DISCUSSION

The purpose of this study was to improve our ability to sub-group international populations of employees on the basis of their work values and attitudes, and to explore the forces underlying the various sub-groups. In addition, it was intended to clarify the interrelationship among the country clusters, and the relative position of the Independent countries with respect to the clusters.

Like geographical mapping techniques, the SSA provides a useful if not totally precise picture of the world we are exploring. The technique is quite flexible in permitting the analyst to partition the map into different regions, requiring only that one be guided by substantive concepts and theoretical frameworks. This flexibility is a strength, but is also a major limitation of method in that subjectivity is clearly admitted. Depending on one's viewpoint and purposes, the map could be sub-divided in different ways. The SSA presents the data points in a visual form so another analyst can draw clusters differently if it seems more suitable.

As stated earlier, our divisions - based largely on language, geography, and prior classifications - seems to fit the data reasonably well. In addition, we have attempted a synthesis of the findings based on our three data sources. Using the self-reported attitudes and expectations from the three sources representing employees from 29 countries, five distinctive clusters can be established. In addition, there were a few countries which

506

appear to be consistently Independent. This composite clustering is offered in Figure 4.

These clusters are labeled Anglo-American, Nordic, Latin-European, Central European, Latin American, and the Independents. Within each of the five central sections the least industrialized nations tend to be placed towards the periphery. This categorization seems to be consistent with the results of the three separate analyses and is suggested tentatively as a guide to future research in this area.

FIGURE 4

A COMPOSITE OF CROSS-NATIONAL CATEGORIES

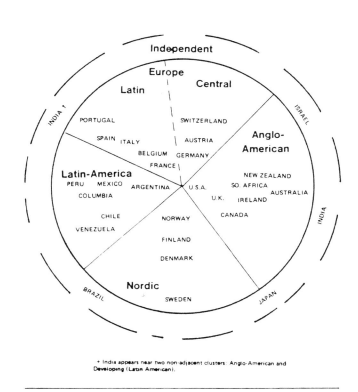

+ India appears near two non-adjacent clusters: Anglo-American and Developing (Latin American).

One basic dimension which seems to underly the distribution in all the preceding figures is the level of industrialization of the countries. Although this dimension is a gross measure, the tie to industrialization supports Webber's proposition, noted earlier; namely, countries with common economic orientation (technology) tend to cluster together while those of different levels of development seem to diverge.

Our findings also support Webber's hypothesis that differences in culture and language are divergent forces. The results leave no doubt that cultural differences, and particularly language, contributed largely to the formation of the clusters, sometimes regardless of geographical proximity (e.g., Anglo-American countries). Among countries at a similar level of industrialization, differences in language seem to be the basis for divergent clusters. For example, this seems to explain the division of continental Europe into two subdivisions, the Germanic countries (Germany, Austria, Switzerland) and the Latin-European group (France, Belgium, Italy and Spain). A common language, of course, often implies similar history, and similar social, economic and religious values.

Even allowing for the impact of language on the questionnaire results, it seems unlikely that artifact alone can account for these relationships. Furthermore, the countries which were found to be independent most often seem to have unique languages and cultures (e.g., Japan, Israel, Brazil).

The SSA technique is especially useful in showing the position of Independent countries relative to various clusters of countries. Japanese employees consistently demonstrate dissimilar attitudes to all other clusters. Still, the results indicate that Japan in most cases is closer to the highly industrialized countries (Anglo-American and European) than to the Developing countries. Less industrialized countries, such as Israel and India, were in most occupational groups closer to the Anglo-American cluster, although relatively far away from the more highly developed Anglo countries.

Some countries do not cluster close to others although they can be meaningfully grouped with them. An example would be Chile, which we put in the Latin-American group, although it is relatively far away from other countries in the cluster. This distance may be due to smaller samples yielding less stable results. Or there is a possibility that employees in less developed countries are highly variable on specific issues such as work goals. By contrast, Haire et al., explored a broad variety of managerial attitudes and found that Developing countries cluster together. Of course, the clusters will vary with different sets of countries. As we have seen, a country relatively close to others may be closer or further away when new countries are introduced.

CONCLUSION

An important aspect of this study is the potential for practical application by multinational organizations. For example, knowledge of relative similarities among countries can guide the smooth placement of international assignees, the establishment of compatible regional units, and predict the ease of implementing various policies and practices across national boundaries.

We suggest that future studies may work with regional/cultural groups of countries for effective analysis without the necessity for a laborious and expensive data collection from the whole world. Researchers who wish to compare very different sorts of countries could sample from the domain represented by various clusters. Researchers who wish to minimize cultural differences could restrict their work to a small number of clusters.

In addition, the SSA method could be applied to economic, political, and social data, as well as to attitudinal reports. An interdisciplinary approach to clustering countries is likely to be especially fruitful in the long run, and should advance understanding of management theory and practice around the globe.

NOTES

[1] The authors thank Ms. Chaya Kibelis for her considerable help in the literature review preceding this research. We also appreciate the extensive comments by Professor Robert Dubin on an earlier version of this paper.

[2] This is an extended version of a paper presented at the Annual Convention of the American Psychological Association in Chicago, Illinois, August, 1975.

[3]Webber, R.A. "Convergence or Divergence." Columbia Journal of World Business, Vol. 4 (May-June 1969), 75-83.

[4]Ajiferuke, B. & Boddewyn, J. "Culture and other explanatory variables in comparative management studies." Academy of Management Journal, Vol 13 (1970), 153-165.

[5]Nath, R. "A Methodological Review of Cross-Cultural Management Research." International Social Science Journal, Vol. 20 (1968), 35-61.

[6]Bass, B.M. "A preliminary report on manifest preference in six cultures for participative management." Technical Report No. 21 (1968), University of Rochester.

[7]Bass, B.M. & Eldridge, L.D. "Transnational differences in the accelerated manager's willingness to budget for ecology." Technical Report No. 50 (1972), University of Rochester.

[8]Harbison, F. & Myers, C.A. Management in the Industrial World: An International Study. (New York: McGraw-Hill, 1959).

[9]Hinrichs, J.R. & Ferrario, A. "A Cross-National Study of Manager's Job Attitudes," presented at the Eighteenth International Congress of Applied Psychology, Montreal, Canada, August 1974.

[10]Mouton, J.S. & Blake, R.R. "Issues in Transnational Organization Development." In Bass, B.M., Cooper, R., & Hass, A.H. (Eds.), Managing for Accomplishment. (Lexington, Mass.: Heath Lexington, 1970), 208-224.

[11]Porter, L.W. & Siegel, J. "Relationships of Tall and Flat Organization Structures to the Satisfaction of Foreign Managers." Personnel Psychology, Vol. 18 (1965), 379-392.

[12]Ryterband, E.C. & Barrett, G.V. "Managers' Values and Their Relationship to the Management of Tasks: A Cross-Cultural Comparison," in Bass, B.M., Cooper, R., & Hass, J.A. (Eds.), Managing for Accomplishment. (Lexington, Mass.: Heath Lexington, 1970), 226-260.

[13] Haire, M., Ghiselli, E.E., & Porter, L.W. _Managerial Thinking: An International Study_. (New York: Wiley, 1966).

[14] Sirota, D. & Greenwood, M.J. "Understand Your Overseas Work Force," _Harvard Business Review_, January-February 1971, 53-60.

[15] Guttman, L. "A General Nonmetric Technique for Finding the Smallest Coordinate Space for a Configuration of Points." _Psychometrika_, Vol. 33 (1968), 469-478.

Canada's Culural Barrier: A Dangerous Deterrent to Canadian Industrial Growth

by
Y.T. Kee
Associate Professor
University of Manitoba

Can two distinctly different cultural groups see eye-to-eye in one business firm, ignoring personal differences in deference to company goals? In terms of the current Canadian industrial impasse, the answer may be negative – unless both groups can acquire fresh understanding. Such understanding could be the decisive factor in Canada's quest for increased industrial expansion. Yet surprisingly few individuals seem fully aware of the crisis, and its insidious effect upon firms in which broad misunderstandings flourish.

Much of Canada's modern industrial management is simultaneously staffed by both French Canadians and English Canadians. These two groups neither think alike in terms of basic issues, nor tackle the philosophy of management similarly. This fact, long suspected, has been verified by several recent studies.

In 1964, the Royal Commission on Bilinguism and Biculturism in Canada set up a committee to support and encourage research projects to determine the effect of broad bilcultural differences upon Canada's present and future. We are indebted to Auclair and York[1] for their important studies of differences in attitude toward industrial leadership, as well as to those of Haire, Ghiselli, and Porter,[2] and Carlisle[3] in the 1960's.

More recently, this author was privileged to direct, with aid from Dr. T.S. Major,[4] an in-depth study into prevalent differences in managerial attitudes on the part of French Canadian and English Canadian managers within a large financial institution maintaining offices in both Montreal and Toronto.[5] We are especially indebted to Douglas Jones[6] for his superior handling of this assignment, to L.M. LaFleur[7] for detailed investigation of the relationships between personality characteristics and specific motivational variables, and to Alan Willey[8] for assisting in the analysis of tables and graphs. Minus the findings of these and other bicultural studies, one might believe a certain variation in managerial viewpoint could create a healthy business climate, perhaps even acting as a deterrent to stagnation in company thinking. But in Canada's bicultural situation, research shows such hypotheses to be quite incorrect.

Before discussing results from aforementioned studies, let us examine in broad terms some of the major emerging differences in viewpoint. To dramatize these, we list not specific responses but overall impressions created by the collective results:

- Should an industry consider making money to be its primary purpose?

Most English Canadian managers and supervisors might reply, " Certainly!" ... Most French Canadian managers and supervisors would say, "Putting money first is crass! Service to the community and humanity-at-large has far more import."

- Should a person's salary reflect his on-the-job productivity?

The majority of English Canadians would say, "Of course; that's the only fair measure."... Their French Canadian peers would probably reply, "Unfair! ... Employees should be paid according to family responsibilities."

- Should one's subordinates share in goal-planning and decision-making?

The average English Canadian manager or supervisor would say, "Certainly; this will encourage individual development, and utilize fresh, young organizational thinking." ... A typical French Canadian manager or supervisor might answer, "No indeed! My subordinates must do what I recommend. As their superior, I am responsible for all planning and major decisions."

- Should all managers within a company function as a team in discussing problems, making decisions and sharing departmental goals and progress?

English Canadian managers might expectedly say, "Right! This works to everyone's advantage." ... But many French Canadian managers would insist, "Managers must be autonomous. Group discussions waste time."

● Do most persons enjoy working, and receive personal satisfaction from doing a good job?

The average English Canadian, manager or subordinate, would probably reply, "Of course. Seeing the company grow, and acknowledging one's peronal contiributions to this growth, is highly rewarding." ... Yet his French Canadian counterpart is more apt to say, "Not so! People enter industry because circumstances force them to. Only doctors, lawyers, teachers, and clergymen pursue noble, satisfying work."

Certainly it is possible that members of both cultural groups at work in Canada today might reflect attitudes somewhat modified by personal experience in a bicultural working atmosphere. However, the foregoing hypothetical quotations represent the more significant findings of most Canadian bicultural industrial research conducted within the past two decades. The majority of French Canadian and English Canadians, working side-by-side, reflect vast divergencies of opinion toward company goals, monetary rewards, development of subordinates, inter-managerial teamwork, personal goals and personal satisfaction.

Is the "language-barrier", produced by continued use of the French tongue in certain sections of Canada, the major cause? While the most obvious dissimilarity and undoubtedly a deterrent to full communication, this language difference cannot be held totally accountable for all problems. It is, in fact, rather likely to disappear of its own accord. In Jones' study, recently conducted among French Canadian and English Canadian bank managers,[9] only 3% of all respondents (employed in the Montreal area) reported speaking French exclusively). Fluency in both English and French was claimed by 31% with all others noting English as the primary spoken tongue.

Thus, we must assume the marked philisophical differences may be rooted in the deeper, more subtle, less eradicable area of cultural background.

In 1962, Clyde Kluckhorn gave the following definition of "culture":

> That part of human life ... learned by peoples as a result of belonging to some particular group ... our special legacy, as contrasted with our organic heredity... the main factor of which permits us to live together in a society, giving us ready-made solutions to our problems, helping us to predict the behavior of others, and permitting us to know what is expected of us.[10]

Unfortunately, this cultural heritage aids us in predicting another's behavior and knowing what is expected of ourselves, only when we are inter-relating with members of our own cultural society. Arming us with little instinctive foreknowledge of those outside our group, it may quite innocently precipitate misunderstandings and disappointments when we deal elsewhere.

The other fellow from a completely different culture may react quite differently form our preconceived expectations, as his own cultural background causes him to perceive the very situation differently! Despite ever-growing global communication, few persons are yet adequately prepared to understand the attitudes, loyalties, thought patterns and acquired habits arising from another's lifelong exposure to foreign culture.

We may somewhat appreciate this phenomenon when viewing the rather violent misunderstandings which arise at so-called peace conferences" between conflicting world powers. It is more difficult to accept the fact that members of two cultural groups reated within one great Canadian nation are still arriving at business conferences with attitudes similarly divided.

Auclair and York[11] found that this is, indeed, a common corporate occurrence. Auclair defined the major responsibility of management as achievement of the aims of the enterprise through effective coordination and direction of people, postulating that when marked divergencies in attitudes and values toward the process of leadership exist, the creation of a unified working climate becomes impossible.

He and York explored the consistency of these differing attitudes, to determine whether disparities in opinion might be attributed to basic cultural influences. They studied 1,505 French Canadians and 1,600 English Canadians at three levels of management, within three large Canadian manufacturing organizations and four large Canadian service organizations. The research represented various levels of administration plus such important sub-groups as staff, line, marketing and engineering.

To delineate lower, middle and higher management and any attitudinal divergencies therein, they used in the final sample three early-1960's salary levels:

Lower Management: $8,999.00 or less annual salary
Middle Management: $9,000.00 to $17,999.00 annual salary
Higher Management: $18,000.00 or more annual salary

They used as final subjects naturalized Canadians whose first language was French or English and whose parents were correspondingly French or English, plus native Canadians whose first language was French or English irrespective of parental origin. Distribution of four main variables, age, marital status, educational level, and religious affiliation, were maintained at all managerial levels. (Religious affiliation emerged as the only measurable difference between the ethnic groups. Further research determined this does not contribute significantly to relevant divergency in managerial attitude). To ensure accuracy, they used six bilingual translators, and later submitted the translated respondent replies to a series of statistical analyses which determined the questions equally meaningful to both cultures. Their major findings in summation:

(1) English Canadian managers value company goals to a far greater extent than do French Canadian managers, who tend to stress social humanitarianism. English Canadians showed stronger preference for "profit" and "service" as key objectives. French Canadians favored "human relations", "reduction of unemployment", and "development of social institutions".

(2) The French Canadian expresses significant role conflict in terms of self actualization, personal contributions to society, monetary gain, personal harmony at home as a result of job goals, and perceived relationships between remuneration and family ob-

ligations. He seems to feel "Big Business" regards the individual as a tool of production; that it is somewhat dishonorable to pursue financial gain; that persons with greater family obligations deserve larger salaries; and that accomplisment of managerial duties is incompatible with attainment of a normal family life. In light of far lesser expression of such views by English Canadians, Auclair and York determined French Canadians do not readily identify with the organization's primary function within an industrial society, while English Canadians welcome industrial goals and take personal satisfaction from company accomplishments.

(3) In management of people, the French Canadian tends to regard the authority of his status as absolute, viewing subordinates' doubts, complaints and disagreements as direct threats to his personal authority. The English Canadian takes a more flexible view of personal authority, and appears far less defensive about management prerogatives.

(4) Because the French Canadian does not find the industrial milieu intrinsically need-fulfilling, he feels people as a whole dislike work, are inherently lazy, primarily motivated to accomplishment only by remuneration, and not totally trustworthy in job interaction. The English Canadian is more apt to believe that people derive personal satisfaction from task activity itself, viewing money as but one of several motivators; thus they perform well when given the opportunity and may be expected to interact with others in a climate of mutual trust.

(5) The authenticity of the foregoing is further exemplified by differing ethnic attitudes toward task achievement. The French Canadian exerts great pressure upon subordinates in order to attain minimum standards and volume productivity. (Auclair suggests this may result from a belief that subordinates have only limited interest and personal involvement in the job, hence must be driven to uniform performance.) Conversely, the English Canadian manager sets higher standards of performance and output, believing subordinates to be personally motivated toward their achievement. Yet, he tends to be more tolerant of failure to reach top goal levels.

(6) While both managerial groups outwardly value harmonious work relationships, high morale, and over-all congeniality, they differ considerably in the handling of subordinates. In a marked

517

departure from originally expressed principles, French Canadian managers appeared to take a tough, critical approach towards employees, condoning personal practices of sarcasm and accusation which could produce serious employee frustrations. By contrast, English Canadian managers placed less emphasis on theory, and appeared to practice more sensitivity in subordinate relationships, again demonstrating confidence.

(7) These divergent views again emerge regarding subordinate participation in decision-making. Three to four times as many French as English Canadians tend to exclude subordinates from decision-making, adhering to "the manager's right to manage" and suggesting that subordinates may be best utilized for efficient handling of routine work, requiring little or no information concerning policy decisions until they become practice. English Canadian managers seem to favor more opportunities for subordinates to participate in decision-making, thereby fostering personal development and greater job motivation.

(8) In terms of supervisory control, French Canadian managers tend to favor a regulatory, closer and more restrictive system, while English Canadians express belief in further subordinate freedom and autonomy. Hence, employees exposed to bicultural management may be forced to operate under two opposing regimes: one permitting little or no freedom, the other encouraging freedom and demanding greater autonomy and participation.

(9) With the two managerial groups' widely differing views in regard to development, deployment and utilization of human resources, it would appear quite impossible for company leaders to reach agreement on personnel policies, training and development, allocation and performance of tasks, and departmental decision-making.

(10) Unable to embrace a common philosophy of management, the two ethnic groups may experience great difficulty in communication at the managerial level. The French Canadian's seemingly "aura of infallibility", fostered by his personal view of job status and an innate distrust of other's motivations, may discourage group interaction. The English Canadian, favoring egalitarian standards and organizational teamwork, may assume there is no common ground for frank discussion of company problems with his French Canadian peers.

Auclair speculates that bicultural problems in lateral company communication may portend serious difficulty in vertical communication. Coming from an essentially non-economically-oriented society, the French Canadian subordinate may experience tension and self-devaluation through inability to identify with corporate economic goals. This fosters general apathy, which is reinforced by French Canadian superiors' distrustful, authoritative behavior. Such fears and conflicts render the subordinate incapable of response to English Canadian superiors anticipating eager participation in return for a working freedom actually foreign to his nature.

The English Canadian subordinate fares no better; he is simultaneously encouraged by English Canadian superiors and frustrated by French Canadian superiors! Each group suffers in the bicultural business climate - simply through inability to fully comprehend the other's feelings.

Such findings are supported by some four decades of bicultural behavioral research. As early as 1943 E.C. Hughes[12] theorized that French Canadian attitudes toward economic matters (developed in that life period when career expectation is formed) might be responsible for a tendency of French Canadians to reject powerful economic institutions and thus develop large French Canadian-owned enterprises at a slower rate.

P.K.D. Naegele[13] remarked that French Canadians learn both at home and school to value service in the church, the professions, and government over business, while the entrepreneurial spirit is a dominant characteristic of English Canadian upbringing. F. Roussel[14] suggested that French Canadian businessmen's sons are seldom encouraged to pursue business, while English Canadian youths are generally trained to value the corporate life both economically and socially. In a 1966 study of international managerial values, Haire, Ghiselli and Porter[15] noted that French managers reflected more dissatisfaction in terms of self-actualization than did either English or American managers.

Trudeau[16] suggested in 1956 that French Canadian culture seemed essentially authoritarian and traditionalistic, while English Canadian social structures tended strongly toward egalitarianism, a contrast also stressed by Falardeau[17] and Naegele[18]. Studies by both Rioux[19] and Garigue[20] indicated that the profound respect for authority brought into industry by French Canadians tended to affect relationships with both subordinates and superiors, while the network of familial relationships was also transferred as a major reference for interaction.

Faucher[21] and Taylor[22] each mentioned the French Canadian tendency to deal with work-mates on the basis of social, rather than business, status. Trudeau contrasted tight French Canadian upbringing with that of English Canadians, who learn early to become independent of parental control, de-emphasizing authority and status relationships in favor of a group-centered approach to problem-solving.

While the foregoing reports generally reflect tendencies toward business apathy and marked distaste for corporate success on the part of French Canadians, research, conducted under the supervision of Douglas Jones[23] at the University of Manitoba, in 1970 and 1971, produced a slightly different picture. Comparing the characteristics of branch managers in the Toronto and Montreal offices of a large Canadian financial institution, Jones found that French Canadian bank managers seemed to place somewhat more emphasis on the importance of success, material gain and hard work than did their English Canadian counterparts!

The findings also seem to indicate that the French Canadian promoted to bank manager is generally better educated, usually bilingual, and often from a better-income family ... a series of factors perhaps implying that banking appears closer to the field of service in the average French Canadian viewpoint.

Once on the job, French Canadian bank managers appear to voice dissatisfaction with the amount of pay received, and self-actualization realized, in a ratio nearly identical to that of English Canadian peers.

They differ significantly only in unsatisfied need. In findings closely paralleling Auclair's,[24] responding French Canadians seemed to demand more authority and status, and appeared less ready to believe them received. They also appeared to be slightly more vocal; on the thirty-two completed questionnaires Jones received (from a possible 125), twenty-two were from managers working under the Montreal office.

While 69% of all respondents had no formal schooling beyond high school, an additional 25% had engaged in some further education beyond this point. Although just 6% of all respondents were college graduates, 31% of all Montreal respondents (in contrast to 10% from Toronto) had some training after high school. It is difficult to determine whether this differential resulted from personal ambition, or the ability and desire of better-income families to foster further education.

Responding French Canadians also appeared to receive managerial appointment when slightly younger, perhaps denoting certain success or drive status. (Average present age of Montreal respondents: 33.4, Toronto average: 36.8). On the basis of Jones' comparatively small sample, this surge of ambition may be of rather recent origin - or might reflect improving French Canadian opportunities, although Montreal respondents had over 15 years' employment with the firm, while 50% of Toronto respondents claimed this amount. However, 39% of Montreal managers appeared within the 5 to 15 years' employment category, contrasted by just 10% of Toronto respondents. The divergency narrowed with those employed 5 to 6 years: 33% from Montreal; 40% from Toronto.

Familial pride may have colored French Canadian responses regarding parental economic background. While no respondent claimed an "Upper Class" background, 4% of Montreal managers designated "Upper Middle". English Canadian (Toronto) managers were equally divided between "Middle" and "Lower Middle" backgrounds. 64% of Montreal managers selected "Middle, while just 27% chose "Lower Middle" class. The remainder specified "Lower Income".

Importance of status to the French Canadian emerged in responses regarding present-income level. One would expect branch managers within the same company and range of experience to receive similar remuneration. Significantly, 23% of the French Canadians classified present income as "Upper Middle". Another 64% selected "Middle Income", while 80% of responding English Canadians chose this category. A smaller group (20% of those from Toronto against 9% from Montreal) classified present income as "Lower Middle".

Surprisingly few attitudinal differences between ethnic

groups appeared in terms of perceived personal needs. Pay, self-actualization, and security seemed most significant to all respondents irrespective of parental background, job location, or years of experience. In satisfaction, "pay" represented the highest perceived deficiency - a finding perhaps attributable either to basic human nature, or to a tendency of both Canadian and U.S. financial institutions to provide comparatively moderate salaries. Self-actualization claimed second place among presently-unfulfilled needs. The study verified earlier research in regard to French Canadian managerial attitudes: Montreal respondents place dissatisfaction with present "authority" and "status" side-by-side with "pay".

While Auclair seemed to believe prolonged exposure to another culture (within the corporate entity) might not greatly modify original attitudes, Jones' findings appear to indicate that French Canadian bank managers move a bit closer in attitude to their English Canadian peers as years multiply within the organization. When asked for point ratings of 1 to 7 on "success", "material gain", "innovation", "hard work", and "change", French Canadian respondents employed 5 to 6 years placed "material gain" first. Those with 5 to 15 years gave greater importance to "success" (although one might assume elevation to management represented this to some degree). And, surprisingly similar to replies anticipated from Anglo-Saxon manager, Montrealites with the firm 15 years or more placed most emphasis on "innovation".

To further utilize Jones' findings and relate their significance to the over-all cultural study (as well as to the organization employing his respondents) L.M. LaFleur[26] conducted a detailed study of the relationships between personality characteristics displayed by significant attitudinal trends and certain motivational variables apparent (or lacking) in the manner in which the parent organization appears to motivate employees to motivate employees with management capabilities.

Disregarding technical considerations, individual productivity is dependent upon ability, motivation to perform, and the prerequisite of environmental opportunity. Thus LaFleur chose as his main objective an exploration of the effects of selected personality characteristics upon individual motivation, hoping the findings might aid the parent firm in creating a climate of optimum organizational effectiveness. To accomplish this, sets of seventeen "Independent Variables" (personality characteristics) and "Dependent Variables" (motivational variables) were chosen for detailed analysis.

The selected personality characteristics included education, location of education, years of education, degrees held, business experience, type of experience, number of professional affiliation, age, area of adolescence, province of adolescence, economic status of parents, family banking tradition, ethnic background, language proficiency, present economic status, recreation and hobbies and communal activity.

Motivational variables included the area of bank interest, importance of pay, importance of self-actualization, importance of autonomy, importance of authority and status, importance of security, importance of success, importance of hard work, importance of material gain, importance of change, importance of innovation, authority and status in position, opportunity for participation in goal setting in position, opportunity for independent thought and action, pay in position, opportunity to utilize talents and abilities, and security in position.

The sets of variables were constructed so that data from respondents to the original questionnaire might be of two basic types, (1) individual personality traits and (2) motivational variables within their parent organizations. This was done believing that while personality is an important variable determining organizational climate, this climate is simultaneously the variable determining organizational effectiveness.

The questionnaire itself was constructed by this writer. Its initial portion was designed to pinpoint personality traits under consideration, proposing to disclose the traits we find primarily important after more than a decade of research and study in the field of bicultural business philosophy and behavior. Its latter portion, concerned with motivational variables, was composed to specific questions selected from questionnaires formulated earlier by Rensis Likert[28] and Lyman W. Porter.[29]

LaFleur's Chi-square test compared the distribution of values of each selected motivational variable for two different levels of each selected personality trait (i.e., apparently "French Canadian" of "English Canadian" in character, as determined by freqency of appearance from the cities of origin, and the provinces of adolescence, education and employment). These tests disclosed that in terms of motivation...

1. Education affects managerial attitudes toward "Importance of Pay".[30]

2. Location of education affects attitudes towards "Importance of Security" as a performance incentive.

3. The province of education affects managerial attitudes toward "Opportunity for Authority and Status".

4. The area of the majority of the "growing up" years affects the manager's subsequent value of "Autonomy".

5. The area of adolescence affects his ultimate value of "Security", "Opportunity for Authority and Status", "Pay", and "Material Gain".

6. The province of adolescence affects attitudes toward "Authority and Status of Present Position", as well as "Opportunity for Independent Thought and Action".

7. Parental economic status significantly affects ultimate attitudes toward "Material Gain". (The wealthier the family, the more materialistic the manager appears).

8. Parental economic status affects one's ultimate value of "Authority and Status", "Opportunity for Participation in Goal Setting" and "Opportunity for Independent Thought and Action".

LaFleur's tables and graphs were further analysed and interpreted by Alan Willey[31] who found the exercise generally to be reliably and logically interpreted. Thus, we conclude the University of Manitoba study of Montreal and Toronto bank managers produced significant evidence that cultural differences indeed color the managerial philosophy. Managers appear to be influenced by financial background. However, length of service in the firm (at least in the financial field, which might be broadly interpreted as closer to community service) seems to modify and even partially erase some originally divergent viewpoints between the ethnic groups.

Like Auclair, we found that some personality traits distinguishing members of a given group (from humanity as a whole) may derive from biological heritage. In general, however, these traits seem traceable less to constitutional factors than to formative influences of the environment to which all group members were subjected. Personality is also, of course, directly molded by parents, teachers and others to whom one is exposed during the formative years.

Thus is may be quite logical for the child of wealthy parents to later accept material wealth as a personal standard, while not likewise accepting the corporate goal of material gain as appropriate. Similarly, the child from a higher-income home learns to expect more in all life phases, hence may anticipate responsibility and authority relative to his personal image of his job status or title, and thus finds closely-held corporate reign particularly frustrating. While these might seem logical reactions for anyone raised in similar circumstances, the French Canadian may cling more tightly to the status role he perceives fitting to his position.

One must also conclude that the French Canadian has by background been forced into certain psychological "identity crises". Campau explained:

> The majority of Canada's 20,000,000 people live either in English-speaking Ontario or French-speaking Quebec. The rest for the most part are strewn across 4,000 miles close to the Southern border. It is a hard country to weld together, not only because of its formidable geography and different languages and culture, but also because it has had such emotionally cohesive elements as the common cause of revolution or the common danger of large-scale enemy invasion.[32]

Caloren further suggested:

> Ethnic nationalism has been a constant in French Canadian life since the conquest of Quebec by the British in 1759 ... The French Canadian social institutions and values are, themselves ... the product of a minority which seeks to compensate for its dependence on a dominant majority by avoiding competition with that majority.[33]

We may assume that these and other reasons, inherent in French Canadian managers, influence their tendency to avoid excessive communication with members of that "English majority" even when playing tandem roles in business. But like Auclair, we see such barriers to communication as cultural, rather than bilingual. He stated:

> ...the French Canadian manager cannot effectively utilize his talents and personal resources ... because industrial work does not have the same value or meaning for him that it does for an English Canadian. He cannot reconcile his role as a responsible member of an organization with the concept of himself as a useful member of society ... This is the basic conflict that the French Canadian must face head-on and solve above all others, if he is to be a member of a management team which fosters organizational behavior in others.[34]

How, then, might members of both cultural backgrounds find common pathways to understanding? Auclair saw little merit in attempting to teach English Canadians in bicultural organizations to speak French, insofar as English continues to be the dominant tongue in day-to-day business communication. Our findings in this regard (only 3% of all respondents to the University of Manitoba bank managers' study speak French exclusively) lead us to concur.

Auclair also warned that one must not expect "field" training (outside the French Canadian atmosphere) to change basic cultural attitudes, nor will French Canadian students substantially alter basic philosophies toward management simply by attending business schools primarily Anglo-Saxon in climate. (He cited one study of 577 French Canadian and 533 English Canadian business school students which found managerial philosophies of both graduates and undergraduates to be highly similar to those among managers already in industry).

Yet, any lasting solutions must assuredly come through educational programs designed to increase English understanding of French cultural philosophies, and French understanding of English cultural philosophies, in the Canadian nation. Other programs must be created to help French Canadians to fully comprehend – and adapt to – Canada's current corporate climate for the good of the economy.

BIBLIOGRAPHY

1. Auclair, Gilles A., Ph.D. "Cultural Differences in Attitudes Toward Industrial Leadership: their existence and impact upon managerial styles and organizational climate in large Canadian industrial organizations", Ecole des Hautes Etudes Commerciales, University of Montreal. (Pre-publication draft). Read, Professor W., York University; Dr. Auclair's partner in the original major study sponsored by the Royal Commission on Bilingualism and Biculturalism in Canada, 1964.

2. Haire, Masons, et al., Managerial Thinking: an International Study, N.Y., John Wiley and Sons, 1966.

3. Carlisle, A. "Cultural Differences and Supervisory Styles", Relations Industrielles, 23, 1, pp. 48-56, Universite Laval.

4. Major, T.S., Ph.D. Faculty of Commerce, University of Manitoba.

5. The financial institution herein referred to would prefer to remain publicly anonymous; however, individuals desiring personal knowledge with no intention of publishing the name may request information from this author.

6. Jones, D., "A Study of Characteristics of Branch Managers", a paper submitted to Dr. Y.T. Kee, Faculty of Commerce, University of Manitoba, 1971, in partial fulfillment of the requirement for the Degree of Master of Business Administration.

7. LaFleur, L.M., "An Investigation into the Relationship Between Personality Characteristics and Certain Specific Motivational Variables", a paper submitted to Dr. Y.T. Kee, Faculty of Commerce, University of Manitoba, 1971, in partial fulfillment of the requirement for the Degree of Master of Business Administration.

8. Willey, A., "An Interpretation of Tables and Graphs in the Practicum Entitled 'An Investigation into the Relationship between Personality Characteristics and Certain Special Motivational Variables' (by L.M. LaFleur)", a paper submitted to Dr.

Y.T. Kee, Faculty of Commerce, University of Manitoba, 1971, in partial fulfillment of the requirement for the Degree of Master of Business Administration.

9. Ibid.

10. Kluckholn, Clyde, <u>Culture and Behavior</u>, The Free Press of Glencoe, New York, 1962, p. 25.

11. Ibid.

12. Hughes, E.C., <u>French Canada in Transition</u>, University of Chicago Press, Chicago, Illinois, 1943.

13. Naegele, P.K.D., "Canadian Society: Some Reflection in B.R. Blishen & Others": <u>Canadian Society</u>, MacMillan, Toronto, Ontario, 1961, pp. 1-53.

14. Rouseel, F., <u>Comment le fils Voit-il a Profession de son Pere Homme D'Affaires?</u> Association professionelle des industriels, 1961.

15. Ibid.

16. Trudeau, P.E. <u>La Greve de L'Amainte, une Etape de the Revolution Industrielle</u> au Quebec, Cite, Libre, Montreal, Quebec, 1956.

17. Falardeau, J.C. <u>Essais sur le Quebec Contemporain, Les Repercussions Sociales de Industrialisation dans le Province de Quebec</u>, Presses Universitaires de Laval, Quebec, 1953.

18. Ibid.

19. Rioux, M. "Remarques sur les Valeurs et les Attitudes des Adolescents d'une Communaute Agricole au Quebec", <u>Contributions a l'Etude des Sciences de l'Homme</u>, 3, Montreal, Quebec, 1956: 133-143.

20. Garigue, P., <u>L'Option Politique du Canada Francais: une Interpretation de la Survivance Nationale</u>, Edit. due Levrier, Montreal, Quebec, 1963.

21. Faucher, A. "La Daulite Canadienne et l'Economique: Tendances Divergentes et Tendances Convergentes", in M. Wade & J.C. Falardeau: La Dualite Canadienne, Presses Universitaires de Laval, Quebec, 1960: pp. 222-238.

22. Taylor, N.W., "La Psychologie de Entrepreneurs Canadiens-Francais", Recherches Sociographiques, 2, Presses Universitaires de Laval, Quebec, 1961.

23. Ibid.

24. Ibid.

25. Ibid., p. 36.

26. Ibid.

27. Kee, Y.T., Business Across Boundaries: A Laboratory Experiment to Analyze the Decision-Making Behaviour of Groups from Different Cultures, University of Minnesota, Minneapolis, Minnesota, 1970.

28. Likert, Rensis, The Human Organization: Its Management and Value, McGraw-Hill, Inc. New York, N.Y., 1967.

29. Porter, Lyman W., "A Study of Perceived Need Satisfactions in Bottom and Middle Management Jobs", Journal of Applied Psychology, February 1961, pp. 1-10.

30. Mr. Lafleur's Questionnaire.

31. Ibid.

32. Campau, Dubarry, "Is Canada Cultured?" The Saturday Review, Vol 50, April 2, 1967, p. 58, as quoted by Dr. Auclair, ibid.

33. Caloron, Fred., "Nationalism in Quebec, 1967". Christian Century, Vol. 84, June 12, 1967, pp. 914-915, a condensation of the quotations used by Dr. Auclair, ibid.

34. Ibid., pp. 38-39.

The Multinational Executive: Patriot or Traitor

by
George Moller
Consultant

Your lordship, presiding judge, ladies and gentlemen of the jury. The jury here has been selected and assembled to sit in judgment over our defendant: Mr. Goodman, who is the executive of a Canadian company, wholly owned by a United States corporation aspiring to multinational character. The jury will understand that I will have to speak under certain restraints. Not being admitted to the bar of the state of Ohio, I have been called here as an expert witness for the defense and have been assured of extraterritorial status for anything I may say which is not in complete accordance with the laws of this country. I beg your indulgence in this respect. His lordship will indicate whenever I get beyond the boundaries of politeness in my presentation to you and I beg your indulgence if I should detail to you, a jury with a high level of fundamental understanding, that which may be boring or trite.

---

  * A mock trial before an imaginary United States court.
  ** George Moller, D. Juris (University of Prague), Dipl. Comm. (Vienna), F.C.A., R.I.A., practiced law and was manager of a bank in Czechoslovakia. He also was employed as a public accountant (Chartered Accountant) in Toronto and served for 20 years as the Vice-President of a large world-wide U.S. corporation until his recent retirement. He is now employed as a consultant. Dr. Moller is a keen observer of the phenomenon of the multi-national corporation. As the chairman of the planning committee of the International Association of Financial Executives Institutes, he continues his interest in international financial relations. He has authored numerous papers on management, accounting, taxation and international problems, taught at McMaster University (Hamilton, Ontario), and is a frequent conference and seminar speaker.

Our defendant, Mr. Goodman, is a Canadian. He is a professional accountant and financial officer of a company operating under the laws of Canada. Canada is a neighbor of the United States of America. I would like to repeat a picture drawn by the present prime minister of Canada, who compared the United States to a big elephant and stated that if that big elephant grunts, Canada has an earthquake.

I wish to repeat for your sake the serious accusations which have been made by the state prosecutor (the crown attorney in Canada) against our defendant who has been apprehended on a visit to the headquarters of his parent company here in the United States and accused of a number of transgressions against the laws of the United States of America. He is accused of having violated tax laws in the United States and he may have seriously violated the balance of payment guidelines which have been issued here, not to mention the compliance with foreign exchange control regulations and the application of social concepts which are not exactly cherished here, e.g., disregarding the Trading with the Enemy Act.

CONFLICTS OF INTEREST

Let me deal with each of these conflicts of interest of which our friend and defendant has been accused. For my legal source I will rely on the article "Conflict Resolution and Extraterritoriality," by Professors Litvak and Maule (now Ottawa, Canada).

Mr. Goodman considered himself the executive of a multinational corporation, not the executive of a subsidiary of an international corporation, much less of a United States company. The difference is that a multinational corporation is presumed to have the interest of the population of the entire world in mind, and it must take this interest into consideration when making management decisions. An international corporation is, in effect, a national corporation with investments in subsidiaries and affiliated companies in other parts of the world. From a legal viewpoint, an international corporation is, therefore, a domestic corporation subject to the laws of the country in which it is incorporated and has its seat of business.

Why is Mr. Goodman before this court? Mr. Goodman is here because he was caught in a conflict of interest. He tried to abide by the precepts of a multinational corporation but is now being judged under the precepts of national corporation subject to the laws of the United States of America.

What is he then? Is he really a traitor - guilty of treason, one who is false to his trust or betrays his country or his cause? I submit that Mr. Goodman has never betrayed his country, Canada. He has never betrayed his cause, the multinational corporation. But he could be considered guilty of disregarding the laws of the United States of America if we accept the concept that, as an executive of the subsidiary of a corporation in the United States, he owes allegiance and loyalty to the laws and legal concepts of the United States.

Let us accept the fact that multinational corporations, although widely discussed in the literature, cannot in effect exist because multinational corporations would require a concept of supranational law and a body of supranational laws which would give these corporations firm boundaries and a concept of legal existence.

We have some supranational institutions in this world, the foremost being the United Nations. But we immediately must admit that the United Nations, which significantly has its headquarters in the United States of America, has not really succeeded in establishing international and supranational law. We have a world court in The Hague which may make fourth or fifth page news. I do not remember having ever seen any headlines describing the judgments of this venerable institution. We have the International Monetary Fund (IMF) and quite a number of other international organizations, but we have no body of law of any kind which would be respected by even a majority of countries under which a multinational corporation could operate. There may be a small beginning in the European Economic Community but it does not solve our problem. Therefore, ladies and gentlemen of the jury, Mr. Goodman had really no guidelines, no moral or, still less, legal concepts to which he could have adhered when making the decisions which brought him before this high court.

Let us examine for a few minutes the issues which the prosecutor has so aptly brought into the confines of the written and venerable law of this country. The antitrust laws of this country have been violated because Mr. Goodman has advocated and was instrumental in the combine (merger) of several Canadian manufacturing companies for the purpose of export. You may not be familiar with the fact that the Canadian anticombines law, which, in many respects, is as strict and as difficult to interpret as the merger laws in this country, permits (by an amendment passed in the early 1960s) the combination of manufacturers for the purpose of becoming more efficient and effective in exporting their products. Mr. Goodman advocated and was instrumental in his company joining in such a legal combine. It is legal in Canada but not in the United States. The extraterritoriality of the Canadian company was completely disregarded by the prosecuting attorney here in claiming that, regardless of what the Canadian Anti-combines Act may state, it is clear under the laws of this country that any combination for the purpose of fixing market participation in other countries is illegal.

Let us have a look at the economic aspects of Mr. Goodman's alleged transgression in this respect if you, the independent jury, should decide that he is guilty of a breach of the law here. His interest was to make, within the statute of Canadian law, his company a prosperous one which would yield a reasonable return on its investments. To do that, he was obligated, in my opinion, to use every avenue open to him under the laws of his country to enhance the profits of the Canadian enterprise, and to assist in making production more efficient by pooling the know-how and technology of several manufacturers in the same line. In this case these manufacturers have combined to divide between them the lines of production, so that each one could become more efficient and effective in producing the product to be exported to underdeveloped countries. We have here a clear-cut multinational aspect in the structure of the production goals and objectives of Mr. Goodman's Canadian company.

I would like to rest my case by posing the question: Has the United States of America the right to judge the actions of a company which is incorporated under the laws of Canada and has not violated these laws in any respect?

The defendant is furthermore accused of having disregarded a prohibition from the parent company preventing the Canadian company from exporting its products to a country which by some interpretation falls under the U.S. Trading with the Enemy Act. Again the question arises: Is this country to which the products have been exported really an enemy of Canada's? Could it be considered an enemy in the multinational society? Is such an expression applicable to any country in an effectively regulated society not strictly divided by natural boundaries?

I would like to leave this case to your own good judgment and come to the next accusation against Mr. Goodman, which perhaps is more technical.

THE SECOND CHARGE

Mr. Goodman refused to implement a mock agreement made between his parent company and the Canadian subsidiary to pay royalties based on a turnover basis for certain products originating from the parent company. The parent company wanted to impose this royalty on the Canadian company for the simple reason that the Canadian tax rate for corporations was 4 percent higher than the tax rate effective in the United States and that the profits of the Canadian company would be subject to 4 percent more tax than if they were transferred as royalties which are only subject to a 15 percent withholding tax in Canada recoverable in the United States. The defendant also resisted the transfer of profits in the form of interest when it would have helped the tax situation of the parent company (but not, naturally, the Canadian company) if these interest payments had been grouped with other earnings transferred from other foreign associated companies in the pool of foreign earnings for the purpose of tax assessment for the parent company in the United States.

But the worst crime of which Mr. Goodman was accused was that he did not comply with, and, in fact, knowingly resisted compliance with, the Balance of Payment Guidelines issued by the United States of America. An attempt was made, I am told, to obviate these guidelines by channeling funds to Europe which were in excess of the permissible maximum of investment abroad under the guidelines. As you all know, these guidelines provide that you may not invest more than in a certain basic period. It is not necessary to discuss this in detail here; the principle is known to you. He did not want to borrow, in Canada, money which was not needed for the Canadian enterprise and transfer it to a European-affiliated company as working capital because this European-affiliated company was unable to raise working capital in the currency of Canada for its operations.

Actually, this court should not only not find him guilty but should honorably discharge him from this accusation because he actually was obeying the guidelines as they are understood by resisting an attempt to obviate these guidelines.

He also may have been guilty of transgression because he did not obey foreign exchange control regulations of subsidiaries in other countries (in this case, France) in permitting certain transactions to be channeled through Canada which could not be channeled directly in the exchange between France and the United States. He is not accused of this transgression in this court, but I mention it to show that Mr. Goodman was adhering strictly to the concepts of a multinational corporation and was trying to achieve a satisfactory performance from each of the companies forming the multinational corporation of which his Canadian company was a part, in the intrest of preserving the common goal for which a multinational corporation is supposed to strive.

Mr. Goodman, and this is the last example we want to bring before you, was advocating also the sale of shares of the Canadian corporation to Canadians to an extent which would have created at least an interested minority in the country in which his company is operating. He believed that this step, leading to the formation of a public company in Canada, would contribute to the multinational character of the corporation and would simply create a true Canadian interest in this corporation and thus assure the compliance with the Canadian interest in the execution of management responsibilities in Canada. He was doing so because there are not yet any legal restrictions in Canada on the operation of wholly owned foreign subsidiaries, and I want to place before this jury the theoretical question of whether any condemnation of Mr. Goodman would not lead to an increase in the already widespread tendencies to ask for such laws where voluntary compliance is not taking place. Is the United States really eager to bring about conditions such as in Mexico, where Mexicanization is a concept which has found widespread attention in the world and where it is virtually impossible to operate wholly owned subsidiaries of an American or any other foreign corporation?

Ladies and gentlemen of the jury, I have taken enough of your time to describe for you the motivation which led Mr. Goodman to his actions, which he took in good faith and in the unfortunately mistaken opinion that he is allowed to act and should be allowed to act as a good citizen of the world and as a good executive of a true multinational corporation. As Sir Duncan Oppenheim noted: "I do not think the fact can be hidden that there is a fear in some countries of foreign investment by big international companies, and this fear is not confined to the so-called developing countries. These anxieties are of a primarily emotive and nationalistic kind and are more likely to produce consequences directly opposed to the national interests." Mr. Sidney Rolfe also asked: "How much economic benefit does a nation give up to add to its psychological sense of security?" In answer to this question I would ask you, how much security can a Canadian company assume if you, ladies and gentlemen of the jury, should come to a verdict of guilty?

REFERENCES

Drucker, Peter F., The Age of Discontinuity - Guidelines to Our Changing Society. New York: Harper & Row, 1969.

Knortz, Herbert C., "Controllership in International Corporations," Financial Executive 37, 6, June 1969: 54-60.

Litvak, I.A. and Maule, C.J., "Conflict Resolution and Extra-territorality," The Journal of Conflict Resolution 13, 3, September 1969: 305-19.

Perlmutter, Howard V. "The Torutous Evolution of the Multi-national Corporation," Columbia Journal of World Business 4, 1, January-February 1969: 9-18.

Rolfe, Sidney E., "The International Corporation," Twenty-second Congress of the International Chamber of Commerce held in Istanbul, Turkey, May 31-June 7, 1969.

Tomb, John O. "The Multinational Corporation in the Seventies," Executive, May 1970.

VII
The
Future

The Canadian Role: Bridge Builder
or Fence Sitter
by
The North South Institute

...Some developed countries have given indications
of movement at particular stages in the discussion
only to have their national positions pulled back
because they have to proceed at the pace of the
slowest within the developed world. That is a great
pity, and this is my great worry about a country
such as Canada that has tended to take relatively
progressive and advanced positions within the councils of the developed world. It would be a great pity
if debate has now become so polarized that the G-8
position was, in fact, holding Canada back.

Remarks by Mr. Shridath S. Ramphal, Commonwealth
Secretary General to the Canadian Parliamentary
Subcommittee on International Development, 31
March, 1977.

...The heat is on Canada. The developing world regards us as a "fat cat." We like to look good at international conferences but without straining our economic relations with the major western powers - particularly the United States - that do not accept the
new order. Canada's posture is ambivalent. We recognize our role as a bridge between the various fac-
tions but we do not exert leadership because we are
neither convinced of the validity of structural
changes nor have we determined what form they
should take. Moreover, there is very little public
support for such changes. Hence we stumble along
with bits and pieces of programs with the various

departments of government operating from totally
different perspectives.

Douglas Roche, MP, "Canada and the Third World:
The Future," Text prepared for national speaking
tour, 1977.

Generally, and sometimes with outstanding eloquence (as in
Prime Minister Trudeau's internationally-noted Mansion House
speech), senior spokesmen for the Canadian Government have endorsed the idea that the existing international economic structure
needs to be transformed to redistribute wealth and opportunity in
the world. But this rhetoric has not yet been translated into any
clear programme of action or even a consistent sense of direction.
The issues of the new economic order involve different subject-
matter, different actors, different forums, and different styles
from those of traditional foreign policy in the industrial countries.
In most of these countries, including Canada, the adjustment required to handle these new conditions has been slow.

When Canadian policy-makers defend Canada's policies, they
emphasize first, the difficulty of ensuring that both the international and the domestic implications of various options are fully
considered, and second, the problem in finding a proper balance
between the needs of the Third World, the needs of Canadians
and the needs of Canada's closest international partners. They
frequently suggest that international constraints are imposed by
the requirement for Canada to maintain credibility and good relations with its major trading partners - the United States, the
European Community, and Japan - and that the reactions of these
countries to Canadian positions must be considered and weighed
against other benefits and costs. At the domestic level they
point to the need to give great attention to such factors as the
state of the Canadian economy, the concerns of Canadian industry, the maintenance of public support for Canadian initiatives,
and the consistency of Canadian policies.

When this combination of potential constraints is allowed to
predominate, it is not surprising that Canada's actions do not
always match the lofty international pronouncements of its spokesmen. On such issues as the Common Fund for commodities and
willingness to take some general action to relieve the debt burden
of the poorest countries, Canada is often found within (or at least

close to) the group of industrial countries most responsive to the Third World's demands. However, there are also wide gaps and inconsistencies which are not even traceable to a pattern of Canadian self-interest. In such areas as the Canadian reluctance to move on certain individual commodity negotiations, aid tying, foreign investment, and the transfer of technology, the explanation for Canadian stances must be sought, at least partly, in the decision-making structure itself.

POLICY FORMULATION

It is still not widely recognized in Canada that a number of Federal Departments share jurisdiction over Canadian relations with developing countries and that, on the "non-aid" issues now so important in international negotiations, ministries such as Finance, Industry, Trade and Commerce, and External Affairs, generally have the dominant influence in setting Government policy. CIDA lacks full departmental status and, even in the aid programme, the Agency is subject to formal interdepartmental structures as well as the general control of the Treasury Board and the more-or-less strict tutelage of CIDA's "parent" department, External Affairs. When the developing countries forcibly widened the international negotiating agenda, the monopoly over policy of these core departments was somewhat reduced, with at least sporadic inputs by departments such as Agriculture; Environment; Energy, Mines and Resources; Consumer and Corporate Affairs; and Science and Technology. From time to time, the Privy Council Office and Prime Minister's Office have also taken active and influential roles.

While perhaps ensuring more breadth of perspective and expertise, this expanded participation has not simplified the process of deciding on Canadian action in areas where departmental objectives and biasses differ. Given the need to obtain a proper blend of national, international and Third World concerns, what steps has the Government taken to ensure that sound and balanced Canadian policies are being formulated?

In October 1974, in a climate of urgency, the Canadian Government recognized the importance of changes in North-South relations brought about by OPEC's success and by the bitter Sixth Special Session of the United Nations General Assembly. Accepting the obvious need to give greater consideration to these relationships, the Government set up an Interdepartmental Committee on Economic Relations with Developing Countries and gave it a mandate to:

1) direct a continuing review of policies as they affect Canada's economic and other relations with developing countries;

2) consider the consistency of Canada's international economic and other policies with Canada's development policies; and

3) ensure the preparation of policy positions for major international meetings affecting Canada's economic and other relations with developing countries.[1]

It was expected that the committee would play a major role in preparing and coordinating the Canadian Government's response to North-South issues and in raising the priority of the Third World concerns within the govrnment apparatus.[2] The Secretary of State for External Affairs, Allan MacEachen, stressed that the creation of the committee was ".. an indication of our desire to be as sympathetic and as constructive as possible."[3]

Three-years after it was set up, it is possible to assess whether the operations of this coordinating committee fulfilled these hopes, and exemplified the sympathy and constructiveness referred by by Mr. MacEachen. In theory the Committee, which consists of representatives from twelve departments, ministries and agencies, is set up at the deputy minister level, but in practice it has almost always functioned at lower echelons. It has met infrequently since its inception, has not had a standing secretariat or research staff of its own, and has allowed much of the responsibility for researching and formulating policy proposals to fall to individual departments, particularly Finance, External Affairs, and Industry, Trade and Commerce. While others may be formally consulted or may be intermittently influential, these three departments (through a combination of expertise, bargaining strength, and political leverage) continue to be responsible for Canada's stance on most of the critical non-aid issues of the current North-South debate - commodity trade, debt, market access, foreign investment, transfer of technology, and the Law of the Sea.

In addition to the irregularity of meetings and the lack of independently-based research staff, there are a number of factors that inhibit the ability of the committee to forge an integrative approach to North-South issues. The committee is geared more to conference preparation than to a broad overview of development cooperation. This tends to make its work reactive rather than innovative and directed to conference agendas rather than to overall policy coordination and the development of long-range initiatives. It must also be conceded that the sheer number of conferences is enough to strain the ability of any preparatory committee. (The calendar of major events at the end of this book testifies eloquently to this problem.)

CANADIAN APPROACHES

Canada's approach to North-South issues has reflected a continuing struggle to balance responsiveness to Third World demands with the maintenance of credibility among the major industrial countries. Not surprisingly such a balancing act frequently leads Canada to adopt policy stances not too far removed from the lowest common denominator among Western countries. This preoccupation is based on the perception that Canada can do little for the South if it loses the confidence of the industrial countries - a situation, Canadian spokesmen claim, in which Sweden now finds itself.[4] This kind of perception was made explicit by CIDA President Michel Dupuy in an appearance before the Commons Subcommittee on International Development. He noted that Canada would support the convening of a debt conference but would not "press" for such a conference as Sweden had done because this action had reduced the effectiveness of Sweden's advocacy.[5]

A related preconception of Canadain officials is that the substantive outcome of North-South negotiations depends on the United States, Japan and the European Community, and that the contributions of other industrialized countries are of subordinate importance. In the words of CIEC co-chairman Allan MacEachen "if the rest of us moved (excluding the U.S., Japan and the European Community) it would not make very much difference. So it depends on them."[6]

While these discreet and modest Canadian approaches may have a sound diplomatic rationale in the long-term, they lead to certain distinct problems. There seems to be an over-emphasis of this "role-identity" to the detriment of innovative analysis. Canada seems content to assume positions close to those of the industrial countries most responsive to the Third World demands, but not too far removed from the centre of the Western group, and then wait for events to unfold. Since Canadian officials believe that Canada has, in this way, maintained its credibility in the industrialized world, it seems reasonable to ask at which points it would be appropriate to "cash in" some of the accumulated goodwill and act forcefully to achieve movement by the group as a whole.

There are a number of areas where such Canadian advocacy could prove highly effective if well-supported by research in those issues in which Canada has no obvious vested interest. It is apparent that Canada's co-chairmanship of the North-South dialogue offered some of these opportunities, and that they were used to a certain extent. Co-Chairman MacEachen, for example, is credited with easing tension by finding a compromise formula that allowed talks to proceed beyond the dangerous July 1976 stalemate.

The lack of integrative Canadian analysis is painfully obvious, even when compared to the United States with its much wider range of interests, interest groups and ideological positions to defend. Since 1975, the United States Development Coordination Committee (consisting of twelve agencies) has submitted to Congress extensive reviews on development issues and the impact of U.S. actions in the Third World.[7] Canada's own interdepartmental committee, which bears resemblance to the U.S. committee, has not provided any report that could match the U.S. document.[8] Except for rather spotty oral testimony by departmental representatives before Parliamentary Committees, it has produced nothing on a regular basis to try to integrate policy questions for public consumption. While the compilation of such material may not lie within the present mandate of this committee, which certainly lacks the resources to undertake the task, such a venture would at least force the interdepartmental group to assess the consistency of its own performance, set forth some of its analysis and policy options and, in the process, help generate greater Parliamentary/media/public discussion of North-South issues.

Another problem with the Canadian approach is that the stress on Canada's modest international influence may cause Canadians to sit back and wait for things to develop rather than attempt to influence their outcome. For instance, Mr. Allan MacEachen, in assessing Canada's position at CIEC, told the Subcommittee on International Development:

> For example, on commodities and on the common fund I think our position is quite adequate at the moment, and that if the Americans and the community [European Community] came forward, we would not have any difficulty in meeting them. [9]

This is clearly a reactive Canadian approach and it may be fair to suggest that it characterizes a wider range of Canadian responses than those to which the Minister specifically referred.

In summary, while Canadians in general, and Canadian policy-makers in particular, like to view Canada as being in (or close to) the vanguard of the industrial countries, this self-image is more flattering than accurate. Canada, on occasion, has taken positions that have put this country among the leaders of the North. However, as far as proceeding with in-depth and innovative analyses or offering proposals that could facilitate substantive agreement between the North and the South, Canada has neither called upon enough of its resources nor come close to realizing its potential.

FOOTNOTES

[1] Canada, House of Commons, Subcommittee on International Development, 1st Session, 30th Parliament, Issue No. 6 (November 25, 1975), p. 8.

[2] It is noteworthy that as early as its May 27, 1972 Report to the House of Commons, the Subcommittee on International Development Assistance emphasized that because "the challenge of development ... is not an isolated exercise or programme" there is a major need for "much greater consistency and much-improved coordination." It was not until the externally-precipitated crisis of 1974 that the government attempted to establish consistency and coordination by going beyond the old coordinating machinery of the "Aid Board" and aid committees. Canada, Parliament, House

of Commons, <u>Proceedings of the Standing Committee on External Affairs and National Defence</u>, 3rd Session, 28th Parliament, Issue No. 29 (May 27, 1971), p. 38.

[3] Canada, House of Commons, <u>Standing Committee on External Affairs and National Defence</u>, 1st Session, 30th Parliament, Issue No. 6 (March 13, 1975), p. 18.

[4] Other commentators have noted the importance of the "convergence" of opinion between Third World and medium-scale or small industrial countries (see for instance, Editorial "Another Development and the Third Development Decade", <u>Development Dialogue</u> No. 2 (1976), pp. 5-6), and the Secretary-General of the Commonwealth has warned against "entrapment in such hard-line positions which polarize the world debate". See Canada, House of Commons, <u>Subcommittee on International Development</u>, 2nd Session, 30th Parliament, Issue No. 2 (March 31, 1977), p. 9.

[5] Canada, House of Commons, <u>Subcommittee on International Development</u>, 2nd Session, 30th Parliament, Issue No. 3 (April 1, 1977), p. 10.

[6] Canada, House of Commons, <u>Subcommittee on International Development</u>, 2nd Session, 30th Parliament, Issue No. 1 (March, 30, 1977), p. 25.

[7] For instance see: U.S. Development Coordination Committee, <u>Development Issues: U.S. Actions Affecting the Development of Low-Income Countries</u>, the Second Annual Report of the President, transmitted to the Congress (May, 1976).

[8] Interdepartmental committees did, of course, have a role in the protracted negotiations and approval of the Government's <u>Strategy for International Development Cooperation, 1975-80</u>. The nature of this document, however, was very different from the kind of integrated progress report prepared in the U.S.

[9] Canada, House of Commons, <u>Subcommittee on International Development</u>, 2nd Session, 30th Parliament, Issue No. 1 (March 30, 1977), p.18.